African American History For Dummies®

Cheat Sheet

African American Cultural Institutions

Whether you desire a general overview of the culture, feel like marveling at a few wax miracles, or want to embrace the African Diaspora, somewhere in the U.S. is a facility that caters to your interests. These suggestions can get you started.

Institution	Location	Features	Contact Information
American Jazz Museum	Kansas City, MO	Historical exhibits, live music, and performing arts center	1616 E. 18th Street, Kansas City, MO 64108; www.american jazzmuseum.com
Rosa Parks Library and Museum	Montgomery, AL	Historical exhibits, children's wing	1276 Rosa L. Parks Ave, Troy State University, Montgomery, AL 36108; http://montgomery.troy.edu/museum/
Amistad Center for Art & Culture	Hartford, CT	Historical and art exhibits, Juneteenth celebration	600 Main Street, Hartford, CT 06103; www.amistadart andculture.org
Buffalo Soldiers National Museum	Houston, TX	African American military history and wartime memorabilia	1834 Southmore, Houston, TX 77004; www.buffalosoldier museum.com
California African American Museum	Los Angeles, CA	Historical and art exhibits	600 State Drive, Exposition Park, Los Angeles, CA 90037 www.caamuseum.org
Negro Leagues Baseball Museum	Kansas City, MO	Memorabilia, multimedia and film exhibits	1616 East 18th Street, Kansas City, MO 64108; www.nlbm.com
National Center of Afro-American Artists	Boston, MA	Art exhibits featuring artists of African descent from around the world	300 Walnut Avenue, Boston, MA 02119; www.ncaaa.org
National Civil Rights Museum	Memphis, TN	Site of Martin Luther King, Jr.'s assassination, historical displays	450 Mulberry Street, Memphis, TN 38103; www.civilrights museum.org
National Great Blacks In Wax Museum	Baltimore, MD	Wax displays of historical events	1601-03 East North Avenue, Baltimore, MD 21213; www.ngbiwm.com
National Underground Railroad Freedom Center	Cincinnati, OH	Historical exhibits and interactive displays	50 East Freedom Way, Cincinnati, OH 45202; www.freedomcenter.org
Museum of the African Diaspora	San Francisco, CA	Historical exhibits and multimedia displays	685 Mission Street (at Third), San Francisco, CA 94105; www.moadsf.org

Lift Ev'ry Voice and Sing

Following is the first verse of the African American National Anthem, composed in 1900 by brothers James Weldon Johnson and John Rosamond Johnson:

Lift ev'ry voice and sing,
'Til earth and heaven ring,
Ring with the harmonies of Liberty;
Let our rejoicing rise
High as the list'ning skies,
Let it resound loud as the rolling sea.
Sing a song full of the faith that the dark past has taught us,
Sing a song full of the hope that the present has brought us;
Facing the rising sun of our new day begun,
Let us march on 'til victory is won.

For Dummies: Bestselling Book Series for Beginners

BESTSELLING BOOK SERIES

African American History For Dummies®

Cheat Sheet

Important Dates in African American History

1619	The first Africans arrive in Jamestown, Virginia.
1662	Virginia law establishes that a mother's status determines a child's freedom.
1789	U.S. Constitution designates African Americans as only three-fifths of a person.
1803	Louisiana Purchase increases size of the United States, opening up the argument over admitting slave and free states.
1810	Busiest period of the Underground Railroad begins.
1820	Congress approves the Missouri Compromise, designed to admit slave and free states into the Union.
1831	Nat Turner leads a slave rebellion in Virginia.
1850	The Compromise of 1850, which includes the Fugitive Slave Act requiring the return of runaway slaves to slavery, passes Congress.
1857	*Dred Scott* decision designates slaves as property, not citizens.
1861	The Civil War starts.
1863	Abraham Lincoln issues the Emancipation Proclamation.
1865	*April:* The Civil War ends, Abraham Lincoln is assassinated, and the Freedmen's Bureau is established. *December:* Congress ratifies the Thirteenth Amendment, abolishing slavery.
1867	Reconstruction begins.
1868	Congress ratifies Fourteenth Amendment, making African Americans full citizens.
1870	Congress ratifies Fifteenth Amendment, which prohibits preventing any U.S. citizen from voting based on race, color, or previous slave status.
1877	Reconstruction ends.
1896	In *Plessy v. Ferguson*, the Supreme Court sanctions the "separate but equal" doctrine of Jim Crow.
1914	The period known as the Great Migration begins.
1916	Marcus Garvey brings his Universal Negro Improvement Association to the United States.
1926	Carter G. Woodson begins Negro History Week, which becomes Black History Month in 1976.
1941	President Franklin Delano Roosevelt bans racial discrimination in government employment, defense industries, and training programs.
1947	Jackie Robinson breaks Major League Baseball's color barrier.
1948	President Harry S. Truman desegregates the military.
1954	*Brown v. Board of Education* decision rules that "separate is unequal," ending school segregation.
1955	*August:* 14-year-old Emmett Till is murdered. *December:* The Montgomery Bus Boycott begins.
1957	A white mob prevents nine black students from integrating Central High School in Little Rock, Arkansas. Eisenhower later sends in federal troops to escort the students.
1960	Student sit-ins begin in Greensboro, North Carolina, to integrate eating facilities.
1963	*May:* Medgar Evers is murdered. *August:* Martin Luther King, Jr., delivers his "I Have a Dream" speech. *September:* Four black girls are killed in a Birmingham church bombing.
1964	Congress passes the Civil Rights Act of 1964. Three civil rights workers are found dead in Mississippi during Freedom Summer.
1965	*February:* Malcolm X is assassinated. *March:* King leads the march from Selma to Montgomery. *August:* Congress passes the Voting Rights Act of 1965.
1968	Martin Luther King, Jr., is assassinated in Memphis on April 4.
2005	Rosa Parks dies.
2006	*January:* Coretta Scott King dies. *November:* Ground is broken on the National Mall for a Martin Luther King, Jr., Memorial, a first for an African American or a civilian.

For Dummies: Bestselling Book Series for Beginners

African American History

FOR

DUMMIES®

by Ronda Racha Penrice

BICENTENNIAL
1807
WILEY
2007
BICENTENNIAL

Wiley Publishing, Inc.

African American History For Dummies®

Published by
Wiley Publishing, Inc.
111 River St.
Hoboken, NJ 07030-5774
www.wiley.com

Copyright © 2007 by Wiley Publishing, Inc., Indianapolis, Indiana

Published simultaneously in Canada

WILEY

About the Author

Ronda Racha Penrice is a Chicago native with deep Mississippi roots who has worked with various publications, including *The Quarterly Black Review of Books*, *Rap Pages*, *Essence Online*, *Nia Online*, *Creative Loafing*, *Africana.com*, *AOL Black Voices,* and *Uptown*. The Columbia University alumna, who also attended graduate school at the University of Mississippi, has a lifelong interest in African American history and culture. She currently resides in Atlanta, GA. This is her first book.

Dedication

I humbly dedicate this book to my grandparents, Dessie Ree Shannon Stapleton Beard (1925-1998) and Willie Beard (1920-2002), who taught me honor, integrity, pride, and humanity by example. Because of their unconditional love and support for me and my love of reading and writing, I am here today always striving to make them proud.

I also dedicate this book to my great aunt, Ada Beard Humphries (1918-2000). In her frequent retellings of transporting me from Chicago to Mississippi, when I was just six weeks old, she made my humble beginnings appear almost as magical as the birth of Jesus Christ and convinced me that I could do and be anything.

In Memoriam: My uncle, John Curtis Beard (1957-1978) and his son, Curtis Rodriguez Beard (1977-1999); and Dr. Endesha Ida Mae Holland (1944-2006).

Author's Acknowledgments

All thanks go to God first. I haven't always been the most faithful servant but He's blessed me anyway.

Tonya Bolden, I owe you so much. You exemplify the values my grandparents deemed most important. You've always been supportive and have never hesitated to share an opportunity, including this amazing one. Keep blessing the world.

I can't say enough about my agent, Matt Wagner of Fresh Books, who championed me every step of the way. Thank you, Stacy Kennedy of Wiley Publishing, for taking a chance and sticking with me even when it looked like a mistake. My first project editor Mike Baker put in the initial work to get me started. Senior copy editor Elizabeth Rea added valuable insight throughout the project. Words of gratitude are so inadequate to express my eternal debt to the absolutely amazing Tracy Barr, who finally whipped me into shape. I just hope the final product has made all those headaches distant memories.

I have to thank my village because, without them, I would be lost. My former employer, surrogate mother, and frequent sponsor, Roz Stevenson has been my angel on earth; my mother, Tyrethis Beard Penrice, and my brothers, Raefeael Tylin Penrice and Darryl Russell Penrice. My aunts Willie Ann Beard Benjamin, Carolyn Beard Humphries, their husbands Lawrence and Kirby,

Dorethen Beard Holman, Alberta Beard Ford, and my uncle Lawrence Lee Beard and his wife Nellie; first cousins, Cedric Beard, Dwayne Beard, James Beard, LaShawnda Benjamin, Kristy Holman Dixon, Sharleatha Smith Beard Gayten, Trelva Humphries Harvey, Kendall Holman, Kerwin Holman, and their families. My innumerable friends: Joane Amay, Paula Stokes, Tiaka Hurst, Cantranette McCrimmon, Chianti Phillips, P.E. Cobb, Ebonette Bates, Sharon Collins, Debra Brown, Sabrina Fuller, Bomani Jones, Deborah Cook, Tony Murphy, Sheree Renee Thomas, LaTanya Marble, Michael Andre Adams, Ken Gibbs, Jr., Dorothy Stefanski, Roni Sarig, Lumumba, Allen Gordon, Jevaillier Jefferson, (cousin) Carol Wheeler, Leslie Lockhart, (cousin) Danny Ray, Isoul H. Harris, Kym A. Backer, Scharla Ash, Hikmah Housson, Landras Mitchell, Merrell Gantt, Gil Robertson, David Webber, and the never forgotten Rodney Crump, Patrik Henry Bass, Burt Murray, Ms. Etha Robinson, Serese Teate, (cousin) Vernon Rucks, (cousin) D.V. Rucks, Peter Pazzaglini, and David F.A. Walker; I apologize to anyone I did forget. It wasn't intentional.

Publisher's Acknowledgments

We're proud of this book; please send us your comments through our Dummies online registration form located at www.dummies.com/register/.

Some of the people who helped bring this book to market include the following:

Acquisitions, Editorial, and Media Development

Project Editor: Tracy L. Barr

Acquisitions Editor: Stacy Kennedy

Senior Copy Editor: Elizabeth Rea

General Reviewer: Venetria K. Patton

Editorial Manager: Michelle Hacker

Editorial Supervisor and Reprint Editor: Carmen Krikorian

Editorial Assistants: Erin Calligan Mooney, Joe Niesen, Leeann Harney, David Lutton

Cover Photos: © Todd Gipstein/National Geographic/GettyImages

Cartoons: Rich Tennant (www.the5thwave.com)

Composition Services

Project Coordinator: Adrienne Martinez

Layout and Graphics: Claudia Bell, Denny Hager, Joyce Haughey, Heather Ryan, Alicia B. South

Anniversary Logo Design: Richard Pacifico

Proofreaders: Aptara, Melanie Hoffman, Jessica Kramer, Charles Spencer

Indexer: Aptara

Publishing and Editorial for Consumer Dummies

Diane Graves Steele, Vice President and Publisher, Consumer Dummies

Joyce Pepple, Acquisitions Director, Consumer Dummies

Kristin A. Cocks, Product Development Director, Consumer Dummies

Michael Spring, Vice President and Publisher, Travel

Kelly Regan, Editorial Director, Travel

Publishing for Technology Dummies

Andy Cummings, Vice President and Publisher, Dummies Technology/General User

Composition Services

Gerry Fahey, Vice President of Production Services

Debbie Stailey, Director of Composition Services

Contents at a Glance

Table of Contents

Introduction

• •

*B*lack history is American history," Oscar-winning actor Morgan Freeman said in a 2005 interview, explaining why he doesn't support Black History Month. Interestingly, Carter G. Woodson, the man who created Negro History Week, which evolved into Black History Month, envisioned a time when general American history would incorporate African American history.

African American history, to be clear, is so much more than a handful of extraordinary individuals or practices like slavery, Jim Crow, and civil rights. A lot of it is painful, but it's also inspiring and triumphant. "We will be able to hew out of the mountain of despair a stone of hope," Martin Luther King, Jr., said in 1963.

It took the Civil War, the civil rights movement of the 1960s, and a lot of struggle in between to secure African Americans the basic right to citizenship that white Americans took for granted. *African American History For Dummies* isn't a big sermon on this struggle; instead, it's a straightforward, interesting (I hope!), and honest overview of African American history from Africa through the transatlantic slave trade, slavery, the Civil War, Reconstruction, Jim Crow, and the 1960s civil rights movement until now. Along the way, that history birthed a culture that includes the black church and education as well as sports, music, literature, television, and film.

About This Book

Making this book as comprehensive (within the page limit my editor demanded) and as engaging as possible has been a top-priority for me. So consider *African American History For Dummies* an introduction to a vast and vastly interesting subject. I hope it will inspire you to seek out more information. At the very least, you'll look at the contributions of African Americans with new eyes.

Of course, in deciding what to include, I tried to be as objective as possible. I sifted through many history books, paid many library fines, viewed many Internet pages, and checked and double-checked many dates and name spellings (and missed more than a few deadlines in the process!) so that you can trust the information contained in this book.

I must admit that I have a personal connection to the book. My grandfather, a Mississippian from birth to death, came from a family of sharecroppers. My great aunt sang blues songs at family gatherings and told the best stories, some of which I later found in a book of African American folklore. My grandmother never tired of sharing family stories with me, even a tragic one about the unsolved murder of her brother who migrated to Chicago in the 1930s. Of course, my whole family has plenty of stories about the civil rights movement, and, yes, I wish I had first learned about the Ku Klux Klan in books or on television.

I've lived a lit bit of African American history myself, too. I was a middle school student when Harold Washington became Chicago's first black mayor, and, wouldn't you know, David Dinkins became the first black mayor of New York City when I moved there for college. Did I know that LL Cool J would become a global rap star when I bumped into him at clubs? Certainly not, but in Los Angeles, I did know that meeting Fayard Nicholas of the legendary Nicholas Brothers dance duo was a big deal. I also cherished seeing Halle Berry, Will Smith, and Denzel Washington at the Academy Awards luncheon the year Berry and Washington won. Still, my biggest thrill was meeting Muhammad Ali when I was just a kid.

African American History For Dummies is the actual history behind these personal experiences that explains why these events mean so much. In an effort to reveal the interesting side of history (believe me, there is one!), I favored cold, hard facts over generalities and consciously strayed away from the same old stories. After all, the ultimate aim of this book is to make African American history accessible without sacrificing the history.

Foolish Assumptions

In writing *African American History For Dummies,* I had to make some assumptions about you, the reader. In addition to my main assumption — that African American history is important for everyone, not just African Americans — here are a few others:

- ✔ You suspect that African American contributions to American history ran deeper than you learned in required history classes but don't know how to prove it.

- ✔ At one point, you tried to read about African American history, but you just couldn't find enough of what you needed to know in one spot and don't like the idea of having to dust off your college research skills.

✔ You picked up bits and pieces of African American history here and there, but want an accessible reference where you can go to find out more.

How This Book Is Organized

Of course, I would love you to read this book from cover to cover, but that's most certainly not required. Maybe African American music suits your fancy or the Civil War and Reconstruction have always fascinated you. If so, go straight to the chapters that cover those topics. Feel free to mix and match chapters or simply read them all at a leisurely pace.

This book is divided into six parts that are a mix of topical and chronological approaches. To make it easier for you to find the information you seek, I've broken the information into parts, each with chapters relating to the part's topic.

Part I: Coming to America

Before launching into the nuts and bolts of African American history, I give you a brief overview of African American history and its significance in overall American history. The African American's journey to the present began with Spain's discovery of the New World and institution of slavery there. This doesn't necessarily mean that the first Africans to Jamestown were slaves; the chapters in this part show how that change took place and traces slavery's development to the American Revolution, which founded two Americas — one slave and one free — and set the stage for the dramatic events that followed.

Part II: Long Road to Freedom

There was a lot of struggle between slavery and emancipation. The official end of the slave trade only intensified the domestic institution of slavery. This part provides an overview of slavery and illustrates the various ways that African American slaves resisted the institution. It also delves into the movement to abolish slavery, highlighting the Underground Railroad and other organized efforts of resistance. When the showdown finally took place in the form of the Civil War, its purpose wasn't as clear to white Americans as it was to African Americans. Although freedom finally came to African Americans, in the most important ways it was a mere technicality.

Part III: Pillars of Change: The Civil Rights Movement

It took some pretty strong forces to propel the nation from Jim Crow to the civil rights movement to the present, and this part addresses that progress. It covers the institution, reality, and overthrow of Jim Crow and examines the grand history of the civil rights movement. And because the history of America and African Americans didn't come to a screeching halt in the 1960s, this part addresses both the good and the bad of what followed the civil rights movement.

Part IV: Cultural Foundations

At a number of points in history, the debate over how much African American culture retained its African roots has been among the biggest and most contentious debates around. This part shows that African American culture is indeed both African and American by highlighting family roles, food, and language, among other elements. The chapters in this part also delve into two of the primary foundations of African American culture — the black church and education — and trace their development from slavery to the present.

Part V: A Touch of Genius: Arts, Entertainment, and Sports

This part delves into the amazing accomplishments that can only result from striving to be the best. In literature, African Americans have gone from slave narratives to a Nobel Prize. At one time, the American stage meant only racist roles in blackface for African Americans; today, it's Tony Award–winning performances. Musically, African Americans have transformed slave songs into unique creations such as jazz and hip-hop that the whole world celebrates. In film and television, actors who would have been cast as maids and butlers only a handful of decades ago now star in blockbusters and win Oscars. And in the sports arena, African Americans have gone from being the last players allowed to play to among the best to ever play.

Part VI: The Part of Tens

One of my favorite features of *For Dummies* books is this part, which is a quick glimpse of interesting lists and tidbits. In the case of *African American History For Dummies,* these lists include ten classic literary works by African American writers; ten fascinating African American firsts, ranging from medicine to fashion; and ten important and remarkable African American artists.

Icons Used in This Book

The little pictures you see attached to paragraphs throughout the book are another of the standard, helpful *For Dummies* features. They're intended to flag information that's special and important for one reason or another. *African American History For Dummies* uses the following icons:

This icon accompanies information that explains where something — an organization, an event, and so on — originates from. Perhaps you didn't know, for example, that other civil rights activists used sit-ins before they became popular in the 1960s.

This icon brings to light the details of African Americans, especially those not typically spotlighted, who did some outstanding things that warrant further explanation.

In my opinion, words say a lot. Surely, an escaped slave can better tell you how scary running away really was or what freedom truly means than I can. Besides, many of the quotations and excerpts that carry this icon are just outright inspiring.

Although I find everything in this book enlightening, I admit that it isn't all necessary information that you must read in order to understand the topic. That's where this icon comes in; it points out what you may want to read but don't have to. It also highlights some interesting facts you might not know like the fact that Mississippi didn't ratify the Thirteenth Amendment abolishing slavery until 1995.

This icon points to facts or ideas that you should, well . . . remember. Essentially, it's important stuff that's had a major impact on African American and American history and therefore shouldn't be overlooked.

Where to Go from Here

Now's the time to dive into this book in the way that best suits you: I can't tell you which chapter to choose or part to read. Flip to the Table of Contents and find a topic that interests you. Skip around. Fast forward ahead or travel back in time. Within each chapter, sidestep sidebars or read only the text with Remember icons. Or, if you like, read *African American History For Dummies* from cover to cover. It's completely up to you.

Part I
Coming to America

The 5th Wave   By Rich Tennant

"I think I know who the ones with the helmets
are, but I'm not sure about the other ones.
You know, the ones in the back of the boat."

In this part . . .

African slavery didn't originate in the English colonies: Portugal was the first country to trade Africans as slaves, and Spain was the first to establish slavery in the Americas. But the first Africans who came to the English colonies in 1619 weren't slaves — they were closer to indentured servants. By the 1660s, that status had changed.

This part examines early African American history: how Africans found themselves in the New World; what horrors they had to endure as the commodity that helped build America and make Britain a world power in the process; and how, despite the disappointment of the American Revolution that promised freedom to all but denied it to them, they managed to become a nation within a nation and continue the fight for freedom that lasted about 100 years.

Chapter 1

The Soul of America

· ·

In This Chapter

▶ Capturing the African American experience throughout history

▶ Examining advances and challenges

▶ Exposing all Americans to African American history

▶ Remaining conscious of unresolved issues

· ·

Countee Cullen's question, "What is Africa to me?," from his 1930 poem "Heritage," should resonate with more than African Americans. European interaction with the African continent profoundly changed the world, black, white, and otherwise, and nowhere else is that fact more evident than in the United States.

With the exception of South Carolina, Africans were largely the racial minority in early America, partially because white colonists adamantly restricted their numbers. Even in small numbers, though, Africans had an enormous impact on American history; the truth is that America has a dual history rooted in both Europe and Africa.

This chapter presents a general overview of African American history, underscoring why that history is important to all Americans.

A Peek at the Past

It's been said that "to know your past is to know your future." Is it inconceivable that the problems of the present stem from the past? Certainly, the United States has undergone tremendous change in the last six decades. If Americans believe that those changes affect them now, then the circumstances leading up to those changes must affect them, too. Americans felt that connection to a certain degree when Alex Haley's book *Roots* (1976) and the subsequent television miniseries a year later sparked a nationwide fervor among African Americans and others to learn more about African Americans and their connection to Africa. Long before Haley's tome, however, historians pondered African American history and its relationship to Africa and the United States.

Prophets looking backwards: African American historians

If, as German scholar Friedrich von Schlegel observed, "the historian is a prophet looking backwards," then a number of prophets have emerged from African American history. Celebrated African American intellectual W.E.B. Du Bois, the first African American to receive a PhD from Harvard University, chose the African slave trade as the subject of his doctoral dissertation and, in 1896, published *The Suppression of the African Slave Trade to the United States of America*. Thirteen years prior to Du Bois's work, George Washington Williams, the first "colored" member of the Ohio legislature, published *History of the Negro Race in America From 1619 to 1880*.

Despite the scholarship of these men, Carter G. Woodson, the man frequently referenced as the Father of Black History, became one of the foremost advocates of African American history. The son of former slaves, he wrote some of the most influential works on the African American experience. He also established Negro History Week, which blossomed into Black History Month, with the hope that, one day, general American history would rightfully include the vital and numerous contributions of African Americans.

Woodson's successors include:

- John Hope Franklin, author of the most widely used African American history textbook, *From Slavery to Freedom* (1947)

- Lerone Bennett, former executive editor of *Ebony* magazine and author of *Before the Mayflower* (1963)

- David Levering Lewis, Pulitzer award–winning historian known for *When Harlem Was in Vogue* (1981) and his two-part biography of W.E.B. Du Bois

- Paula Giddings, author of *When and Where I Enter* (1985) and *In Search of Sisterhood* (1988)

- Nell Irvin Painter, noted biographer of Sojourner Truth

- Robin D.G. Kelley, coeditor of *To Make Our World Anew: A History of African Americans* (2000) and author of *Hammer and Hoe: Alabama Communists During the Great Depression* (1991)

Carter G. Woodson, the man behind Black History Month, believed that preserving African American history was essential to African American survival. "If a race has no history, if it has no worthwhile tradition," Woodson reasoned, "it becomes a negligible factor in the thought of the world, and it stands in danger of being exterminated." He also felt that omitting African American contributions from general American history sanctioned and perpetuated racism. "The philosophy and ethics resulting from our educational system have justified slavery, peonage, segregation, and lynching," he noted. Looking at matters from this perspective, it's little wonder that African Americans have been so vilified.

However, it didn't begin that way. History acknowledges that the first Africans who came to Jamestown held a status closer to indentured servants. Yet in fewer than 50 years, African and slave became interchangeable. Therefore, racism against African Americans is 300 years old, *at the very least*. Because the dismantling of Jim Crow, an institutionalized system of segregating African Americans generally associated with the South, only began in the 1950s and 1960s, the U.S., as a nation, has only legally acknowledged African Americans as full citizens for about 50 years. The only way to correct the past and move forward is to recognize this reality. "I want American history taught," celebrated writer James Baldwin once demanded. "Unless I'm in the book, you're not in it either."

Life before slavery

Despite many history lessons to the contrary, African American history didn't begin with slavery; like other Americans, African Americans have a beginning that predates the Americas. Africans transported to the Americas through the slave trade generally hailed from Western and Central Africa, an area that includes present-day Ghana, Nigeria, the Ivory Coast, Mali, Senegal, Angola, and the Congo. Of Africa's many empires, Ghana, Mali, and Songhay are the most important to African American history. Some unique features of these empires included religious tolerance, attempts at representative government, and somewhat egalitarian attitudes concerning the contributions of women.

Although Egypt attracted European attention centuries before the slave trade began, tales of Africa's enormous riches reignited European interest in the continent. Portugal, which beat other European countries to Africa, didn't go there looking for slaves but rather for material wealth. And although the Portuguese captured Africans during those early trips, they weren't doomed to a lifetime of enslavement. Columbus's "discovery" of the New World and Spain's claim on the land changed that; when Spain instituted slavery to capitalize on cash crops like sugar, Portugal served as the primary supplier of Africans. As Chapter 3 explains, England entered the slave trade relatively late but excelled quickly.

Life before emancipation

The first Africans to arrive in Jamestown in 1619 held a status similar to indentured servants. Although the situation had changed drastically by the 1660s, there's no evidence that Africans ever resigned themselves to slavery. Even before the United States' official birth, African slaves appealed to the courts as well as the moral consciences of colonists.

Slave life was harsh, with human beings reduced to nothing more than property. Laws ensured that slaves had absolutely no control over their own lives. Slaveholders had the legal right to dictate their every move and mistreat them with no recourse. Consequently, slaveholders separated families without a second thought, and rapes and unwanted pregnancies were far from unusual occurrences for slave girls and women.

Still, in the greatest moments of despair, free blacks and their enslaved brethren never abandoned their hope for freedom. Whether they ran away, rallied sympathetic whites toward emancipation, or snuck slaves to freedom using the Underground Railroad, they did whatever they could to force the new nation to live up to its promise of freedom and equality. Less than a century into the new nation's existence, the inevitable finally happened with the rise of the Civil War.

Life before civil rights

Long before Lincoln's Emancipation Proclamation and the ratification of the Thirteenth Amendment abolishing slavery, African Americans firmly set their minds on attaining freedom. When Lincoln wavered about ending slavery during the Civil War, African Americans like Frederick Douglass continued lobbying for freedom. Reconstruction (the period of recovery, particularly in the South, following the Civil War) revealed that most white Americans had never seriously entertained the idea of African American freedom. White Congressman Thaddeus Stevens was the grand exception. As he and others battled to right the wrongs of the past with the aid of newly inaugurated African American congressmen, white Southerners refused to change the status quo, and the North sat back and watched.

When Reconstruction ended, African Americans didn't give up the fight for racial equality as white mob violence corruptedtheir freedom and Jim Crow ruled their lives. In the 20th century, African American leaders like W.E.B. Du Bois and Ida B. Wells-Barnett pounced on every opportunity to challenge the "white only" claim on the U.S. The African American masses weren't silent either; in search of better jobs and a life free of Jim Crow, they migrated North with new urgency. Although the Promised Land wasn't all they imagined, they didn't abandon each other. Battling mob violence in the North, the nation saw that African Americans never accepted lynchings and Jim Crow; there wasn't really a "New Negro" at work but rather the old one in plain view. Marcus Garvey capitalized on that spirit when he launched his brand of Black Nationalism and Pan-Africanism. (You can read about Du Bois, Wells-Barnett, Garvey, and others, as well as the Great Migration, in Chapter 7.)

The demographic shift created a new power base for African Americans. Prompted by the shameful treatment African Americans received during the Great Depression, black leaders demanded a piece of Roosevelt's New Deal program and switched from the Republican to the Democratic Party. By the time World War II rolled around, strong leaders, remembering the broken promises of World War I, wouldn't back down from their new demands. By the time the 1950s and 1960s came (see Chapters 7 and 8), the weapons critical to winning the battle against inequality were in place.

Being Black in America Today

The Supreme Court ruling in *Brown v. Board of Education* dealt a powerful blow to the Jim Crow bully, but Emmett Till's brutal murder in Mississippi as the result of an innocent encounter with a white woman shook thousands out of their complacency. When Martin Luther King, Jr. emerged on the scene a few months later, "Ain't gonna let nobody turn me 'roun'" became an anthem for change. The nonviolent, direct action favored by Gandhi, which Martin Luther King, Jr. followed, also worked in the U.S. However, Malcolm X, the Black Panther Party, and eventually the Student Nonviolent Coordinating Committee (SNCC) felt that black power was a more effective strategy and refused to turn the other cheek. Despite their differences, the two factions had the same ultimate goal: equality.

Throughout the 1970s and 1980s, African Americans amassed a vast assortment of incredible achievements. From serving as mayors in major cities like Los Angeles, New York, and Chicago to selling millions of records worldwide, African Americans excelled in both expected and unexpected areas. Also, black household incomes consistently soared to record heights. The picture wasn't rosy for everyone, however. The effects of crack cocaine use literally ravished black neighborhoods, gun violence robbed mothers of their children, and prisons often sucked up those who survived.

So much has changed for the better for black Americans since King and Malcolm X lost their lives. Visible "colored only" and "white only" signs no longer exist, and black people aren't physically assaulted for daring to vote. Most of the obstacles that limited opportunities for African Americans at one time are gone. Yet vestiges of racism linger. On the one hand, hip-hop moguls such as Sean "Diddy" Combs and Jay-Z turn themselves into global brands; on the other hand, news cameras document black men, women, and children stranded on rooftops for days while elected officials place blame instead of expedite rescue efforts.

What's in a name? "Negro," the N-word, and many others

"African," "Afro-American," "colored," "Negro," "black," and "African American" are just some of the names used to describe people who trace their roots to the African continent. The constantly evolving terms largely reflect developments in African American culture and its relationship to the dominant white culture. The changes also reveal African Americans' ongoing quest for self-identity and self-determination.

Surprisingly, "Negro" didn't always refer to black people. At times, it also included Asians and, in the New World, Native Americans. In 19th-century runaway announcements, the term "negro" identified black Americans. Progressive institutions such as the African Methodist Episcopal Church preferred the term "African," but "colored" was widely used. In 1829, David Walker addressed his famous appeal to the "coloured citizens of the world." The use of "colored" by the National Association for the Advancement of Colored People (NAACP) indicates the term's positive value in the early 20th century; in the years between the two world wars, the NAACP actually spearheaded the use of "Negro" with a capital "n," and that usage persisted into the 1960s.

As the civil rights movement gave way to the black power movement, "black" replaced "Negro." The 1980s ushered in the use of "African American," which supporters such as Jesse Jackson insist is a reflection of both an African and American identity. However, some argue that it isn't specific enough because white Africans such as actress Charlize Theron are technically African American. Today, people often use "African American" and "black" interchangeably, and this book is a perfect example.

Slaves sometimes referred to themselves as "niggers" in front of whites to indicate their servility, and the term was widely used in early European and American history to refer to African Americans, including usage in novels such as Mark Twain's classic *Adventures of Huckleberry Finn* (1884). Although widely used, "nigger" was rarely a positive term, a point underscored in the midst of the civil rights movement when newspapers and television frequently quoted hostile white Americans using the word freely.

Some black Americans make distinctions between "nigger" and "nigga." African Americans almost never view the former positively. On the other hand, some African Americans view the latter more positively when used among African Americans, although saying it aggressively can indicate hostility. While hip-hop songs and comedy routines use the term liberally, it's generally unacceptable for non-African Americans to use "nigga" or "nigger" under any circumstances. The unwritten rule is that blacks can use the term and nonblacks can't. Of course, many black Americans, such as Oprah Winfrey, believe that absolutely no one should use the word under any circumstances.

Contributions

African American contributions to American history are tremendous. It's not a stretch to say that African slave labor, for example, is one of the main reasons the U.S. exists today. In the colonies, Africans cleared land and built houses in addition to cultivating cash crops such as rice, tobacco, and cotton. African Americans weren't absent in the U.S. expansion westward either. In the North, African American slaves worked in the shipping industry as well as early factories. African American soldiers fought in the American Revolution, the War of 1812, and the Civil War.

African American contributions in music are celebrated the world over. Few authentic American music genres are without African American roots, including rock-and-roll, which counts Chuck Berry, Little Richard, the infamous Ike Turner, and the lesser-known Roy Brown and Wynonie Harris among its early pioneers. African American dance has influenced American culture since slavery. Literature and sports have also played key roles. So have less well-known contributions in medicine and architecture, among other fields. The following is a brief sampling of those contributions.

In music and dance

Trying to keep up with African American contributions in music and dance is dizzying. Jazz is an indigenous American art form birthed from African American culture, as are hip-hop, blues, ragtime, and spirituals. Many argue that jazz put the U.S. on the world's culture radar. Few musicians of any color have matched jazz maestro Duke Ellington's volume of compositions. And are there many gospel singers more well-known than Mahalia Jackson? "Precious Lord, Take My Hand" is easily one of the most popular gospel songs. On a similar note, Motown's catalog grows more timeless each year. To read more about African American music and musical influences, go to Chapter 16.

Throughout history, white Americans have borrowed African American dances. Actually, the dance that gave Jim Crow, America's caste system, its name originated with an African American performer. Both the Lindy Hop and the Charleston got a lift from African Americans, and many scholars have great reason to believe that tap dancing, as it's known today, was developed during slavery. In contemporary terms, black artists never seemed to run out of new dances in the 1950s and 1960s, and dancers and choreographers Katherine Dunham and Alvin Ailey garnered international praise for their mastery and innovation in the fields of ballet and modern dance. You can find out more about African American dance in Chapter 15.

In literature

Toni Morrison's 1993 Nobel Prize in Literature wasn't an anomaly in the context of the tradition from which she hails. To start, slave narratives captivated readers in America as well as abroad. White Americans may have questioned the talent of Phillis Wheatley, the remarkable slave poet, in court, but the English accepted her talent with ease. Richard Wright, James Baldwin, Alice Walker, and so many other African American writers are American treasures whose voices have carried throughout the world. Chapter 14 discusses African American literature in detail.

In sports

Many African Americans have excelled in all types of sports. Muhammad Ali, Tiger Woods, Venus and Serena Williams, Michael Jordan, Arthur Ashe, Wilma Rudolph, Jesse Owens, and Major Taylor are just a few of the African American sports greats. (Read about African American athletes in Chapter 18.)

African American athletes have also played crucial roles in key social issues. Jackie Robinson helped the nation take a critical step toward racial desegregation when he broke Major League Baseball's color line in 1947. Muhammad Ali's refusal to fight in Vietnam boosted antiwar efforts. And, in recent years, record-setting achievements by golfer Tiger Woods and real-life tennis sisters Venus and Serena Williams have diversified two international sports not generally associated with athletes of color.

Other contributions

African American contributions outside of sports, entertainment, and the arts are usually less known but are equally substantial. Dr. Charles Drew pioneered the blood bank. Based on his doctoral dissertation about "banked blood," he spearheaded the "Blood for Britain" project, which ultimately saved many of those wounded in World War II's critical Battle of Dunkirk. In 1941, he served as the director of the American Red Cross's plasma storage program for U.S. armed forces.

Both Colin Powell and Condoleezza Rice fit into their individual appointments as secretary of state so easily that most Americans spent little time pondering the historic appointment of an African American to the critical position, nor the unprecedented succession of an African American by another African American. It's safe to assume most travelers to the Los Angeles International Airport are completely unaware that black female architect Norma Merrick Sklarek designed Terminal One.

Is it mere coincidence that Lewis Latimer served as draftsman for both Alexander Graham Bell and Thomas Edison for the two inventions that people take for granted today? There's no doubt that Latimer's version of the light bulb using a carbon filament helped it stay bright longer. Without Garrett A. Morgan, the traffic light and the gas mask might not exist.

Discounting the enormity of African American contributions to American history and culture overall is a big mistake. African Americans have used their talents to benefit not just African Americans, but all Americans.

Challenges

Unfortunately, great achievements by African Americans haven't come easy. It's an understatement to say that African Americans have excelled against tremendous odds. Few cultures have produced as many titans who hail from such humble backgrounds as slavery and Jim Crow. Former slaves Frederick Douglass and Booker T. Washington were among the most prominent Americans of their day. Billionaire Oprah Winfrey, born poor in the Jim Crow South, was raised in a time when doing laundry for wealthy whites was as far as most African American women ever got.

With each of these extraordinary individuals, education was the difference maker. Yet, for much of American history, African Americans haven't had access to the ladders by which most Americans ascend to success.

Getting equal education

Securing a solid education has been crucial in the overall fight for equality. Education has provided the critical foundation from which African Americans have waged their fight against countless other inequities, be it inferior housing, discriminatory hiring practices, or police brutality.

Despite hard-won battles against inequities in education, affirmative action, one of its main corrective measures, is a constant target. Civil rights activists have charged that Proposition 209, an amendment to the California constitution purportedly aimed at ending racial discrimination in public education and other public areas of interest, has resulted in the enrollment of fewer disadvantaged students of color in higher education.

Ward Connerly, who classifies himself as multiracial, and other supporters of Prop 209, have taken their fight nationally and succeeded in helping similar measures pass in other states, including Michigan in 2006. Some institutions have discontinued scholarships for black students from disadvantaged backgrounds as well as dismantled programs exposing minority high school and college students to professions such as science, which boast far too few professionals of color.

The United States is at a critical crossroads. While school desegregation efforts throughout the nation, especially the South, only began in earnest in the 1970s, many Americans believe that the ills of 200-plus years of slavery and nearly 100 more of Jim Crow can be erased in less than 50 years.

Achieving the American dream

Historically, the American dream eluded African Americans. Immediately following the civil rights and black power movements, that no longer seemed true. African Americans began voting and electing African American politicians. Poverty levels among African Americans began falling as the black middle class began expanding. Better yet, a larger number of African Americans became wealthy without hitting the lottery.

In recent years, there's been less to cheer about. Shaking the vestiges of slavery and Jim Crow hasn't been easy for all. And while there are African Americans who continue to excel financially and otherwise, so many others are backtracking. As civil rights activist Rev. Jesse Jackson often reminds Americans, the playing field is still unequal in many ways:

- ✔ **Income:** While the white poor constitute 8 percent of the total white population, nearly 25 percent of the African American population lives in poverty. African American household income has been 60 percent of white American household income since 1980. According to the Census Bureau, in 2005, average income for white Americans was $50,622 compared to $30,939 for black Americans.

- ✔ **Continuing discrimination:** Revelations of unwritten discriminatory policies against African Americans by corporations and other entities have come to light. In 1997, Avis Rent-A-Car paid a $3.3-million settlement for allegations, primarily because it ignored numerous complaints about a North Carolina franchisee that required higher credit card maximums and proof of employment from prospective African American customers, but not other customers. Additionally several studies have claimed that it's not rare for African Americans with the same credit history and assets as white Americans to pay more for a home mortgage.

- ✔ **Healthcare:** Healthcare disparities are even broader. According to the Centers for Disease Control, in 2004, the cancer death rate for African Americans was 25 percent higher than that of white Americans. Black infants are twice as likely to die than white infants.

- ✔ **Incarceration rates:** According to the Sentencing Project, an advocacy group aimed at achieving a more equitable criminal justice system, there were 98,000 African Americans incarcerated in 1954 and 884,500 in 2004. Even given the obvious population growth, that statistic is substantial.

Fighting for civil rights

Those dismayed by the erosion of civil rights gains argue that the fight is more difficult now because dismantling covert racism isn't as galvanizing as dismantling overt racism. During the 1950s and 1960s, activists could point to "colored only" water fountains, public schools, and other visible manifestations of racial discrimination as clear evidence of racial injustice. Convincing Americans that the disproportionately high incarceration rates for African American men are rooted in slavery and Jim Crow is less compelling.

If most Americans, as various state referendums indicate, aren't interested in affirmative action programs and if proven early-education programs like Head Start consistently face budget cuts, what is the solution? Historian and political theorist Manning Marable, well-known for his scholarly work surrounding racism, and other civil rights activists consistently argue that recognizing that the events of the past are indeed connected to our present is the first step in creating a 21st-century strategy that will result in a more equitable American society for all its citizens.

Embracing the Past

During the 1960s, an especially turbulent time for the nation in general, African Americans appeared to vocalize racial pride more, although that impression may have been the result of increased media attention. (In the 1920s, for example, large numbers of black people were members of Marcus Garvey's Universal Negro Improvement Association, which emphasized racial pride.)

James Brown's hit 1968 single "Say It Loud — I'm Black and I'm Proud" ended the usage of "colored" or "Negro" among African Americans and others. Slogans such as "Black is beautiful" helped define the early 1970s. African Americans began to expect more of other Americans, and total ignorance of African American culture was no longer acceptable. Today, it's customary for the president of the United States to acknowledge Black History Month at the very least. Increasingly, more and more people of various races believe that embracing the past can move the nation forward.

Celebrating black heritage

Contemporary African Americans celebrate their heritage in various ways. Here are some prominent examples:

- *The Cosby Show,* which aired from 1984 to 1992, exposed an entire nation to a rare slice of African American life. Creator and star Bill Cosby showed television audiences that African Americans could be financially successful without losing touch with their heritage by incorporating jazz, African American art, and African American colleges into the show.

- NBA great Kareem Abdul-Jabbar turned his attention to African American history in his post-basketball life, as evidenced by his book *Black Profiles in Courage: A Legacy of African-American Achievement* (1996).

✔ Congresswoman Maxine Waters collects African American memorabilia, including images of the controversial Aunt Jemima, the head-ragged pancake spokeswoman.

"Aunt Jemima is the black woman who cooked and cleaned, struggled, brought up her own family and a white family," Waters explains. "And if I'm ashamed of Aunt Jemima — her head rag, her hips, her color — then I'm ashamed of my people."

Of course, interest in African American history has spread beyond a few individuals. Demand for more information about African American history has resulted in corporate-funded PBS breakthrough series such as *Eyes on the Prize, Africans in America, The Rise and Fall of Jim Crow,* and *Slavery and the Making of America.* New scholarship and public demand has inspired increasingly more in-depth coverage of critical aspects of African American and American history that have revealed, among other things, that slavery was an American institution and not just a peculiarity of the South.

General American culture is also embracing African American culture. Many consider Martin Luther King, Jr., one of this nation's greatest Americans, and, some white Americans even wear Malcolm X T-shirts. It isn't rare to find Black History Month celebrated in schools with few or no African American students. In the world of academia, American literature classes include the works of African Americans. *The Narrative of Frederick Douglass* is widely read in high schools, and general Southern literature courses include the work of black Southern writers Zora Neale Hurston, Ernest Gaines, and Alice Walker. In fact, Ernest Gaines is arguably one of the most celebrated Southern writers since William Faulkner, and Nobel Prize–winner Toni Morrison is one of this nation's greatest writers. Awareness and appreciation of African American culture by all is certainly on the rise.

Increasing demand for African American exhibits and museums

A boom in cultural or heritage tourism reflects the growing interest in the African American experience. People of all races have attended landmark exhibits such as the New York Historical Society's "Slavery in New York." Almost every state has uncovered enough information of specific relevance to African Americans to create an African American heritage tour. Exhibits have even gone online; for example, you can explore the Library of Congress's "The African American Odyssey: A Quest for Full Citizenship" exhibit at memory.loc.gov/ammem/aaohtml. The New York Public Library's Schomburg Center for Research in Black Culture also has several online exhibits, including "Malcolm X: A Search for Truth" and "Harlem 1900–1940: An African-American Community" (`www.nypl.org/digital/digitalcoll_allcollections.htm`).

Cultural tourism specifically addressing slavery is increasingly popular, even in the South where the institution of slavery was more pervasive. This heightened interest has resulted in unique museums such as

- ✔ The Slave Relic Museum in Walterboro, South Carolina
- ✔ The Slavery and Civil War Museum in Selma, Alabama, which offers a slave reenactment experience
- ✔ The National Underground Railroad Freedom Center in Cincinnati, Ohio, which gives visitors a taste of the Underground Railroad and various escape strategies used by slaves

African American communities across the nation have a long history of creating institutions to preserve their history. Notable museums include the Smithsonian's respected Anacostia Museum and Center for African American History and Culture in Washington, D.C., and Chicago's venerable DuSable Museum of African American History, named for the Haitian fur trader Jean Baptiste Pointe du Sable, the city's first permanent settler. Two museums commemorating Martin Luther King, Jr.'s life and death, the King Center in Atlanta, spearheaded by Coretta Scott King, and the National Civil Rights Museum in Memphis (located at the Lorraine Motel, the site of King's assassination), are the efforts of committed citizens that remain top tourist destinations in the United States, especially among African Americans.

In 2003, President George W. Bush signed a bill to create the National Museum of African-American History and Culture under the direction of the Smithsonian on the National Mall. This new museum, an expansion of the work of the Anacostia Museum, underscores the greater significance of African American history and culture to the nation as a whole.

Hard Lessons to Learn

Slavery remains a topic chock-full of emotions for many Americans, as former Virginia governor L. Douglas Wilder, the first elected black governor in the nation and the grandson of slaves, learned in his quest to launch the United States National Slavery Museum in Fredericksburg, Virginia. Attracting the support of both corporate and individual donors proved difficult for Wilder because many people don't consider a museum about slavery a healing mechanism that can foster reconciliation with the past.

Slavery as an American (not Southern) institution

Despite the nation's tremendous gains, many people still fail to acknowledge the magnitude of slavery within the United States. They either don't understand or refuse to acknowledge that it was the economic backbone of the colonies and later the country. Although some businesses, such as Philip Morris and Wachovia Bank, have acknowledged their ties to slavery, many others have not. Slave labor, for example, helped build early railroad lines and institutions such as Brown University.

Deadria Farmer-Paellmann, a pioneering force behind the Corporate Restitution Movement (see the section "A question of reparation" later in this chapter), began tracing corporate ties to slavery in 1997. She rose to national prominence in 2000 when insurance giant Aetna apologized for its ties to slavery after learning that a subsidiary of the company insured slaves at one time. Since then, Farmer-Paellmann, an attorney, has uncovered similar links for over 50 companies. Because of Farmer-Paellmann's actions, several local and state governments now require that companies seeking public contracts disclose any links to slavery.

Flagging the issue

The Confederate flag flew during Civil War battles fought by the Confederacy to preserve its right to practice slavery. Yet many nonblack Americans, and a few African Americans as well, don't understand why the presence of the Confederate flag, particularly in government facilities, bothers so many African Americans. Those who defend displaying the Confederate flag charge that African Americans are too sensitive and that the flag represents Southern heritage and honors the Confederate dead and veterans, not racism or Jim Crow. Supporters fail to address the link between white Southern heritage and slavery and Jim Crow. While they defend the gentility of the antebellum South in the symbol of the Confederacy, others can't ignore the savagery of slavery that's part of the story as well.

Compounding the issue is the fact that the Confederate flag resurfaced in the South during the intense struggle to dismantle Jim Crow. South Carolina, for example, erected the Confederate flag atop the statehouse in 1962. It wasn't removed until 2000, after the NAACP spearheaded an economic boycott of the state until the flag was taken down.

A question of reparation

While there is certainly no lack of evidence that slavery was indeed real, those who support the reparations movement, which seeks to obtain acknowledgment and compensation for the descendants of slaves and, in some instances, Jim Crow, have encountered tremendous resistance. Simply pondering a formal apology for slavery created a furor during the Clinton presidency.

The reparations argument isn't a new one. For example, the U.S. government offered the following reparations after the Civil War:

✔ Many Confederate slaveholders who lost their land during the war got it back.

✔ Slaveholders in Washington, D.C., who emancipated their slaves received compensation for their losses.

Other precedents for reparations include a settlement by the federal government to Japanese Americans wrongfully interred during World War II. In 1994, Florida compensated survivors and descendants of the 1923 Rosewood Massacre, in which white Floridians attacked black Floridians. Read more about the Rosewood Massacre in Chapter 7.

The "forty acres and a mule" that General William Sherman promised to African Americans after the Civil War didn't really pan out (refer to Chapter 6), and no form of reparations were paid on a systematic scale to former slaves who later endured Jim Crow. Those who advocated compensation for ex-slaves include Alabama native William R. Vaughan, a white Democrat who proposed an ex-slave pension and, from 1890 to 1903, succeeded in getting nine such bills introduced in Congress, but none ever passed.

Callie House

Born a slave in 1861, Callie House was a washerwoman and widow living in Nashville, Tennessee. She was an important force in the ex-slave pension or reparations movement through her work with the National Ex-Slave Mutual Relief, Bounty and Pension Association, which began in the 1890s. Basing her argument on the fact that ex-Union soldiers received pensions, House specifically targeted the $68 million collected in taxes on rebel cotton to compensate ex-slaves. Trumped-up charges of postal fraud erroneously suggested that her organization, which succeeded in galvanizing 300,000 ex-slaves across several states, was without merit. House's imprisonment in 1917 on postal fraud ended her fight but not her legacy.

Historian and law professor Mary Frances Berry brought the efforts of Callie House into heated contemporary reparations debates with her book *My Face Is Black Is True: Callie House and the Struggle for Ex-Slave Reparations* (2005).

Advocates of reparations say that the movement is about more than money. According to respected historian and political theorist Manning Marable, reparations efforts serve a greater purpose. "What it's about is an effort to reengage the American people in a discussion of racism in American life," Marable explains. "It's not about the money. [We want to] restart a genuine dialogue about racism and the economic consequences of slavery." Citing the black-white income gap and denied access to capital, among other injustices, some economists estimate that racism costs African Americans as much as $10 billion annually.

Fitting Tribute — At Last

On November 13, 2006, not far from the Capitol building (which African American slave labor helped build) and Pennsylvania Avenue (where African American slaves were once sold), three of Martin Luther King, Jr.'s children were present for the groundbreaking of the Martin Luther King, Jr., National Memorial, the first such memorial for an African American. "We give Martin Luther King [Jr.] his rightful place among the many Americans honored on the National Mall," President Bush told a crowd of several thousand that included former president Clinton, who signed the bill authorizing the memorial; poet Maya Angelou; and King's longtime civil rights friends and comrades Jesse Jackson and Ambassador Andrew Young.

Congressman John Lewis, who spoke at the historic March on Washington when King delivered his majestic "I have a dream" speech, broke ground on the memorial in an emotional moment. Not so many decades before, police violently beat Lewis, a former president of the Student Nonviolent Coordinating Committee (SNCC), as he marched with King from Selma to Montgomery seeking only the justice to which all Americans are entitled.

Conceived by his Alpha Phi Alpha fraternity brothers in 1983, the Martin Luther King, Jr., Memorial is a promising step in the right direction that symbolizes much more than a fitting tribute to a man President Bush said "redeemed the promise of America." Such an honor goes beyond one person. "It's because of them that I can be heard," media titan Oprah Winfrey said, referring to the countless African Americans who struggled against incredible odds in the name of freedom for us all.

Chapter 2

From Empires to Bondage: Bringing Africans to the Americas

Slavery is perhaps the most profound consequence of Columbus's so-called "discovery" of the New World. European nations, led by Portugal and Spain, came to the New World in search of riches, but they lacked a work force necessary to procure them. Attempts to use the indigenous population proved unsatisfactory, so the eventual solution was to import Africans. This decision changed the complexion of what became the Americas. Spain and Portugal's early dominance inspired England and other countries to seek their fortunes in the New World, ultimately leading to the establishment of African American culture in what became the United States.

Before delving into the specifics of African American history, it's necessary to recognize the chain of events that brought Africans to the Americas and weigh the impact of those events. Africa was rich with history long before Europeans began pillaging it. When Europeans arrived there, they found three main empires: Ghana, Mali, and Songhay (also spelled Songhai). This chapter explores these African empires. It also examines the launch of the slave trade as well as the implementation of slavery in Latin America and the Caribbean.

Touring African Empires

Modern-day Africa is comprised of *no fewer* than 50 countries, 784 million people, and 1,000 languages. The majority of African Americans, however, trace their roots specifically to West Africa and Central Africa. Countries in this area include Ghana, Cote d'Ivoire (Ivory Coast), Nigeria, and Senegal, as well as Angola and the Congo.

The African continent had a tremendous history before Europeans ever set foot there. Three empires — Ghana, Mali, and Songhay — are particularly important in African American history because many enslaved Africans hailed from these regions (see Figure 2-1).

Figure 2-1:
The Ghana, Mali, and Songhay Empires.

Although slavery existed in early Africa, it greatly differed from the form of slavery practiced in the United States (discussed in Chapter 3). It's important to acknowledge that African Americans, like all other Americans, have a story whose beginnings extend before life in the Americas.

Ghana

Located in West Africa, north of the Niger and Senegal valleys (500 miles from its modern-day namesakes — eastern Senegal, southwest Mali, and southern Mauritania), Ghana, populated by the Soninke, began its rise in the 8th century when the camel revolutionized trade. Its capital city Kumbi Saleh (also Koumbi Saleh) became the center of the important trans-Saharan trade connecting West Africa with Mediterranean countries between the 8th and 16th centuries. Trading gold and salt, in particular, made Ghana rich.

Historians often single out the rule of Tenkamenin (sometimes Tunka Manin), who came to power in 1062, because of his expert governance. Every day, Tenkamenin went among the people and listened to their concerns, giving them an audience until justice prevailed. Although Ghana tolerated Islam during that time, particularly because Muslim traders generated wealth, it hadn't converted, unlike other parts of Africa. The Almoravids, a band of Muslims, first attempted to bring Ghana under Islamic rule in 1068, but Ghana fought them off until 1076. Eventually the Soninke regained control of Ghana, but it was too late to prevent its complete decline by the 13th century.

Ghana's people, the Soninke, know Ghana as Wagadou, meaning "Land of Herds." Europeans, however, took their lead from the term "ghana," meaning "warrior king" — a term used to describe Wagadou's ruler — and renamed the region the Ghana Empire. The European term is the more commonly used one.

Mali

According to oral history, between 1235 and 1238, Sundiata Keita (sometimes Mari Jata) defeated Sumanguru, Ghana's last great ruler, to end Ghana's dominance and begin the Mali Empire, which included parts of Nigeria and the Guinea forests. Mansa Musa (sometimes Mansa Moussa), Mali's Muslim ruler from roughly 1307 to 1332, however, attracted the most attention for Mali outside of Africa with the empire's tremendous wealth, largely accumulated through Ghana's salt and gold mines.

In 1324, Mansa Musa's Hajj, the annual pilgrimage to Mecca, became legendary. As the legend goes, Mansa Musa traveled with a caravan of 60,000 — including 12,000 slaves, 500 of them equipped with staffs of gold — and distributed 80 camel loads of gold dust to the poor. He gave so much gold away in Egypt that gold prices reportedly plummeted.

During Mansa Musa's rule, elaborate mosques were built in Timbuktu, Jenne, and Gao, among other places. Eventually Timbuktu became a highly respected intellectual and commercial center. Good government is cited frequently as one of the main reasons behind Mali's relatively long reign as an important African empire. But in the 15th century, Europeans, captivated by Africa's wealth, began penetrating the continent. These incursions coincided with Mali's decline.

Which way to Timbuktu?

Prosperous trans-Saharan trade routes transformed Timbuktu into a major economic and cultural powerhouse beginning in the 13th century. A city on par with ancient Rome, Timbuktu grew even more in stature during the Mali Empire, which controlled the wealthy gold-salt trade routes in the area. It was during the Songhay Empire, however, that Timbuktu really emerged as the spiritual and intellectual center of the Muslim world. Its great Koranic Sankore University not only attracted some of the world's best minds but also garnered praise from many non-Muslims.

Sadly, when the Songhay Empire declined in the late 16th century, so did Timbuktu. When the slave trade set in, Portugal traders ended Timbuktu's reign as a major commercial center. Contemporary Timbuktu hasn't fared well either. In 1990, because of increasing desertification that has destroyed the vegetation and water supply, Timbuktu made UNESCO's List of World Heritage in Danger. (UNESCO is the United Nations Educational, Scientific and Cultural Organization.) Sand threatens to bury the city and its great monuments completely.

Songhay

By the 15th century, the Songhay Empire emerged and, under the leadership of Sonni Ali (sometimes Sonni Ali Ber), took over the Niger region and encompassed the once-mighty Mali Empire. Taking advantage of Mali's declining empire, Ali conquered Timbuktu in 1469; this move immediately established Songhay as a major power. In 1493, Askia Mohammad, a powerful general, overthrew the government. During his rule, Songhay became an intellectual center, and he used his Hajj to connect with scholars and other heads of state in his efforts to strengthen the Songhay Empire and assist Islam's expansion into West Africa. With that knowledge, he standardized trade, policed trade routes, and instituted a bureaucratic system of government. His son, Askia Musa, overthrew him in 1528. The Songhay Empire fell in the 16th century when the Moroccans overtook it.

Interaction with the rest of the world

Africans weren't isolated from the rest of the world. European and Asian contact with Africans was substantial, as evidenced by the following facts:

- East African societies were in contact with their Asian counterparts very early on, and the interaction was markedly strong.
- Ethiopians lived in Greece around the 5th century BC.

The Egypt-Ethiopia link

Although the Africans who came to the New World as slaves can't trace their direct ancestry back to Egypt, historians have proven that early Ethiopian and Egyptian history is intermingled. Ethiopians and Egyptians married, fought, and traded with each other for centuries. In the 8th century BC, Ethiopia, which some scholars call Kush (or Cush), conquered Egypt. Ethiopian ruler Piye (also Piankhi and Piankhy) was the first to rule both Egypt and Ethiopia completely, from 747 to 716 BC, and began the 25th Dynasty. His son, Taharqa, who dubbed himself Emperor of the World and began his rule in 690 BC, was the last great ruler of the 25th Dynasty.

Discussing Egypt and Ethiopia in terms of African history that relates to African Americans is extremely controversial. Traditional scholars are more comfortable discussing the Ghana, Mali, and Songhay Empires because most of the Africans involved in the slave trade hailed directly from these areas. Yet there's no denying that Egypt's reputation as one of the world's greatest civilizations fed European curiosity regarding Africa.

✔ Because of trade on and off the continent, Africans traveled to many European countries for business.

✔ In 711, the Moors, Muslims who hailed from North Africa, began their rule over the Iberian Peninsula (present-day Spain and Portugal). Portugal freed itself from Moorish rule in the late 13th century, but Spain didn't completely free itself of Moorish rule until 1492.

There's also reason to believe that West African traders established commercial relationships with the indigenous American people long before Columbus's famous 1492 voyage. Mali, according to some Arabic records, sent at least two expeditions across the Atlantic between 1305 and 1312. Some scholars also claim that Columbus, in his journals, noted that Africans were already in the New World when he arrived. Certainly the discovery of skeletal remains resembling those of Africans in Central America, coupled with the African features found in the art of indigenous Americans and the similarities between the language patterns of early Americans and Africans, strongly suggest that Africans could preceded Columbus to the Americas. Mainstream history, however, has been slow to investigate these claims.

Tracking the Slave Trade

Portugal's search for wealth and its settling, along with Spain, of the Americas launched the very lucrative transatlantic slave trade. As other European countries began scrambling for their own pots of gold in the New World, the African slave trade became more competitive. By 1650, the Dutch, English, and French seriously challenged Portugal's monopoly. Africans also aided the slave trade.

Because Europeans arrived in Africa during its declining years, the slave trade generated wealth for some of Africa's poorer states. That wealth became so attractive that Dahomey, a West African kingdom that had vowed not to participate in the Atlantic slave trade, eventually became a key trading center. When Africans began resisting slavery in the 18th century, Europeans, who possessed gunpowder and other warfare advantages, easily repelled them. Initially Africans participated in the slave trade primarily because slavery, on and outside the continent, had been a common practice for centuries.

Slavery in Africa

Unfortunately, every major civilization and almost every ethnic group has been guilty of practicing slavery in one form or another. Africa was no different: Slavery existed on the African continent long before it became one of Europe's hottest enterprises. No matter who practiced it, however, there's little evidence that slavery was ever pleasant. Masters in ancient Greece, Rome, India, and China beat and killed their slaves at will, and the Aztecs may have cut out the hearts of their slaves during elaborate rituals. For the majority of these ancient civilizations, however, war, not race, determined one's slave status. Prior to Portugal's initiation of the slave trade, this was largely the case in Africa.

Captors either sold or kept Africans they captured. Usually these Africans became the property of the chief or the head of the family. Some slaves served as human sacrifices in royal ceremonies. For the most part, children couldn't be sold and often became trusted family members. When the Muslims invaded Africa, the system changed slightly. Purchasing slaves became more common than capturing them. The Muslims seized women for their harems and forced men to serve in the military and perform menial services. Some slaves ended up in Arabia and Persia, among other Islamic strongholds. Still, even under Muslim rule, slavery wasn't as harsh as it would become in the Americas, particularly in the U.S. Slave labor in Africa was used mainly for servitude, not as a means of commercial production, and it wasn't determined by race. This changed with the European slave trade and its development in New World.

Elmina Castle

Built in 1482 by the Portuguese and owned by the Dutch and the British at different points in its history, Elmina Castle may be the oldest European structure south of the Sahara. A monument in the deadly transatlantic slave trade, Elmina Castle saw at least 30,000 African captives pass through its halls annually until the 18th century. Held in dungeons and packed on top of each other, often for days, these Africans marched to slave ships through "the door of no return." Elmina Castle was such an important outpost during the height of the slave trade that it housed cannons to protect itself from other European slave traders.

England, Elmina's last owner, seized control in 1872 and relinquished the fort to Ghanaian leader Kwame Nkrumah in 1957. During the 1990s, Ghana began an exhaustive renovation of the site and the surrounding area, which includes Cape Coast Castle, another important fixture in the slave trade. Today, Elmina Castle is a tourist attraction and a World Heritage Monument.

Launching the European slave trade

Moved by tales of Africa's great wealth, the Portuguese prince known as Henry the Navigator sponsored several voyages to Africa as early as the 1420s. These voyages followed Portugal's 1415 seizure of Ceuta, a Moor stronghold in Morocco, which halted the spread of Islam and promoted Christianity in the region instead. In 1441, Henry's explorers penetrated Africa deeper than previous Europeans had and brought back 12 Africans caught near the coast of northern Mauritania. Most sources cite the 1444 voyage that resulted in the capture and eventual sale of around 240 Africans in Lisbon as the first slave voyage to Africa. Within ten years, Portugal imported roughly 1,000 Africans a year to meet the tremendous demand for domestics, stevedores (dockworkers to load and unload ships), and agricultural workers. Because Henry the Navigator considered himself a devout Christian, his ships sailed under the Order of Christ. Therefore, those African captives often converted to Christianity.

Initially Europeans captured Africans themselves. They didn't involve other Africans until later. Additionally, the first Africans enslaved by Portugal weren't subjected to race-based discrimination because race didn't predetermine their servitude at that time.

Even though the success of these voyages stimulated more competition, the Portuguese ruled the slave trade for nearly a century. The 1479 Treaty of Alcáçovas settled the Castilian succession of Spain, allowing Isabella to become queen; in return, Spain conceded the slave trade to Portugal in addition to allowing Portugal to supply her with slaves. Settling those concerns allowed Portugal to expand its dominion over the slave trade; one example of this expansion was the construction of the fort Elmina Castle in 1482 in what is now Ghana.

When Columbus gave Spain a claim to the New World in 1492, it took little time for Spain to introduce slavery there. By 1501, the governor of Hispaniola (the island now occupied by Haiti and the Dominican Republic) was already requesting African slave labor. The first African slaves arrived to Hispaniola in 1502. Reportedly these slaves, relatively few in number, came directly from Spain, which had a long history of slavery. Once the cultivation of sugar began in the New World, the demand for slave labor increased. By 1518, Portugal was supplying Spain with African slaves in large numbers. As Portugal established its own colonies in the Americas and Spain expanded hers, the slave trade grew.

As the Renaissance swept across Europe, new ideas took hold. The end of feudalism resulted in the emergence of cities and a greater reliance on commercial trade. By the time the Industrial Revolution hit its stride in the mid to late 18th century, a culture of greed and profit already existed. These changes created a greater demand for African slave labor. Although Spain, Portugal, France, England, and the Netherlands, among other countries, played major roles in the slave trade and slavery, the Catholic Church and Africans weren't innocent bystanders.

Africans hitch a ride with New World explorers

While many scholars refuse to entertain the idea that Africans beat Columbus to the New World, they do concede that Africans were prominent in conventional stories of the New World's discovery. It's widely believed that Pedro Alonso Niño, Columbus's navigator on his 1492 voyage uncovering America, was African. Because of a Spanish ban against Africans traveling to the New World, though, some have doubted Niño's race. There's no denying the many Africans who traveled to the New World when Spain lifted its ban in 1501, however.

Accounts of Africans accompanying explorers include the following:

✔ Thirty Africans were present when Vasco Núñez de Balboa discovered the Pacific Ocean.

✔ Africans were with Cortés in Mexico.

✔ Esteban (sometimes Estevanico) was pivotal to Alvar Núñez Cabeza de Vaca's exploration of the modern-day southwestern U.S. Although Native Americans killed Esteban, his travels to the southwestern interior greatly aided the Spanish conquest of the Southwest.

✔ French explorations, especially voyages to the Mississippi Valley and Canada, included Africans.

African Slavery in Latin America and the Caribbean

Following the arrival of the first African slaves to Hispaniola in 1502, it didn't take long to institute slavery into other colonies such as the Spanish-controlled islands of Puerto Rico, Cuba, and Jamaica as well as Mexico, Peru, Venezuela, and the Portuguese-controlled Brazil. By 1620, 300,000 Africans had arrived in the Americas. Portugal, which supplied an estimated 130,000 slaves to Brazil alone, and at least 80,000 slaves to Mexico, was initially the largest importer of slaves.

Columbus crossed the Atlantic to find wealth, so Spain, which claimed one-fifth of the wealth discovered, had ample incentive to sanction slave labor for mining copper, gold, and silver. Work in the mines was very taxing, but Africans seemed in greater supply than the quickly dwindling indigenous population. When mining appeared to be a financial bust, cultivating sugar seemed lucrative. Hispaniola built the Caribbean's first sugar mill in 1516. Spain had a number of sugar mills in various locations of its European empire, so it already had an African slave population experienced in cultivating sugar. The industry grew so rapidly and slaves died so quickly that Spain didn't have enough European slaves to feed the New World demand.

Working in the sugar mills was almost as grueling and dangerous as working in the mines. Being poorly fed didn't help. Unbelievably, many slaves in Latin America (the region comprised of South and Central America) weren't given food to eat and were expected to find food in between their many working hours. Despite the toll on human life, the sugar industry flourished in the Americas, with Brazil and Mexico initially leading the way. By the 17th and 18th centuries, the Caribbean islands of Jamaica, Barbados, and Cuba were also significant sugar producers and exporters.

African slave labor wasn't used just on sugar plantations or in discovering wealth. Africans helped build the New World by working as bricklayers, plasterers, and blacksmiths. They planted and maintained crops as well as tended to sheep and cattle. As they had in Spain, both slave and free Africans worked as domestics, caring for children and handling cooking and cleaning. (Flip to the section "Seeking freedom" for more on free Africans in the colonies.) There were few areas in the New World devoid of African contributions.

By paving the way for slavery in the New World, Spain and Portugal specifically established the economic framework tying slave labor to industrial enterprises. American slaveholders, to a certain degree, took cues from Latin American and Caribbean slavery and, as a result, regulated slave behavior much more rigorously than either Spain or Portugal.

Sanctioning and opposing slavery

Europeans didn't immediately turn to African slave labor as the solution to their labor challenges in Latin America and the Caribbean. At first, Europeans used both Native Americans and Africans for labor, but the hard work and European diseases such as smallpox decimated the Native American population. In one part of Hispaniola, the native population went from one million to only a few thousand in two decades. By contrast, Africans became the ideal solution because they seemed plentiful.

Pope Nicholas V invested Portugal's King Alfonso V with the authority to enslave non-Christians in 1452, so early on, the slave trade had the Catholic Church's blessing. Spain's King Carlos I permitted the slave trade from Africa to the Americas in 1513.

Ironically, the biggest boost to the African slave trade came from a man who fervently opposed slavery — for the native population, anyway: Bishop Bartolomeo de Las Casas supported importing African slaves but only because he saw it as a means to keep Native Americans free and alive. Later, he regretted his decision.

There was, however, early opposition to enslaving Africans.

- Pope Pius II issued a letter in October 1462 condemning the slave trade.
- Pope Leo X decried both slavery and the slave trade in 1514. When Christian pirates presented him with the captured Granadan Leo Africanus, who later wrote about Africa, the pope freed him.
- Pope John III issued the *Sublimus Dei* in 1537, which decried enslaving Native Americans and others simply because they weren't Christians.
- The Archbishop of Mexico, Alonso de Montufár, wrote the Spanish Crown in 1560 questioning African enslavement.
- Friar Tomás de Mercado not only denounced the slave trade in 1569 but also discouraged his fellow Spaniards from participating in it.
- Mexican professor Bartolomé de Albornoz cast doubt on the legality of the slave trade when he published *The Art of Contracts* in 1573.

Although it's certain that many Africans opposed slavery, few are on record. Dom Alfonso, the ruler of the Congo kingdom and a Christian convert, is an exception. Wanting to modernize his kingdom, Dom Alfonso sought the advice and counsel of the Portuguese. When he realized the harmful effects of the slave trade, he wrote to Portugal's King John III in 1526 to end the trade:

[W]e need from [your] kingdoms no other than priests and people to teach in schools, and no other goods but wine and flour for the holy sacrament: that is why we beg of Your Highness to help and assist us in this matter, commanding the factors that they should send here neither merchants nor wares, because it is our will that in these kingdoms [of the Congo] there should not be any trade in slaves nor market for slaves.

Dom Alfonso's pleas were futile. Portugal was the main slave supplier, and demand for slaves was increasing. Spain already had flourishing colonies in the New World, and the French, Dutch, and English, along with Portugal, later established successful colonies. As commercial enterprises such as the sugar industry increased, slavery became further entrenched in the New World. It would be at least a few hundred years more before ending slavery and the slave trade received serious consideration.

Dealing with life as a slave

Racial and class distinctions existed among the Spanish and Portuguese who settled in the New World; the breakdown was as follows, in this order:

1. **White elite**

2. **Mestizos:** Those of mixed European and Native American heritage

3. **Mulattos:** Those of mixed European and African heritage

4. **Native Americans**

5. **Africans**

    1. **Ladinos:** Those born in Africa but who had lived in Spain long enough to know some Spanish and familiarize themselves with Spanish culture

    2. **Bozales:** Those coming straight from Africa to the Americas; they could become ladinos by learning Spanish and converting to Christianity

    3. **Criollos (Creoles):** Those born in the Americas

Soon after their arrival in the Americas, African slaves received Spanish or Portuguese first names. Popular names include Fernando, Juan, Ricardo, and José for men and Mariá, Louisa, and Ana for women. Very rarely did slaves receive a last name. Rather, in paperwork, the country of their origin usually followed their first name, as in Ricardo Angola. Learning Spanish or Portuguese was also necessary in some colonies, especially among domesticated slaves.

Marriage among slaves was acceptable and sanctioned by the government and the Catholic Church, which bestowed married slaves with official documentation. When applying for marriage licenses, slaves had to declare their ethnic backgrounds. Interestingly, slaves had a tendency to marry people with the same backgrounds. In theory, married slaves weren't subject to separation through sale, so perhaps that made marriage more appealing; but overall, slaves desired family life. Cohabitation was greatly discouraged, and bigamy was disdained, but there's evidence that some Africans continued to practice polygamy in the New World. In their culture, if men outnumbered women, it was acceptable for a man to have more than one wife. Colonial authorities broke up these unions whenever possible.

Because African men outnumbered African women in the Americas, the men often became involved with Native American women, another practice discouraged by colonial authorities. Known as *zambos*, the children of free Native American women and African men were born free. To prevent such relationships, authorities passed many restrictions, including keeping Africans and Native Americans from living in the same areas and not allowing them to trade with one another. Because Native Americans and Africans outnumbered whites, it wasn't always easy to enforce such laws.

Even today, Latin America and the Caribbean generally demonstrate a higher retention of African cultural values, and this is mainly because Africans greatly outnumbered whites. Unlike the U.S., which carefully regulated the ratio of whites to Africans and often had white slaveholders directly supervise slave labor, Latin America and the Caribbean teemed with non-whites. Absentee owners weren't at all uncommon and many overseers were *mestizos*. This population imbalance, coupled with Spain and Portugal's early tendency not to separate ethnic groups, allowed for greater cultural retention. For example, in religious practices, Africans simply mingled their own religious beliefs and practices with Catholicism.

Seeking freedom

Despite being able to retain key characteristics of their African culture, Africans enslaved in the New World still desired freedom. And there were various ways through which freedom could be secured.

Grants and purchases of freedom

Slaves could be granted freedom by their masters. Some masters freed elderly and loyal slaves as well as their children with slave mistresses and sometimes the mistresses themselves. There were also slaves who purchased their freedom. Because the Spanish felt that Africans were inferior, freedom, itself, was relative. The Spanish believed Africans required supervision and, therefore, regulated African behavior, sometimes extremely. In Lima, Peru, for example, free blacks weren't buried in coffins because coffins were reserved for whites. Interestingly, skin color also distinguished free Africans, with the higher social status accorded to those with lighter skin.

Escapes

For the men aged 14 to 25 who were most needed in the labor force, freedom was hard to attain, so many of them escaped. Africans actually began escaping as soon as they reached the New World. In 1503, a colony governor complained to Spanish officials in Spain about fleeing slaves. Eventually the Spanish labeled those escapees *cimarrones*. The escaped slaves later formed maroon communities in remote areas. As long as these maroons lived quietly, the Spanish, who seemed to anticipate a certain number of runaways, seemed unconcerned. It wasn't at all uncommon for maroons to attack their former masters and help other slaves escape slavery. Sometimes authorities insisted on re-enslaving maroons. The British fought the maroons in Jamaica for decades before agreeing to a treaty. One of the earliest and most well-known maroon communities is Yanga in Mexico. In 1609, Yanga and the Spanish came to an agreement that allowed the maroon community to continue.

Yanga, Mexico

One of the New World's earliest maroon communities, San Lorenzo de los Negros, was renamed Yanga in 1932 after its founder, former African slave Gaspar Yanga. Revolting against the Spanish near Veracruz, Mexico, in 1570, Yanga, who was also a Muslim, led a group into the highlands, where they established their free colony. In 1606 and again in 1609, the Spanish colonial government sent troops to destroy the community, but each time encountered greater resistance than they anticipated.

When Yanga became too elderly to lead the resistance, Francisco de la Matosa, an Angolan, continued to protect the community against the colonial government. When Spanish troops burned the community, Yanga and his crew resettled nearby. Eventually, the Spanish agreed to a treaty, and the town established itself officially in 1630.

Thanks to Mexican author and historian Vincente Riva Palacio, a former mayor of Mexico City and grandson of Mexico's "Black President" Vincente Guerrero, who brought the story to widespread attention in the 1870s, Yanga is known today. A statue of Yanga stands near Veracruz, Mexico, where the town remains.

Rebellions

In addition to escaping, Latin American and Caribbean slaves plotted their freedom through rebellions. The Spanish were especially quick to quell any rebellious activity, often hanging those even rumored of conspiring. The most famous slave revolt is the Haitian Revolution (1791–1803), in which Africans (slave and free) embraced the ideals of the French Revolution and fought the French for their right to citizenship in what would become the free republic of Haiti on January 1, 1804.

The official abolition of slavery

While many Caribbean and Latin American colonies wouldn't earn their independence until the 20th century, the European powers did abolish slavery in Latin America and the Caribbean in the 19th century. Slavery ended in the British colonies in 1833 and in the French colonies in 1848. In Puerto Rico, Cuba, and Brazil, slavery wouldn't end until 1873, 1886, and 1888 respectively.

Chapter 3

The Founding of Black America

The year 1619 marks the official arrival of Africans to what would evolve into the United States of America. Even though African slaves weren't uncommon in other parts of the Americas, including some areas that would later comprise the United States (refer to Chapter 2), historical sources indicate that these Africans were closer in status to the early white indentured servants who could become free. In time, that equality in status would disappear. The American Revolution, despite its philosophical underpinning of the equality of all men, did not improve matters much for black Americans.

This chapter explores slavery's early development in British North America, touching upon the transatlantic slave trade and its horrible Middle Passage before turning attention to how white colonists, in the course of their own fight for freedom, established a democracy rooted in the bondage of others.

From Servitude to Slavery

Until recently, no one was certain where the ship carrying the first documented Africans to arrive in Jamestown, Virginia, in 1619 originated. Recent scholarship traces those Africans back to the *San Juan Bautista,* a Portuguese slave ship that was raided by two British ships. One of those ships, the *White Lion,* which flew a Dutch flag, landed in Jamestown in 1619 and, according to John Rolfe, Jamestown's most well-known early settler, swapped "20 and odd Negroes" (presumably taken from the *San Juan Bautista)* for "victuale."

After the arrival of these first Africans, the black population grew steadily. Although historical records show that parents Isabella and Antoney baptized their son, William, the first black child born in the English colonies, in 1624, the vast majority of early Africans, like those early white settlers, arrived by boat. Approximately 300 Africans lived in Virginia in 1649, at a time when race still didn't predetermine one's slave status.

While historians are still uncertain about the true status of these early Africans, it is clear they weren't enslaved for life. Instead, their treatment resembled that of indentured servants who worked a number of years before obtaining their freedom. A 1673 Virginia court case forcing Andrew Moore's master to set him free for service confirms the indentured status of early Africans.

The Virginia colony wasn't an anomaly. When the ship *Desire* arrived in Massachusetts in 1638, the Africans on board weren't automatically slaves for life. The same was true in New York, then a Dutch colony known as New Netherland. In 1644, 11 blacks filed a petition for their freedom and secured it. In fact, records from 1651 and 1652 show that some black people owned their own property and even had indentured servants themselves. This indentured status would be short-lived, however. During the same time that many Africans gained their freedom through indentured servitude, measures leading to the lifelong enslavement of Africans based solely on race were falling into place.

Inching toward slavery

The 1640 sentencing of John Punch to a lifetime of servitude to his master was a pivotal event in the eventual enslavement of black people based solely on race. Punch's sentence is noteworthy because, although he ran away from his Virginia master with two white servants — and the only offense cited was running away — the white servants received only four additional years of servitude, not a lifelong sentence. It wasn't completely unexpected, however; a year before Virginia passed a statute to distribute arms and ammunition to "all persons except Negroes."

Laws inching the colonies closer and closer to enslaving Africans based solely on race followed in both Virginia and Maryland, especially in the 1660s:

  ✔ A 1662 Virginia statute established that the mother's status determined a child's freedom.

✔ Both Virginia, in 1667, and Maryland, in 1671, established laws that Christian conversion didn't change one's slave status (heathenism was once a justification for slavery).

✔ A 1669 Virginia statute specifically equating "negroes" and "slaves" stated that a master wasn't responsible if a slave died while he was administering punishment.

Virginia's Slave Codes of 1705, a series of laws defining and regulating slave status and behavior, left no speculation regarding how the colonists viewed Africans. Ultimately, a number of factors contributed to the formal adoption of African slavery in the colonies.

Why Africans?

Like the Spanish (refer to Chapter 2), the English found that enslaving Native Americans wasn't plausible. Not only were Native Americans sickly due to their inability to ward off the foreign pathogens that the colonists brought, but they also knew the lay of the land and could escape easily. In the free-labor system that included both blacks and whites, whites (designated as English, Irish, or Dutch and not by race then) proved inept workers. They also had the protection of a government, and if they managed to escape, they could blend in with other non-African settlers. From a slave proponent's perspective, Africans offered several advantages:

✔ Because of their dark skin, Africans were easily identifiable.

✔ Africans were strong as well as adept at agriculture.

✔ Granted a monopoly on the British slave trade, the success of the Royal African Company, formed in 1672, made African labor more accessible and affordable to colonists.

Slave trading became one of Britain's most competitive enterprises. All this activity coincided with the increased commercial production of rice, tobacco, cotton, and other goods, which made slavery an indispensable means to economic wealth in the North American colonies.

The Triangular Trade

Slavery's formal acceptance by the colonies significantly changed the lives of Africans, and the slave trade, coupled with the goods produced by her colonies, made England a superpower. For England, the slave trade reached its peak during the 18th century as a very profitable three-way exchange, known as the *Triangular Trade,* developed. Here's how it worked:

- ✔ **Leg 1:** Typically, a shipment of goods, which could include beads, cloth, hardware, rum, salt, and guns, left England (particularly London, Bristol, or Liverpool) for West Africa.

- ✔ **Leg 2:** In West Africa, the goods were swapped for captured Africans who were packed into slave ships by the hundreds to journey across the Atlantic Ocean to the Americas — first to the Caribbean and sometimes on to North America.

- ✔ **Leg 3:** In the Americas, Africans were unloaded and replaced with molasses, rum, sugar, tobacco, or any other hot commodity before heading back to England.

The term *Triangular Trade* stemmed from the fact that the route, which could take a full year to complete, actually formed a triangle on a map. In time, however, the "triangle" referred more to the route's three-way exchange system of goods for slaves for goods.

Not all ships that sailed back and forth to Africa originated in England, as the colonies set up a triangular trade of their own, which bypassed England: New England distilled sugar and molasses from Caribbean plantations and then shipped them to Africa in exchange for slaves who, in turn, produced more sugar in the Caribbean before beginning the process again. Some slaves also wound up in New England; by 1755, New England had more than 13,000 slaves.

The first slave voyage from British North America left Boston in 1644; by the 1670s, Massachusetts traders regularly carried slaves from Africa to the Caribbean. Rhode Island entered the slave trade around 1700 and had as many as 20 ships sailing from Newport to Africa by the 1750s; an estimated 60 percent of the North American ships involved in the slave trade were from Rhode Island. The arrival of slaves to British North America reached its peak during the 18th century. Overall, it's believed that between 500,000 and 550,000 slaves came from Africa, mainly via the Caribbean, to what is now the United States.

The Middle Passage

Named for the middle leg of the Triangular Trade from Africa to the Americas, the *Middle Passage,* which involved hundreds of Africans packed into ships for months, claimed the lives of many Africans. Death toll estimates vary widely, but approximately 1 to 3 million of the estimated 11 to 18 million Africans reportedly transported to the Americas and the Caribbean through the transatlantic slave trade between the 16th and early 19th century died before ever reaching land.

The capture

By the slave trade's peak in the 18th century, European nations had established an intricate system of trading posts and forts along the West African coast. Largely ignorant of the African interior, European traders relied on Africans to capture other Africans deep in the continent.

Although African slavery differed greatly from the form of slavery that took hold in the Americas, greed still motivated the Africans who assisted European traders in exchange for goods or even guns to give them an advantage over other Africans with whom they were at odds.

Principal regions from which Africans were captured included Senegambia, Sierra Leone, the Windward Coast, the Gold Coast, Bight of Benin, Bight of Biafra, and Central Africa (primarily Angola). Among the Africans captured — some were the spoils of war; others kidnapping victims — there was no discrimination. They hailed from various racial groups with no distinctions made between servants and royalty. No one was safe: Even the Africans selling other Africans could become slaves.

Ayuba Suleiman Diallo, or Job ben Solomon

Born in Bondou, West Africa, around 1702, Ayuba Suleiman Diallo, better known as Job ben Solomon, is one of the rare African captives who returned to Africa. Kidnapped while heading home after selling two Africans for 28 cattle, Solomon, a merchant from a wealthy family, found himself sold to the captain of the *Arabella,* moored on the Gambia River. Immediately after his capture, Solomon sent a note to his wealthy father for help, but the ship on which Solomon was loaded sailed before his father could respond.

In Annapolis, Maryland, Alexander Tolsey, a planter from Queen Anne's County, purchased Solomon, whose job as a cattle herder gave him the opportunity to plan his escape. Easily caught, Solomon went to jail. Not giving up, Solomon, a Muslim, wrote a letter in Arabic to Vachell Denton, the man who had sold him on the auction block. Curious, Denton forwarded the letter to William Hunt, an investor in the *Arabella,* in London.

Believing that Solomon's powerful relatives could prove beneficial for future African trading ventures, James Oglethorpe, a Royal African Company official, purchased Solomon's freedom. By 1733, Solomon was on a ship from Annapolis to London. He returned to the Gambia River in August 1734, four years after he left, only to find his once prosperous country poor, his father dead, and his wife living with another man. Still Solomon, unlike many, many others, returned home to Africa. Biographer Thomas Bluett recorded his remarkable story in *Some Memoirs of the Life of Job,* published in 1734.

Capture was only the beginning. Some African captives had to walk 500 miles to the coast, often naked and barefoot and sometimes in chains, to reach the dungeons or "negroe houses" they occupied at the forts and factories that dotted the coast. After surgeons examined them, acceptable captives were marked on the breast by a hot iron bearing the imprint of the respective company that may have purchased them for as little as $25 in goods.

The voyage

Branded and chained, newly purchased slaves were packed into ships with literally no room to move for a voyage that could last anywhere from six to ten or more weeks (see Figure 3-1). Length of voyage (the shorter the better) rather than ship size (smaller ships were more common than larger ones) determined survival rates. Diseases such as dysentery and smallpox only exacerbated already horrifically unsanitary conditions. Crews threw so many dead bodies overboard that sharks often followed slave ships. Even worse, when the journey ended, some captives remained chained to dead bodies.

Figure 3-1:
Slave deck
of the
Wildfire.

© Bettmann/Corbis

The wreck of the *Henrietta Marie,* a slave ship

In 1972, in his search for the sunken Spanish ship *Nuestra Senora de Atocha* off the coast of Key West, diver Moe Molinar, a member of renowned treasure hunter Mel Fisher's team, didn't quite know what to make of the shackles he uncovered instead.

A decade after Molinar's discovery, archaeologist David Moore and salvor Henry Taylor arranged to inspect the ship more closely. They found a bell inscribed "THE HENRIETTA MARIE 1699." Further study revealed that the ship was a 120-ton British slave ship that had set sail from London in 1700 for Africa's Guinea Coast, which spanned modern-day Sierra Leone to Lagos, Nigeria. In Africa, the ship took on 250 men, women, and children before heading to Jamaica and its wealthy sugar plantations. Fourteen weeks later, the *Henrietta Marie* reached Port Royal, Jamaica, with 190 captives for sale. It's estimated that the ship's cargo grossed over $400,000. In June 1700, on its way back to England, the *Henrietta Marie* shipwrecked near Key West, Florida.

Today, the *Henrietta Marie* is the only fully recovered slave ship in the United States. More than 7,000 artifacts, including shackles, Venetian glass trade beads, and ivory "elephant's teeth," make up the U.S.'s first major museum exhibition devoted to the transatlantic slave trade. For more info on the *Henrietta Marie,* visit www.melfisher.org/henriettamarie.htm.

It's estimated that two out of every ten Africans who left the African coast didn't survive the Middle Passage. White crewmembers didn't fare well either. Yet even with the high death tolls, these voyages were still very profitable.

Safe arrival

A captive's transatlantic journey could be torturous due to trade winds or storms, but the last leg was usually the most pleasant. With the intended destination in close proximity, captives received more food to fatten them up for sale. Once docked, doctors examined captives either on the ship or in quarantine stations, locations holding Africans before sale. Slave brokers determined price, discounting those captives who weren't in great health.

In the Caribbean, especially on smaller islands, buyers purchased survivors straight from the ships. Most British ships, however, headed to Jamaica and Barbados, two of Britain's largest slavery strongholds in the Caribbean. Slave traders often sold captives who reached North America in public auctions in Virginia and New England, where taverns and stores could sell slaves; Figure 3-2 shows a poster announcing the arrival of slaves.

Gorée Island and Sullivan's Island

On Gorée Island near Dakar, Senegal, the House of Slaves, a prime holding station for Africans prior to their dispatch to the Americas in the transatlantic slave trade, has become a popular tourist destination for many African Americans partaking in heritage tours. The majority of African Americans, however, can't trace their ancestors directly back to this holding station, which was controlled mostly by the French, unless they're from Louisiana, which was once a French territory.

Sullivan's Island, just north of Charleston Harbor in South Carolina, is a more accurate heritage spot for most African Americans. According to respected historian Ira Berlin, almost 400,000 African slaves entered the United States through the Lowcountry or South Carolina region. Between 1787 and 1808, the year importing slaves became illegal, slave owners purchased over 100,000 Africans. Therefore, a substantial number of African Americans, anywhere from 40 to 75 percent depending on the source, can trace their ancestors' entry into the United States to Sullivan's Island.

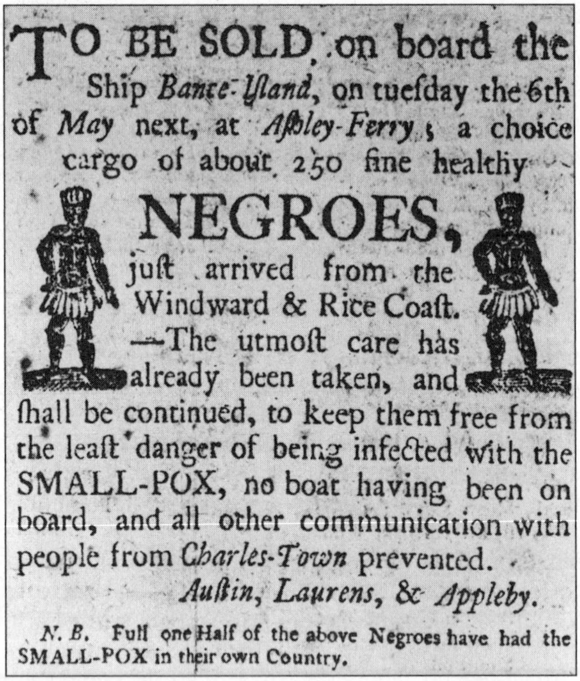

Figure 3-2:
Poster announcing the new slave arrivals.

TO BE SOLD, on board the Ship *Bance-Island*, on tuesday the 6th of *May* next, at *Ashley-Ferry*; a choice cargo of about 250 fine healthy

NEGROES,

just arrived from the Windward & Rice Coast. —The utmost care has already been taken, and shall be continued, to keep them free from the least danger of being infected with the SMALL-POX, no boat having been on board, and all other communication with people from *Charles-Town* prevented.

Austin, Laurens, & Appleby.

N. B. Full one Half of the above Negroes have had the SMALL-POX in their own Country.

© Bettmann/Corbis

At the auctions, such as the one depicted in the print shown in Figure 3-3, slaves sold for $150 or more. Women of childbearing age often yielded higher prices. Usually, families were broken up prior to the voyage, and if they remained intact, those who oversaw the auction made little effort to keep them together. In the early 19th century, when the domestic slave trade replaced the transatlantic slave trade, prices and the ruthlessness of traders both rose considerably.

Figure 3-3: A slave auction.

© Leonard de Selva/Corbis

African Americans and the Revolution

By the time of the American Revolution, slavery was entrenched in British North America. During this time, not one colony banned it. Despite this dim reality, when the colonists began to describe their relationship with England using the master-slave paradigm, freedom had to seem attainable to many African Americans. Surely, those who *felt* enslaved could empathize with those who *were* enslaved. Therefore, many African Americans embraced the American Revolution.

A bit of background

Because of various countries' extensive investment in the New World, Europe's battles for power didn't exclude the Americas. During the French and Indian War (known as the Seven Years' War in Europe), Americans such as George Washington got their first taste of military action. Although England emerged from the battle with possession of Florida and Canada, the war changed how the English interacted with the colonists.

Prior to the French and Indian War, English intrusion in the colonists' lives had been minimal. The war, however, created a lot of debt. Because England felt it couldn't afford additional wars, King George III mandated that colonists not settle beyond the crest of the Appalachian Mountains. The problem was that many colonists had supported the British precisely so that they could expand westward.

Making matters worse, the British passed a series of laws — the Revenue Act, also known as the Sugar Act (1764), the Stamp Act (1765), and the Townshend Act (1767) — that taxed the colonists for the first time. With their political and economic freedom threatened, the colonists began to entertain new ideas regarding their relationship with England, frequently referring to themselves as slaves to English tyranny.

Recognizing the colonists' hypocritical position, Abigail Adams bluntly expressed her sentiments in a 1774 letter to her husband John Adams, who would become the second U.S. president: "It always appeared a most iniquitous scheme to me to fight ourselves for what we're daily robbing and plundering from those who have as good a right to freedom as we have."

Fighting for freedom

In 1770, at the Boston Massacre, a black man named Crispus Attucks was not only the first to die but also encouraged those around him, whites included, to stand their ground against the British. Because of the former slave, unarmed American colonists stood eye to eye against armed British soldiers. Yet Attucks was far from the only African American who stood up for freedom. Four Boston slaves petitioned the colonial legislature in Massachusetts for their freedom in 1773, and a year later, blacks in Massachusetts asked Governor Thomas Gage to abolish slavery. So when the fighting began in the American Revolution, African Americans sided with freedom.

AFRICAN AMERICAN FACES

Crispus Attucks

A runaway slave for more than 20 years, Crispus Attucks instigated the Boston Massacre of 1770, a pivotal event that led to the American Revolution. The son of an African father and Indian mother, Attucks worked on a whaling crew that sailed out of Boston Harbor. His animosity toward the British was the product of a number of factors, including the competition he faced from British troops who took part-time jobs during off-duty hours for lower wages and his fear of being drafted into the British navy.

Three days prior to the fateful March 5, a fight erupted between ropemakers and three British soldiers. Thus, when a British soldier entered a pub looking for work, he found a group of angry seamen, including Attucks, instead. About 30 men tormented the job-seeker before soldiers came to his rescue. Despite being unarmed, Attucks and his crew didn't back down, and

Attucks was the first of five to die. The significance of Attucks's actions wasn't lost on those who dubbed the incident the Boston Massacre and elevated Attucks to martyr status. Despite laws and customs restricting the burial of blacks, Attucks's body rested with the others in Park Street Cemetery.

Ironically, John Adams, later a U.S. president, painted Attucks a rogue in court to defend the British soldiers, who won an acquittal. That outcome outraged the colonists more and made the American Revolution even more attractive. In 1858, black abolitionists honored the revolutionary with Crispus Attucks Day. Thirty years later, objections from both the Massachusetts Historical Society and the New England Historic Genealogical Society, which considered him a villain, couldn't prevent the erection of the Crispus Attucks Monument in Boston Common.

At the same time that Attucks and Peter Salem, who distinguished himself enough at Bunker Hill to grace a postage stamp, were siding with the Americans, George Washington, who would later become the new country's first president, took steps to bar blacks from the American forces. In July 1775, he sent an order to recruiting officers instructing them not to enlist black soldiers. (Existing black soldiers remained in service.)

Months later, Lord Dunmore of Virginia countered by declaring free all black indentured servants or slaves who could fight for the Crown. As a result, other blacks, such as Southerners Thomas Jeremiah and a dockworker named Sambo, joined the British camp. On December 31, 1775, Washington, backed by the Continental Congress days later, reversed his policy slightly to allow free blacks to serve.

Some states like New Hampshire and New York offered freedom to slaves who fought with the Americans, and many slaves, no doubt motivated by the possibility that their status would improve in victory, joined in the efforts. Georgia and South Carolina refused to enlist slaves even when the Continental Congress offered to pay for every slave recruited. Yet there were some black sailors in the South who served bravely on several vessels.

In all, about 5,000 African Americans fought for the American cause. Massachusetts, Connecticut, and Rhode Island even had a few all-black companies. Black soldiers Prince Whipple and Oliver Cromwell were with Washington when he crossed the Delaware on Christmas Day in 1776. Free black Haitians even came to fight for the patriots' cause. There's no denying that Africans made substantial contributions to the victory that established the United States of America.

Hope and disappointment

Prior to the actual start of the American Revolution, African Americans had many reasons to believe freedom was near. Although John Locke, whom the colonists admired, had recognized slavery in his *Constitutions of Carolina,* John Woolman's *Considerations On Keeping Negroes*, along with works by James Otis and Thomas Paine, showed that more whites were questioning slavery. Even without a passage specifically decrying slavery in the Declaration of Independence, African Americans had every reason to feel encouraged by the declaration's proclamation that "all men are created equal, that they are endowed by their Creator with certain unalienable Rights, that among these are Life, Liberty and the pursuit of Happiness."

And there were a few encouraging signs: Some whites extended the revolutionary ideology to African Americans, and manumission (freedom) societies sprouted with the intent of emancipating those still enslaved. This spirit directly resulted in the freedom of the many black soldiers who fought in the war and their families. On a larger scale, Massachusetts, Connecticut, and Rhode Island made early moves to abolish slavery, and New York and New Jersey weren't far behind. In 1775, the Quakers began establishing antislavery organizations.

Still it was clear that independence from England alone wouldn't change conditions for the majority of African Americans. Despite signs that the new Constitution would live up to the promise made in the Declaration—that all men are created equal — compromises that undermined the promise of freedom were also made. The Constitution included a provision to ban the slave trade in 1808, but it also included the designation of a slave as three-fifths of a person (an agreement reached to appease Southern delegates). It was clear that the road to ending the American institution of slavery would be long and arduous.

The suppressed passage

Thomas Jefferson wrote the following passage, which condemns slavery but did not make it into the Declaration of Independence:

"[George III] has waged cruel war against human nature itself, violating its most sacred rights of life and liberty in the persons of a distant people who never offended him, captivating and carrying them into slavery in another hemisphere, or to incur miserable death in their transportation thither. This piratical warfare, the opprobrium of *infidel* powers, is warfare of the Christian king of Great Britain. Determined to keep open a market where MEN should be bought and sold, he has prostituted his negative [veto] for suppressing every legislative attempt to prohibit or to restrain this execrable commerce: and that this assemblage of horrors might want no fact of distinguished die, he is now exciting these very people to rise in arms among us, and to purchase that liberty of which he deprived them, by murdering the people upon whom *he* also obtruded them; thus paying off former crimes committed against the *liberties* of one people, with crimes he urges them to commit against the *lives* of another."

The Free African Society and the Birth of Black America

As black Americans — even those who had fought for American independence — were excluded in efforts to create the new nation, eight black men took matters into their own hands and helped form the basic foundation of black America.

On April 12, 1787, a month before the U.S. Constitutional Convention, Absalom Jones and Richard Allen and six others gathered in Philadelphia to create the Free African Society, a non-denominational organization formed to address the needs of the larger black community. Unlike the Newport, Rhode Island–based Free African Union Society that preceded it, members of the Free African Society weren't interested in repatriating to Africa. "This land," Richard Allen declared years later, "which we have watered with our tears and our blood is now our mother country."

The creation of the Free African Society was a pivotal first step in establishing black America. Its mission and duties, coupled with the black church (which you can read more about in Chapter 12) and social and fraternal organizations such as the African Lodge, the main organ of black Masons, began to address critical issues regarding African Americans. These efforts recognized the unique position African Americans held in the United States, a position W.E.B. Du Bois labeled *"double consciousness,"* his belief that African Americans possessed a "twoness" that made them both American and African.

An African American lodge

The African Lodge traces its roots back to March 6, 1775, when a British Lodge of Freemasons near Boston initiated 15 African Americans, including Prince Hall who hailed from Barbados. Following a rejection from white Americans to establish an African American chapter for Masons in Boston, an appeal by Hall and others to the Grand Lodge of England in 1784 resulted in African Lodge No. 459, which received its full charter in 1787. Under Hall's leadership, black Masons organized Grand Lodges and their movement, which often took on civic causes such as education, steadily grew. Today, to honor its pioneer, this form of Freemasonry is labeled Prince Hall Masonry.

Part II
Long Road to Freedom

The 5th Wave   By Rich Tennant

"Frederick Douglass wanted to set up a meeting with you, Mr. President. I asked him when he would be free, and he said only you would know that."

In this part . . .

As the United States started to grow in the 19th century, the question of slavery became more contentious. Impatient with how long the government was taking to end slavery, countless folks began working to free slaves via the Underground Railroad, and slaves staged violent rebellions. In response, Southern slaveholders pushed for stronger fugitive slave laws.

This part examines the escalation of the slavery issue, from the Underground Railroad to the passing of fugitive slave laws and from the election of President Lincoln to the secession of Southern states and the outbreak of the Civil War. It also explores the war's outcome in terms of the emancipation of slaves and the effect that efforts made to rebuild the union during Reconstruction had on African Americans.

Chapter 4

American Slavery, American Freedom

- -

In This Chapter

▶ Contrasting slavery in the North and the South

▶ Plotting for freedom

▶ Living with conditional freedom

- -

*B*anning the importation of slaves in 1808 did little to reduce slavery's intensity in the United States. Despite being founded on a platform of freedom, the U.S. wasn't ready to leave slavery behind. During the early 19th century, the domestic slave trade proved as inhumane and ruthless as the transatlantic slave trade had been. Major economic changes contributed to slavery's proliferation.

The Industrial Revolution in England eventually created a greater demand for cotton in the booming textile industry. Similar developments in the North added to that demand, and the South eagerly responded to the call. With the advent of the cotton gin in 1793, cotton plantations began to boom, requiring more slaves to perform the labor-intensive work of cultivating cotton. The low cost of slave labor coupled with the payoff of increased cotton production, in addition to staple cash crops such as rice and sugar, meant planters needed more slaves.

This chapter explores the intricacies of the domestic slave trade and the ins and outs of slave life in the North and the South, as well as the tenuous life free blacks experienced, even in the North. These circumstances fueled the tug of war between slavery and freedom that eventually led to the Civil War.

American Bondage

The first Africans didn't come to the North American colonies as slaves, but less than a century later their skin color was synonymous with the institution (refer to Chapter 3). Being born black generally meant a lifetime of slavery, and there were no exceptions for those of mixed race. Those who managed to win their freedom weren't safe either.

In the U.S., the law designated slaves as property, with a value no greater than furniture, yet how slavery was practiced in the United States differed by region. The next sections describe slavery in both the North and South.

An estimated 500,000 to 550,000 slaves came to the United States via the transatlantic slave trade, but the slave population increased mainly through birth rates. In 1800, the slave population was just over one million. By the onset of the Civil War, the slave population numbered approximately four million.

Northern slavery

Today many still view slavery as a Southern institution, but in reality, it was an American institution. Slavery was big business that involved much of the nation either directly or indirectly. Therefore, blame doesn't rest solely with the South.

The lucrative domestic slave trade

"I wish you may visit me early this Spring to make some arrangements about your Negroes. If they continue high I would advise you to sell them in this country on one and two years credit bearing 8 per ct interest. The present high price of Negroes can not continue long and if you will make me a partner in the sale on reasonable terms I will bring them out this Fall from VA and sell them for you and release you from all troubles. On a credit your Negroes would bring here about $120 to $130,000 bearing 8 per ct interest. My object is to make a fortune here as soon as possible by industry and economy, and then return [to Virginia] to enjoy myself. Therefore I am willing to aid you in any way as far as reason will permit."

(Henry A. Tayloe of Marengo County, Alabama, to "Dear Brother" [B.O. Tayloe] on January 5, 1835)

Universities' ties to slavery

Some of the North's and the world's most prestigious universities also have ties to slavery. Perhaps the most prominent is Brown University. The Brown family, an early benefactor to its eventual namesake, owned several businesses tied directly and indirectly to slavery. Family member John Brown was actually a prosecuted slave trader. In addition, slave labor built Brown's University Hall. Cognizant of this history, Brown's president Ruth Simmons, the descendant of slaves and the Ivy League's first African American president, took proactive measures and organized a committee to examine those ties as well as propose how Brown could reconcile that history in 2004.

Although three Yale graduate students helped spark Brown's introspection with their 2001 report questioning Yale's ties to slavery, Yale resisted further inspection. According to Yale President Richard Levin, "American history is full of embarrassments. We know today that slavery was very widespread in the North as well as the South, at least prior to the Revolutionary War. There are a number of early leaders of this institution who were slave owners. It's simply a fact of history."

Northern slave owners: A sampling

Douglas Harper, author of several books on the Civil War who maintains a Web site about slavery in the North, notes how some well-known Northern families profited from slavery. According to Harper, "A list of the leading slave merchants is almost identical with a list of the region's prominent families: the Fanueils, Royalls, and Cabots of Massachusetts; the Wantons, Browns, and Champlins of Rhode Island; the Whipples of New Hampshire; the Eastons of Connecticut; Willing and Morris of Philadelphia." Other prominent Americans owned slaves. Benjamin Franklin owned slaves at one time but later became a leading antislavery activist. Abraham Lincoln's immediate family opposed slavery, but he had paternal ancestors who owned slaves in colonial Pennsylvania in the 18th century.

Life as a Northern slave

Slavery in the North wasn't necessarily any less cruel than slavery in the South. As in the South, Northern slaves were sometimes purposely bred for market, families were separated (as evidenced by a 1732 advertisement announcing that a 19-year-old black woman and her child could be sold together or separately), and Northern slaves suffered maltreatment at the hands of their owners. Philadelphia brickmaker John Coats, for example, reportedly kept his slave workers in iron collars with shackles.

Slavery and marriage

Although the law didn't recognize slave marriages, many slaveholders encouraged them mainly because settled slaves with families were less likely to flee. *Broad marriages,* marriages between slaves with different owners, were less desirable, however. While it wasn't uncommon for slave masters to perform marriage ceremonies, that recognition didn't necessarily protect slave women from sexual assaults. Young slave women were even more vulnerable, and children fathered by slave masters weren't uncommon. It was even a ritual among some young white men to have their first sexual experience with a female slave.

In the U.S., slave families, either from the North or the South, didn't often remain intact. Indebted slaveholders sold slaves or traded them to settle their accounts. A slaveholder's heirs didn't always honor his or her intention to keep slaves together. In other instances, wills scattered slaves throughout the family. Circumstances such as these separated children from their mothers, husbands from their wives.

Much is unknown about the specific duties of Northern slaves. Because the North was largely rural during slavery's early days, it's assumed that most slaves worked the land alongside their owners. Smaller households had fewer slaves, which meant that slaves often lived in their masters' households instead of in separate quarters. As cities emerged, many slaves, particularly women and children, worked as domestics.

Northern slavery after the Revolution

Northern slavery declined following the American Revolution, in part because a number of slaves won their freedom during the war. Increased industrialization and wage labor also contributed to slavery's decline in the North even though some companies did operate with slave labor.

Although most of the North legally abolished slavery following the American Revolution, that fact is misleading: Gradual emancipation was far more common than immediate freedom. According to the 1800 census, New England was home to 1,488 slaves. Connecticut, for example, didn't completely abolish slavery until 1848, and in 1850, there were still 236 slaves in New Jersey. In addition, New England–based slave ships carried almost all the 156,000 slaves who entered the United States between 1801 and 1808. Even after the slave trade legally ended in 1808, such shipments continued, albeit to a lesser degree, because of poor enforcement of the edicts. Northern ships, however, carried slave goods to various destinations up until the Civil War. Northern factories also transformed Southern cash crops such as cotton into marketable consumer goods.

Southern slavery

Slavery wasn't a hidden institution in the South, but the reality wasn't quite the same as traditional depictions in the years since. For example, large plantations resembling those seen in *Gone with the Wind* and the *North and South* miniseries weren't the norm. In reality, relatively few Southerners owned huge plantations with large numbers of slaves. Of the 8 million whites who lived in the South in 1860, 384,884 were slave owners, with 200,000 of them owning five slaves or fewer. Yet even white Southerners who didn't own slaves generally felt invested in the slave system.

Even though the majority of Southern slave owners had five or fewer slaves, very little information exists regarding the intricacies of slave life on smaller farms. There's much more information about slave owners with plantations of 20 or more slaves. Larger slave owners not only kept better records; they were also more influential, economically and politically. This is why they dominate American popular culture.

Labor on plantations

The complexion of the American plantation changed tremendously between the late 17th century and the 19th century. Plantation size and the crops cultivated greatly affected slave culture. Backbreaking labor, however, was consistent regardless of plantation size or crop cultivation, with slave duties extending well beyond planting and harvesting crops.

Rice plantations

On South Carolina's rice plantations, slaves taken largely from the Sierra Leone region of Africa and from the West Indies were often more skilled in rice cultivation than their owners. To these slaves fell the backbreaking work of carving rice fields out of the tidal swamp area; clearing cypress and gum trees from low-lying lands; and building canals, dikes, and small floodgates that drained and flooded the fields in correlation to the high and low tides. On top of these tasks, they also planted, maintained, and harvested the crop.

Rice plantations, particularly in South Carolina and Georgia, worked on the *task system,* in which slaves received and performed specific duties. Tasks could include clearing the land for rice, draining the rice fields, harvesting rice, and milling the rice. Uncompleted tasks warranted punishment, usually whippings. Grueling work, as well as rampant malaria and fever, killed many slaves young. Life in South Carolina was so hard that few whites survived it, especially in its early years. As a result, blacks, some of whom became immune to malaria, greatly outnumbered whites in parts of South Carolina, sometimes by as much as a three-to-one ratio.

Smoking: Not the only way tobacco kills

Tobacco cultivation included as many as 36 steps. Planting, weeding, and harvesting tobacco wasn't a simple undertaking. Beginning in January and February, slaves selected seedbeds, cleared them, and burned them. In mid-March, they sowed tobacco seeds into a layer of ashes and covered the plants with pine branches to protect them. Since slaves eventually transplanted the successful plants, they cleared a field and plowed it into knee-high hills that were 3 to 4 feet apart. Slaves couldn't transfer the plants until it rained and, even then, they might not take. Because of the fragility of the tobacco plant, slaves would sometimes have to do these tasks several times to ensure a decent crop.

To ward off weeds and deter cutworms, slaves cultivated the plants weekly with a hoe and their hands and removed leaves at various stages before harvesting the crop in late August or early September. The crop then cured for four to six weeks. Before the tobacco leaves shipped, they had to "sweat" for another week or two and then go through sorting.

Tobacco plantations

Cultivating tobacco was labor-intensive, falling between rice and cotton in terms of difficulty, but topping each with the level of detail, and slaveholders needed large numbers of slaves for the long process. They also needed skilled slaves to make the shipping barrels, build the tobacco barns, load the barrels into the ships, and, later, to work in the factories that manufactured tobacco products. In the late 1700s, however, soil depletion and falling tobacco prices tempered Virginia's once mighty tobacco plantations.

Cotton and sugar plantations

With Eli Whitney's invention of the cotton gin in 1793 and the advent of the Industrial Revolution, cotton became a boom crop. By efficiently separating cotton fibers from seedpods and sticky seeds, the cotton gin greatly increased cotton production from 10,000 bales in 1793 to more than 400,000 by 1820. Greater productivity created a greater demand for slave labor: Every 100 acres of cotton required 10 to 20 slaves. Jean Etienne de Bore added to that demand when he opened a successful sugar mill in Louisiana in 1794. Others followed, giving the South two huge crops with cotton and sugar.

American cotton and sugar plantations adopted the popular *gang system* of labor favored in the Caribbean and used on tobacco plantations. Considered more productive than other work systems, the gang system organized slaves into three groups based on physical abilities. The groups were highly supervised by an overseer, usually white, and a driver, usually black, with slaves told when to work, when to eat, and when to stop. In general, there was one slave for every three acres of cotton. Clearing land, burning underbrush, spreading fertilizer, and breaking soil were just some of the duties performed, in addition to planting, cultivating, and picking cotton.

Clearing land as well as cutting and carrying the sugar cane for milling may have been the easiest part of working on a sugar plantation. The dangerous part came with transforming the sugar cane into sugar. Using a method known as 'the Jamaica Train," sugar cane was boiled in four to five open kettles, arranged from largest to smallest. Teams of slaves ladled the hot liquid from kettle to kettle until it reached the right temperature and consistency to crystallize. Even with a large number of slaves dying, huge amounts of sugar lost, and the enormous quantities of wood needed to provide heat, sugar plantations were still hugely profitable.

The multiple effect evaporator, an invention by Norbert Rillieux, the free off-spring of a slaveholder and a slave, made sugar plantations more efficient and even more profitable. The multiple effect evaporator, still used today in various other industries, reduced the manpower and danger of making sugar by piping the juice from one container to the next. Instead of heating all the containers, the first one received heat and the other chambers relied on latent heat. Around 1845, Louisiana plantations began implementing the new system.

House slaves and field slaves

On larger plantations, slave duties were typically specialized, with the main division being between field and house slaves.

- ✔ **House slaves:** House slaves were dedicated to the master's house and other duties outside the field. Unlike other slaves, they interacted with the master's family and his associates. Their primary duties included cooking and cleaning. Some slave women served as *mammies*, caring for and, in some cases even nursing, white children, and others served as *aunties*, caring for slave children while their mothers worked. Because the work of house slaves placed them in close proximity to the white power structure, they received intense scrutiny. Sometimes, the benefits of domestic work included better quarters, more food, hand-me-down clothes from the master's household, and even an education.

  To serve the needs of the master's household, house slaves often lived in the "big house" or at least stayed overnight frequently. In some cases, loyal slaves received their freedom when a master or mistress died, but more often than not, heirs inherited house slaves as cherished and prized possessions.

- ✔ **Field slaves:** Field slaves often reported to work at sunup and worked until sunset. Eighteen-hour days were typical during harvest time, with women working the same hours as men and pregnant women working until childbirth. Children were sent into the fields sometimes as early as age 5 or 6; beginner tasks included carrying water to the fields. Even though field slaves usually received less food and poorer clothing and performed harder tasks, many preferred the field to the big house, because of the camaraderie of the field. Working in the house led to a greater sense of isolation from the rest of the slave community. (You can find more details on the slave community in Chapter 11.)

Regardless of whether they worked in the big house or in the fields, slaves typically received very little food. Weekly meal rations usually consisted of a few pounds of meat (usually salt pork) with rice, peas, corn, and/or sweet potatoes, among other vegetables. Sometimes slaves were fortunate enough to have their own gardens and raise chickens, but many masters discouraged such activities that could divert attention away from the slaves' primary duties.

Overseers

On plantations with 20 slaves or more, an *overseer,* usually a white man who owned no land and no slaves, supervised the slaves. Sometimes the overseer system yielded dramatic results. For example, in 1830, 14 Mississippi slaves picked an average of 323 pounds of cotton when 150 pounds was typical. Yet plantation owners and overseers frequently complained of slaves being lazy and punished those they felt weren't working hard enough or whom they considered otherwise disruptive. Backbreaking work and cruel treatment only intensified the desire to be free, with slaves frequently taking matters into their own hands to achieve it.

Drivers

Drivers, usually physically imposing black male slaves, assisted overseers in supervising slave labor and frequently administered whippings. Although former slaves often deemed the slave driver as the "meanest" black man on the plantation, in recent years, historians have argued that the slave driver wasn't simply the master's or overseer's flunkey. In the gang system, it wasn't uncommon for the driver to serve as the lead worker. He often set the tone and rhythm for work, even leading the group in songs.

Ultimately, the driver worked as the middleman between the master, overseer, and slaves and sometimes negotiated perks as well as punishment. Drivers usually came to power during their late 30s, and they usually served long tenures that could last as long as 20 years. The master and overseer frequently trusted the driver's judgment regarding agricultural matters. In addition, the driver policed the slave quarters (where he also resided) for potential escapes and rebellions. For these services, he received special privileges for himself.

Before I Die a Slave: Fighting the System

Africans were never content with slavery and rebelled from the start. Revolts were so common on slave ships that traders could even get insurance against it, and many of the first Africans who reached land committed suicide. Two boatloads of Africans who arrived in Charleston in 1807, for example, starved themselves to death. Even after slavery was firmly established, Africans still didn't submit to it and were among the first to use the court system to secure their freedom, even though the results rarely favored them. Laws declaring that Christian conversion didn't change one's slave status, for example, emanated from slave challenges for freedom.

Most slaves didn't turn to the justice system for help, but they resisted slavery on a daily basis nonetheless. Some feigned illnesses to avoid work, and some even harmed themselves by cutting off fingers or shooting themselves in the foot or hand. In many cases, masters still found something for them to do. Mothers sometimes killed their infants to prevent them from living a life of slavery; countless others induced miscarriages.

Slaves also resisted slavery by directly harming their masters. It wasn't uncommon for a slave (usually female) to poison the master. Some slaves stabbed or choked unusually cruel masters, despite the punishment. Any slave who murdered or harmed a master in any way rarely escaped death. Hanging was most common, but there's at least one report about a slave being burned alive.

With courts ruling that slaves were property, the law, which couldn't restrict the treatment of one's property, offered no relief from cruel masters. Because whites feared rebellion the most, they took great measures to prevent it.

The Slave Codes

American slave masters believed in heavily regulating slave behavior; they also believed that maintaining a careful balance between slaves and white supervisors curtailed violence against whites. In 1705, Virginia passed what's known as the Slave Codes. These laws emphasized slaves as property and greatly restricted slave behavior to safeguard the white population.

The Slave Codes included the following laws:

- ✔ Slaves couldn't leave plantations without authorization.
- ✔ Slaves couldn't bear weapons.
- ✔ Slaves could never strike a white person under any circumstances.

Whenever word of a conspiracy surfaced or an actual attempt at rebellion occurred, colonists passed more laws such as these.

To enforce the Slave Codes, militia-like slave patrols were set up in which free white men served usually for one-, three-, or six-month periods. Those who didn't want to serve were fined. These patrols returned slaves to plantations, conducted random searches of slave quarters, and generally policed slave behavior. During times of perceived or demonstrated danger, a vigilance committee that generally disregarded caution took over, often killing any blacks, slave or free, guilty or innocent, found during the group's rampage. These patrols were a precursor to the Ku Klux Klan, which historically had two incarnations, one in 1866 and another in 1915.

Rebellions

The Slave Codes made it difficult for slaves to rebel, but they didn't prevent insurrection. The four rebellions that historians generally consider most important are the Stono Rebellion (1739), Gabriel's Rebellion (1800), Denmark Vesey's Uprising (1822), and Nat Turner's Rebellion (1831).

Stono Rebellion

On September 9, 1739, an Angolan slave named Jemmy led 20 slaves gathered at the Stono River outside of Charleston, South Carolina, in a rebellion. First they marched to a local shop and armed themselves before killing the two shopkeepers. From there, they marched to the home of a local man, killing him and his son and daughter. Although they stopped at Wallace's Tavern, they spared the owner, reportedly because he was kind to his slaves. The people at the next six or so houses weren't so lucky. As they continued their march, their numbers grew, as large as 100 according to some historians' claims.

By the time the former slaves reached the Edisto River the following afternoon, they had killed 20 to 25 whites and had a gang of whites hot on their trail. In the ensuing gunfire, at least 30 members of the Stono Rebellion lay dead while 30 others escaped. Colonists captured and executed most of them within a month, however. The Negro Act, which reinforced restrictions against blacks assembling in groups and reading, among other things, quickly passed after the Stono Rebellion.

The timing of the Stono Rebellion and the fact that it occurred on a Sunday has led some to suggest that it triggered the Security Act, which required all white men to carry guns on Sundays to ward off possible slave insurrections. Those who didn't were fined. The Stono Rebellion also resulted in a ban against drums. Slaveholders discovered that slaves used them to communicate between plantations.

Gabriel's Rebellion

Gabriel Prosser was a slave and trained blacksmith on Thomas Prosser's tobacco plantation in Henrico County, Virginia. When the elder Prosser died, his son took over the plantation operations and hired out Gabriel and his brother Solomon. While working outside the plantation in Richmond, Gabriel encountered other slaves, free blacks, and working-class whites, who exposed him to the ideas of the American Revolution and alerted him to the slave uprising in Haiti (1791–1803), which inspired him.

Following a month spent in jail for stealing a pig, Gabriel started plotting an outright rebellion. He recruited several slaves and at least two Frenchmen. His plan included seizing Capitol Square in Richmond and taking Governor James Monroe hostage.

Originally, the rebellion was to occur on August 30, 1800. More than 1,000 slaves gathered at the appointed meeting place on that day, but heavy rain forced them to postpone action until the next day. In the interim, two slaves gave them away. Within days, authorities captured 30 slaves, but Gabriel remained at large. To crack the case, officials offered pardons in exchange for testimonies. Assisted by a former overseer who had since changed his mind about slavery, Gabriel attempted to escape by boat, but a slave with hopes of buying his own freedom with the reward money alerted white authorities of Gabriel's presence. After a speedy trial, Gabriel was hanged.

Estimates of the number of slaves involved ranged from 2,500 slaves to 50,000! In all, authorities tried at least 65 slaves, executing an estimated 35 of them, for participating in the rebellion. They then transported arrested slaves and free blacks they hadn't executed out of the area. Because slaves couldn't testify in court against free people, some gained their freedom by testifying. Still the silence of the majority of the participants astounded and scared whites. Like Gabriel, most accepted their deaths and refused to divulge any significant information regarding the rebellion. Long after discovering the plot, Virginians remained paranoid.

Denmark Vesey's Uprising

Denmark Vesey's unsuccessful 1822 plot captivated many historians, not for its effectiveness but rather for its organization. A successful carpenter and property owner, Vesey, who purchased his own freedom in 1800, plotted for several years to free others in the Charleston, South Carolina, area. He carefully selected his collaborators, even reaching out to Haitians for assistance. Vesey reportedly collected 250 pike heads and bayonets along with 300 daggers. When details of his plot leaked, he moved up the original July date for action, but whites had already started responding. Although estimates of involvement in Vesey's Uprising ran as high as 9,000 and included slaves, free blacks, and a few whites, authorities arrested approximately 130 blacks and killed 35, including Vesey.

The far reach of the Haitian Revolution

Once known as Saint-Domingue, modern-day Haiti traces its roots back to a slave rebellion that began in 1791 when black slaves murdered their white masters for refusing to extend the same freedoms white Frenchmen were fighting for in the French Revolution. France sent forces immediately to Haiti, but the conflict lasted at least two years. In 1794, Haitian slaves received their freedom, and relative calm returned under the rule of Toussaint L'Ouverture, a self-educated former house slave. However, in 1800, Napoleon, anxious to dominate the entire Western Hemisphere, sent additional French troops to Haiti and ousted L'Ouverture. With L'Ouverture gone, France believed it had won back control, but when Napoleon tried to reinstitute slavery, others took up the fight. Aided by a number of factors, including yellow fever, which decimated the French troops, Haiti remained free and, on January 1, 1804, Haiti declared its independence to the world.

The U.S. watched the events in Haiti intensely. Thomas Jefferson denounced the revolution and later refused to engage in trade with Haiti. Of course, American slaveholders, fearing their slaves would also rise up, placed more restrictions on them. Efforts to keep word of the Haitian Revolution from slaves in the U.S. failed. Gabriel Prosser and Denmark Vesey weren't the only African Americans inspired by the Haitian Revolution; although they all didn't attempt rebellions of their own, many others were inspired to keep the struggle for freedom alive.

With his 2001 article, "Denmark Vesey and His Co-Conspirators," published in *The William and Mary Quarterly,* an academic journal dedicated to early American history, historian Michael P. Johnson questioned whether Denmark Vesey ever plotted a slave insurrection. According to Johnson, Charleston's ambitious mayor used the alleged plot to discredit his political rival and advance his own career. Since Johnson's article, historians have vigorously debated the issue. Johnson, however, does assert that Vesey opposed slavery.

Nat Turner's Rebellion

Without a doubt, Nat Turner's Rebellion is the most well-known American slave revolt. Unlike other leaders of slave rebellions, Nat Turner left little to speculation and provided his own version of events that fell in line with his Christian beliefs. Although born a slave in Virginia, Nat Turner successfully escaped slavery at age 21 but later returned to fulfill a greater vision. A deeply religious man and a powerful figure, Turner's alleged mystical powers, coupled with his distant and pious nature, made an impression on both blacks and whites.

Driven by a vision he saw during a rare solar eclipse on February 12, 1831, Turner, labeled a prophet by some, concluded, "I should arise and prepare myself and slay my enemies with their own weapons."

Turner quickly chose his four disciples and decided that July 4 would be the fateful day as he headed toward Jerusalem, Virginia. Turner postponed his plan when he became ill. Another sign received on August 13 prompted him to take action on August 21.

Convening on the banks of Cabin Pond, Turner, his disciples, and two other men, armed with a hatchet and a broadax, first went to the home of Turner's slave master, Joseph Travis. They killed Travis, his wife, and three children before moving on to other white homes. (One poor white family who didn't own slaves was spared.) Traveling by horse, Turner and his crew continued on to Jerusalem, picking up more participants along the way. Three miles from Jerusalem, they encountered a group of armed whites, but Turner escaped, waiting for his disciples at Cabin Pond before digging a cave for his hide-out.

Meanwhile, overseers received orders to single out slaves they distrusted and shoot them if they tried to escape. By the time they captured Turner on October 30 (see Figure 4-1), 60 whites and more than 100 slaves had died. Turner was executed on November 11.

Figure 4-1:
Print showing the discovery of Nat Turner.

© Bettmann/Corbis

They didn't just kill Turner on November 11; they skinned him as well. Legend has it that one white man owned a money purse made of Turner's hide and another one kept his skeleton for years.

Nat Turner's Rebellion sent ripples throughout the South and the nation. Whites everywhere, North and South, passed even more laws restricting slaves' actions. Fearing another insurrection of this magnitude, some slave-holders tried to improve how they treated their slaves. One of the major turning points in American history, Nat Turner's Rebellion underscored slavery's true cycle of viciousness.

Running away

Running away was far more common than rebellions as a form of slave resistance. Sometimes slaves who could read and write forged papers of freedom and left slave life behind them. Many others took their chances in the unfamiliar swamps and forests. Hiding during the day and scouring for food with bloodhounds on their trails, slaves had little more than the North Star to guide them as they traveled at night. Most failed in their escape attempts. Once captured, most times within days, they often received severe punishment — some unsuccessful runaways suffered more than 100 lashes for their effort (see Figure 4-2). These conditions are the reason runaway slave Harriet Tubman, who operated the Underground Railroad (discussed in greater detail in Chapter 5), is so heralded. Not only did she make it to the North, she repeatedly risked her own life and freedom to free 300 others. She and noted abolitionist Frederick Douglass are perhaps the two best-known runaway slaves.

Although many runaway slaves traveled to the North, some remained in the South (particularly North Carolina and Florida), in some cases forming com-munities of runaway slaves known as *maroon communities*. One such commu-nity was the Black Seminoles, slaves from coastal South Carolina and Georgia who fled to Florida and lived among the Seminole Indians as early as the 1600s. Another maroon community was discovered in North Carolina in March 1811, but the fugitive slaves living there refused to be captured and fought for their freedom.

Escaping slavery was extremely difficult, and some slaves developed inge-nious plans. There was no end to the lengths slaves would go to obtain their freedom. Here are a few examples:

- Harriet Jacobs, a slave born in North Carolina, was no longer able to cope with her master's sexual advances. To escape molestation, she hid in a crawl space in her grandmother's attic for seven years before finally fleeing to Philadelphia.

- Husband and wife William and Ellen Craft escaped slavery in Macon, Georgia, when the fair-skinned Ellen posed as a young and sickly master accompanied by his slave.

- Henry "Box" Brown placed himself in a box with a jug of water and some biscuits and mailed himself from Richmond, Virginia, to Philadelphia.

It's been estimated that 89 percent of all runaway slaves were male, with 76 percent of them under age 35. Women, especially mothers, rarely ran away, and husbands often were reluctant to leave their wives, children, and other close family members, which is why many historians now argue that slaveholders encouraged family life on their plantations. More closely supervised house slaves rarely had opportunities to flee.

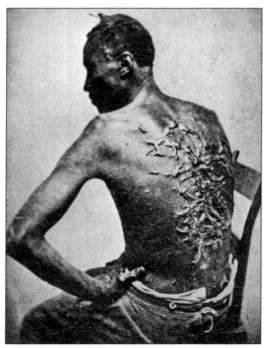

Figure 4-2:
Scars from
a brutal
beating.

© Bettmann/Corbis

The experience of a captured runaway slave

"Some weeks after his escape, he was captured, tied, and carried back to his master's plantation. This man considered punishment in his jail, on bread and water, after receiving hundreds of lashes, too mild for the poor slave's offence. Therefore he decided, after the overseer should have whipped him to his satisfaction, to have him placed between the screws of the cotton gin, to stay as long as he had been in the woods. This wretched creature was cut with the whip from his head to his foot, then washed with strong brine, to prevent the flesh from mortifying, and make it heal sooner than it otherwise would. He was then put into the cotton gin, which was screwed down, only allowing him room to turn on his side when he could not lie on his back. Every morning a slave was sent with a piece of bread and bowl of water, which were placed within reach of the poor fellow. The slave was charged, under penalty of severe punishment, not to speak to him. . . . When he had been in the press four days and five nights, the slave informed his master that the water had not been used for four mornings, and that a horrible stench came from the gin house. The overseer was sent to examine into it. When the press was unscrewed, the dead body was found partly eaten by rats and vermin. Perhaps the rats that devoured his bread had gnawed him before life was extinct."

(Harriet Jacobs, *Incidents in the Life of a Slave Girl*, published in 1861)

"Free" Blacks

Not all African Americans in the U.S. were slaves. But "free" African Americans were far from free; often resented by whites (both slaveholders and nonslaveholders), free blacks faced tremendous restrictions. In the South especially, they had to carry papers proving their freedom to avoid enslavement. In addition, slave codes regularly included restrictions on free blacks.

Different ways to be free

Blacks became free in several ways:

- ✔ By running away from their masters and moving to the North.
- ✔ By being freed by owners who became Christians and had a change of heart regarding slavery. As the years wore on, however, some states discouraged this activity, which sometimes resulted in as many as 400 slaves receiving their freedom at once.
- ✔ By being freed upon their owners' deaths.

✔ By being fathered by slaveholders, who sometimes felt compelled to free their children and their children's mothers. Some scholars believe that Thomas Jefferson, in his will, freed at least one of his children with his slave Sally Hemings.

✔ By performing exceptional acts, such as fighting valiantly in the American Revolution.

✔ By purchasing their freedom. With the permission of their owners, skilled slaves such as blacksmiths and carpenters hired themselves out, collected pay for their work, and purchased their freedom. The price could range from $800 to more than $1,200. Husbands in the North sometimes labored for years to purchase the freedom of their children and wives.

✔ By being born to a free mother. The mother's condition determined freedom (laws dictated that children born to free women were free). For this reason, many black men who could purchase their freedom opted to free their wives first, particularly if they hadn't had children yet, so that their children would be free.

✔ Be being born to a white mother. There are a few documented incidences of white women fleeing with their black lovers, although this was very uncommon.

Perhaps free, but not equal

Regardless of how free blacks came to be free, they did enjoy some of freedom's benefits. In 1800, Philadelphia's free black community owned almost 100 houses and lots. In 1837, New York's black community owned $1.4 million in property. Free blacks in the South also owned property, with some amassing considerable amounts. Despite the backlash following Nat Turner's Rebellion in 1831 (see the section "Nat Turner's Rebellion" earlier in the chapter), Virginia's free blacks owned 60,000 acres of farmland in 1860. By far, New Orleans had the wealthiest community of free blacks: In 1860, they owned in excess of $15 million worth of property. Thomy Lafon, a wealthy New Orleans real estate broker born free in 1810, was so philanthropic the Louisiana State Legislature commissioned a bust of him following his death in 1893.

Some wealthy blacks also owned slaves. Many purchased their own families to remove them from bondage, but a few others, like Mississippi's William Johnson, known as the Barber of Natchez, owned slaves outright. However, a larger number of wealthy free blacks helped fund various antislavery causes.

Amassing wealth wasn't easy, but many African Americans were very industrious. Free blacks in Massachusetts (Boston in particular) worked as engravers, tailors, teachers, and lawyers. African American blacksmiths and carpenters weren't uncommon in such Southern cities as Charleston, Atlanta, and Richmond. There were also black shopkeepers, barbers, and builders. Domestic work was common as well. Whites who objected to blacks working in factories or in the shipyards relented when western expansion created a shortage of white workers. European immigrants who began coming to the U.S. in droves, however, greatly threatened the economic stability of free blacks.

Despite the wealth free blacks amassed or the industriousness with which they worked and lived, they weren't equal to white Americans. In order to sell corn, wheat, or tobacco in Maryland in 1805, for example, free blacks needed a license; whites didn't. Although states such as Maryland, Tennessee, New York, and Pennsylvania had given free blacks the right to vote prior to the American Revolution, that privilege ended in the 19th century. Maryland's free blacks lost the vote in 1810, while those in Tennessee and North Carolina lost the right in 1834 and 1835 respectively. Thomas Jefferson signed an 1802 bill that banned free blacks from voting in the nation's capital of Washington, D.C., and in 1821, New York instituted a voting-related property qualification that applied only to blacks. Ironically, even without the right to vote, blacks were still required to pay taxes and sometimes more than their white counterparts who could vote.

Toward the middle of the 19th century, some Southerners advocated enslaving all blacks. Already this new nation based in freedom had purchased the liberty of its white citizens by denying the same right to its black citizens. Perhaps no other group recognized this hypocrisy as clearly as free blacks. Throughout the early 19th century, proslavery and antislavery camps galvanized. In the decades leading up to the Civil War, the majority of African Americans, slave and free, assisted by some moral and courageous whites, inched closer and closer to ending slavery.

Black slaveholder William Johnson

Born a slave in 1809 and emancipated by his slave owner (who probably was also his father) in 1820, William Johnson, a barber by trade, established a barbershop and bathhouse in Natchez, Mississippi, and acquired several landholdings. He has become a notable figure not because of his achievements but because his personal journals are a rare glimpse into the life of a black slaveholder.

In his diaries, Johnson, who owned 15 slaves when he died in 1851, details attending auctions as well as purchasing slaves. He even discusses whipping them. Sometimes, being cognizant of the limitations placed on his race, Johnson arranged for white associates to attend slave auctions to make purchases on his behalf. He also recounts witnessing a free black kidnapped into slavery.

To historians' dismay, Johnson never explored his own feelings regarding his contradictory status. In 1951, Johnson's diaries were published in the book *William Johnson's Natchez: The Ante-Bellum Diary of a Free Negro*.

Chapter 5

Bringing Down the House: Marching toward Civil War and Freedom

. . . .

In This Chapter

▶ Organizing to end slavery

▶ Spreading the abolitionist message

▶ Considering the emigration option

▶ Going underground

▶ Stretching the divided nation too far

. . . .

*T*he American Revolution, discussed in Chapter 3, awakened many white Americans to the paradox of American slavery and American freedom. That awakening profoundly affected African Americans and the nation over-all. As a number of white Americans enlisted in the fight to end slavery, emo-tions rose considerably in the new nation. After the War of 1812, antislavery and proslavery arguments grew more intense. While the North moved decid-edly toward manufacturing and away from slavery, the South remained com-mitted to agriculture and slave labor. Those two disparate economic realities created a form of sectionalism from which the nation has never rebounded. Expanding the new nation westward only exacerbated those tensions. With lines drawn, mainly along the lines of North and South, tensions spilled over into many facets of American life. Nowhere was the animosity more dramatic than in the halls of government.

This chapter explores the abolition movement and its impact on westward expansion and vice versa. It delves into the Underground Railroad and the founding of the African American press, as well as examines the key legal cases and governmental showdowns that finally brought the nation to civil war.

Picking Fights

Prior to the American Revolution, some white colonists began questioning the institution of slavery. James Otis of Massachusetts wrote a response to the Sugar Act in 1764 in which he argued that all men, white and black, were born free. The Quakers, popularly known as the Society of Friends, were the first white people in this country to organize against slavery. They began speaking out against slavery as early as 1688 and published their first antislavery tract in 1693. Most of the Quakers' antislavery activity filtered through the Society of Friends, which championed religious freedom, education, and egalitarianism. Abolitionist societies such as the following were formed (interestingly, abolition and manumission societies, especially early organizations, didn't necessarily include African American members):

- ✔ **Pennsylvania Abolition Society (PAS):** Founded by well-known Quaker Anthony Benezet in 1775, the Society for the Relief of Free Negroes Unlawfully Held in Bondage was the first acknowledged American abolition society. The organization suspended meetings during the American Revolution, but reorganized itself as the Pennsylvania Abolition Society (PAS) in 1784. Benjamin Franklin, a former slaveholder himself, served as president of the Society.

- ✔ **New York Manumission Society:** This organization succeeded in ending slavery in New York.

- ✔ **New England Anti-Slavery Society:** Massachusetts, particularly Boston, became another abolition stronghold. Prominent white abolitionist William Lloyd Garrison helped establish this society in 1832. The Society's goals were to abolish slavery in the U.S. and secure equal civil and political rights for African Americans.

- ✔ **American Anti-Slavery Society:** Established in Philadelphia in 1833 and led by William Lloyd Garrison, the society's stated goal was to end slavery in the United States.

Although relatively few in number, antislavery organizations weren't uncommon in the South during the early 19th century. That changed in time, particularly following Nat Turner's Rebellion (refer to Chapter 4), when all abolitionist activity in the South came under fire and the mere suspicion of antislavery behavior invited retaliation.

Of course, proslavery forces sprouted to counter antislavery activity. Prominent proslavery supporters included Southern politician John C. Calhoun, who proclaimed slavery "a positive good" before the U.S. Senate in 1837, and Samuel F.B. Morse, the man behind the telegraph and Morse code. Like antislavery advocates, white Southerners had a number of proslavery organizations, but the American Colonization Society, an organization to send African Americans back to Africa, was among their more interesting efforts.

During this charged period, antislavery and proslavery forces defined and refined their arguments. With sides clearly drawn, they fought steadily, well into the Civil War. The following sections outline key arguments for both sides.

Arguing against slavery

Ironically, much of the credit for the increased intensity in antislavery efforts goes to the English and other Europeans, who began to question slavery as an institution. Scottish philosopher and economist Adam Smith, the author of fundamental texts on capitalism, free trade, and economics in general, claimed that slavery wasn't profitable and that it actually retarded progress. Smith wrote, "From the experience of all ages and nations, I believe, that the work done by free men comes cheaper in the end than the work performed by slaves. Whatever work he does, beyond what is sufficient to purchase his own maintenance, can be squeezed out of him by violence only, and not by any interest of his own."

Other arguments against slavery included the following:

- ✔ **It was anti-Christian.** Many antislavery advocates were deeply religious and used Christianity to argue against slavery. They insisted Jesus Christ taught universal brotherhood and established the equality of all men as a cardinal principle of Christianity.

- ✔ **It violated American values.** Antislavery factions argued that slavery violated the core American value of freedom that Americans fought for and won during the American Revolution.

- ✔ **It threatened the security of the nation.** Slavery was not only inefficient but also threatened the peace and security of the nation since white Southerners lived in fear of slave revolts such as Nat Turner's Rebellion in 1831 (see Chapter 4 for more on this and other rebellions).

Arguing for slavery

African American inferiority formed the cornerstone of the proslavery argument. According to slavery's strongest supporters, African Americans weren't quite full human beings and retained childlike qualities even in adulthood. Because African Americans weren't equipped, intellectually and socially, for freedom, continued the argument advocating *social paternalism,* slavery was a public good borne out of necessity. Proslavery supporters often denied slavery's brutality, insisting that only extreme misbehavior prompted extreme force.

Thornton Stringfellow, a staunch proslavery supporter and minister, who used his many writings to justify slavery, especially from a biblical perspective, proclaimed that "the African remains, at the end of that time, a mere child in intellectual and moral development, perfectly incapable of performing the great functions of social life."

Following are other arguments supporting slavery:

✔ **It was biblical.** Proslavery proponents noted the many instances of slavery in the Bible. For them, the "curse of Ham" (more accurately the "curse of Canaan"), when Noah punished Ham's son Canaan to life as a servant, was immediate proof of God's intention that African Americans, then often referenced as the "children of Ham," be enslaved. Jesus, according to proslavery supporters, never specifically denounced slavery.

✔ **It allowed American advancement.** According to Edward Brown in *Notes on the Origin and Necessity of Slavery* (1826), "slavery has ever been the stepping ladder by which countries have passed from barbarism to civilization." South Carolina Governor and one-time U.S. Senator James Henry Hammond added, in his 1858 address to the U.S. Senate, that "In all social systems there must be a class to do the menial duties, to perform the drudgery of life."

✔ **It ensured the security of the nation.** Proslavery forces contended that slavery helped maintain the social order. Without it, they argued, violence would erupt and white people, especially white women, would be unsafe. Slavery, in their assessment, was a positive good.

Leading the Antislavery Assault: Key Abolitionists

Some of the most outspoken black antislavery advocates were runaway or former slaves. Frederick Douglass and Isabella Baumfree, better known as Sojourner Truth, are perhaps the most well-known former slaves turned abolitionists, but author William Wells Brown and activist Henry Highland Garnet were also very popular. African Americans born free also identified with the struggle against slavery. Free blacks such as siblings Charles Lenox Redmond and Sarah Parker Redmond as well as author Frances E.W. Harper frequently lectured against slavery. Noted mathematician Benjamin Banneker, who was born free, even sent a plea for justice and equality to Thomas Jefferson.

Although African Americans spearheaded their own efforts to end slavery, the nation was predominantly white. Therefore, white abolitionists and their resources were critical in the fight to end slavery. Two such abolitionists,

Anthony Benezet and William Lloyd Garrison, were among the abolitionist movement's most revered figures. This section provides details about a handful of the many abolitionists who were particularly influential in the fight against slavery.

As free blacks increased their resources, they became more vocal not just about ending slavery but also about attaining true equality for African Americans. The latter was especially important since white abolitionists didn't necessarily believe that African Americans should receive the same treatment as white Americans.

Anthony Benezet

Anthony Benezet, whose family fled religious persecution in France, was one of the first figures in the abolition movement. A Quaker convert who studied Africa to better aid his cause, Benezet wrote several influential antislavery pamphlets. His *A Short Account of That Part of Africa, Inhabited by the Negroes* (1762) helped British antislavery leader Thomas Clarkson clarify his position on slavery. Methodism's founder John Wesley incorporated Benezet's *Some Historical Account of Guinea* (1771) into his sermons in Britain against the slave trade. Benezet, a pioneering force behind the nation's first abolition society better known as the Pennsylvania Abolition Society (refer to the section "Picking Fights"), also worked overtime to ensure the passage of the Act for the Gradual Abolition of Slavery by the Pennsylvania Assembly in 1780.

David Walker

Few abolitionists, black or white, matched David Walker's revolutionary spirit, especially in the 1820s when calls for gradual emancipation prevailed.

In 1829, David Walker, born in North Carolina to a free mother and a slave father, published his highly controversial *Walker's Appeal*. In his *Appeal,* Walker praised slaves who defended themselves against their masters. At a time when many African Americans, even abolitionists, refrained from advocating violent and rebellious action against slavery, Walker dared to suggest that slaves kill their masters for their freedom. Of course, this scared many slaveholders who already feared slave rebellions. It also scared many white abolitionists who usually favored gradual emancipation. Walker's direct address to enslaved and free African Americans to take the fight for freedom into their own hands, even if it meant using violence, distinguished his *Appeal* the most.

Walker's message was so incendiary that a bounty of $3,000 was placed on his head, and some Southern states offered $10,000 to anyone who brought him in alive. In some places in the South, those caught with *Walker's Appeal* risked fines and imprisonment. When the slave Nat Turner and others later rebelled, white Southerners didn't blame slavery for the rebellion, but rather

Walker's Appeal for encouraging it. Despite the risks, Walker refused to hide and instead produced more editions of the controversial treatise. Shortly after the third edition was distributed in 1830, Walker was found dead. At the time, it was assumed to be murder, but many historians today believe that he died of tuberculosis.

William Lloyd Garrison

Born in Massachusetts, William Lloyd Garrison, mentored by abolitionist publisher Benjamin Lundy, initially advocated for gradual emancipation and supported efforts to settle African Americans in Africa. By the 1830s, however, he supported immediate emancipation and distanced himself from the American Colonization Society.

To reinforce his newfound advocacy of *militant abolitionism,* or the immediate abolishment of slavery without violence, Garrison launched his own antislavery publication, *Liberator,* in 1831. Garrison didn't relegate his brand of militant abolitionism (also known as *Garrisonism)* to his newspaper. Instead, he established the New England Anti-Slavery Society in 1832 and spearheaded the American Anti-Slavery Society, which began publishing the *National Anti-Slavery Standard* in 1840.

Over the years, Garrison rejected not only slavery but the Constitution as well. He and Frederick Douglass didn't speak for years because Garrison supported burning the Constitution, which he contended was a proslavery document, while Douglass favored using it as a tool to end slavery. Undoubtedly, the House of Representatives' 1836 decision to ignore petitions against slavery, a policy that lasted until 1845, only reinforced Garrison's point.

Frederick Douglass

Born into slavery in Maryland in 1818, Frederick Douglass, shown in Figure 5-1, is perhaps America's most well-known abolitionist. One of the first truly prominent African Americans on both a national and international level, Douglass, the son of a slave mother who died when he was 7 and an unknown white man, learned to read and write at an early age. Set on freedom, Douglass, after one failed escape attempt, finally succeeded in 1838. After spending a brief time in New York where he was also married, he and his new wife settled in New Bedford, Massachusetts.

A *Liberator* subscriber, Douglass went to see its publisher William Lloyd Garrison speak in 1841 and impressed Garrison who became a mentor. Days after that meeting, Douglass delivered a speech of his own, and his career as a master orator began. Encouraged to write about his personal experience with slavery, Douglass published his classic text *Narrative of the Life of Frederick Douglass* in 1845. Fearing that the text could prompt his re-enslavement, Douglass went to Europe, where he lectured in England, Scotland, and Ireland.

Figure 5-1:
Frederick
Douglass.

© Corbis

Back in the United States, Douglass began publishing his own newspaper and developing his own ideas about freedom. He campaigned relentlessly to end slavery and procure equal rights for African Americans. Thus, he became a titan within the African American community until his death in 1895.

Fighting with Words

Many black abolitionists favored moderate and strategic action over violence to end slavery. Since white Americans outnumbered black Americans, violence just wasn't a viable option. Even in communities where African Americans weren't outnumbered, their behavior was so restricted that amassing substantial firepower would have been difficult. Therefore, violence wasn't practical. So the pen became one of the biggest weapons against slavery.

Proslavery factions feared African American literacy and passed many laws restricting the teaching of reading and writing to African Americans. Mere suspicion of being able to read and write posed a danger to many black Southerners, slave or free (read more about African American education in Chapter 13).

Slave narratives

Most white Americans were completely unfamiliar with how slaves were treated. Slave narratives were open testimony from those who actually survived the horrors, and they enlightened those who were clueless about life in bondage. Slave narratives such as *Narrative of the Life of Frederick Douglass* (1845) and Solomon Northrup's *Twelve Years a Slave* (1853) were important antislavery treatises that sold well both in the United States and abroad.

Douglass's narrative stood out because, more than other narratives, it created an emotional connection with readers. He not only detailed slavery's horrors; he made readers feel how horrible slavery felt. Other narratives outlined the injustices, but Douglass tugged at readers' heartstrings. His work underscored the fact that African Americans were indeed human beings. Slave narratives' ability to create a human connection also played an important role in the early development of African American literature, which you can read about in Chapter 14.

Origins of the black press

White abolitionists proved that newspapers such as Benjamin Lundy's two publications, *The Philanthropist* and *The Genius of Universal Emancipation,* and Garrison's *Liberator* could be very effective tools in the fight against slavery. African American publishers found that newspapers specifically targeting African Americans created forums in which blacks could truly express who they were and where they were going. Early African American newspapers began the important legacy of providing the African American community with a voice that celebrated African American milestones as well as agitated for equal rights. The black press also became an important mechanism for galvanizing African Americans nationally.

Prior to the Civil War, more than 40 such newspapers emerged, but *Freedom's Journal,* launched by Samuel E. Cornish and John B. Russwurm, and *The North Star,* launched by Frederick Douglas, were two of the most important.

✔ *Freedom's Journal:* The nation's first black newspaper, *Freedom's Journal* pushed for an end to slavery, as well as informed the more than 300,000 free blacks in the U.S. about national and international news. The newspaper included profiles of great African Americans as well as stories about often-ignored historic achievements.

At its height, *Freedom's Journal*'s distribution spanned 11 states, Washington, D.C., Haiti, Europe, and Canada. Unfortunately, it folded in March 1829, in part because coeditors Russwurm and Cornish disagreed over the issue of colonization.

✔ ***The North Star:*** Frederick Douglass's *The North Star,* first published in 1847, became the most prominent of all early African American newspapers mainly because of Douglass's stature. *The North Star* went beyond just advocating slavery's end and equal rights for African Americans; it also championed equal rights for women. Its motto was "Right is of no Sex — Truth is of no Color — God is the Father of us all, and we are all brethren."

Within these pages, Douglass expanded his vision of freedom and, like *Freedom's Journal,* provided a forum for critical African American issues overlooked by white abolitionist papers. The paper was far from a financial success, however. To stay afloat, Douglass continued lecturing. In 1851, he merged his paper with the *Liberty Party Paper* to form *Frederick Douglass' Paper,* which published until 1860. Douglass published a monthly before settling into political life in the 1870s.

Cornish and Russwurm address their readers

"We wish to plead our own cause. Too long have others spoken for us. Too long has the publick been deceived by misrepresentations, in things which concern us dearly, though in the estimation of some mere trifles; for though there are many in society who exercise towards us benevolent feelings; still (with sorrow we confess it) there are others who make it their business to enlarge upon the least trifle, which tends to the discredit of any person of colour. . . .

"Our vices and our degradation are ever arrayed against us, but our virtues are passed by unnoticed. And what is still more lamentable, our friends, to whom we concede all the principles of humanity and religion, from these very causes seem to have fallen into the current of popular feeling and are imperceptibly floating on the stream — actually living in the practice of prejudice, while they abjure it in theory, and feel it not in their hearts. Is it not very desirable that such should know more of our actual condition; and of our efforts and feelings, that in forming or advancing plans for our amelioration, they may do it more understandingly? In the spirit of candor and humility, we intend by a simple representation of the facts to lay our case before the publick, with a view to arrest the progress of prejudice, and to shield ourselves against the consequent evils."

(Comments made in "To Our Patrons," *Freedom's Journal,* Volume 1, Number 1, March 16, 1827)

The Colonization (or Emigration) Movement

Proslavery Southerners frequently argued that liberating African Americans would create chaos and endanger the republic. Ironically, many white abolitionists didn't necessarily intend for African Americans to live among them. For members of both camps, *colonization* answered the question of what to do with emancipated blacks.

Colonization became one of the main objectives for the Connecticut Emancipation Society, and in 1777, Thomas Jefferson headed a Virginia legislative committee intended to gradually emancipate and deport slaves. Interestingly, some of the most definitive steps taken toward colonization came first from African Americans, who preferred the term emigration.

Early resettlement efforts

Prompted by the poor treatment free blacks received, leaders of the Free African Union Society (founded in Newport, Rhode Island, in 1780) decided in January 1787 to create their own settlement in Africa.

The Free African Union Society eventually connected with free blacks in Boston whose goals matched their own. Led by Prince Hall, founder of the first black lodge of Freemasons (refer to Chapter 3), 75 black Americans had already petitioned the Massachusetts legislature for its assistance in relocating them back to Africa. The Society also connected with London's Granville Sharp, who was working with the proposed Sierra Leone settlement intended to rid England of unemployed Africans, many of whom were former American slaves freed by the British during the American Revolution.

Despite its best intentions, the Free African Union Society never succeeded in its goal to resettle blacks in Africa. The efforts of Paul Cuffe, a successful black maritime entrepreneur and whaling captain with Native American roots, met with different results, however.

Cuffe: Man on a mission

Dismayed by the treatment of free blacks, Paul Cuffe (sometimes Cuffee), a converted Quaker, felt that, for most African Americans, returning to Africa would be better than remaining in the United States. Cuffe consulted with the African

Institution, a British organization established in 1807 to address the welfare of Africans and the suppression of the slave trade with special interests in Sierra Leone, before traveling to Sierra Leone with a crew of nine African American seamen. There, he met with chiefs and other local officials to assess Sierra Leone's potential as a home for American blacks. From there, he visited England, which received him well. Pressured by the African Institution, England granted Cuffe a trading license as well as land in Sierra Leone.

The War of 1812 and family trials delayed but didn't destroy Cuffe's plans. In December 1815, using his own money, Cuffe departed the United States for Sierra Leone. In February 1816, he delivered 38 black American settlers, nine families comprising 18 adults and 20 children, to Sierra Leone.

Although Cuffe, who died in 1817, never emigrated himself, his success in resettling others prompted white colonization proponents to form the American Colonization Society in 1816. In 1820, the American Colonization Society, whose membership included prominent white Americans such as Henry Clay, sent its first group of free blacks to Sierra Leone. By 1830, 1,420 black Americans had settled near Sierra Leone in their own colony, Liberia, whose capital Monrovia they named in honor of U.S. President James Monroe.

Questioning motives

Public positions on the issue of black colonization varied. Slaveholders supported colonization efforts, primarily because they viewed colonization as a solution to the problem they had with free blacks. Many free blacks opposed colonization because they felt that their removal would allow slavery to flourish in the U. S. Black abolitionist and politician Martin R. Delany didn't oppose emigration for African Americans but did object to the American Colonization Society. Delany, who later established his own organization to resettle African Americans in Liberia, charged that the society's goal was to eliminate blacks from the U.S. and labeled its leaders "anti-Christian" and "hypocrites."

Some free blacks participated in colonization efforts in Africa in order to spread Christianity, but overwhelmingly, African Americans refused to leave the United States and chose to fight for the emancipation of all black people.

The Effects of Proslavery Politics

Of course, antislavery activity didn't sit well with proslavery factions. Each year, proslavery and antislavery forces appeared more divided. Those tensions only intensified as new territories sought entry into the union. As the antislavery factions tried to tilt the nation toward freedom, proslavery supporters put more pressure on the government and the legal system. They focused their efforts on the U.S. Constitution and the new Western territories.

Constitutional backup: The Fugitive Slave Clause

Since antislavery activity began prior to the American Revolution, slavery was a major issue during the formation of the United States. Some Northern states had already made the decision to abolish slavery before the Constitution became a reality.

Vermont, with its 1777 constitution, has the distinction of being the first state to ban slavery.

Unlike the three-fifths compromise and the agreement to abolish the slave trade in 1808, the Fugitive Slave Clause came late in the proceedings at the Constitutional Convention and curiously invited little resistance from Northerners. Without specifically using the terms "slave" or "slavery," Article IV, Section 2 of the Constitution established the following protocol:

> No person engaged in service in one state could escape that service by fleeing to another state. Once the person to whom service was due made a claim, that person had to return.

Stronger fugitive slave measures: Fugitive Slave Act of 1793

It didn't take long for Southerners and Northerners to clash over the fugitive slave issue. When three Virginia men kidnapped a fugitive slave living freely in Pennsylvania, the governor there demanded that Virginia expedite them. Virginia's noncompliance prompted Pennsylvania to appeal to President George Washington who referred the matter to Congress. In response, Congress passed the Fugitive Slave Act of 1793, which made the recovery of fugitive slaves a federal matter.

With the federal government's blessing, slaveholders could follow escaped slaves to the North, seize them, and appear before a judge who could side with them without allowing the fugitive slave to present his or her side of the story. This one-sidedness also left free blacks and children born to fugitive slaves vulnerable to slavery. That reality compelled more Northerners to join the Underground Railroad.

Battling over the slave status of new land

Originally, the Northwest Ordinance of 1787, passed under the Articles of Confederation a few months before the ratification of the U.S. Constitution, banned slavery in new territories but mandated the return of fugitive slaves.

As the U.S. expanded, however, that policy changed, with new territories becoming fair game for slavery or freedom. Westward expansion, a move-ment largely facilitated by the Louisiana Purchase of 1803, ignited tension between the North and the South. The purchase garnered the U.S. land encompassing all or parts of modern-day Arkansas, Iowa, Kansas, Louisiana, Missouri, Montana, Nebraska, New Mexico, North Dakota, Oklahoma, South Dakota, Texas, and Wyoming, among other areas.

The issue of whether these areas were free or slave came to a head in 1819 when Missouri applied for statehood. Attempts to balance the number of slave and free states and various territories only created greater division between the two sides of the argument.

The Missouri Compromise

When Missouri sought statehood in 1819, Northerners attempted to block its entry as a slave state, a major problem since slavery already existed in the territory. New York Congressman James Tallmadge introduced an amendment that limited slavery in Missouri and even proposed to free the children of those already enslaved. The measure passed the House but failed the Senate. Complicating matters further, Alabama gained admission to the Union as a slave state in 1819, creating parity between slave states and free states. Known as the Missouri Compromise of 1820 (sometimes the Compromise of 1820), Maine entered the Union as a free state thus allowing Missouri to enter the Union as a slave state, making the count 12 slave states and 12 free states.

The Missouri Compromise extended the Mason-Dixon line, which divided the North from the South, free states from slave states, westward.

The Underground Railroad

In the face of Constitutional amendments protecting slavery and rancorous debate over whether new states would be free or slave (as described in the preceding section), some abolitionists decided to take even more proactive measures to end slavery by helping runaway slaves escape to freedom.

Runaway slaves from the South often found freedom in Northern states, espe-cially as the North began to ban slavery. Yet the odds of successfully eluding a slaveholder and actually making it to the North weren't high, especially if one were unassisted. To increase the success rate of such bold action, the Underground Railroad developed. Although scholars believe that this com-plex system of escape tactics and routes, secret agents, and safe houses began in 1787, it reached its height between 1810 and 1850. An estimated 30,000 to 100,000 slaves escaped via the Underground Railroad over the course of its operation.

Heavily staffed by Quakers, the Underground Railroad evolved over time. Initially some slave owners permitted the purchase of runaway slaves, so members of the Underground Railroad gathered funds to facilitate freedom in that manner. As more slaves fled, however, slave owners insisted on their return. Underground Railroad supporters remained undaunted. Sometimes entire towns backed up the Underground Railroad and stood firm against slaveholders or their agents who tried to retrieve fugitive slaves.

Operation Freedom

To avoid capture, runaway slaves typically traveled at night, using the North Star as their guide. Therefore, the Underground Railroad became most useful during the day, so abolitionists established secret stations along the way to provide places for slaves to rest.

These stations were particularly critical in the South where the free black population remained relatively small and slave recovery efforts were particularly intense. Either someone took runaway slaves to stations or safe houses, or the runaway slaves usually identified the safe houses by the quilt hanging in the window, a lit lantern at the front of the house, or other signs. Secrecy was required within the safe houses as well, so they often contained secret passageways and attics where runaway slaves could hide.

Usually, it was the responsibility of the slave to plan his or her own escape. Sometimes, free blacks, posing as slaves, came to plantations to help slaves flee. Other times runaway slaves had to reach certain points where agents known as conductors greeted them. The journey north was usually a combination of travel by foot, by horse and buggy, and even by boat. For example, Calvin Fairbanks, a white man who developed his distaste for slavery while attending Oberlin College, regularly transported fugitives who made it to Kentucky across the Ohio River to freedom. Since slave catchers also patrolled the North, some runaway slaves settled in Canada.

Escaping slavery was just one aspect of the process. Money, food, and clothes were also necessary. Participating in the Underground Railroad was very dangerous, even for white people. Calvin Fairbanks spent over a decade in a Kentucky prison for his role in aiding fugitive slaves. It was also costly. Thomas Garrett of Wilmington, Delaware, went bankrupt paying a $10,000 fine for his admitted role in assisting fugitive slaves.

Key people along the line

Historians believe that the Underground Railroad may have originated with the Quakers in the late 1780s, so it's no surprise that Quakers comprised a large portion of white Underground Railroad supporters. White participants, even those who weren't Quakers, tended to be very religious and included Presbyterians, Baptists, Methodists, Episcopalians, and Catholics. For them, God's law superseded man-made laws. Their occupations ranged from preachers and politicians to ordinary citizens. Jacob M. Howard, a Michigan Underground Railroad supporter who later became a Republican senator, introduced the Thirteenth Amendment, which abolished slavery, to the Senate.

Ohio, Pennsylvania, Illinois, and Michigan were just a few Underground Railroad strongholds. It wasn't completely uncommon for entire towns to participate. Oberlin and Ripley in Ohio had a large number of participants, many of them unknown. Levi Coffin and John Fairfield were two of the more prominent white participants of the Underground Railroad:

- **Levi Coffin:** Sometimes called "the President of the Underground Railroad," for nearly 20 years, North Carolina–born Coffin and his wife Catharine used their strategic location in southern Indiana, the modern-day Fountain City, to help more than 2,000 former slaves escape to freedom. A successful merchant, Coffin personally helped finance many Underground Railroad efforts. So many fugitive slaves came through his home that people renamed it "Grand Central Station." Coffin's reputation as a model citizen inspired other white people to become involved with the Underground Railroad. His 1847 relocation to Cincinnati, Ohio, where he died many years later, didn't end his Underground Railroad activities.

- **John Fairfield:** Hailing from a slaveholding family in Virginia, Fairfield, who abhorred slavery, became involved in the Underground Railroad when he helped a slave friend escape to Canada. Subsequently other black people, presumably in the Ohio area where he spent a lot of time, sought him out and paid him to help their relatives and friends escape. Posing as a slaveholder, a slave trader, and sometimes a peddler, Fairfield was able to gain the confidence of whites, which made it easier for him to lead runaway slaves to freedom. One of his most impressive feats was freeing 28 slaves by staging a funeral procession. While he led many of his charges to Canada, others he delivered to Levi Coffin, who handled the remainder of their escape.

African Americans were intrinsically involved in the Underground Railroad beyond just being fugitives. It was understandably harder for white participants to convince other African Americans to flee. Fugitive slaves were particularly convincing and a large number risked their own freedom to free others. Besides, it was also easier for African Americans to blend in, especially on large plantations.

African Americans had a higher emotional investment since many had relatives and close friends still in bondage. Their job didn't end with the escape, though. More often than not, fugitive slaves stayed with other African Americans. They frequently settled in black communities where they learned where to look for work as well as how to conduct themselves, among other things. Despite the tremendous risks of recapture or becoming a slave for the first time, African Americans on all levels vigorously participated in the Underground Railroad and other antislavery efforts. Frederick Douglass's Rochester, New York, home was a well-known station. Other courageous figures of the Underground Railroad include:

- ✔ **William Still:** Philadelphia abolitionist Still, revered as "the Father of the Underground Railroad," assisted as many as 60 slaves a month. Despite the great need for secrecy, the New Jersey–born Still kept meticulous records. Those biographies and details of how each individual escaped later comprised the book, *The Underground Railroad* (1872).

- ✔ **Elijah Anderson:** Following a conviction for violating the Kentucky law against "enticing slaves to run away," Anderson, a fugitive slave who reportedly led 1,000 slaves to freedom, died in a Kentucky state prison.

- ✔ **Jane Lewis:** New Lebanon, Ohio, resident Lewis rowed countless former slaves across the Ohio River to freedom.

- ✔ **John Mason:** A fugitive slave once recaptured only to escape again, Mason helped more than 1,300 slaves to freedom. In just 19 months, he reportedly delivered 256 slaves to William Mitchell, a black missionary in Canada.

- ✔ **Harriet Tubman:** No Underground Railroad figure matches the legendary status of Harriet Tubman, one of its rare female conductors (see Figure 5-2). Even as a young slave, Tubman, born in Maryland around 1820, selflessly protected others: While shielding a field slave from an angry overseer, she received a blow on the head that made her prone to fall into a deep sleep at times throughout her life. Unwilling to be sold, Tubman fled north in 1849. She got a job in Philadelphia but traveled back the next year to free her sister and her sister's two children. Tubman made an amazing 19 trips back south, personally freeing over 300 slaves, including her parents.

Often dubbed "Moses" for leading "her people" out of bondage, Tubman died in 1913. "[I]n the point of courage, shrewdness, and disinterested exertions to rescue her fellowman," wrote William Still, "she was without equal."

LC-05262- 7816

Harriet Tubman (1823-1913)
nurse, spy and scout

Figure 5-2:
Harriet
Tubman.

© Corbis

Because runaway notices couldn't be posted until Monday, Tubman favored traveling on Saturdays, often carrying a drug to silence crying babies and a gun to urge on fugitives who wanted to give up along the way. By 1856, her exploits were so notorious that her capture would yield $40,000. Tubman, who reportedly made her last trip south in 1860, was never caught, however. Never one to rest, during the Civil War she served as a both a nurse and a spy.

Message in the music

When it came to the Underground Railroad, spirituals were much more than songs of worship. As Frederick Douglass indicated in *My Bondage, My Freedom,* spirituals held deep meaning. Just as the drums had allowed slaves to communicate from plantation to plantation, so did the spirituals. Countless numbers of slaves were able to escape slavery along the Underground Railroad in part because of spirituals.

Certain songs delivered messages about secret meetings or clues about escape routes. "Follow the Drinkin' Gourd" directed runaways to travel in the direction of the Big Dipper while "Steal Away" and "Swing Low, Sweet Chariot" often signaled that a slave was going to flee. To disclose her presence to slaves and let them know to prepare to leave, Tubman reportedly sang "Dark and thorny is de pathway/Where de pilgrim makes his ways/But beyond dis vale of sorrow/Lie de fields of endless slaves." Another song, "Go Down Moses," with the lyrics "Go, down Moses way down in Egypt's land/Tell old Pharoah, Let my people go," is often sung in tribute to Harriet Tubman, the Moses of her people. Read more about African American music in Chapter 16.

The Breaking Point

Marching into the 1850s, the divide between slavery and freedom became harder to manage. Foreseeing victory in the Mexican War (1846–1848) and the new territory that would come with it, political leaders sought ways to determine the status any new territory:

- ✔ The Wilmot Proviso proposed to outlaw slavery in any annexed territory.

- ✔ Some leaders insisted that new territory follow the precedent of the Missouri Compromise and be equally divided into slave and free states (refer to "The Missouri Compromise" earlier in the chapter)."

- ✔ Illinois Congressman Stephen A. Douglas championed popular sovereignty as a way to allow the people of those territories to side with slavery or freedom.

- ✔ Proslavery stalwart John C. Calhoun argued that slavery couldn't be excluded anywhere.

Straining North-South relations

The Fugitive Slave Law (or Fugitive Slave Act) caused the most aggravation for African Americans (refer to the earlier section "Stronger fugitive slave measures: Fugitive Slave Act of 1793"). Previously, claiming fugitive slaves was difficult for Southern slaveholders, but the Fugitive Slave Law mandated that officials arrest fugitive slaves and return them to their owners or be fined heavily. This law threatened the success of the Underground Railroad, which often depended on the lax enforcement of fugitive slave laws. For many militant abolitionists and those straddling the fence, the Fugitive Slave Law spurred them to greater action. As Southern slaveholders intensified their efforts to capture fugitive slaves in the North, many Northerners chose to stand their ground, which only flamed the seething tensions between North and South.

Harriet Beecher Stowe's abolitionist novel *Uncle Tom's Cabin* (1852) further strained North-South relations. Not only did the influential book sell more than 300,000 copies in its first year, but the theatrical counterpart also did well. By humanizing the suffering of those enslaved, Stowe took many white Americans beyond the facts of slavery. Proslavery supporters denounced the book as fervently as antislavery proponents welcomed it. Many proslavery supporters contended that Stowe exaggerated slavery's brutality. Still Stowe's novel became the rallying cry that shocked more white Americans into action against slavery.

The Compromise of 1850

When California petitioned for statehood, there were 15 slave states and 15 free states. Accepting California as a free state would have tilted that balance, and that proposition angered Southerners. The situation was so critical that several Southern states, led by elder South Carolina statesman John C. Calhoun, seriously considered seceding from the Union. A series of dramatic debates produced the pivotal Compromise of 1850 under which

- California entered the Union as a free state.
- Other territories deferred the slavery question until later.
- Texas received compensation for ceding land to New Mexico.
- The District of Columbia abolished the slave trade.
- A more strident fugitive slave law passed to appease Southern slaveholders.

Only a temporary fix to the country's much larger problem, the Compromise of 1850 couldn't stop the Union from unraveling.

The Kansas-Nebraska Act

In 1854, Illinois Senator Stephen A. Douglas accelerated the probability of civil war with the Kansas-Nebraska Act, which repealed the Missouri Compromise and allowed the legislatures of territories that should have been free to determine their own slave or free status. Kansas literally became a battleground as proslavery and antislavery factions flocked there.

In the midst of this chaos, the Northern Whigs, Free Soilers, and antislavery Democrats united to form the Republican Party, which set out to attract both antislavery and indifferent voters. Unlike the South, where many non-slaveholders vehemently defended slavery, a sizable number of Northerners opposed to slavery were reluctant to end it. Thus, attracting those voters would strengthen the Republicans and their political base.

Still trafficking slaves

Southerners pushed the envelope beyond just insisting upon slavery's expansion; they also demanded that the slave trade reopen, a sore spot since the slave trade's illegal continuation already agitated Northerners. As late as 1836, entire ships containing African slaves sailed from Cuba to Texas. Other instances include:

- ✔ The *Wanderer,* which sailed between New York and Africa, delivered almost 500 slaves to Jekyll Island, Georgia, in 1858. Although charged for the crime, a conviction never followed, to the dismay of antislavery supporters.

- ✔ Timothy Meaher, a wealthy shipyard owner in Mobile, Alabama, bet a Northerner that he could easily defy the slave trade ban without punishment, so he sent the *Clotilda* to Africa. In 1860, the ship returned with over a hundred Africans. Officials apprehended Meaher and his cohorts but later dismissed the charges. (Some say they got off because of the beginning of the Civil War.)

Following the Civil War, passengers from the *Clotilda* joined with others from the same West African region to form Africatown, a section of Mobile, Alabama. There, they maintained many of their cultural traditions, including aspects of their language. Once interviewed by the Harlem Renaissance writer Zora Neale Hurston, Cudjoe Lewis, who died in 1934, was the last *Clotilda* survivor. Today, Africatown still serves as a reminder of both slavery and Africa's cultural richness.

Dred Scott: A strike against freedom

The Supreme Court's 1857 Dred Scott decision showed the Civil War's inevitably. In 1847, Scott went to trial in Missouri to gain freedom for himself and his wife Harriet. Under the Missouri Compromise, Scott claimed he was entitled to freedom because his master Dr. John Emerson (since deceased) had taken him into Illinois and other free areas. When a lower court ruled that Scott and his family were free, the Missouri Supreme Court reversed the decision, and the United States Circuit in Missouri upheld Missouri Supreme Court's decision. Scott and his lawyers appealed it to the United States Supreme Court, but fared even worse at the hands of the highest court in the land.

Stacked with proslavery justices, the Supreme Court decided that, because Scott was African American, he wasn't a citizen and therefore couldn't sue anybody. To top it off, the Court ruled that the Missouri Compromise was unconstitutional. While the South cheered, abolitionists struggled to remain optimistic.

Henry Highland Garnet's "Call to Rebellion"

"Brethren, arise, arise! Strike for your lives and liberties. Now is the day and the hour. Let every slave throughout the land do this, and the days of slavery are numbered. You cannot be more oppressed than you have been — you cannot suffer greater cruelties than you have already. Rather die freemen than live to be slaves. Remember that you are FOUR MILLIONS!"

(Given at the National Negro Convention, Buffalo, New York, 1843)

Defining events at Harpers Ferry

If it wasn't already clear that the nation was headed toward civil war, John Brown and his actions in Harpers Ferry, Virginia, left little doubt. A stalwart abolitionist, Brown was born into a religious family in Connecticut in 1800. Although never rich, Brown did not let lack of funds prevent him from supporting the antislavery cause. He helped finance the publication of *Walker's Appeal* (refer to the earlier section "David Walker") and was among the few who supported Henry Highland Garnet's very radical "Call To Rebellion" speech at the 1843 National Negro Convention in Buffalo, New York. Apparently, Brown took Garnet's message for slaves to rebel against their masters to heart.

With Kansas up for grabs (courtesy of the Kansas-Nebraska Act), Kansans had to determine whether their state would have a free or slave status. To sway the decision, Brown and five of his sons went there and fought proslavery forces in Lawrence, with Brown killing five proslavery settlers in another town. Still these feats paled in comparison to his plan for Harpers Ferry.

Increasingly convinced that only violence would end slavery, Brown raised money throughout the North for a dramatic scheme to arm his own army against slavery. On October 16, 1859, Brown and 21 men (5 African Americans and 16 white Americans) raided the federal arsenal at Harpers Ferry. They planned to secure enough firepower to battle Virginia's slaveholders, but they didn't get very far. Federal and state troops swooped in almost immediately and captured Brown, who was hanged on December 2, 1859. Although the plot failed, Brown's actions terrified Southerners and inspired Northerners.

Before his hearing sentence, John Brown addressed the court: "Now, if it be deemed necessary that I should forfeit my life for the furtherance of the ends of justice, and mingle my blood further with the blood of my children, and with the blood of millions in this slave country whose rights are disregarded by wicked, cruel, and unjust enactments, I submit: so let it be done."

Facing the Moment of Truth

A year prior to John Brown's 1859 rebellion at Harpers Ferry, Virginia, Abraham Lincoln delivered his famous declaration that "a house divided against itself cannot stand" when he accepted the Republican nomination to represent Illinois in the Senate:

"A house divided against itself cannot stand. I believe this government cannot endure permanently half slave and half free. I do not expect the Union to be dissolved — I do not expect the house to fall — but I do expect it will cease to be divided. It will become all one thing, or all the other."

A pivotal figure in establishing a strong Republican party, Lincoln, known for his antislavery stance, became the Republican nominee for president in 1860. When he won with nearly 40 percent of the vote, Southern states didn't secede immediately. Speculation regarding their actions ended on April 12, 1861, when shots rang out at Fort Sumter, South Carolina, to launch the Civil War.

States' rights notwithstanding, the Confederate States of America and its president Jefferson Davis made it clear that the Civil War was about enslaving African Americans. Lincoln wasn't as clear. In 1862, *New York Tribune* editor Horace Greeley wrote an open letter to Lincoln urging him to end slavery. Lincoln responded: "If I could save the Union without freeing any slave, I would do it; and if I could save it by freeing all the slaves, I would do it: and if I could save it by freeing some and leaving others alone, I would also do that." Lincoln wasn't alone. Many white Northerners weren't sure how slavery factored into the Civil War. In time, the North changed its course, and waged a war to not just save the Union, but to finally end slavery.

Chapter 6

Up from Slavery: Civil War and Reconstruction

. . . .

In This Chapter

▶ Observing Lincoln's balancing act on the issue of slavery

▶ Seeing the impact of emancipation on the war effort

▶ Constructing a new union with freed blacks in mind

▶ Tracking the demise of Reconstruction

. . . .

*A*fter decades of trying to balance slavery and freedom, the United States finally reached the breaking point and ended up at war with itself. Although the Confederacy was clearly of the view that slavery was at the heart of the disagreement (even if later cries for states' rights veiled that sentiment), President Abraham Lincoln initially refused to acknowledge slavery's role at all. Many African Americans knew that the Civil War ran deeper than keeping the Union together, and they fought hard off and eventually on the battlefield to determine their own destiny.

This chapter delves into the struggle to make the Civil War a final blow to the institution of slavery. It also discusses the issues that initially prevented African Americans from fighting. The African American resolve for freedom manifested itself during Reconstruction, the nation's brief experiment to achieve true democracy following the war. The Union victory in the war, however, was only the beginning of change in the U.S., so in this chapter, you also find out about the complex struggles between Lincoln's successor and Congress, the North and the South, and white Southerners and the newly freed slaves.

The Question: End Slavery or Not?

To the dismay of African Americans and white abolitionists, Abraham Lincoln, during the early part of his presidency and in the early years of the Civil War, refused to take a firm stance about ending slavery. But Lincoln felt trapped; to save the Union, he had to avoid pushing slave states that hadn't seceded (and which physically separated the North from the South) into the ranks of the Confederacy. Not offending other white Southerners further wasn't Lincoln's only worry. He also had to avoid riling proslavery factions and Northerners fearful of ending slavery. Eventually, however, Lincoln moved toward emancipation, one of the defining triumphs of his presidency.

Teetering on a tightrope

Before Lincoln took office in February 1861, seven states had already seceded. Aware that the nation was at stake, Lincoln hoped to prevent further defection and took care in his inaugural address to condemn individuals for secession and not the South overall. His guarded words, however, didn't prevent the new nation of seceding states, the Confederate States of America (CSA) led by Mississippian Jefferson Davis, from firing the shot that launched the Civil War on April 12, 1861.

Initially, the North, even those who voted against Lincoln, lent their support to restoring the Union. Because the North had more people and greater resources, Lincoln and his supporters felt the war would end quickly, with the Union victorious. As the Union lost several battles, that support began to fizzle. White and black Northern abolitionists wanted the war to end slavery, but that prospect scared other Northerners, many of whom feared a slave insurrection.

In addition, slavery was alive and well in the border states that stuck with the Union. Lincoln understood that keeping these states was critical to the Union's success, and he worked overtime not to lose them.

The key border states were Maryland, Missouri, Kentucky, and Delaware. Some historians also include West Virginia, even though it didn't officially become a state until 1863.

Lincoln hoped the Crittenden-Johnson Resolution would reassure slave border states. The resolution, sponsored by Kentucky senator John J. Crittenden and Tennessee's Andrew Johnson (the only Southern senator not to quit his post even when Tennessee seceded) emphasized that the federal government was fighting to preserve the Union and not to disturb any institutions already in practice.

The first Confiscation Act, 1861

As the war progressed, the issue of what to do about slavery became even more relevant. When Union forces began penetrating the South, able-bodied male slaves sought refuge, but Union generals didn't know what to do with them. Their varying reactions, as evident in the following, only underscored that there was no federal policy pertaining to slaves:

- Some generals proclaimed the fleeing slaves free.
- Some generals seized the slaves as contraband and put them to work.
- Some refused to take the slaves in and forced them to leave.
- Some actively returned the slaves to their previous owners.
- One Union general requested permission to allow slaveholders to cross Union lines and recover their slaves.

In response to all this confusion, Congress passed its first Confiscation Act in August 1861. This act established a federal policy for dealing slaves. With this Act, it became federal policy to seize slaves directly used in military action in support of the Confederacy, but the Act made no direct mention of freeing any slaves. Instead, it simply deprived rebelling slave owners of slave labor used against the Union. Even with no mention of freeing any slaves, Lincoln worried how the Union's bordering slave states would react to the legislation.

Blacks in the Early Days of the Civil War

As Lincoln pondered how slavery factored into the Civil War and moved toward emancipation, many African Americans never doubted that this was the war to end slavery. When the Civil War began, African Americans were eager to contribute.

Even though blacks wanted to fight for the Union and freedom, the War Department initially turned them away. Lincoln and other Unionists feared that allowing black men to fight would imply that the war was about ending slavery and not preserving the Union, an action that would alienate the critical border states. Also there was a fear that allowing African Americans to fight would turn the Civil War into a slave insurrection and force white soldiers to battle both African Americans and the Confederacy. Thus, African Americans had to fight to enlist in the Union army. A few African Americans did serve in the navy early on, however; others formed military clubs such as the Hannibal Guards of Pittsburgh and the Crispus Attucks Guards of Albany, Ohio, to prepare for battle should the call come.

Serving the Union

The rising death toll of white Union soldiers convinced white Northerners that white soldiers shouldn't be the only ones sacrificed to win the war. In addition, slim Union victories like Shiloh and defeats such as the Second Bull Run threatened recruitment. When a voluntary call for 300,000 Union soldiers only yielded 90,000, Lincoln had to consider his other options.

With the Militia Act passed in July 1862 (essentially overturning a 1792 law prohibiting black men from bearing arms), Lincoln and Congress started paving the way for African Americans to join Union forces. Several sections of that act specifically addressed African American enlistment, establishing pay rates as well as potentially emancipating the mothers, wives, and children of these soldiers.

Surviving in the South

The Confederacy faced its own crisis: As slaves realized that their freedom was indeed within reach, instead of running away, some slaves just walked off the plantation. Many of those slaves ended up in Union camps and eventually enlisted with the Union to defeat the Confederacy. Some slaves who didn't leave refused to submit to white authority.

Tempering slaves' reactions to what was happening with the war became a big concern for the Confederacy, so strengthening slave patrols, militia-like units that regulated slave behavior, including hunting down runaways, was first on the list (go to Chapter 4 for more information about slave patrols). All the proslavery rhetoric from previous decades about slaves loving their masters flew out the window. Exemptions from patrol duties ended as the Confederacy instituted punishments in the form of fines and imprisonment to those who didn't attend to their duties.

Moving toward the Emancipation Proclamation

Long before becoming president, Lincoln favored setting aside money for African Americans' voluntary emigration to Haiti or Liberia and compensating slaveholders for their losses. That position didn't change with the Civil War, especially since Lincoln needed to keep the Union's bordering slave states loyal. His repeated pleas to Delaware, Maryland, Kentucky, and Missouri in 1862 to accept compensated emancipation may have gone unheard, but the wheels of emancipation were already in motion.

Shutting down the illegal slave trade

Shutting down the slave trade was one of Lincoln's first moves toward eventual emancipation. Despite numerous bans spanning several decades, an illegal slave trade continued well into the 1850s, with the last official slave ship to the U.S., the *Clotilda,* arriving in 1860 (refer to Chapter 5). To stop the trade, Lincoln did the following during the first half of 1862:

- ✔ **Sanctioned the hanging of Captain Nathaniel Gordon, a known slaver from Portland, Maine.** Gordon was the first slave trader ever executed under the Piracy Act of 1820, which defined slave trading as piracy.

- ✔ **Launched negotiations to allow Britain, which had become one of the world's leading antislavery forces, to search American ships.** For decades, the U.S. had refused these searches; as a result, the illegal slave trade flourished. The resulting treaty with Britain (signed April 25, 1862) helped kill the slave trade. More importantly, the treaty attracted British sympathy to the Union's cause.

- ✔ **Approved a bill to end slavery in Washington, D.C.** This bill was the Civil War's only instance of compensated emancipation: $1 million was set aside to pay D.C. slaveholders up to $300 per slave, and there was another $100,000 to fund voluntary emigration.

- ✔ **Signed a law outlawing slavery in the territories.** The debate about the status of slavery in the territories had arguably led the country to the Civil War in the first place (check out Chapter 5 for more).

Passing the Second Confiscation Act

With the illegal slave trade finally quashed, the nation's priority was to get through the Civil War. The Second Confiscation Act became a pivotal turning point. Signed by Lincoln in July 1862, the Second Confiscation Act was an important step toward the Emancipation Proclamation because it freed the slaves of rebelling citizens, in addition to allowing for the seizure of other property. (The First Confiscation Act purposely avoided any reference to emancipation.)

Courting England's support

The Confederacy was actively seeking England's support. Cotton was one of the primary reasons the Southern states had been so quick to secede: Because the South enjoyed a virtual monopoly over one of the world's most dominant crops, leaders figured that world powers had to side with their main cotton supplier, even if they opposed slavery. Obviously, if England supported the South, the Union would be at a distinct disadvantage.

Lincoln believed that European powers, particularly England, wouldn't support a slave government; the problem was the Union didn't necessarily stand for freedom. Officially, federal forces were fighting to keep the United States unified rather than to end slavery. Winning England's support became another factor leading Lincoln toward the Emancipation Proclamation.

Free at Last (Well, Sort of): The Emancipation Proclamation

On July 22, Lincoln surprised his cabinet members by reading a preliminary draft of his executive order for emancipation. Only two cabinet members fully endorsed the Proclamation, and one cabinet member suggested that Lincoln share his decision with the public after a Union battle victory, advice Lincoln heeded.

His moment came after the September 17, 1862, Battle of Antietam (also known as the Battle of Sharpsburg), in which Major General George B. McClellan successfully pushed back Confederate forces commanded by General Robert E. Lee. Lincoln readdressed his cabinet on September 22 for advice on the document's wording, not on the issue of whether he should deliver it or not, and shortly thereafter, issued a preliminary Emancipation Proclamation. He issued the formal Emancipation Proclamation 100 days later on January 1, 1863.

What the Proclamation did

In the Emancipation Proclamation, Lincoln vowed that, if rebellion continued, "all persons held as slaves within any State, or designated part of the State, the people whereof shall be in rebellion against the United States, shall be then, thenceforward and forever free."

Although many people assume the Proclamation freed all the slaves in the U.S., it actually didn't. Here are the finer points:

✔ The Proclamation declared slaves in *rebelling* states free.

✔ It did *not* free slaves in the border states or areas within Confederate territory already under Union control.

✔ It welcomed acceptable freed slaves to join the armed services.

Reaction to the order

Despite Lincoln's great strategic pains in taking the Emancipation Proclamation public, he pleased no one at first:

✔ **Northern whites:** The perceived shift from saving the Union to ending slavery so angered many Northern whites that some soldiers resigned. During the fall elections, Republicans lost key seats to Democrats who didn't generally support such so-called radical changes, narrowing the Republican advantage in the House to just 18 votes.

✔ **Abolitionists:** Because Lincoln's proposed emancipation was more than he had committed to since the war began, white and black abolitionists didn't criticize it publicly. Privately, they didn't think Lincoln had gone far enough and wished that he had abolished slavery completely. Still they considered the Proclamation a step in the right direction.

✔ **The English:** The proclamation didn't move the English populace. Commenting on Lincoln's proposed emancipation, one London newspaper wrote, "the principle is not that a human being cannot justly own another, but that he cannot own him unless he is loyal to the United States."

In fact, England may have never committed to either side in the U.S. Civil War had Jefferson Davis, the president of the Confederate States, not demanded the return of captured slaves back to states, where death awaited them, with his own proclamation. After that, Manchester, England's working population let Lincoln know that their sympathies rested with the Union. A short time later, England supported the Union.

✔ **African Americans:** While many blacks, especially in the targeted South, were unaware of the Emancipation Proclamation, those knew of it assigned the document greater value than Lincoln intended. Although heralded as "the Great Emancipator" throughout history, that title stems from the war's end result and not from any definitive stance Lincoln took against slavery as president.

Finally in the Fight

After the Emancipation Proclamation, it became easier for African American soldiers to join the Union army. Many historians agree that these extra bodies, along with a few other factors, ultimately secured a Union victory.

With the ground cleared for African American military enlistment, recruitment became ferocious. Luminaries such as Frederick Douglass served as recruiting agents, and recruitment rallies took place throughout the North. A number of black soldiers were already prepared for war and quickly stepped up. An estimated 180,000 African Americans — roughly 10 percent of total forces — joined the Union cause.

As Union soldiers

Bringing about an end to slavery may have become the Union's new direction in the Civil War, but many African Americans didn't feel the love. The War Department established the U.S. Bureau of Colored Troops and created the U.S. Colored Troops to segregate black and white soldiers. White Americans doubted the courage of black soldiers early on, but were proved wrong when black soldiers repeatedly demonstrated the depths of their courage. The first such display occurred just days after the official establishment of the U.S. Colored Troops, at Port Hudson, Louisiana, when two African American units charged the Confederate enemy repeatedly, suffering 200 casualties.

Their role

While large numbers of African Americans served as cooks and performed other duties, the establishment of the U.S. Colored Troops created more combat opportunities for African Americans. On the field, African Americans fought fiercely and bravely, giving Union forces a significant and much-needed lift. Serving as spies and scouts by passing themselves off as slaves, African Americans also offered the Union unique advantages.

In the last stages of the Civil War especially, African Americans were present and critical in key battles, including the Battle of Vicksburg in Mississippi, Milliken's Bend in Louisiana, and the all-important surrender at Appomattox Courthouse on April 9, 1865, in Virginia. A few soldiers such as Decatur Dorsey and James Daniel Gardner (sometimes Gardiner) did receive medals for their services, but some received their just due posthumously.

Susie King Taylor: African American women and the Civil War

In *A Black Woman's Civil War Memoirs* (1902), Susie King Taylor provides an unmatched insight into the life of an African American woman during the Civil War. Born a slave near Savannah, Georgia, the former Susie Baker secretly learned to read and write as a child. When the Union forces arrived in 1862, her uncle took her along with his family to safety behind Union lines.

King Taylor's many talents served the Union well; she worked as a laundress, nurse, and teacher, among other things. Not content to share her accomplishments only, King Taylor, who married a Union soldier, noted, "There were hundreds of them who assisted the Union soldiers by hiding them and helping them escape. Many were punished for taking food to the prison stockades for the prisoners." King Taylor, who died in 1912, believed "these things should be kept in history before the people."

Black soldiers participated in 410 military battles overall, 39 of them major. According to some scholars, over 38,000 black soldiers died during the Civil War, a figure some argue is almost 40 percent greater than that of white soldiers.

Their pay

Black soldiers received $7 a month for service while white soldiers received $13. Members of the 54th Massachusetts Regiment protested the discriminatory policy by serving for an entire year uncompensated. The protests worked, and in 1864, the War Department granted black soldiers equal pay.

Soldiering alongside whites

White and black soldiers served in separate regiments. Even in segregated units, however, black officers rarely led black soldiers. Exceptions included two regiments of General Butler's Corps d' Afrique that were led by Major F.E. Dumas and Captain P.B.S. Pinchback. Major Martin R. Delany, Captain O.S.B. Wall, Captain H. Ford Douglass, and First Lieutenant W.D. Matthews were also black officers. Black surgeons and chaplains were a bit more numerous.

Convincing whites to lead all-black forces wasn't easy at first. Those who were willing usually became officers. Thanks to the film *Glory* (1989), Colonel Robert Gould Shaw, the 54th Massachusetts Regiment commander who wrote over 200 letters to family and friends during the Civil War, is the best-known white leader of black troops.

Thomas Morris Chester: Civil War correspondent

Liberian émigré Thomas Morris Chester, the college-educated son of an ex-slave, served an important and unique function during the Civil War. An early U.S. Colored Troops recruiter, Chester, who helped form the Massachusetts 54th and 55th Regiments as well as two black companies in his native Harrisburg, Pennsylvania, was reluctant to join the military himself because African Americans rarely rose above the rank of sergeant. Instead, Chester served as a Civil War correspondent for *The Philadelphia Press* in 1864 and 1865; in that position, he covered African American troops in Virginia, especially during the critical fall of Richmond.

Captured in the book *Thomas Morris Chester, Black Civil War Correspondent,* his observations are the only detailed, firsthand accounts of African American soldiers in combat during the Civil War. In addition to describing camp life for black troops, Chester also wrote about how Confederate soldiers and civilians reacted to them. After the war, Chester, who died in 1892, also helped with Reconstruction.

The dangers they faced

Fighting for the Union was particularly dangerous for black soldiers because Confederate forces didn't take kindly to them. In 1862, Jefferson Davis threatened to return all slaves captured in arms to the slave states to which they belonged. Lincoln countered that for every Union soldier killed in a manner that violated the laws of war a Confederate soldier would also die. For those enslaved by the Confederates, Lincoln promised that a Rebel soldier would also endure hard labor.

Still, Confederate soldiers treated black prisoners of war differently. By war's end, there were many black prisoners of war, but to make examples of them, Confederates killed African Americans more readily than they did white prisoners. Sometimes black captives weren't even reported. When Fort Pillow fell to Confederate forces in April 1864, black soldiers weren't even allowed to surrender; Confederates shot some and burned others alive.

As Confederate soldiers

Some African Americans also served with the Confederacy. Determining their actual numbers, however, is difficult because many were slaves, especially early in the war. Gauging how many African Americans fought for the

Confederacy after Lincoln issued the Emancipation Proclamation is especially difficult given that many Southern blacks didn't learn of the Proclamation until months after it went public.

African Americans in the Confederate military often served as cooks, musicians, guards, and in other noncombatant positions. Some like Charleston's Robert Smalls, who along with his wife Hannah successfully delivered a Confederate boat to Union forces, operated as double agents.

Well into 1864, the Confederacy was understandably reluctant to arm slaves. Early in the war, many white Southerners feared slave insurrections. But with an ever-growing number of wounded and dead, the Confederacy, like the Union, had little choice but to turn to African Americans. Although the 1865 Confederate Senate committed to enlisting 200,000 African Americans, there's little evidence that the Confederacy ever reached anywhere near that number. Continued fear of armed slaves prompted Jefferson Davis to sign a bill on March 13, 1865, mandating that enlisted slaves not exceed 25 percent of the total able-bodied male slave population of each state. It's especially important to note that enslaved African Americans who fought for the Confederacy were promised their own freedom.

The End of the War and the Thirteenth Amendment

With Lincoln newly reelected in 1864 and the South's surrender, the future looked bright for all American citizens in 1865. On January 31, 1865, Lincoln proposed the Thirteenth Amendment abolishing slavery. On April 9, 1865, General Robert E. Lee surrendered to Union General Ulysses S. Grant. But five days later, John Wilkes Booth, a Confederate sympathizer, crept into the presidential box of Ford's Theatre in Washington, D.C., and shot Lincoln, who died the next day, April 15.

As the constitutional amendment made the rounds from state to state seeking the critical three-fourths vote needed for ratification, African American citizens, like those shown in Figure 6-1, realized that their world had changed. The Civil War was over, but the important work of reconstructing the nation was only beginning. Tensions ran as high in peace as they had in conflict.

Mississippi, a state that sent two African American men to the U.S. Senate and a few more to the House of Representatives during Reconstruction, didn't ratify the Thirteenth Amendment abolishing slavery until 1995, not 1895.

© Corbis

Figure 6-1:
Freed
slaves.

(Re)constructing Democracy

Reconstruction, the period roughly spanning 1865 to 1877, presented the United States with the unique opportunity to exercise true democracy. For his part, Lincoln devised a plan to reestablish the Union long before the Civil War ended. On December 8, 1863, he proposed his Proclamation of Amnesty and Reconstruction, which carried these key points:

- ✔ Amnesty didn't extend to high-ranking Confederate government and military officials or soldiers who had abused black and white prisoners of war.

- ✔ In accordance with the Ten Percent Plan, a state could gain readmission to the Union if no less than one-tenth of the number of its citizens who voted in the 1860 election took an oath of loyalty to the Union and accepted emancipation.

Lincoln's assassination profoundly affected black Americans, and they had reason to worry. Andrew Johnson, Lincoln's Southern vice-president, didn't share Lincoln's views. Johnson proclaimed, "This is a country for white men, and by God, as long as I am President, it shall be a government for white men." Unfortunately, he was true to his words.

Undermining Lincoln's plan

In May 1865, President Johnson issued his own plan for Reconstruction. On paper, the plan differed little from Lincoln's plan. By issuing his plan while Congress wasn't in session, however, Johnson showed that he intended to act by presidential authority alone, eliminating Congress from the process. Some refer to Johnson's proposal as *Presidential Reconstruction.* Congress not participating in Reconstruction wasn't good for African Americans.

Abraham Lincoln and the Republican Party had selected Johnson as their vice-presidential candidate in order to appeal to the more moderate Democrats who didn't support emancipation. He was a former slave owner and the only Southern senator not to resign during secession.

Still, there were those in Congress who continued to work toward the original intent of Lincoln's plans for reconstruction. Thaddeus Stevens and Charles Sumner, labeled Radical Republicans, were the key forces behind much of the progressive legislation benefiting African Americans. Stevens, a Northerner whom white Southerners considered a *carpetbagger* (usually a white Northerner active in Republican politics who "interfered" with the South after the Civil War) had been critical in repealing the 1861 Crittenden-Johnson Resolution, a bill cosponsored by then-Senator Johnson that emphasized the Union's intention to preserve the Union and not to end slavery.

The Black Codes

With a president sympathetic to ex-Confederates, Reconstruction took a turn for the worse. Southern states may have been willing to concede to the Thirteenth Amendment (refer to the section "The End of the War and the Thirteenth Amendment"), but they weren't ready to embrace black Americans fully. Insisting as they had in slavery that African Americans required white supervision, Southern states passed the Black Codes in 1865 to regulate African American behavior. Reminiscent of the Slave Codes (refer to Chapter 4), the Black Codes, which varied from state to state, did the following:

- Restricted where African Americans could live
- Regulated their work habits, even arresting and imprisoning them if they quit their jobs
- Prohibited blacks from testifying against whites

Presidential vetoes

With many of the former Confederacy's top brass in critical Congressional seats again, national politics looked as vulnerable as local politics. Pennsylvania senator Thaddeus Stevens fought to restore Congressional control over Reconstruction, but Johnson used his veto power to quash many of the bills Stevens tried to push through. Luckily, Congress overrode Johnson's veto of the Civil Rights Act of 1866. Intended to counter the Black Codes, this act reaffirmed the rights of *all* citizens to sue and be sued; testify in court against anyone, regardless of race; and buy or rent any piece of property anywhere, among other things.

Emergence of white supremacist groups

Angry Southerners refused to back down in the face of federal legislation. Just as they had resurrected the Slave Codes in the form of the Black Codes, they brought back the essence of slave patrols. In no time, white supremacist organizations emerged, such as the Knights of the White Camellia, the White Brotherhood, and the Ku Klux Klan (KKK), to name only a few.

As Reconstruction continued, these organizations' membership numbers increased, and new organizations formed. If they couldn't intimidate African Americans legally, they were determined to do it with violence, regularly beating and lynching African Americans they felt stepped out of line. With law enforcement personnel in their ranks as well as a willingness by nonmembers to turn a blind eye, the pre- and post-Civil War South differed little for many African Americans.

Taking back the power: Reconstruction Act of 1867

Thaddeus Stevens, who didn't take the turn of events in the South lightly, established the Joint Committee on Reconstruction. At around the same time, more Radical Republicans won offices in the 1866 elections. With the Reconstruction Act of 1867, Congress took back the reins. The act

- Divided the South into five military districts ruled by a governor
- Declared that, in order to have federal troops removed, Southern states had to ratify the Fourteenth Amendment, which maintains that all persons born or naturalized in the U.S. are citizens of both the U.S. and the state in which they reside and are subject to equal protection under the law

Things looked brighter for African Americans with Congress back in control. For example, when Johnson wanted to pull the plug on the Freedmen's Bureau, which provided much-needed assistance for newly freed African Americans, Congress revived it. That light wouldn't shine long, however.

A Mixed Bag of Hope and Despair

Leading abolitionists such as Frederick Douglass worked so hard to end slavery that they'd given little thought to what freedom would actually mean. What would newly freed blacks do to support themselves? Private Northern mutual aid societies were among the first to address the need and descended on the South in droves as early as 1861. For them, education and religious piety was a positive start, and African Americans poured themselves into both. (Read more about education in Chapter 13 and religion in Chapter 12.) Yet the leaders of these organizations realized that only government intervention could sufficiently address the problems confronting African Americans. Some began appealing to the government as early as 1863 for a government organization that could fulfill this purpose.

The Freedmen's Bureau

Just before the war officially ended, the Bureau of Refugees, Freedmen, and Abandoned Lands, better known as the *Freedmen's Bureau,* came into formal existence in March 1865. Assisting former slaves and transitioning them to freedom was the Freedmen's Bureau's main priority, and its duties varied widely. For example, many former slaves wanted to make their marriages official, so the Bureau issued countless marriage licenses. But the Bureau also helped a small number of poor whites as well. A laundry list of primary functions included:

- **Food rations:** Hunger was a major problem among ex-slaves, so the Bureau distributed food rations. Between 1865 and 1869, the Bureau distributed approximately 21 million food rations, with an estimated 5 million going to poor whites.

- **Education:** Illiteracy was a major problem among the recently freed, so establishing schools became one of the Bureau's main functions. Expanded educational opportunities didn't just benefit former slaves; they also helped poor white Southerners who were also mostly illiterate.

- **Hospitals:** Many ex-slaves needed medical care but had no money to pay for it nor facilities available to them for treatment. Amazingly, the Freedmen's Bureau established 46 hospitals in just two years. By June 1869, over 500,000 patients had received treatment.

- **Labor mediation:** Freedmen were concerned about working for white Southerners and many tried to avoid returning to the land, mainly because it reminded them of slavery. With little recourse, freedmen often appealed to the Bureau to help negotiate fairer wages with white employers. For serious grievances, the Bureau had its own courts because justice, especially against white Southerners, was difficult for African Americans to achieve in Southern courts.

Dedicated workers and beneficiaries truly appreciated the Freedmen's Bureau, but some white Northerners questioned the need for such an agency since the Civil War had ended. White Southerners simply objected to government intervention of any kind but particularly to an agency whose main intention, they felt, was to enfranchise African Americans.

In addition to trying to sabotage Bureau posts by intimidating its workers or raiding its ration houses, angry white Southerners burned houses, raped black women, boldly robbed hardworking black citizens, and shot at or killed others. In Memphis and New Orleans, whites massacred scores of African Americans, killing nearly 100 men, women, and children and injuring countless others. Shocked by these incidents, Congress authorized an investigation. But, without troops, the Freedmen's Bureau could do little more than file incident reports and document the injustices.

Where's my 40 acres and a mule?

Resolving the issue of abandoned or confiscated land was complex. During the war, Rufus Saxton, Union head of the Department of the South, proposed the general plan of allotting black families two acres per working hand and furnishing them with tools necessary to plant corn and potatoes for their own use as they cultivated a specified amount of cotton for the government. The Treasury Department, however, contested the War Department's right to take such action. When both Lincoln's and Johnson's Amnesty Proclamations returned a large portion of confiscated land back to the original owners, the matter was complicated further.

Special Field Order No. 15

On January 16, 1865, General William T. Sherman issued his Special Field Order No. 15 in which approximately 40,000 African Americans received roughly 400,000 acres of confiscated land in South Carolina, Georgia, and Florida. Section 4 of the Freedmen's Bureau Act (passed in March 1865) supported Sherman's order by allowing for the lease of not more than 40 acres of land for a period of three years to freedmen who could purchase the land when the lease ended. But by the summer of 1865, President Johnson, who had promised to return confiscated land to those he had pardoned, ordered the Freedmen's Bureau to comply with his promises. He ignored the fact that black families were already living on the land in question.

Freedmen's Bureau Chief General Oliver Howard came face to face with some of those families in October 1865 on South Carolina's Edisto Island. As expected, the bad news wasn't well-received. When Howard suggested that the families "lay aside their bitter feelings" and "become reconciled to their old masters," one response was, "You only lost your right arm in war and might forgive them."

For his part, Saxton stood by the freedmen and helped them fight to keep their land. Those with deeds from government sales were able to keep their land. Ironically, the government sent in black soldiers to remove many black South Carolinians from their land. By the end of 1866, only 1,565 out of 40,000 who received land through Sherman's Special Field Order remained on that land in South Carolina.

Some scholars contend that the government never promised African Americans 40 acres and a mule, that the policy was just a rumor borne from Sherman's Special Field Order and the Army's practice of loaning extra mules out to African American families.

Southern Homestead Act of 1866

Some freedmen received land through the Southern Homestead Act of 1866 when the government placed 46 million acres of public land in Alabama, Arkansas, Florida, Louisiana, and Mississippi up for sale. Many black Southerners benefited, as evidenced by the following statistics:

- In Florida, ex-slaves gained possession of around 160,960 acres in just one year.
- In Arkansas, ex-slaves possessed 116 of the 243 homesteads granted.
- In Georgia, African Americans held more than 350,000 acres in 1874.

By June 1876, however, Congress repealed the Southern Homestead Act, along with other Reconstruction-era legislation. Acting independently of the federal government, South Carolina, which enjoyed a black majority and a high number of African American state legislators, helped freedmen purchase land. As plantations came up for sale, a local land commissioner bought, divided, and sold the land, often on credit.

The Treaty of 1866

In the Treaty of 1866 with various slaveholding Native American nations like the Choctaw, Cherokee, and Chickasaw, Congress forked over a large sum of money on the condition that these nations would adopt African Americans as citizens and issue 40 acres of land to each person. Although others complied, the Chickasaw continued to resist, not seeing why they should comply with something the U.S. refused to do. As stated in a resolution, "The Chickasaw people cannot see any reason or just cause why they should be required to do more for their freed slaves than the white people have done in the slave-holding states for theirs."

Back to the land

During Reconstruction, most African Americans received no land and had to return to agricultural work, many to the same plantations they fled as slaves. Interestingly, a model for what would become sharecropping emerged during the Civil War.

Working for hire

At the end of the Civil War and into Reconstruction, many ex-slaves agreed to work contracts in which they were to receive monthly wages ranging from $9 to $15 for men and $5 to $10 for women. The contracts often included provisions for food and shelter.

Work contract agreements trace their roots to 1862 when General Grant delegated fugitive slaves to John Eaton who set up a special camp for them at Grand Junction, Tennessee, where he supervised hiring them out. General Benjamin Butler did the same in Louisiana.

Work contracts weren't always honored, even those negotiated by the Freedmen's Bureau. Some had loopholes, but quite simply, good faith was essential to the agreements' success, and it was in short supply. As power returned to white Southerners (many of them former high-ranking Confederate officials), African Americans had no recourse if the contracts were broken.

Sharecropping

Sharecropping, a system in which blacks and some poor whites worked the land in exchange for anywhere from a quarter to half of a crop (usually cotton or corn) eventually became the more dangerous system compared to work contracts. Sharecroppers received land and housing as well as seeds, animals, and equipment, but they had to wait until harvest time to receive any payment for their share of a crop.

Martin R. Delany, the second-highest-ranking African American at the Freedmen's Bureau, worked overtime to safeguard freedmen's rights. In addition to distributing copies of fair contracts for sharecroppers to use, Delany also negotiated more favorable cotton prices for freedmen. When a Freedmen's Bureau agent ran off with some of those funds, however, Delany's Cotton Agency closed. By September 1868, Delany was out of the Freedmen's Bureau.

As time went on, the dangers of sharecropping became more apparent. Sharecroppers faced the unavoidable evil of purchasing necessities on credit at local stores, often owned by their landowners. High interest rates made it nearly impossible for sharecroppers to bury their debt, which often meant that they had to continue working for the landowners. Falling cotton prices and a depression in 1873 only worsened the sharecropper's plight. From Reconstruction into the early 20th century, sharecropping adversely affected black Southerners.

Finding a new way

Moving north wasn't a much better option for African Americans in the South than working the land because white workers in the North feared an influx of black labor. Employers pounced on these fears and purposely hired black workers to undermine white labor unions. Suspicious of black workers, many white labor unions refused to accept black workers. Unable to join the National Labor Union, African Americans founded the National Negro Labor Union in 1869. Blacksmiths, bricklayers, and other artisans had trouble finding work because white employers favored white immigrant labor, thus forcing skilled black men to work menial and low-paying jobs. Black women usually became domestics or independent washerwomen.

Many black men chose to move west to work as cooks, cowboys, and cattle drivers. Some used the Homestead Act to become farmers, whereas others joined the U.S. Army, which formed the all-black 9th and 10th Calvary in 1866 and the 24th and 25th Infantry, more popularly known as Buffalo Soldiers, in 1869. In addition to protecting settlers mainly from Native Americans being forced from the land, black troops built roads, installed telegraph lines, and performed other duties that further aided westward expansion. Some became railroad workers, miners, and sailors.

As an indication that conditions in some areas of the West were slightly more progressive for African Americans, 26 of the 46 original settlersof Los Angeles were black.

Banking on wealth

Even before the Civil War ended, former slaves were encouraged to save their money. More popularly known as the Freedmen's Bank, the Freedmen's Savings and Trust Company was the primary beneficiary of this thrifty spirit. By 1872, the bank had 34 branches, mostly in the South, as well as $3,299,201 in total deposits in 1874. Unfortunately, poor accounting, speculation, and bogus loans by its white board, led by Henry Cooke (brother of Jay Cooke, a Union financier whose dubious financial practices helped bring on the nation's 1873 depression), sank the Freedmen's Bank.

When the board bailed in 1873, Frederick Douglass stepped in and, when he realized the extent of the financial difficulties, even pumped some of his own money into the bank to keep it afloat. He was too late. In 1874, the Freedmen's Bank failed, literally swallowing up the nickels and dimes of countless ex-slaves. While the public blamed many of the nation's black leaders for the crash, the real culprits, Cooke and his gang, got off scot-free.

Taking office

Politically, African Americans fared better when Congress controlled Reconstruction. To regain admission to the Union, states were required to draft new constitutions, and African Americans were present at the constitutional conventions held to accomplish this task. Only South Carolina boasted a black majority, but even states like Texas, which had a small black population, had African American representation. In addition to abolishing slavery, many of these new state constitutions further enhanced the democratic process by ending property qualifications for voting and holding office.

Attending state constitutional conventions was just the beginning of the black political presence. At one point, the South Carolina legislature had 87 black and just 40 white members. African Americans Alonzo J. Ransier and Richard H. Gleaves served as lieutenant governors of the state in 1870 and 1872, respectively. In 1872 and 1874, the speaker of the house was African American, and a black man, Francis L. Cardozo, served as secretary of state and treasurer between 1868 and 1876.

Mississippi also had a significant number of black politicians. A.K. Davis, James Hill, T.W. Cardozo, and John Roy Lynch served as lieutenant governor, secretary of state, superintendent of education, and speaker of the house, respectively. (Years later, Lynch published *The Facts of Reconstruction* in 1913.) Louisiana didn't match South Carolina and Mississippi in great numbers of significant political positions held by African Americans, but Oscar J. Dunn, P.B.S. Pinchback, and C.C. Antoine served as lieutenant governors of the state. Pinchback even became the governor for 43 days after Henry C. Warmoth's removal in 1872.

Despite these early political gains, a black man wasn't elected governor in the U.S. until Virginia's Douglas Wilder, who served from 1990 to 1994. In 2006, Massachusetts elected Deval Patrick its governor.

Many of these black leaders rose to national prominence. Ironically, in 1870, the nation's first African American senator, Hiram Revels, filled a seat vacated by former president of the Confederate States Jefferson Davis. Blanche K. Bruce, another Mississippian, became the first African American elected to a full Senate term in 1874, a feat not matched again until Massachusetts elected Edward Brooke in 1966. With his knack for amassing public offices, P.B.S. Pinchback got himself elected to the U.S. House of Representatives in 1872 and to the Senate in 1873. After a long debate, however, the Senate denied Pinchback his seat.

The U.S. House of Representatives was more colorful and, at various times, included South Carolina's J.H. Rainey (the nation's first black Congressman), war hero Robert Smalls, Robert De Large, and Robert Brown Elliott, as well as John Roy Lynch, Florida's Josiah T. Walls, Alabama's Benjamin Turner, and Georgia's Jefferson Long, among others. At least one African American remained in Congress until 1901.

The Fifteenth Amendment

Civil War general Ulysses S. Grant won the 1868 presidential election, which was a fortuitous turn of events in the fight for equal rights. Had Grant not been elected, it's doubtful if the all-important Fifteenth Amendment, giving black men the right to vote, would have made it to the ratification phase.

But Grant did win and the Fifteenth Amendment was ratified in 1870. This amendment states, "The right of citizens of the United States to vote shall not be denied or abridged by the United States or by any State on account of race, color, or previous condition of servitude."

The Fifteenth Amendment created a rift between longtime women's rights' supporter Frederick Douglass and prominent suffragists Susan B. Anthony and Elizabeth Cady Stanton. Anthony and Stanton believed that Douglass should have supported women receiving the vote alongside black men; when he didn't, they refused to support the ratification process for the Fifteenth Amendment.

A Turn for the Worse: The End of Reconstruction

Despite the ratification of the Fourteenth and Fifteenth Amendments, all was not well in the fight for civil rights. White Southerners were determined to regain power and turn back civil rights advances, and white Northerners were growing weary of the fight.

The "Redeemers"

Known as "Redeemers," white Southerners determined to seize back power from African Americans by any means unleashed another reign of violence throughout the South. During elections, they intimidated black voters at the polls and at their homes. If that didn't work, murder was also an option. Frequently outgunned, African Americans often suffered as they tried to defend themselves:

- ✔ **Massacre at Colfax Courthouse, Louisiana (1873):** When Louisiana's progressive-minded Radical Republican governor William Kellogg replaced the sheriff and judge from the opposing party with Radical Republicans, black men, anticipating trouble, went on the offensive and turned the courthouse into a fortress. Almost 200 members of the White League descended on the courthouse on behalf of the ousted sheriff, shooting and setting the building on fire. While only two whites died, more than 50 black men, including those who surrendered, died.

- ✔ **Attacks in Opelousas, Louisiana (1868):** Angered by blacks coming to the rescue of a white editor of the local Republican newspaper and a Freedmen's Bureau teacher whom three local whites attacked, a mob killed as many as 200 African Americans in days.

- ✔ **Murders in Coushatta, Louisiana (1874):** When white Northerner and Union veteran Marshall Twitchell attempted to extend black civil rights, members of the White League rounded up black and white Republicans, forced them to leave town, and then murdered at least 24 of them on their way out.

The murders in Coushatta, Louisiana, prompted President Ulysses Grant to send in federal troops, a move unpopular with white Southerners and many white Northerners who had grown tired of Reconstruction. Months later, when the White Man's Party went on a killing spree in Vicksburg, Mississippi, in an attempt to oust the black sheriff Peter Crosby, Grant sent troops to Mississippi.

The Mississippi Plan

As Mississippi marched into the critical 1875 elections, white Democrats enacted the *Mississippi Plan* to gain back the government from the more progressive Republicans. Because Mississippi had a black majority population that was solidly Republican, Democrats used economic intimidation such as firing those who voted Republican and violent attacks such as riots and burning homes to either keep African Americans from the polls or force them to vote Democrat. There were some claims that whites actually held guns on African Americans brave enough to go to the polls to ensure they voted for Democrats.

Mississippi Governor Adelbert Ames asked President Grant several times to send federal troops to Mississippi to stop the Mississippi Plan but Grant, scarred by white Northerners' criticism of his earlier use of federal troops, refused Ames's requests in order to protect Republican chances for the presidency in 1876. Not so coincidentally, Democrats won big at the polls that November, carrying a 30,000 or more margin of votes in a state considered a Republican stronghold. Not only did Mississippi's Democrats practice this intimidation tactic in elections well into the 1960s, but Louisiana, South Carolina, and other Southern states emulated the plan.

Civil Rights Act of 1875

Distressed by the harsh reality of his Reconstruction efforts, President Grant, no doubt unsure of his options, made a frustrated appeal to Congress in January 1875 for some type of action. They responded with the Civil Rights Act originally proposed in 1870. Although school desegregation was no longer included in the bill, it did contain an important provision regarding equal access to public accommodations.

By the time it passed, however, there wasn't much fight left in Congress as far as Reconstruction was concerned. Both Stevens and Sumner were dead. White Southerners opposed to Reconstruction were regaining congressional and Senate seats. Worse yet, white Northerners appeared less and less interested in Reconstruction.

Pulling the plug

By 1870, the Union was back together, but as President Grant's trials attest, it was far from smooth sailing. After winning reelection in 1872, scandal rocked Grant's administration, and with him out of the race for the 1876 election, white Democrats and Redeemers knew that ending Reconstruction was within reach. Discontinuing the Freedmen's Bureau in 1872 wasn't enough. The process of ending Reconstruction really began to take form in 1873, 1874, and 1875 with confrontations like Colfax and Coushatta in Louisiana and various disturbances in Mississippi (refer to the earlier section 'The "Redeemers"'). With the Democratic candidate Samuel Tilden, former governor of New York who rose to national prominence for crushing a corruption ring there, and the Republican candidate Rutherford B. Hayes, whose scrupulousness also scored him points, both opposed to Reconstruction, the end was inevitable.

Reconstruction was essentially over before its official ending as white Southerners killed and terrorized African Americans and some white Republicans with impunity. In its March 1876 decision in the case *United States v. Cruikshank*, the Supreme Court overturned the federal convictions of the Colfax Massacre participants and undermined the Enforcement Act of 1870, which sought to repel the KKK and other white supremacist organizations and which had made the Colfax convictions possible.

The Supreme Court's decision under Chief Justice Morrison Waite set the dangerous precedent that only local and state authorities could prosecute individual crimes against others. The Supreme Court maintained that the due process and equal protection clauses of the Fourteenth Amendment only permitted federal government intervention when states denied rights to citizens.

Another critical blow came in the case of *United States v. Reese* regarding the Kentucky voting tax intended to prevent African Americans from voting. The Supreme Court ruled that the Fifteenth Amendment, which guaranteed black men the right to vote, only meant that citizens couldn't be denied the right to vote based on "race, color, or previous condition of servitude."

With this ruling, the United States sanctioned — or rather encouraged — the development of poll taxes, grandfather clauses, and other strategies later used to disenfranchise African Americans, therefore undermining Reconstruction's purpose.

With slavery abolished, key pro-Reconstruction activists dead, and President Hayes opposed to Reconstruction, white Americans willing to wage the good fight on behalf of African Americans were hard to find. After the Civil War and 12 long years of wrestling for democracy, African Americans were again out in the cold. Adding insult to injury, Jefferson Davis, who led the Confederacy, spent just two years in jail and never stood trial for treason. Other key ex-Confederates also escaped significant punishment.

In 1877, a year after the U.S.'s centennial celebration of independence, African Americans didn't know how far the tide would turn. They were free and educating themselves and each other in record numbers, but the war wasn't over. Although temporarily scorned, the Fourteenth and Fifteenth Amendments would prove to be invaluable building blocks for true democracy. Despite the disappointment of Reconstruction's end, African Americans continued the fight for equality, even when despair greatly overshadowed hope.

Part III

Pillars of Change: The Civil Rights Movement

The 5th Wave   By Rich Tennant

"Hey man, I thought you paid the power bill!"

In this part . . .

With riots, the threat of lynching, and the segregation of Jim Crow holding African Americans down, freedom following the Civil War and into the mid-20th century wasn't exactly as African Americans had envisioned it.

This part tracks the early days of Jim Crow, noting the oppression of African Americans as well as the community leaders, such as Booker T. Washington and W.E.B. Du Bois, who stepped up and proposed ways of executing change. It then moves on to the civil rights era and covers the various organizations formed to bring about change by publicizing injustices against African Americans. Key figures including Martin Luther King, Jr., and Malcolm X are addressed in the context of the civil rights movement and black power movement.

Chapter 7

Living Jim Crow

. . . .

In This Chapter

▶ Experiencing the daily impact of Jim Crow

▶ Finding ways to escape segregation in the South

▶ Surveying African American leaders of varying positions

▶ Falling in line behind Marcus Garvey

▶ Taking a turn in the mid–20th century

. . . .

African Americans soon felt the pinch of Reconstruction's end. White Southerners made it no secret that they longed for the good old days, and although slavery's return was doubtful, racial equality eluded African Americans. In the South, an official caste system known as Jim Crow emerged, making African Americans free in name only. In the North, the situation was only slightly better.

This chapter addresses the legal institution of Jim Crow and the effect it had on the lives of African Americans, particularly in the South. But more than just dwell on the injustices perpetrated against African Americans, this chapter also shows the various ways African Americans fought Jim Crow, even highlighting how they disagreed with one another on which direction to take. Most important, it connects the fight to abolish slavery with the fight to abolish inequality and sets the stage for the culmination of these struggles in the 1950s and 1960s.

Post-Reconstruction Blues

As turbulent as Reconstruction had been (refer to Chapter 6), there were many hopeful moments. African Americans were pursuing education; joining the professional ranks as teachers, congressmen, and doctors; becoming landowners; and voting in record numbers for the first time. Throughout Reconstruction, especially toward its end, some white Southerners began to employ dubious means to disenfranchise African Americans. With the federal government's withdrawal from the South in 1877, black Southerners were largely on their own. White Southerners knew this and went to extreme lengths to return the nation as closely back to slavery as possible.

African American historian Rayford Logan called the period spanning from Reconstruction's end in 1877 to roughly around 1901, the *nadir,* or the "lowest point" of race relations. Other scholars have stretched the nadir's end to the 1920s.

Expanding *sharecropping,* a system in which farmers worked the land first in hopes of "sharing the crops" (and/or profits) later, and completely disenfranchising African Americans became the two chief strategies used by white Southerners to turn back the clock. In addition to threatening economic repercussions such as firing workers or using violence to prevent black Southerners from voting Republican (which, for white Southerners, allowed white Northerners to rule them), white Southerners began to institute poll taxes, literacy tests, and grandfather clauses to keep black Southerners from voting.

Wealthy white Southerners also feared the rise of the Populist Party, also known as the People's Party, which advocated poor whites and African Americans setting aside their racial differences in favor of economic self-interest for both parties. In 1888, for example, black farmers in Lovejoy, Texas, formed the Colored Farmers' National Alliance and Cooperative Union, which later aligned itself with similar white organizations in the South and Midwest to improve conditions for all farmers.

When some African Americans thrived economically, white Southerners used lynching as a warning to other blacks to stay in their place. White Southerners also began to pass laws mandating racial segregation in restaurants, on railroad cars, and in any other areas of social interaction. As during slavery, white Southerners forced African Americans to defer to them or suffer the consequences. Some African Americans didn't wait for things to get worse to make a move — literally.

The Exoduster Movement

As conditions worsened in the South, many African Americans began to believe that leaving the South was the only solution. Former slave Benjamin "Pap" Singleton was one of the many African Americans who believed that greater freedom awaited African Americans elsewhere (specifically, in the Great Plains). He and his partner Columbus M. Johnson established a colony for African Americans near Dunlap, Kansas.

Known as the *Black Exodus* (as well as the Great Exodus or the Exoduster Movement of 1879), thousands of black Southerners responded enthusiastically to such efforts. Between 1879 and 1881, at least 50,000 African Americans fled Southern states for Kansas, Missouri, Indiana, and Illinois.

The sheer numbers of the Black Exodus shocked white Northerners. In 1880, the U.S. Senate conducted hearings to discern the forces behind the exodus. In addition to Singleton, who dubbed himself the "Moses of the Colored Exodus," former slave and exodus supporter Henry Adams testified. Adams explained that he based his support for the exodus on the findings by a secret council of African Americans who, after Reconstruction ended, traveled the South to investigate the true conditions of black Southerners. Adams also claimed he and his group sent President Rutherford Hayes and Congress a petition reportedly signed by 98,000 black Southerners asking that territory be set aside for them to live in peace. When the petition went unanswered, Adams encouraged African Americans to leave the South for Kansas without the government's support.

Not all African Americans supported the exodus. Established black leadership such as Frederick Douglass felt that leaving the South acknowledged defeat and, to win their freedom, African Americans had to stand their ground and remain. Many others disagreed. Less than three decades later, African Americans would once again turn to migration to escape the South's injustice.

Black Town U.S.A.

Celebrated writer Zora Neale Hurston wrote often about Eatonville, Florida, the all-black town where she grew up, but it was far from the only such town. Between 1865 and 1900, African Americans founded over 100 predominantly black towns. Still, all-black towns got a boon from the Exoduster Movement.

In Oklahoma, over 50 black towns or settlements sprouted from 1865 to 1920. Oklahoma had so many black towns, in fact, that Edwin T. McCabe, who founded all-black Langston, Oklahoma, tried to convince President Benjamin Harrison to designate Oklahoma a black state. Ironically, Jim Crow laws immediately followed Oklahoma's statehood.

Founded in 1887 by former slaves Isaiah T. Montgomery and his cousin Benjamin T. Green, Mississippi's Mound Bayou was one of the most prosperous all-black towns. Designated the Jewel of the Delta by President Theodore Roosevelt, Mound Bayou, home to the nation's only black-owned cottonseed mill, boasted a nearly 100 percent literacy rate before 1900.

REMEMBER

A philosophy of self-help and self-reliance permeated the black town movement. As the focus of the American economy moved from agriculture to industry, black towns, which were largely agricultural, declined around 1910. Already hard-hit, surviving towns couldn't withstand the later onset of the Great Depression.

Lynchings and riots

Rural areas in the South were vulnerable to riots during and after Reconstruction. Investigations by Ida B. Wells-Barnett (refer to the sidebar "Ida B. Wells-Barnett" for more about her) revealed that, from 1881 to 1901, at least 100 African Americans were lynched each year (see Figure 7-1). Particularly angered by claims that black male lynching victims often raped white women, Wells-Barnett found that success, not rape, often prompted a lynching. She also discovered that bogus rape charges masked consensual sex between black men and white women, who often pursued black men. Equally important, Wells-Barnett exposed the lynchings of black women. She published her findings in *The New York Age* in 1892 and later also wrote *Southern Horrors: Lynch Law in All Its Phases.*

Most often, riots and lynchings went hand and hand, and there were plenty major ones from 1898 into the early 1920s.

Figure 7-1:
An all-too-common sight in America during the early 20th century.

© Underwood & Underwood/Corbis

Wilmington, North Carolina (1898)

The Wilmington Riot, also known as the Wilmington Massacre, erupted in North Carolina in 1898. Black Republicans successfully teamed with white Populists to win the 1896 local election; two years later, white Democrats vowed not to lose another election. To prey on white fears, the town's white newspaper published inflammatory quotes about black men raping white women; the black newspaper responded. Consequently, on election day, emotions ran high. Despite a large black voter turnout, white Democrats stuffed the ballot boxes and stole the election. Victory emboldened them as men of influence — bankers, lawyers, merchants, and even clergymen — initiated the violence against Wilmington's African American population that killed at least 11 African Americans.

Atlanta, Georgia (1906)

To gain favor with white voters, Georgia's two gubernatorial candidates debated how best to manage Atlanta's growing black populace, which had grown from roughly 9,000 in 1880 to 35,000 in 1900. Meanwhile, local newspapers boasted of lynchings and called for a revival of the Ku Klux Klan, which, despite its secrecy, was generally well-regarded among segregationist whites (see Figure 7-2). Reports of four assaults of white women, presumably by black men, drove whites to mob action. On September 22, thousands of whites from the country and the city gathered in downtown Atlanta and began randomly assaulting innocent African Americans. For three days, the Atlanta Race Riot of 1906 continued. When it ended, at least 25 African Americans had died.

Walter White, who would become an important civil rights activist, was just a boy at the time of the riot, when he witnessed a mob club a defenseless young boy to death outside a black-owned barbershop. Evelyn Witherspoon, a 10-year-old white girl, awakened in the middle of night and joined her sister and mother kneeling by the window. "And there I saw a man strung up to the light pole," she remembered. "Men and boys on the street below were shooting at him, until they riddled his body with bullets. He was kicking, flailing his legs, when I looked out."

Springfield, Illinois (1908)

Violence erupted in Springfield, Illinois, in 1908 when a white woman, not wanting to admit that a white man had beaten her, accused an African American of the crime. Police arrested George Richardson and moved Richardson and a black man connected to the murder of a white man to a neighboring town. The move angered the mob that had developed. They seized guns and other weapons and burned buildings. Over the course of the riot, two black men were lynched, four white men died, and over 70 people sustained injuries. Hundreds of Springfield's black residents fled for safety, but many later returned to rebuild their lives.

Figure 7-2:
A family
affair for
white segre-
gationists.

East St. Louis, Illinois (1917)

In July 1917, an aluminum plant in East St. Louis hired African American workers to break a strike, and white trade unionists met with the mayor and demanded that the city stop African Americans from migrating there. After the meeting, a rumor circulated that a black man intentionally shot a white man in an altercation that included insults against white women. Unchecked by local officials, white mobs took to the streets and drove through black neighborhoods firing shots indiscriminately. In the end, 30 African Americans were dead and hundreds more injured. The riot drove an estimated 6,000 black people from their homes and destroyed at least 300 buildings.

Various cities, the Red Summer of 1919

So many race riots — 26 to be exact — took place in the summer and fall of 1919 in the North and the South, that writer and civil rights activist James Weldon Johnson dubbed it "the Red Summer of 1919." Following are just two that transpired:

- **Longview, Texas:** Angered over a *Chicago Defender* article about the body of a bullet-riddled black youth that turned up near Longview, white townspeople pounced on a high school teacher; they ordered him and a local doctor to leave town. Instead, a group of armed black men gathered at the teacher's house and fired back during the second attack, killing four whites and wounding several others. White townspeople then burned several houses and murdered the doctor's father-in-law before the governor restored order.

- **Chicago, Illinois:** When several black youths drifted into the waters of a public beach whites claimed as their own, white bathers threw rocks at the boys, one of whom drowned during the attack. When a black man was arrested and a white man identified as the rock thrower wasn't, blacks attacked the arresting officer and the riot was on. For five days, violence raged on Chicago's South Side. When the violence finally abated, 15 whites and 23 blacks were dead, 537 people were injured, and more than 1,000 people, mostly black, were homeless.

Riots also erupted in Knoxville, Tennessee; Omaha, Nebraska; and Elaine, Arkansas. Although differing in specifics, all the riots that occurred during Red Summer highlighted the growing racial divide, and in all, African Americans actively fought back against their attackers. Inspired by the summer's tumultuous events, Claude McKay summed up this "New Negro" at the end of his classic poem "If We Must Die": "Like men we'll face the murderous, cowardly pack/Pressed to the wall, dying, but fighting back!"

Tulsa, Oklahoma (1921)

When a local newspaper published a story exaggerating the details of an alleged sexual assault of a white woman by a black man, a white mob of nearly 2,000 surrounded the jail that night intending to lynch the accused black man. A group of armed black men, determined to prevent the man's lynching, showed up. Trouble escalated when a member of the white mob asked a black man for his gun and was refused. In the ensuing scuffle, a shot was fired, and the mob went wild, assaulting African Americans on the streets and burning down Greenwood, which had a reputation as the Negro's Wall Street of America for its prosperity. By the time the National Guard stepped in, most of the Tulsa Race Riot had ended. The official death toll was 39, but experts have estimated the number to be closer to 300. The homeless numbered into the thousands. Using its own resources, black Tulsa eventually rebuilt itself. (This incident inspired West Coast rapper The Game to name his record label The Black Wall Street.)

We're sorry — well, some of us are, anyway

On June 13, 2005, the majority of the U.S. Senate formally apologized for the body's failure to pass the nearly 200 anti-lynching bills presented to it to curb the despicable act that claimed the lives of 4,749 known victims. "There is a power in acknowledging error and mistake," Illinois Senator Barack Obama stated. "It is a power that potentially transforms not only those who were impacted directly by the lynchings, but also those who are the progeny of the perpetrators of these crimes." More than a dozen senators, including Mississippi Senators Trent Lott and Thad Cochran, however, declined to cosponsor the resolution, even as nearly 200 descendants of lynching victims looked on from the visitors' gallery.

Rosewood, Florida (1923)

The massacre that occurred in Rosewood, Florida, in January 1923 began after a white woman reported an attack by an unidentified black man. During the two weeks of violence that ensued, a white mob apprehended one black man, whom the sheriff got out of town, and then later killed another black man. A couple of days later, a white mob attacked a house of black people. During the attack, two white men died; meanwhile the people in the house were either killed or seriously injured, prompting other black people in the area to flee into the swamps. Over a course of days, white people from surrounding areas converged on Rosewood, killing African Americans and burning churches and houses. When the attacks finally ended, a grand jury convened to investigate the incident but found "insufficient evidence" to move forward. (John Singleton directed the 1997 film *Rosewood* about the Rosewood Massacre of 1923. Florida paid reparations to nine Rosewood survivors in 1994.)

Instituting Jim Crow: Plessy v. Ferguson

Quite literally, as noted scholar and political activist W.E.B. Du Bois wrote in his classic work *The Souls of Black Folk* (1903), "The problem of the Twentieth Century is the problem of the color-line." This was certainly evident in the efforts to deny African Americans full rights as citizens. Their rights under attack, African Americans looked to the courts for redress. Yet in 1896, instead of protecting those rights, the Supreme Court's *Plessy v. Ferguson* ruling legalized the color line that divided America.

For years, the Supreme Court had been inching toward legalizing segregation, but with its devastating *Plessy v. Ferguson* decision in 1896, the Supreme Court formally sanctioned Jim Crow, not only in the South, but across the nation.

The term *Jim Crow* comes from a popular tune by white minstrel show performer Thomas "Daddy" Rice. See Chapter 15 for more on minstrel shows.

Court cases before Plessy

With its 1876 rulings in the *United States v. Cruikshank* and the *United States v. Reese,* the Supreme Court curtailed the Fourteenth and Fifteenth Amendments' protection over African Americans. According *Cruikshank,* the Fourteenth Amendment gave the federal government jurisdiction over state actions, not individual actions. Therefore, the federal government couldn't prosecute individuals for intimidating African Americans at the polls; the state had to address it. *Reese* allowed states to enact poll taxes (refer to Chapter 6 for the details surrounding these decisions).

If that weren't enough, in the *Civil Rights Cases of 1883,* a consolidation of five lower court cases, the Supreme Court declared the Civil Rights Act of 1875 prohibiting private institutions from discriminating against African Americans unconstitutional. Justice Joseph P. Bradley noted that neither the Thirteenth nor Fourteenth Amendment allowed Congress to address racial discrimination in the private sector. John Marshall Harlan, in his lone dissent, noted that Congress was only attempting to secure the same rights of white citizens for African Americans.

Plessy v. Ferguson

When the Louisiana Separate Car Act of 1890 requiring "equal but separate" accommodations for whites and blacks passed, New Orleans's Creole community attacked the law in various ways, including newspaper editorials. Enlisting the help of Homer Plessy, whom authorities arrested in 1892, the Creole community never anticipated that the U.S. Supreme Court would rule in favor of such discriminatory law.

Although "separate but equal" doesn't actually appear in the decision, the court upheld the 1890 law, stating that "We consider the underlying fallacy of the plaintiff's argument to consist in the assumption that the enforced separation of the two races stamps the colored race with a badge of inferiority. If this be so, it is not by reason of anything found in the act, but solely because the colored race chooses to put that construction upon it." As in the Civil Rights Cases of 1883, Justice John Marshall Harlan was the lone dissenter.

Ida B. Wells-Barnett

Segregated railroad cars served as Ida B. Wells-Barnett's formal induction into the African American fight for equality. In May 1884, Wells-Barnett refused to move when a railroad conductor insisted she leave the first-class car she paid for simply because of her race. To enforce the 1882 Tennessee law requiring separate accommodations for whites and blacks, the conductor and two other railroad employees literally dragged Wells-Barnett off the train. Confident of a victory, Wells immediately filed suit, but the December 1884 decision in her favor was short-lived. In 1887, the Tennessee Supreme Court overturned the decision.

When angry white Memphians lynched her friends Thomas Moss, Calvin McDowell, and Henry Stewart, successful grocers in direct competition with a white grocer, Wells-Barnett, a partner in *The Free Speech,* an African American newspaper in Memphis, became one of the foremost authorities on lynching, investigating 728 of them by traveling to actual sites and interviewing eyewitnesses. After the publication of her editorial questioning the "moral reputation" of Southern white women, Wells couldn't return to the South and eventually settled in Chicago.

After the ruling, Southern states passed even more Jim Crow laws. "White Only" and "Colored Only" eventually marked everything from restaurants to railroad stations. Although racial discrimination also existed in the North, the South wore its discriminatory practices like a badge of honor. From lynchings (death by a mob without due process of the law) to political disenfranchisement via poll taxes and literacy tests (not to mention the pettiest of human degradation), African Americans, an overwhelming 90 percent of whom lived in the South, bore the brunt of "living" Jim Crow.

Strategies for Achieving Equality

How to address racism's latest tactics became the primary question facing black leadership, which was undergoing tremendous change at the turn of the 20th century. In February 1895, Frederick Douglass died at the age of 77, and two African American intellectuals — Booker T. Washington and W.E.B. Du Bois — came to the fore with what would eventually become diametrically opposed positions. Washington favored *accommodationism,* a policy of foregoing political power in favor of economic progress, while Du Bois advocated *integrationism,* the immediate political agitation to achieve social equality. Quite simply, one accepted Jim Crow, and the other rejected it.

Booker T. Washington: The Accomodationist

A year before the *Plessy* decision, Booker T. Washington, the former slave who built Alabama's Tuskegee Institute into an institution of national renown, delivered his highly controversial address known as the Atlanta Compromise at the Cotton States and International Exposition in Atlanta on September 18, 1895. The Atlanta Compromise articulated Washington's message of accommodation.

Aware of the potential threat European immigrants posed to positions traditionally held by African Americans, Washington emphasized African Americans' loyalty, reminding his audience of who had nursed their children and cared for their dying parents. Washington advised whites and blacks to "cast your bucket down where you are." If whites "cast their buckets" with African Americans, he insisted, the South would progress economically without upsetting the social balance. "In all things that are purely social," he reassured his audience, "we can be as separate as the fingers, yet one as the hand in all things essential to mutual progress."

Taking into account the context of his time, Washington's message wasn't outlandish. "We wear the mask that grins and lies," wrote Paul Laurence Dunbar in his famous poem, "We Wear the Mask." During slavery especially, many African Americans learned to mask their true feelings from slaveholders and other whites. Few wore the mask as expertly as Washington did. In public, he advised African Americans to focus on industrial education and work, not on political injustices, and he ignored or excused lynchings. Privately, Washington supported lawsuits challenging the disenfranchisement of African American voters and consistently funded efforts to pass an anti-lynching bill. Defying Jim Crow laws, Washington often rode alongside whites in first-class train cars, dined in whites-only facilities, and met with President Teddy Roosevelt at the White House.

W.E.B. Du Bois: The Integrationist

W.E.B. Du Bois's criticism of Booker T. Washington's Atlanta Compromise address in *The Souls of Black Folk* (1903) helped establish him as a black leader in opposition to Washington (see Figure 7-3). Du Bois didn't agree with Washington's acceptance of Jim Crow and believed that African Americans should agitate for political change.

At the time of their break, however, there were virtually no black organizations — or any for that matter — dedicated to Du Bois's strategy. There had been various antislavery organizations during slavery, but after slavery ended, they disbanded and nothing concerted sprouted in their place until the early 20th century. In 1905, Du Bois cofounded the Niagara Movement with William Monroe Trotter before later settling in with the National Association for the Advancement of Colored People (NAACP). (Read more about these organizations in the section "Organizing for Freedom.")

Although Du Bois believed in first-class citizenship for African Americans, which included full voting rights, his approach was elitist by some people's standards. Du Bois supported the concept of a "Talented Tenth," first proposed by abolitionist and elder statesman Alexander Crummell in 1897 at the founding of the American Negro Academy, the nation's first major black intellectual society. The Talented Tenth were the best and brightest of the black race charged with the responsibility of leading the masses and shaping their goals and aspirations. These men (although some women were included) also represented African American interests to the white power structure (Chapter 13 has more on the Talented Tenth).

Figure 7-3:
W.E.B.
Du Bois.

© Corbis

Organizing for Freedom

The horrendous experiences of African Americans following Reconstruction's end underscored the absence of any organization to address racial violence, job discrimination, segregated housing, and the many other ills that confronted African Americans. At the turn of the 20th century, that need was recognized and several organizations, such as though outlined in the following sections, emerged. By the time of Booker T. Washington's death in 1915, two of these organizations in particular — the NAACP and the National Urban League — would play especially strong roles in addressing some of black America's greatest challenges in the 20th century.

National Afro-American Council

New York Age publisher T. Thomas Fortune helped spearhead the 1890 formation of the National Afro-American League, a precursor to the National Association for the Advancement of Colored People (NAACP). When the league failed in 1893, Fortune didn't give up. Instead, he helped form the National Afro-American Council in 1898, which adopted a form of militant protest. The council's objectives included

- Investigating and reporting lynchings
- Assisting efforts that tested the constitutionality of laws oppressing African Americans
- Encouraging both industrial and higher education among African Americans

By 1902, followers of Booker T. Washington, known as *Bookerites,* had taken over the organization. They tempered the organization's militancy and diverted its economic initiatives to the National Negro Business League before its demise in 1906.

The National Negro Business League

The National Negro Business League (NNBL) had controversial beginnings. Following an 1899 conference talk entitled "The Negro in Business," in which he documented an estimated 5,000 black entrepreneurs, Du Bois became the director of the Business Bureau of the National Afro-American Council. In what was probably not a coincidence, Washington asked Du Bois for a list of potential members before hosting the first conference of the NNBL in Boston in August 1900, without Du Bois.

Women's work

In addition to supporting general organizations dedicated to racial and social equality, African American women formed their own organizations. The First National Conference of the Colored Women of America resulted in the formation of the National Federation of Afro-American Women, headed by Booker T. Washington's wife Margaret Murray Washington. In 1896, that organization merged with the National League of Colored Women, headed by Mary Church Terrell, and spawned the National Association of Colored Women (NACW) whose membership boasted the nation's most prominent black women.

While the NACW supported the women's suffrage movement, some white women opposed to integration excluded black women from their suffrage efforts, prompting Mary Ann Shad Cary to form the Colored Women's Progressive Franchise Association as an auxiliary of the predominantly white National American Women Suffrage Association (NAWSA). (To keep black female suffragists in the South in the loop, Adella Hunt Logan often passed for white to attend NAWSA's southern meetings.)

The overall goal for black women, as articulated by writer Frances Ellen Watkins Harper at the predominantly white World's Congress of Representative Women, held in Chicago in 1893, was "Demand justice, simple justice, as the right of every race."

Because white Americans weren't interested in employing black Americans, it was only reasonable for black Americans to employ each other. Recognizing the need to cultivate African American businesses, Washington said, in his last annual address to the NNBL, "At the bottom of education, at the bottom of politics, even at the bottom of religion itself there must be for our race, as for all races, an economic foundation, economic prosperity, [and] economic independence."

Under Washington's direct leadership, the NNBL and its national convention in particular served several functions:

- ✔ Fostering economic development as a primary means of obtaining racial equality
- ✔ Uniting African American business owners to fellowship and to exchange innovative ideas to promote economic growth
- ✔ Tracking black business development and growth

NNBL participants such as William Pettiford, who became head of the black-owned Alabama Penny Loan & Savings in Birmingham in 1899, clearly understood their important role in the community. Pettiford, for example, knew that 90 percent of his customers had never held a bank account before, so his bank took great pains to educate customers on how to save and invest wisely. He believed this knowledge stimulated the desire for property ownership and other responsible fiscal behavior that contributed to the overall well-being of the African American community.

The Niagara Movement

Former Harvard schoolmates William Monroe Trotter (who founded the African American newspaper *The Guardian* and who had long opposed Booker T. Washington's accommodationist politics) and W.E.B. Du Bois convened a group of prominent African Americans in June 1905 in Niagara Falls, Canada. The purpose of the conference was to discuss a more proactive strategy to achieve first-class citizenship for African Americans and to launch the Niagara Movement.

This conference marked the official launch of the 20th-century movement for civil rights. More aggressive than previous meetings of African American leaders, the June 1905 meeting of the Niagara Movement had a clear platform that included demands for freedom of speech, full voting rights, and the end of segregation.

Unlike many other African Americans, Trotter routinely criticized Washington. Consequently, Washington planted spies to stay abreast of the Niagara Movement's actions; he even used his influence with the black press to limit the organization's press attention.

Despite having fewer than 200 members and virtually no press attention, the Niagara Movement distributed pamphlets, lobbied against Jim Crow, and even sent protest letters to the president. Ultimately, clashes between the more radical Trotter and the comparatively reserved Du Bois, not scant funding and organizational weakness, led to the Niagara Movement's demise.

Madam C.J. Walker

Of the early black female entrepreneurs, Madam C.J. Walker, born two years after the Civil War ended, is the most famous. Despite being orphaned at age 7 and becoming a widow by age 20, Walker built a national empire around African American hair care and cosmetics by 1917. She was so successful that she owned a manufacturing plant in Indianapolis and employed almost 1,000 sales agents nationally. Arguably the most successful black entrepreneur — male or female — of her time, Walker was also a noted philanthropist who donated to the NAACP and such educational institutions as Tuskegee Institute. Although Walker's former employer, Annie Turnbo Malone, who first patented the straightening comb, might have achieved the millionaire status first, Walker served as the prototype for the African American entrepreneur for many years.

The NAACP

Contrary to popular belief, Du Bois didn't conceive the National Association for the Advancement of Colored People (NAACP). Instead, the NAACP began with a group of white people spurred to action by the horrendous Springfield Race Riot of 1908 (refer to the earlier section "Lynchings and riots"). William English Walling, the son of a former slaveholding family, and his wife were in Illinois when the rioting erupted. Particularly disturbed that such a riot had occurred in the North, Walling wrote an article, "Race War in the North," that provoked a response from Mary White Ovington, a white social worker who worked with African Americans in New York. Early in 1909, Walling, Ovington, and Dr. Henry Moskowitz formed what would become the NAACP. They issued a call for a national conference to tackle the problems of African Americans.

Endorsers of the NAACP included Du Bois, Jane Addams (social reformer and Nobel Peace Prize winner), John Dewey (psychologist and education reformer), and Ida B. Wells-Barnett, among many others. In May 1909, conference attendees laid the groundwork necessary for the NAACP. (Highly suspicious of white people, William Monroe Trotter didn't attend.)

In 1910, the NAACP began formal operations with just one African American member among its officers: Du Bois served as Director of Publicity and Research. Under his leadership, *The Crisis,* the NAACP's official magazine, took a strong stance against lynching and mob violence. People responded enthusiastically and, just three years later, the NAACP had 1,100 members; by 1921, it claimed more than 400 branches.

Spearheaded by Arthur Spingarn, the NAACP's legal team became one of its most enduring legacies. With white and black attorneys working together, the NAACP began a diligent legal assault that chipped away at Jim Crow. Almost immediately, the team won three key Supreme Court cases:

- *Guinn v. United States* (1915) upheld the 15th Amendment, voiding Oklahoma's grandfather clauses.

- *Buchanan v. Warley* (1917) declared Louisville ordinances forcing African Americans to live in certain areas unconstitutional.

- *Moore v. Dempsey* (1923) forced a new trial for an African American man convicted of murder in Arkansas, partially because no African Americans sat on the jury.

The National Urban League

A direct result of black Southerners moving North to escape Jim Crow, the National Urban League (NUL) sought to address the problems of black migrants. It combined the goals of all the civil rights organizations with the economic concerns of the National Negro Business League. As more migrants flooded into the cities, the NUL grew rapidly, opening a Chicago office in 1912; by 1941, it had expanded to 30 cities. During the Great Migration, the NUL was at the forefront of one of black America's most tumultuous times of change and opportunity.

Fulfilling its primary mission of adapting migrants to the North, the NUL battled employment discrimination; poor housing, education, and healthcare; and discriminatory local, state, and federal economic and social policies.

Anticipating the Great Migration, the mass relocation of African Americans from the South spanning roughly from 1914 to 1940, the NUL was the brainchild of Ruth Standish Baldwin, the widow of a railroad magnate, and Dr. Edmund Haynes, a Fisk graduate and Columbia University's first African American PhD recipient. They established the Committee on Urban Conditions Among Negroes in 1910 and merged it with the Committee for the Improvement of Industrial Conditions Among Negroes in New York (founded in 1906) and the National League for the Protection of Colored Women (founded in 1905) and created the National League on Urban Conditions Among Negroes in 1911. It became simply the National Urban League in 1920.

Keep on Moving: The Great Migration

As Du Bois and others argued about top-down black leadership, the black masses didn't wait for the Supreme Court to make decisions. In search of better jobs, educational opportunities, and an escape from racial violence, the African American population of Northern cities swelled. New York City's black population rose 66 percent between 1910 and 1920 — a modest increase compared to Chicago's 148 percent, Philadelphia's amazing 500 percent, and Detroit's unbelievable 611 percent. The Great Migration profoundly changed life in the United States.

Leaving the South

In addition to lynchings and riots (refer to the earlier section "Post-Reconstruction Blues"), two key reasons black Southerners left the South included

> ✔ **Mother Nature:** Beginning in 1898, boll weevils infested cotton crops in Texas and spread that devastation all over the South well into the 1910s. Because the South was slow to industrialize, it couldn't rebound as quickly, and agricultural work became scarce. Next to the boll weevils, the Great Mississippi Flood of 1927 sent Southerners north. Poor treatment after the flood — insufficient relief funds and inadequate or no housing, for example — drove black Southerners out of the South.

Oh, won't you stay, just a little bit longer?

Curiously, white Southerners had difficulty understanding why African Americans wanted to leave the South. During the Great Migration, local authorities blocked white recruiting agents' access to black communities, and they pulled willing migrants off trains. In addition, white employers refused to hire African Americans in order to keep them from earning the money they needed for the trip. In a case of twisted logic, Southern whites felt that terrorizing blacks and keeping them impoverished would make them want to stay.

✔ **Better jobs and opportunities:** World War I significantly curtailed European immigration at the same time that white American men joined the war effort, leaving an abundance of factory jobs unfilled. In Detroit, Henry Ford offered African Americans jobs and equal pay. Some companies were so desperate for workers they paid people's way north. In addition to better wages, schooling was slightly improved. The *Chicago Defender,* with its front-page stories on lynchings and tales of migrants who struck it rich, played such a prominent role in motivating black Southerners to leave that it was banned in many parts of the South.

Hard choices and sacrifices followed the decision to migrate. Potential migrants, typically black men ages 18 to 35, saved money for months. Some families chipped in to help with tickets. Others sold their last possessions. Sometimes migrants stopped en route and worked in smaller towns until they could make it to bigger cities like Chicago or Philadelphia. Children sometimes stayed with grandparents and relatives until their parents could afford to send for them. Unfortunately, for many migrants, the North wasn't as welcoming as they believed.

Life up North

The National Urban League, as well as the Young Men's Christian Association (YMCA) and its sister organization, Young Women's Christian Association (YWCA) were a huge help in providing migrants with housing information and job leads. Yet life in the North was far from grand for most African Americans. Racism, they discovered, was a national problem. Key challenges for African Americans included

✔ **Substandard housing:** Migrants paid substantially more than white workers for housing, most often *kitchenettes,* one-room apartments created by greedy landlords capitalizing on the limited housing for African

Americans. Often four to five adults lived in one room. In addition, land-lords were slow to perform necessary maintenance, but migrants were so afraid of finding other housing that they didn't usually complain.

✔ **Poor healthcare and crime:** Overcrowding, poverty, and inadequate healthcare created innumerable health concerns. Infectious disease raged, and many migrants, especially children under the age of 10, died in high numbers. Black babies often died at twice the rate of white babies. These conditions also produced crime. The hungry stole food. The broke robbed others. Some confrontations turned violent and resulted in death.

In time, migrants and their leaders learned to parlay their significant popula-tion into politics, as astute leaders realized that there was strength in num-bers. At the very least, black Northerners could vote, and they began to use that right more effectively with each passing year.

Marcus Garvey: Man with a Plan

The race pride and self-reliance that were respected qualities during Booker T. Washington's reign reached even greater heights during the Great Migration. Jamaican immigrant Marcus Mosiah Garvey recognized the power of race pride as well as the alienation that migrants felt from middle-class leaders; in response, he offered his Universal Negro Improvement Association (UNIA) movement as the solution. The UNIA was the first mass movement among African Americans in the 20th century.

Garvey brought the UNIA, established in 1914 in Jamaica, to Harlem, New York, in 1916. By 1924, there were over 700 branches of the UNIA in 38 states and over 200 branches throughout the world, including the African continent. Within the United States, the circulation of *Negro World,* the UNIA's official newspaper, reached a height of 50,000 to 60,000 subscribers in the mid-1920s and boasted an overall domestic and international circulation of 200,000 *weekly.*

Advocating race pride

Seizing upon the rhetoric of self-determination surrounding World War I, Garvey spoke strongly of race pride as a basis of global unity among African descendants. "Africa for the Africans at home and abroad" is just one of the slogans he popularized to reinforce his Pan-African perspective.

Garvey encouraged his followers to have black heroes. He also preached Africa's greatness to them and insisted that they possessed that greatness as well. "When Europe was inhabited by savages, heathens, and pagans," he told them, "Africa was peopled with a race of cultured Black men, who were masters in art, science, and literature. Whatsoever a Black man has done, a Black man can do."

Like Washington (refer to the earlier section "Booker T. Washington: The Accomodationist"), Garvey emphasized black self-reliance and solidarity to ameliorate economic conditions for black Americans and African people globally. In 1919, he established the Negro Factories Corporation, which operated several businesses, including grocery stores, restaurants, a printing plant, and a steam laundry.

Going "Back to Africa"

Imperialism thrived during the 1920s as European nations began dividing countries (and continents) among themselves. Garvey believed that it was up to people of African descent to stop them. ". . .[W]hether it is saving this one nation or that one government," he declared in 1923, "we are going to seek a method of saving Africa first. . . because Africa has become the grand prize of the nations. Africa has become the big game of the nation hunters."

Garvey's "Back to Africa" message was more complex than is generally perceived. Unlike the colonization movement of the 19th century (refer to Chapter 5), Garvey didn't necessarily advocate going "back to Africa" to flee white racism. Instead, his message was one of empowerment.

Black Americans and black people from various parts of the world responded strongly to Garvey's message. Regardless of whether they wanted to emigrate to Africa, they believed they had a responsibility to support any efforts to restore her greatness. In June 1919, Garvey established his Black Star Line Steamship Corporation and later purchased three ships to carry Africans back to Africa. Garvey's lack of shipping knowledge, coupled with the incompetence or greed of his accountants, doomed the Black Star Line, however.

Garvey's message of African nations, black businesses, and institutions free of white influence resonated strongly, along with his mantra of "Up, you mighty race, you can accomplish what you will."

Powerful enemies

Established black leadership didn't applaud Garvey's success. His broad appeal confounded them. They couldn't comprehend how he launched so many successful ventures with no white support. Garvey further alienated the established black leadership, some near white in appearance, with charges of "brown" racism (discrimination against African Americans of darker hues). One leader was so angry he sued Garvey for libel and won.

Du Bois and Garvey had a tenuous relationship that developed early. In 1919, Garvey suspected that Du Bois was responsible for the State Department denying passports to special UNIA delegates who were to attend Versailles Peace Conference and blasted Du Bois personally. For his part, Du Bois secretly tried to dig up information on Garvey from the State Department with no success before publishing in *The Crisis* an article on Garvey titled "Lunatic or Traitor."

Garvey's actions also attracted the attention of FBI director J. Edgar Hoover who built a case for Garvey's deportation. In 1923, Garvey received a mail fraud conviction in association with the Black Star Line and served three months. Arrested again 1925, he was sent to an Atlanta penitentiary to serve a five-year sentence. In 1927, President Calvin Coolidge pardoned and deported Garvey, who eventually died in London in 1940.

Can't Catch a Break: The Depression Years and FDR

The Great Depression was especially brutal for African Americans. A drastic drop in cotton prices crushed about 2 million black farmers, and many white Southerners refused to give federal relief to black Southerners. Conditions were only slightly better in cities. The end of World War I halted the wartime economy that had produced jobs for both black and white Americans, but black Americans were especially vulnerable as they competed with unemployed whites. In both the South and the North, white workers demanded that employers replace black workers with white workers, even in the most menial of jobs. African American women lost their lower-level jobs to white women, and the Depression forced black domestics to work for as little as $5 a week.

Relief rates for African Americans in the North and South were as much as four times that of white Americans; in Norfolk, Virginia, for example, an estimated 80 percent of the black population required public assistance. Yet African Americans who received relief got just over half of what white Americans received. Even in the face of national starvation, racism prevailed when many soup kitchens, some run by churches, refused to feed African Americans.

Dissatisfied with President Hoover's response to the Great Depression, white Americans replaced him with Franklin D. Roosevelt. Although African Americans were still largely Republican, black Americans who voted for FDR in the 1932 election foreshadowed black America's Democratic shift.

Mary McLeod Bethune

Born Mary Jane McLeod to former slaves near Maysville, South Carolina, in 1875, Mary McLeod Bethune was a prized student. In 1904, Bethune moved to Daytona Beach, Florida, and founded the Daytona Literary and Industrial School for Training Negro Girls, part of modern-day Bethune-Cookman College. Adding civic leader to her many skills and positions, Bethune led voter registration drives and served as president of the State Federation of Colored Women's Clubs before becoming president of the National Association of Colored Women in 1924. As her reputation grew, Bethune attended several presidential conferences and served on numerous boards. Bethune became a member of Roosevelt's "Black Cabinet," spearheading minority affairs for the National Youth Administration.

A woman of international significance, Bethune received prestigious medals from Haiti and Liberia. Following the landmark *Brown v. Board* decision, Bethune wrote in her *Chicago Defender* column "there can be no divided democracy, no class government, no half free county, under the constitution." Throughout her life, Bethune fully lived her mantra "not for myself, but for others."

FDR: Friend or foe?

Initially, African Americans saw little to encourage them that Roosevelt's policies would address their needs. In lobbying for his New Deal legislation, Roosevelt argued that supporting anti-lynching efforts would alienate Congress's Southern politicians, jeopardizing the crucial legislation needed to battle the Great Depression. In addition, the provisions of some New Deal initiatives didn't necessarily extend to African Americans:

- ✔ **NIRA (National Industrial Recovery Act):** The NIRA attempted to set a minimum wage and standard work hours and recommended that employers recognize unions; however, accepting these changes was voluntary, not mandatory, and therefore offered no real protection for black — or any — employees. In addition, many who accepted the NIRA fired African Americans rather than extend the NIRA recommendations to them. Black domestic workers and those in other menial jobs weren't even covered by the NIRA.

- ✔ **AAA (Agricultural Adjustment Association):** Exclusion from the AAA, which paid farmers not to produce cotton in order to create a shortage that would drive the price up, led black farmers to lose their land and become sharecroppers.

Striking a new deal

At the peak of the Great Migration, African American leaders began to leverage the African American vote. Recognizing the importance of the black vote in his reelection efforts, FDR declared during a national radio broadcast that lynching was murder. He also made two key African American federal appointments — Mary McLeod Bethune to head the Negro Division of the National Youth Administration and *Pittsburgh Courier* editor Robert L. Vann to serve as special assistant to the U.S. Attorney General. Between 1933 and 1946, the number of African Americans employed by the federal government rose from roughly 50,000 to about 200,000.

First Lady Eleanor Roosevelt helped push her husband toward a stronger position on civil rights. New Dealers such as the Harold Ickes, secretary of interior and Public Works Administration administrator, and the Works Progress Administration's Harry Hopkins also pitched in. Ickes ended segregation in the Department of Interior's restrooms and cafeteria while Hopkins ended discrimination in WPA relief efforts.

On June 18, 1941, FDR issued Executive Order 8802, banning racial discrimination in government employment, defense industries, and training programs, and establishing the Fair Employment Practices Committee (FEPC). This order also sealed African Americans to the Democratic Party and set a precedent for government involvement against racial injustice in the 20th century. It also paved the way for President Harry S. Truman to pass Executive Order 9981 in July 1948 desegregating the military.

A. Philip Randolph

Few African American leaders were as forceful as A. Philip Randolph, who helped spearhead and lead the Brotherhood of Sleeping Car Porters, founded in 1925. He also helped found the Harlem-based radical publication, *The Messenger,* which circulated from 1917 to 1928. An expert at compromising without sacrificing his principles, Randolph became one of this nation's most effective civil rights leaders.

Seeking evidence of real change for the African American working class in particular, Randolph threatened a March on Washington by establishing offices in various cities and joining forces with the NAACP, National Urban League, churches, and fraternal and sorority orders. As the momentum for the March grew, FDR buckled. The result: Executive Order 8802.

Can't Fool Us Twice: African Americans and WWII

During World War I, African American soldiers fought alongside the French and strolled Paris and other French cities free of Jim Crow restrictions. These experiences left an indelible impression that made accepting Jim Crow back home even more difficult. That their contributions in the War for Democracy were celebrated only by other black Americans and largely ignored by whites just made matters worse. When World War II broke out, even though African Americans supported the war, they refused to subjugate their own interests again.

The African American press, led by the *Pittsburgh Courier,* refused to remain silent against racial discrimination in the military and at home and, in 1942, waged a "Double V" campaign highlighting the struggle on both fronts. Lobbying — and winning — for black war correspondents, the black press wasn't the only African American entity taking the offensive. Mabel K. Staupers, executive director of the National Association of Colored Graduate Nurses, fought to integrate the Army and Navy Nurses Corps and succeeded when a nurse shortage hit in 1945. The NAACP attacked the racial discrimination practiced by war industries receiving government contracts, charging that African Americans paid taxes for warplanes they couldn't build, repair, or fly.

World War II yielded some other successes, including the Tuskegee Airmen, so-named for their training at Tuskegee Institute. At war's end, the Tuskegee Airmen received two Presidential Unit Citations and 150 Distinguished Flying Crosses, among other honors. Partially acknowledging the racial barriers they battled, Ronald Reagan narrated the 1945 propaganda short *Wings for This Man,* which praised the extraordinary wartime achievements of these airmen.

Chapter 8

I, Too, Sing America: The Civil Rights Movement, 1954–1963

*T*he mid-1950s set the stage for another major revolution in the United States. Just as the Civil War tested the nation's core values almost a century earlier (refer to Chapter 6), the civil rights movement in the mid–20th century tested these values once again.

This chapter examines this era's leaders (greatest among them being Martin Luther King, Jr.), the events that transpired during these volatile years, and the 1963 March on Washington, where King gave voice to millions, black and white, in a speech that defined America as it should be and not as it was.

The Tide Turns: Brown v. Board of Education (1954)

The dramatic battles that set the tone for much of the 1960s didn't just happen. Several events preceded those battles, perhaps none more important than the 1954 Supreme Court decision of *Brown v. Board of Education*. That decision overturned the 1896 *Plessy v. Ferguson* edict, which set the precedent for legalized segregation (refer to Chapter 7 for details about the *Plessy* case).

Before the 1950s, most court cases challenging segregated schooling targeted higher education. Longtime Howard Law School dean Charles Hamilton

Houston, the first African American editor of the *Harvard Law Review,* crafted the brilliant strategy to challenge Jim Crow's "separate but equal" mandate in graduate education in the 1930s when he led the NAACP Legal Defense Fund. Consequently, the NAACP legal team, which had tried many of the key segregation cases since 1935, gained momentum with these 1950 landmark decisions:

- ✔ *Sweatt v. Painter:* Denied admission to the University of Texas School of Law in 1946 despite meeting all requirements but race, Heman Marion Sweatt pursued legal action to force the school to accept him. Because a law school admitting blacks opened in 1947 while his case was still being heard, the Texas courts upheld the University of Texas's denial of admission to Sweatt. The Supreme Court overturned the Texas courts' decision citing that the University of Texas had substantially more professors and students plus a larger law library than the black law school, marking the first time the Court factored in issues of substantive quality and not just the existence of a separate school.

- ✔ *McLaurin v. Oklahoma State Regents:* Although admitted to the University of Oklahoma, doctoral student George W. McLaurin was forced to sit in a designated row in class, at a separate table for lunch, and at a special desk in the library. Oklahoma courts denied McLaurin's appeal to remove these separate restrictions. The Supreme Court overturned the lower court's decision, ruling that Oklahoma's treatment of McLaurin violated the Fourteenth Amendment, which prevents any separate treatment based on race.

In essence, these decisions undermined the rationale behind the Supreme Court's 1896 ruling in *Plessy v. Ferguson:* that separate facilities were equal. In June 1950, NAACP lead attorney Thurgood Marshall, who later became the first black Supreme Court Justice, convened the NAACP's board of directors and some of the nation's top lawyers to discuss the next phase of attack. They decided that the NAACP, which had already initiated some lawsuits, would pursue a full-out legal assault on school segregation.

The 1954 ruling and the reaction

Wanting to form a representative sample of the nation as a whole, the Supreme Court consolidated five cases to form the more popularly known *Brown v. Board of Education* (see the sidebar "The cases the built Brown" for details on these five cases).

To get *Plessy* overturned, Thurgood Marshall and his team knew they had to show that segregation in and of itself actually harmed black children. To do so, he relied on the research of Dr. Kenneth Clark and his wife Mamie Phipps Clark, the first and second African Americans to receive doctorates in psychology from Columbia University. To figure out how black children saw themselves, the Clarks placed white and black dolls before black children and asked them to identify the "nice" and "bad" doll as well as choose the one most like them. Most children identified the white doll as nice and the black doll as bad even when they identified themselves with the black doll. Based on these findings, the Clarks concluded that black children had impaired self-images.

Few expected the unanimous decision finally delivered on May 17, 1954. "[I]n the field of public education the doctrine of 'separate but equal' has no place," ruled the Supreme Court. "Separate educational facilities are inherently unequal." A year later, on May 31, 1955, the case known as *Brown II,* the Court established guidelines to desegregate all public education in the United States.

As the implementation of the *Brown* ruling began, the nation discovered that restoring equality and applying its principle were two different battles. Although many whites didn't fully support the Supreme Court's decision, they abided by it. Others simply refused. In parts of the South, resistance reached dramatic heights.

Crisis in Little Rock: Desegregating Central High School

No one planned on Arkansas serving as a major desegregation battleground. The Little Rock School Board issued a statement that it would comply with the Supreme Court decision and adopted an integration plan. The board selected Central High School as the first school to be integrated at the beginning of the 1957–1958 school year. Careful not to jump hastily into integration's deepest waters, the Little Rock School Board decided to keep its black high school open, allowing just a handful of students to attend Central High that first year. So much for the best-laid plans.

The Little Rock Nine and white resistance

A few black students jumped the gun and tried to enroll in Central High School in January 1956. Because the attempt was made ahead of schedule, a judge denied the students' enrollment, but that made little difference: White citizens opposed to integration took notice and signs of resistance began to show. Months before the September 3, 1957, initiation date, the Capital Citizen's Council (Little Rock's version of the White Citizen's Council, a segregationist group spawned in Mississippi) and the Central High Mothers' League launched an anti-integration media campaign.

Cases that built Brown

Although the decision in the anti-segregation case is commonly referred to as *Brown v. Board of Education,* the final ruling, prompted by the Supreme Court, is a consolidation of several cases:

✔ **Briggs v. Elliott:** In 1947 when the white district superintendent of Clarendon County, South Carolina, schools denied the request of principal Rev. J.A. DeLaine for a school bus to transport black children, black parents filed suit. Eventually the local NAACP, supported by the national organization, helped DeLaine and others file a petition demanding not a bus, but equal schools for black students in Clarendon County. In December 1950, *Briggs v. Elliot* directly challenged the "separate but equal" doctrine established by *Plessy v. Ferguson,* making it the nation's first desegregation case to reach the Supreme Court.

✔ **Bolling v. Sharpe:** To avoid sending their children to dilapidated schools, a group of parents, in a calculated move, marched to the newly built John Philip Sousa Junior High School on September 11, 1950, and attempted to enroll 11 black students. The school's principal turned them away. The resulting case, *Bolling v. Sharpe,* broke with the accepted strategy of demanding equal facilities and directly challenged segregation. The U.S. District Court dismissed the case; the Supreme Court decided to hear the case on appeal. *Note:* When the Court finally rendered its decision, it ruled on *Bolling v. Sharpe* separately because Washington, D.C., wasn't a state and couldn't be grouped as such.

✔ **Brown v. Board of Education of Topeka, Kansas:** Topeka had 4 black elementary schools and 18 white schools. Following a strategy conceived by the Topeka NAACP chapter, black parents attempted to enroll their children in the nearest white school and were turned away. Strengthened by the denied enrollments, the NAACP filed *Oliver Brown et al v. the Board of Education of Topeka, Kansas,* involving 13 parents and 20 children, in the District Court on February 28, 1951. When the District Court ruled in favor of the school board, the NAACP took the case to the U.S. Supreme Court.

✔ **Dorothy Davis v. County School Board of Prince Edward County:** Conditions for black students at R.R. Moton High School in Farmville, Virginia, were horrendous, and the all-white school board consistently refused to allocate more money to the school even though overcrowding meant that some classes were held in an old school bus. Students, led by 16-year-old Barbara Rose Johns (the niece of Vernon Johns, the civil rights leader who helmed Dexter Avenue Baptist Church in Montgomery, Alabama, before Martin Luther King, Jr.), walked out in protest of the school's unacceptable conditions. Johns and fellow organizer Carrie Stokes secured Richmond NAACP counsel Oliver Hill, who filed the case on May 23, 1951. Rejected by the U.S. District Court, the NAACP filed an appeal to the Supreme Court.

✔ **Belton v. Gebhart** and **Bulah v. Gebhart:** In *Belton v. Gebhart,* Ethel Belton and six other parents challenged policies that forced their children to attend run-down, black

Howard High School in downtown Wilmington over the perfectly fine white school in their community. In *Bulah v. Gebhart,* parent Sarah Bulah, dismayed that her daughter had to walk to school when a school bus of white children regularly passed their house, tried to secure transportation for her child. When her attempts failed, she secured council and filed a case. The Delaware Judge Collin Seitz ruled that the circumstances of both grievances violated the "separate but equal" doctrine and ordered the black students admitted to the white schools. This ruling, however, didn't extend throughout the state of Delaware.

Given the increased stakes, the school board solicited volunteers to attend Central High School and selected 17 students. Before any school doors opened, however, anti-integrationists went to work and that number dwindled to nine: Minnijean Brown, Elizabeth Eckford, Ernest Green, Thelma Mothershed, Melba Patillo, Gloria Ray, Terrence Roberts, Jefferson Thomas, and Carlotta Walls. Arkansas NAACP head Daisy Bates served as their personal coach and counselor.

On August 29, a suit filed by a member of the Mother's League prompted the county chancellor to issue a temporary injunction preventing African Americans from enrolling in Central High. Federal District Judge Ronald N. Davies nullified the injunction the next day and ordered the school board to continue with its September 3 plans.

Faubus makes his move

On the night of September 2, the Arkansas National Guard and state police surrounded the school on orders from Arkansas Governor Orval Faubus to admit only white students, teachers, and school officials. A mob of roughly 300 had gathered by morning.

When the nine black students, called the Little Rock Nine, tried to enroll in Central High the next day, members of the Arkansas National Guard turned them away. Frantic, the school board requested a stay of the integration order on September 7, but Judge Davies rejected the request. On September 10, Governor Faubus received a federal summons; he also held a press conference and announced that the armed presence outside the school would remain. Wisely, the Little Rock Nine didn't attempt to enroll again before the hearings. On September 20, Faubus, following a court order, removed the troops.

Eisenhower steps in and the students enroll

On September 23, the Little Rock Nine made another attempt to enroll in Central High, but uncontrolled violence erupted and they left school before it ended, spurring President Eisenhower to intervene. Although far from a drum major for integration, Eisenhower wouldn't permit blatant disregard for the laws of the land.

Political pandering at its worst

Unaware that Governor Faubus had ordered the Arkansas National Guard and state police to block the admittance of the black students into Central High, *The New York Times* predicted on September 3 that integration in Little Rock would go smoothly. After all, Governor Faubus, who grew up racially tolerant, didn't block the desegregation of state buses and other public transportation. In fact, Faubus didn't adopt his anti-integrationist position until his 1956 gubernatorial opponents made it an issue. Although he had vowed to prevent integration to secure his gubernatorial victory, those working to integrate Central High never imagined that he'd take such drastic actions.

On September 24, President Eisenhower addressed the American public on national television to explain his decision to intervene. He said, "The very basis of our individual rights and freedoms rests upon the certainty that the president and the executive branch of government will support and insure the carrying out of the decisions of the federal courts. . . ." He insisted, "The interest of the nation in the proper fulfillment of the law's requirements cannot yield to opposition and demonstrations by some few persons. Mob rule cannot be allowed to override the decisions of our courts."

Protected by federal troops, the Little Rock Nine enrolled in Central High on September 25, 1957, but they continued to be victimized. White students verbally and physically abused them, and segregationists harassed their families and members of the black community in general. Bowing to the pressure, Minnijean Brown poured a bowl of chili over a white student's head and was expelled. Ernest Green, the group's only senior, graduated from Central High on May 27, 1958, but the others didn't get their chance.

Faubus closes the schools

In August 1958, Governor Faubus called a special session of the state legislature and passed a law allowing him to close all the public schools. The schools remained closed until September 1959, when federal authority via the courts finally won out. In the interim, two of the Little Rock Nine had moved away with their families, and the others had graduated from other schools in Arkansas. Governor Faubus served as governor of Arkansas for 12 years before losing the post in the 1970 election.

Following suit: Massive resistance in Virginia

Arkansas wasn't alone in its efforts to circumvent school desegregation. The board of supervisors in Prince Edward County, Virginia, withheld all funding from the county school board, closing all public schools for the 1959–1960 school year. This policy, known as *massive resistance*, stems from U.S. Senator Harry F. Byrd, Sr.'s solicitation of the support of other influential Virginians to prevent school desegregation in 1956.

When the courts reopened the desegregated Prince Edward County schools in February 1959, no white students attended. Instead, their parents enrolled them in *segregation academies,* schools established to prevent integration. This battle waged well into the 1970s, with many Southern schools desegregating in theory but not in practice. Today, many argue that public school education in the North and South operate under a system of *de facto* segregation.

Putting a Face to Racial Violence: Emmett Till

Credited as the birthplace of the White Citizens' Council (WCC), an organization comprised of civic leaders determined to fight integration that spread throughout the South, Mississippi had a reputation for extreme racism. Although African Americans comprised an estimated 45 percent of the state population in the 1950s, only 5 percent were registered voters because both registering to vote and voting itself were so dangerous. Consider these examples: Grocery store owner and NAACP field worker Reverend George Lee was shot and killed in Belzoni, Mississippi, for trying to vote. Weeks later, in Brookhaven, someone shot Lamar Smith dead in broad daylight, with witnesses present, for casting a ballot, but no arrests were made for either murder. These are the conditions Emmett Till, a 14-year-old-boy raised on Chicago's South Side, encountered.

Emmett's murder

Although she was born in Mississippi, Emmett's mother, Mamie Till, grew up in Illinois and, like her son, had limited experience in Mississippi. In August 1955, she sent Emmett, accompanied by family members, to visit his great uncle Mose Wright near Money, Mississippi. Shortly after Emmett's arrival in Mississippi, he and a few others, including his cousin Simeon Wright, went to the general store in Money for candy. After purchasing the candy from Carolyn Bryant, a white woman whose husband owned the store, Emmett whistled at her. Three days later, Bryant's husband Roy and his half-brother J.W. Milam came to Wright's home in the middle of the night and kidnapped Emmett at gunpoint.

The Till case revisited

Prompted by evidence uncovered by Louisiana filmmaker Keith Beauchamp while researching his documentary *The Untold Story of Emmett Louis Till,* the Department of Justice and the Mississippi District Attorney's office for the Fourth District opened an investigation into the 1955 murder on May 10, 2004. Although both Bryant and Milam, who had admitted to killing Till (and even sold details to the magazine *Look* in 1956), were dead, Beauchamp's research pointed to others, black and white, who assisted in the murder. As many as three other people, including Carolyn Bryant herself, may have come to Wright's house the night Emmett was kidnapped.

Ultimately, the investigation yielded no new convictions. The significance of Emmett Till's brutal murder can't be overstated, however. Before her death in 2003, his mother, Mamie Till, said of her son's heartbreaking death, "Men stood up who had never stood up before." Indeed, her son's brutal murder bespoke of hatred's most insidious transgressions against human existence and impelled black and white people to join those committed to freedom.

Although arrested for kidnapping, Bryant and Milam insisted that they had only talked to Emmett and had released him alive. A couple of days later, on August 31, a boy fishing in the Tallahatchie River found Emmett Till's badly decomposed body. Authorities found a 75-pound fan from a cotton gin attached to his neck with barbed wire, a detached eye, and a bullet lodged in the skull, among other atrocities.

The outrage of the nation

Despite attempts by some white Mississippians to bury Emmett there, Mamie Till returned her son's body to Chicago and held an open-casket funeral to expose his brutalization to the world. An estimated 50,000 people viewed Emmett's body.

Photos of the body, published by *Jet Magazine,* hit a nerve with African Americans throughout the nation. White people also responded strongly, as did the world. Emmett's mutilated body exposed the United States' apartheid, prompting thousands of dollars in donations to civil rights organizations.

With most of the nation outraged, Mississippi tried Bryant and Milam for murder. Testifying against the men in court, Wright, Till's uncle, boldly pointed them out. Carolyn Bryant, on the decision of the judge, didn't testify at all. After deliberating for only an hour and seven minutes, the all-white jury in Sumner, Mississippi, acquitted the two men. The acquittal generated more outrage, making Emmett Till a martyr. Many who later joined civil rights movements cited the lynching of Emmett Till as an impetus.

A New Twist in Leadership: Martin Luther King, Jr.

Born in Atlanta, Georgia, on January 15, 1929, Martin Luther King, Jr., shown in Figure 8-1, originally planned to be a scholar and a minister. King attended Morehouse College and excelled at Crozer Theological Seminary in Chester, Pennsylvania, before pursuing graduate studies at Boston University. It wasn't until he accepted the position of pastor at Montgomery, Alabama's Dexter Avenue Baptist Church that King began his journey to become a civil rights icon for the world.

King infused the civil rights movement with a greater moral and philosophical purpose. By insisting that God's law and love truly did conquer all and through his advocacy of *nonviolent direct action,* the process of challenging societal wrongs via protest marches, boycotts, and sit-ins, among other strategies, without the use of violence, he was able to bring an initially reluctant America closer to the dream of true equality for all races.

Figure 8-1:
Martin Luther King, Jr., speaking in Cleveland.

© Bettmann/Corbis

Adopting the philosophy of nonviolence

Sparked by a 1950 lecture about the philosophy of the great Indian activist Mahatma (Mohandas) Gandhi, King began seriously studying Gandhi while a student at Crozer Theological Seminary. He was particularly intrigued by the concept of *satyagraha*. *Satya* means "truth," which also equals love; *agraha* means "force." Therefore, a direct translation means truth-force or love-force.

King found that Gandhi's teachings jelled with his own Christian beliefs (specifically the biblical philosophy to "turn the other cheek" and "love your enemies") as well as his intolerance for racial injustice. He melded these ideas with the concept of nonviolent resistance, which he encountered during his first year at Morehouse while reading Henry David Thoreau's *Essay on Civil Disobedience.* King became convinced that a philosophy based on love could succeed as a "powerful and effective social force on a large scale" and adopted the philosophy of nonviolent direct action.

Even when confronted with violence, practitioners figuratively and some- times literally turn the other cheek and love, instead of hate, those who wrong them. The Montgomery Bus Boycott (see the section "Rosa Parks and the Montgomery Bus Boycott" for details on the boycott) became King's first opportunity to use nonviolent direct action.

As the civil rights movement progressed, King's ideology matured. Although Gandhi's principles provided the foundation for the Congress of Racial Equality (CORE), an active civil rights organization founded in 1942, Martin Luther King, Jr., developed the link between Gandhi and the civil rights movement further. In subsequent writings and speeches, King not only defined the rela- tionship between Gandhi and nonviolent direct action, but he also explained why Christian leaders and all members of society had a moral obligation to rise above the limitations of man-made laws steeped in hatred.

Founding the Southern Christian Leadership Conference (SCLC)

Buoyed by his success in Montgomery (see the section "Rosa Parks and the Montgomery Bus Boycott" for details), King and others founded the Southern Christian Leadership Conference (SCLC), an organization of ministers and others dedicated to duplicating the changes of Montgomery throughout the South. The SCLC

✔ Adopted nonviolent mass action as its chief strategy

✔ Made a commitment to affiliate with local community organizations across the South to widen the reach for social change

✔ Vowed to be open to all regardless of race, religion, or background

In 1957, King invited Southern preachers to the Negro Leaders Conference on Nonviolent Integration. Sixty respondents representing ten states met at Ebenezer Baptist Church, King's home church in Atlanta, and formed the SCLC. Held in Washington D.C., on May 17, 1957, to commemorate the third anniversary of the *Brown* decision, the Prayer Pilgrimage for Freedom, which attracted 20,000 attendees, became the SCLC's first public act. In August of that same year, the organization convened its very first convention in Montgomery. Today, the SCLC is a national organization still based in Atlanta.

Sit-ins, Boycotts, and Marches: The King Era of the Civil Rights Movement Begins

With its rulings regarding school desegregation (see the earlier section "The Tide Turns: Brown v. Board of Education (1954)"), the Supreme Court had spoken loudly, but so too had those opposing justice. Turbulent times lay ahead for the nation. Black people all across America were tired of being "sick and tired." Unlike the NAACP's legal team, they didn't begin with a grand strategy. Instead, ordinary folks challenged racism and racist policies with small, individual acts of defiance — such as drinking from the "white only" water fountain or demanding service at a "white only" restaurant. Actions such as these erupted into a national movement.

Rosa Parks and the Montgomery Bus Boycott

The Montgomery Bus Boycott became the first powerful example of what ordinary black Americans could achieve. *Plessy v. Ferguson*'s declaration of separate but equal permeated every aspect of Southern life. (See Chapter 6 for more on this landmark case.) In Montgomery, Alabama, and other parts of the South, black and white people rode the same public buses but never sat together. Custom and law dictated that whites sit in the front and that blacks sit in the back. The law prohibited a white rider from sharing a seat with a black rider, so if the white section filled up and a white person needed a seat, a black rider had to move back and relinquish his or her seat.

In December 1955, Rosa Parks, shown in Figure 8-2, sat in the fifth row of a bus with three other African Americans. A white man boarded the bus, but there were no seats left in the white section, so the bus driver directed the black riders to move back one row. Three complied. Rosa Parks refused. The driver had her arrested. Attorney E.D. Nixon, former head of the Montgomery NAACP, aided by white attorney Clifford Durr, bailed Parks out and presented their case. The devoted wife had an exemplary background, and with permission from her husband and mother, she agreed to pursue the case.

Figure 8-2:
Rosa Parks.

The popular version of the story is that the 42-year-old Parks, a sometime seamstress and volunteer secretary of the NAACP, was too tired to give up her seat. In her autobiography *Rosa Parks: My Story* (Dial), she explains, "People always say that I didn't give up my seat because I was tired, but that isn't true . . . No, the only tired I was, was tired of giving in." In other words, Rosa Parks didn't stumble into the fledgling civil rights movement unwittingly; she walked into it defiantly.

Organizing — and then extending — the boycott

With Parks on board, Alabama State College professor and Women's Political Council member Jo Ann Robinson and others sprang to action. Black Montgomery received flyers asking them not to ride buses on Monday, December 5. Organizers urged local ministers, one of whom was Martin Luther King, Jr., to speak of the boycott in their Sunday sermons. These efforts resulted in nearly 90 percent of black Montgomery residentsnot riding the buses.

The success of the one-day bus boycott inspired the formation of the Montgomery Improvement Association (MIA), which selected King as its president. After his first address in his new capacity, given at Montgomery's Holt Street Baptist Church on December 5, black attendees numbering in the thousands voted to continue the boycott.

At first, the boycott organizers' demands were modest. As early as December 8, the MIA approached the bus company with a plan, not to eliminate the segregated bus system, but for more equitable bus seating. The bus company refused.

The long haul: Keeping the boycott going despite resistance

As whites in Montgomery tried to end the boycott, blacks strategized ways to keep it going. To counter the ten-cent fare black cabdrivers charged boycott participants, for example, the city passed an ordinance forbidding cab services to charge less than a forty-five cent fare. To keep the boycott going, the MIA organized a private taxi service of black citizens who owned their own cars. Similar to buses, the service had designated routes and pickup times. In another move to divide the black community and end the boycott, city commissioners negotiated with three non-MIA ministers who accepted their terms. A story announcing the boycott's end leaked to the Sunday papers, and word got back to the MIA leadership. To inform the black community that the story was a hoax, MIA members, ministers among them, hit the bars Saturday night. The boycott remained intact.

Unable to stop the boycott through false negotiations, Montgomery officials turned to intimidating the protestors. In January, Montgomery police arrested King, who had begun receiving death threats, for speeding five miles above the speed limit. When the MIA Executive Board filed the federal lawsuit *Browder v. Gayle* challenging the constitutionality of segregated bus laws on January 30, intimidation efforts only increased. King's house was bombed, as was E.D. Nixon's house. When, on February 20, attendees at a mass MIA meeting rejected a settlement from the Men of Montgomery, a group of white businessmen, a Montgomery grand jury indicted King and 88 other bus boycott leaders for violating a 1921 Alabama statute barring boycotts without "just cause." To top it off, the Alabama state legislature introduced bills to *strengthen* bus segregation.

In March, a grand jury tried King on conspiracy charges. Although found guilty, his punishment of a year in jail or a $500 fine was suspended as he appealed the decision. By this time, the Montgomery Bus Boycott was a major national story, and a number of cities observed a National Deliverance Day of Prayer in support of the boycotters.

Death knells for bus segregation

In May, the *Browder v. Gayle* trial challenging the constitutionality of Montgomery's segregated buses finally began in federal district court. Two of the three judges ruled that segregated buses in Montgomery were unconstitutional. On appeal, the Supreme Court unanimously upheld the unconstitutionality of Montgomery's segregated bus system.

The court order ending Montgomery's segregated bus system arrived in Montgomery on December 20. The next day, King, Nixon, and local Baptist minister Ralph David Abernathy (a King comrade who would become a significant figure throughout King's civil rights administration) rode in the front section of a Montgomery bus.

Victory wasn't easy, though. Two days later, a sniper fired shots into King's home. Some passengers became victims of assault by whites who opposed desegregating the buses, and others were the victims of sniper fire. It was clear that, while King and his team had won an important battle, they hadn't won the war.

Sitting in for justice

In February 1960, four black college students — Joseph McNeil, Ezell Blair, Jr., Franklin McClain, and David Richmond — sat at a Woolworth's lunch counter reserved for "whites only" in downtown Greensboro, North Carolina. This simple act added fuel to the burgeoning civil rights movement of the 1960s.

Sit-ins weren't a new civil rights technique. In the early 1940s, the Congress of Racial Equality (CORE) successfully used sit-ins to desegregate public facilities, in Chicago primarily. Howard University students also had success in 1944 when they used the sit-in tactic to desegregate a cafeteria in Washington, D.C. These incidents were more isolated, however. The four students in North Carolina sparked a wave of additional sit-ins throughout the South and set the stage for the creation of a new organization that quickly gained momentum within the civil rights movement: the Student Nonviolent Coordinating Committee (SNCC).

The day after the first sit-in at the Greensboro Woolworth's, more students from North Carolina Agricultural and Technical College, the historically black college that the original four attended, descended on the store. Even though there were no confrontations, the local media covered the second sit-in. When the national media picked up the story, it struck a chord with other students who began to duplicate the sit-ins in other locations.

F.W. Woolworth's was a discount store that represented Americana. One of the nation's few chains, it helped create a national identity. The lunch counters at the front of the stores were popular meeting spots. Civil rights leadership recognized the symbolic power of Woolworth's and acted quickly to organize more sit-ins. Within two weeks, students in 11 cities had staged sit-ins at Woolworth's and S.H. Kress stores. To show their support, Northern students, both black and white, picketed local branches of chain stores that practiced racial segregation in the South.

Sit-ins in Nashville

Nashville was a pivotal city in the sit-in movement. With the national spotlight created by the Greensboro sit-in, students from four predominantly black schools took action in Nashville in February 1960.

The first wave of sit-ins was peaceful, but that changed on February 27, 1960, when a group of white teenagers attacked sit-in participants. Nashville police didn't stop the attack. Instead, they arrested the sit-in participants for disorderly conduct. A new group quickly replaced the arrested students. Nashville police arrested approximately 81 students during this period.

When the black community rallied behind the students with money to bail them out, the students refused the bail money and opted to serve jail terms. Fisk student Diane Nash, a former beauty pageant contestant who became one of the civil rights movement's young leaders, explained, "We feel that if we pay these fines we would be contributing to and supporting the injustice and immoral practices that have been performed in the arrest and conviction of the defendants."

By April, Nashville, long considered a moderate city in regards to race relations, had lost considerable tourist dollars. When segregationists bombed the home of Z. Alexander Looby, the attorney who represented the participating students, 2,500 people, whites among them, marched to city hall and addressed Nashville Mayor Ben West. A turning point in the Nashville movement came when Nash asked West if he believed it was wrong to discriminate against a person solely on the basis of race and West answered "yes." Weeks later, lunch counters in Nashville were desegregated.

Beyond lunch counters

The sit-in tactic helped integrate other facilities. By August 1961, an estimated 70,000 people had participated in sit-ins across the country (more than 3,000 of these were arrested). One of the most important results of these actions was that students from across the country became active participants in the civil right movement.

The sit-ins demonstrated that mass nonviolent direct action could be successful and brought national media attention to the new era of the civil rights movement. Additionally, the *jail-in* tactic of not paying bail to protest legal injustice became another important strategy. For the first time, the battle to end racial injustice combined legal action with direct public protest.

Founding the Student Nonviolent Coordinating Committee (SNCC)

SCLC administrator Ella Baker, a former NAACP and National Urban League worker, convinced SCLC leadership to sponsor a gathering of student sit-in leaders and participants. Baker encouraged the students to form an independent, grassroots unit. The result was the Student Nonviolent Coordinating Committee (SNCC, pronounced *snick*), run by students. Throughout the 1960s, SNCC was an important fixture of the civil rights movement.

Marion Barry, the beleaguered former mayor of Washington, D.C., served as SNCC's first chairman. Other key SNCC leaders included Diane Nash, John Lewis, James Forman, and Stokely Carmichael (later known as Kwame Ture).

Riding for freedom

Under the direction of James Farmer, the Congress of Racial Equality (CORE), an interracial civil rights organization, implemented the influential Freedom Rides of 1961. Organized to test the enforcement of *Boynton v. Virginia* (1960), which desegregated all interstate transportation facilities, including bus terminals, 13 Freedom Riders —7 black (including Farmer) and 6 white — boarded a Greyhound bus in Washington, D.C., on May 4, 1961, with New Orleans as their ultimate destination.

The riders traveled through Virginia and North Carolina with no incident, but John Lewis and another rider were attacked in Rock Hill, South Carolina, for trying to enter a "whites only" waiting room. Upon entering Alabama, the group split in two. According to Birmingham Public Safety Commissioner "Bull" Connor, who would become a poster child for segregation, no officers were available to escort or protect the riders because it was Mother's Day. When a mob of about 200 white people brandishing guns surrounded one of the buses (disabled by blown tires), someone threw a bomb through a broken bus window. As the riders left the bus, the mob set upon them. The second group fared little better. Pictures of the burning Greyhound bus and the severely injured passengers landed on the front pages of national and international newspapers.

President Kennedy demanded that the Freedom Rides end, but Farmer and CORE couldn't stop the determined students. Even after Alabama officials escorted the riders to Tennessee, John Lewis and Diane Nash found a way back to Birmingham, rallying new riders to continue the journey. Aware of the danger, some riders even drafted wills. When Greyhound bus drivers refused to drive them, Robert F. Kennedy called a Greyhound superintendent in Birmingham and demanded a bus, noting that the law entitled the riders to transportation.

When the riders reached Montgomery, Alabama, the police escort accompanying them from Birmingham disappeared. As they stepped off the bus, a group of angry whites attacked them and nearby reporters. Even though a police station was nearby, no local law enforcement appeared at the scene. Eventually federal marshals saved the day. When the riders landed in Jackson, Mississippi, authorities immediately arrested them for attempting to use "whites only" facilities. Yet the riders continued on.

Over the next four months, several hundred more volunteers descended on Mississippi despite the risks. Finally, bowing to pressure from Robert Kennedy, the Interstate Commerce Commission tightened regulations against segregated bus and train terminals, and the Freedom Rides ended.

The Albany Movement: A chink in the armor

Unlike previous movements, where the goal had been to desegregate the buses or the schools specifically, the Albany Movement, founded in 1961, set out to desegregate the entire city of Albany, Georgia, and to challenge the city's white power structure. Albany's black community, hailing from various socioeconomic backgrounds, participated in numerous protest efforts, such as sitting-in at a local bus terminal and contesting police brutality. More than 500 people were jailed before mid-December, prompting organizers to call in Martin Luther King, Jr., to attract more national attention. As soon as King and Ralph David Abernathy joined an Albany protest march on December 16, authorities arrested them, Albany Movement president Dr. William Anderson, and about 200 others.

To undermine the efforts of the protestors, city officials changed their tactics:

✔ Unlike other Southern law enforcement entities, Albany Police Chief Laurie Pritchett, who favored arrests over public beatings, forbade his officers from mistreating anyone in the presence of the news media.

✔ As King vowed to spend Christmas in jail, black leaders and city officials struck a deal to halt the demonstrations in exchange for the release of jailed protestors and other concessions. King didn't spend Christmas in jail, but the city didn't alter any of its segregationist policies, a move that embarrassed King and the SCLC.

✔ When King and Abernathy returned to Albany in July 1962 for sentencing, they couldn't serve their full 45-day sentence because city officials claimed an anonymous black man had paid their fine just two days into their sentence. When King managed another arrest later, Albany officials suspended his sentence.

> ✔ When police beat the pregnant wife of the Albany Movement's vice-president delivering food to black prisoners, members of Albany's black community responded violently. Delighting in this break in nonviolent direct action, Pritchett directed news attention to "them nonviolent rocks," prompting King to call for a day of penance and halt protests. King understood that the retaliation of protesters would help justify action against them and take the attention away from desegregation.

In Albany, city officials made sure that there were no obvious incidents of brutality. With police not beating participants and not permitting King or his close associates to serve jail time, Albany was able to lessen the impact of the protestors and at the same time not make any significant concessions regarding segregation.

In August 1962, King left Albany. Because nothing happened while King was there, his efforts seemed futile. Members of the Albany Movement didn't view their campaign as a failure, however, because much of the city legally desegregated in 1962.

Integrating Ole Miss and Increasing Federal Involvement

By 1962, the nation had experience with university integration, yet James Meredith's entry into the University of Mississippi in Oxford, Mississippi, was especially virulent. Led by Governor Ross Barnett, Mississippi held firmly to its segregationist reputation. Mississippi's obstinacy in refusing to allow James Meredith's enrollment spurred Robert F. Kennedy to extend the federal government's involvement in the civil rights movement further.

The trouble began when the Mississippi-born Meredith decided to transfer from Jackson State, a black college in Mississippi, to Ole Miss. Denied admission twice, Meredith appealed to the courts. Eventually a federal district court ordered Ole Miss to admit Meredith. On September 20, 1962, when Meredith attempted to register for school, Governor Barnett himself blocked Meredith's path. After speaking with Barnett directly, Robert F. Kennedy sent 500 federal marshals to escort Meredith onto the campus and into his dorm room on September 30, but an angry crowd of students and outside agitators gathered in opposition to Meredith's enrollment.

Federal marshals tried unsuccessfully to disperse the rock-throwing crowd with tear gas. More outside agitators poured into Ole Miss and used bottles, bricks, and gunshots to attack the marshals, who heeded Justice Department orders not to use their rifles. In the end, 160 marshals were wounded (28 by gunshot), and two people were killed. Reluctantly, Kennedy sent in the first wave of 5,000 army troops who controlled the crowd without using their rifles. Although the number of troops eventually declined, Meredith attended Ole Miss with federal protection until his graduation in 1963.

The incident at Ole Miss changed President Kennedy's position on dealing with the civil rights movement. He finally realized that federal intervention was necessary and, furthermore, that most of the American voting public didn't view such intervention negatively, even in the South.

1963: A Bloody Year

In 1963, the confrontations and violence associated with the civil rights movement escalated. Black America's patience had worn thin waiting on justice. The Freedom Rides (see "Riding for freedom") and the Albany Movement (see "The Albany Movement: A chink in the armor") hadn't moved the nation as far along as civil rights leaders had hoped. The SCLC, perhaps urged on by criticism from the much younger SNCC, took bolder action.

Not-so-sweet home Alabama: Birmingham

Dubbed "Bombingham" by some for its extreme racial violence, Birmingham became a significant project for civil rights leaders. SCLC executive director Wyatt Tee Walker believed that the South would follow Birmingham; if civil rights protests succeeded there, they could succeed anywhere.

What happened in Birmingham demonstrated that black Americans wouldn't wait any longer for freedom and equality. It was an important turning point in the civil rights war, but it was by no means the last battle.

Project C

On April 3, 1963, the first protest of what Wyatt called *Project C,* for "confrontation," began, and 20 people were arrested. Three days later, a march led by local Reverend Fred Shuttlesworth, founder of the Alabama Christian Movement for Human Rights, also ended in nonviolent arrests, which were uncharacteristic for segregationist Bull Connor. However, on April 7, when Martin Luther King, Jr.'s brother Reverend A.D. King marched with other ministers to City Hall, they encountered dogs and nightsticks. Despite an injunction telling him not to lead a march, on April 13, Martin Luther King, Jr., and buddy Ralph David Abernathy did so anyway and went straight to jail.

Letter from Birmingham Jail

King's "Letter from Birmingham Jail," a response to a letter published by white clergyman denouncing the demonstrations and urging patience, made this jail visit different from others. In the widely published letter, King explained why African Americans could no longer wait for freedom. Written on scraps of paper with a pen smuggled into the jail during King's eight-day stay, the letter articulated the desires of those who marched while also justifying their defiance of unjust laws. "We know through painful experience that freedom is never voluntarily given by the oppressor," he wrote, "It must be demanded by the oppressed."

The children's march

After King left jail on bail, he saw that volunteers in Birmingham had dwindled. James Bevel, fresh from the Nashville sit-ins, suggested using high school students. A dilemma emerged when the students' brothers and sisters of all ages also turned up for nonviolent resistance training. After much deliberation, the decision was made to let the children march on May 2. Although Connor didn't use violence during the march, he and his team arrested an estimated 900 children. When more people marched the next day, Connor ordered the use of clubs, dogs, and fire hoses against the participants. The melee made national headlines, demanding the attention of President John F. Kennedy.

The children kept coming, and the police kept arresting them, making national headlines and filling the jails. In days, police arrested at least 2,000 people, the bulk of them children. As the number of young people increased, the situation became more charged. Negotiating with city officials, civil rights leaders agreed that protests would start around noon on May 7, but the children came early, and some began taunting the police. A disturbance broke out. Fearful of greater violence, civil rights leadership halted the next day's protest. White leadership also feared greater violence and decided to negotiate.

Negotiating for desegregation

May 10, Birmingham's white merchants made a pact with the SCLC to desegregate as well as hire African Americans during the next three months if the organization put a stop to the demonstrations. Not everyone was pleased, however. Some blacks criticized King for yielding to promises.

The Ku Klux Klan (KKK) responded by bombing A.D. King's home and a motel where they believed Martin Luther King, Jr., and his aides were staying. These bombings induced rioting among some blacks. The federal government sent in 3,000 army troops, among other resources, and the bombings ended. Aided by Birmingham's moderate mayor, desegregation in Birmingham finally began.

When Alabama Governor George Wallace vowed to bar two black students from registering at the University of Alabama in Tuscaloosa in June 1963, President Kennedy ended his public silence on civil rights. In a public broadcast that evening, Kennedy stated that "all Americans are to be afforded equal rights and equal opportunities." The support of the federal government for desegregation was finally in place, but turbulent times still lay ahead.

Murder in Mississippi: Medgar Evers

News of President Kennedy's commitment to civil rights only angered segregationists further. White Mississippians refused to give up segregation. The murder of Medgar Evers one day after Kennedy's speech made that clear.

Mississippi NAACP field secretary Medgar Evers kept Mississippi in the fight for civil rights. Evers's work included helping establish NAACP chapters throughout the state, investigating violent crimes against black people, and organizing boycotts of segregated stores in Jackson, as well as Jackson gas stations that wouldn't allow black people to use the restrooms. Just before his death, he began a full-scale campaign to desegregate downtown Jackson. When Mayor Allen C. Thompson went on television asking blacks not to participate, Evers went on television, too. A sit-in at the Woolworth's lunch counter proved successful enough that the mayor publicly promised to desegregate some public facilities. Bowing to pressure from the WCC and other segregationists, however, he backed down from his promise.

Evers's successes, even if they were small in comparison to the successes in other cities, no doubt sealed his fate. On the evening of June 12, 1963, in front of his house, Evers was shot in the back. Seen as a martyr, Evers's death added more urgency to the civil rights movement.

Closing the Evers case

Following Medgar Evers's murder, an all-white jury acquitted his assassin, Byron De La Beckwith. Thanks to the efforts of Evers's widow Myrlie Evers-Williams, Mississippi finally retried and convicted De La Beckwith of murder on February 5, 1994. The 1996 film *Ghosts of Mississippi,* starring Whoopi Goldberg, dramatizes those efforts.

March of All Marches: The March on Washington (1963)

Orchestrated by labor organizer A. Philip Randolph (see Chapter 7) and unsung civil rights activist Bayard Rustin, the March on Washington, held in the nation's capital on August 28, 1963, was the march of all marches. More than 250,000 people, with an estimated 50,000 whites among them, representing various organizations converged on the Lincoln Memorial to demonstrate for black equality.

In addition to King, other participating civil rights leaders included the National Urban League's Whitney Young, Jr., the NAACP's Roy Wilkins, and CORE's James Farmer. Entertainers such as gospel great Mahalia Jackson, Joan Baez, and Bob Dylan were present, as well as movie stars Sidney Poitier, Charlton Heston, and Marlon Brando.

Prior to the March, White House officials warned organizers that such a march could create a conservative backlash against the movement. Adjustments occurred, as the march's site shifted from the White House to the Lincoln Memorial. Organizers also agreed to censor militant speakers.

Freedom Rider and SNCC Chairman John Lewis's speech sparked controversy for its militant message. Lewis voiced his and others' frustration with waiting on the government for hundreds of years for freedom, as well as his pronouncement that black people would no longer wait. He also noted that both the Democrats and Republicans had betrayed the Declaration of Independence.

Considered one of the greatest moments of the 20th century, King's address dispelled any potential for trouble. In his famous "I have a dream" speech, King gave voice to hope: "I have a dream that one day this nation will rise up and live out the true meaning of its creed: 'We hold these truths to be self-evident: that all men are created equal.' . . ." As he continued, the crowd's "amens" grew louder. King's dream that his "four children will one day live in a nation where they will not be judged by the color of their skin but by the content of their character" moved whites as well as blacks.

Some of King's skeptics even acknowledged the power of his vision. King's "I have a dream" speech expanded the focus from black equality to an American society inclusive of all. Those words resonated even more with President Kennedy, who had been lukewarm about the gathering. Afterward, he invited key march organizers to the White House. Unfortunately, the high of the March on Washington didn't last for long.

Chapter 9

Turning Up the Heat (1963–1968)

. . . .

In This Chapter

▶ Mourning the rising death toll in pursuit of the dream

▶ Understanding key civil rights legislation

▶ Risking it all to register black voters

▶ Unleashing black power

▶ Dying for freedom

. . . .

Although civil rights organizations had gathered at the March on Washington in a show of unity, some opponents of integration weren't easily swayed. Still, proponents had much reason to be optimistic. Right before their eyes, the America they had known was finally changing. Throughout the South, "white only" and "colored only" signs began to gradually disappear.

This chapter explores the violence of the civil rights era in the mid- to late 1960s. Particular topics of note are the impact of JFK's assassination, the events of Freedom Summer, and the rise of Malcolm X and the black power movement. This chapter also familiarizes you with the heated civil rights battles in Alabama, the passage of key civil rights legislation, and the impact on the nation of Martin Luther King, Jr.'s murder.

Suffering Two Tragic Blows

Most civil rights participants knew that death was a very real consequence for their actions. In some Southern states, black residents avoided civil rights activity because of the fear of retaliation, but segregationists made no distinctions between participants and nonparticipants. White Americans weren't safe either. Some argue that some white Southerners didn't actively resist desegregation primarily to avoid physical harm. In the fall of 1963, the lengths to which segregationists would go to prevent integration shocked and saddened the nation.

Four innocent victims

When a bomb exploded at Birmingham's Sixteenth Street Baptist Church just minutes before the 11 a.m. service on September 15, 1963, the whole nation felt the jolt. Four little girls — 11-year-old Denise McNair and 14-year-olds Cynthia Wesley, Carole Robertson, and Addie Mae Collins — died instantly from the dynamite blast emanating from the church basement; more than 20 others were injured. Ironically, "The Love That Forgives" was the message planned for the day's service.

A hub for civil rights activity, the Sixteenth Street Baptist Church was a center of Birmingham's African American community and served as a central checkpoint for the first phase of what Southern Christian Leadership Conference (SCLC) executive director Wyatt Tee Walker dubbed *Project C* (the "c" stood for confrontation), waged only a few months prior (refer to Chapter 8). Therefore, the church represented black Alabamans' progress, and that progress didn't sit well with the state's extreme segregationists, including Governor George Wallace.

The community's reaction

Despite King's pleas for nonviolence, black Birmingham reacted violently to the church bombing. Alabama authorities responded with fire hoses, brutal beatings, vicious dogs, and mass arrests. Adding to the already tragic situation, police shot and killed 16-year-old Johnnie Robinson for throwing stones at a car of white people, and two white people killed another black youth, 13-year-old Virgil Ware.

A funeral service was held for three of the four girls killed in the bombing (one family insisted on a separate ceremony). Over 8,000 mourners and clergymen of both races attended the service, but city officials, no doubt fearful of angry and emotionally charged crowds, stayed away. Delivering a stirring eulogy, Martin Luther King, Jr., hoped that "the innocent blood of these little girls may well serve as the redemptive force that will bring new light to this dark city." The holy scripture, he reminded attendees, said "A little child shall lead them."

Just days after the funeral service, Birmingham's Public Safety Commissioner Bull Connor proclaimed to a gathering of White Citizens Council (WCC) supporters that the Supreme Court was responsible for the girls' deaths because of the *Brown v. Board of Education* decision. He even suggested that King's supporters bombed the church themselves.

The aftermath

Instead of stopping civil rights activity, the tragic bombing attracted national and international attention, pressuring the FBI to investigate the incident. Little was done though and, as was later learned, FBI head J. Edgar Hoover blocked the release of critical evidence to prosecutors. Only years later, in

1977, was Ku Klux Klan member Robert Edward Chambliss convicted. A 2000 reopening of the case brought convictions for two others: Thomas Blanton in 2001 and Bobby Frank Cherry in 2002. (The fourth man involved in the bombing, Herman Cash, died in 1994 and avoided prosecution.)

Acclaimed African American filmmaker Spike Lee received a 1998 Academy Award nomination for his documentary *Four Little Girls* about the 1963 bombing and its effects on the nation and the girls' families.

JFK dies

On November 22, 1963, the civil rights movement received another crushing blow. With President John F. Kennedy solidly behind civil rights efforts and actively pushing Congress for the passage of a major civil rights bill, the prospect of achieving full black equality appeared within reach. But during a visit to Dallas, as Kennedy rode with his wife Jackie in a convertible in a parade, three shots rang out, hitting Kennedy in the head and neck. He died shortly thereafter.

Kennedy's absence made the future of civil rights legislation uncertain. Because Vice President Lyndon Johnson hailed from Texas, few pegged him as a civil rights champion. Johnson's actions as president, however, surprised many, especially white Southerners.

The Civil Rights Act of 1964

Ironically, Kennedy's assassination strengthened the proposed civil rights bill. Prior to his death, any civil rights legislation would have required significant compromise to pass both houses of Congress. After his death, President Johnson refused to compromise.

With an upcoming presidential election, Johnson's strong endorsement of the Civil Rights Act would normally have been a huge political risk. Yet with key Republicans emerging as allies and other lawmakers less inclined to squabble over a bill an assassinated president supported, the bill passed both houses of Congress with no significant changes. On July 2, 1964, Johnson signed the Civil Rights Act of 1964 into law. The law did the following:

✔ It prohibited racial discrimination in any public accommodations engaged in interstate commerce.

✔ It enforced public school desegregation.

> ✔ It withdrew federal funding from any institution or program that endorsed discrimination.
>
> ✔ It outlawed all employment discrimination and established the Equal Employment Opportunity Commission (EEOC) to monitor any violations.
>
> ✔ It ensured equal voter registration.

In November 1964, Johnson easily won the presidential election.

Targeting Mississippi for Voter Registration: Freedom Summer

In the summer of 1964, Mississippi, where Emmett Till, Medgar Evers, and countless others were boldly murdered without consequence (refer to Chapter 8), continued its reign as a segregationist stronghold. Just as the SCLC figured that victories in Alabama would significantly pave the way to integrate other Southern cities, Bob Moses, a former SCLC volunteer and a Student Nonviolent Coordinating Committee (SNCC) leader, banked that change in Mississippi would greatly influence the nation. The goal? Register black voters. During that eventful summer, volunteers poured into the state determined to make a difference.

As more and more whites, especially students, signed up for duty in the fight for black equality, civil rights leaders shifted their goal from desegregation to voting rights. Although the Fourteenth and Fifteenth Amendments established voting rights for African Americans, whites in many Southern states either intimidated blacks or established roadblocks such as poll taxes and literacy tests to keep them from voting.

Getting ready

Beginning a voter registration project in Mississippi was daunting, to say the least. On the surface, McComb, a small town in rural Mississippi, wasn't an ideal place to launch a voter registration campaign: Shortly after New York math teacher Bob Moses's arrival, a Mississippi state legislator who shot a black man for registering to vote was acquitted. When an FBI agent tipped off local police that another black man who witnessed the shooting intended to testify, the witness was beaten and killed.

Initially African Americans in McComb, understandably cautious considering the racial climate, welcomed Moses and provided him with financial and other resources. Less cautious than the older community, McComb's black youth eagerly embraced change. One ambitious youth lied about her age and led a sit-in that got her expelled from high school and sent to reform school. Some parents were outraged, but many students kept on agitating, even choosing civil rights work over school. Harassment, murders, and beatings didn't deter them.

Throughout the state, black Mississippians stepped up. Medgar Evers is probably the best-known (refer to Chapter 8 for information about him), but Aaron Henry, Fannie Lou Hamer, Dr. T.R.M. Howard, and Amzie Moore were also noted local leaders in the voter registration campaign, not to mention countless others whose names don't grace the history books. Promised much-needed funding by Robert Kennedy, the Voter Education Project launched in April 1962.

A mock election called Freedom Vote held in 1963 drew almost 80,000 black voters, proving that black Mississippians wanted to vote. Encouraged by this and the presence of white volunteers, Bob Moses proposed Freedom Summer.

Getting out the black vote

Robert Kennedy, who arranged funding for black voter registration campaigns, wouldn't commit federal protection for volunteers. Moses was convinced that placing college students, preferably white, in black communities throughout Mississippi to register black residents to vote as well as teach them reading and math would secure federal protection.

At orientation sessions held in Ohio, Freedom Summer organizers emphasized potential risks such as arrest, jail time, or death to volunteers. The volunteers were also required to bring $500 in bail money and instructed not to antagonize Mississippi police officers who arrested them. In June, hundreds of volunteers, mostly white, poured into Mississippi. Given Mississippi's volatile racial history, the Johnson administration worried about the safety of Freedom Summer participants and the potential impact on the nation.

By the time Freedom Summer kicked off, 900 volunteers had signed up for the fight. The central battleground became Greenwood, Mississippi, situated in the notorious Mississippi Delta region between Memphis, Tennessee, and Jackson, Mississippi, in the notorious Mississippi Delta region.

Mississippi burning

Tragedy struck early for the volunteers pouring into Mississippi. On June 21, after investigating a church bombing in Lawndale, local police stopped two white Northerners Andrew Goodman and Michael Schwerner and black Mississippian James Chaney for speeding and took them to jail. Although reportedly released that same night, the three men disappeared. Instead of investigating, state police claimed that the trio staged their own disappearance as a publicity stunt.

The FBI got involved, and as the investigation dragged on, public outcry pressed the search on. On August 4, just days before the all-important Democratic National Convention, the three bodies surfaced just outside Philadelphia, Mississippi. Their deaths shifted public attention to Freedom Summer and its mission in Mississippi.

By the end of the year, the FBI arrested 18 people, mostly Ku Klux Klan members, in relation to the murders. Although most of the people arrested received convictions, the convictions were for breach of civil rights, not murder (this case is the basis for the 1988 film *Mississippi Burning*). A murder conviction came decades later in January 6, 2005, when mastermind Edgar Ray Killen, a minister, finally received justice.

The success of Freedom Summer

Prior to Freedom Summer, just under 7 percent of Mississippi's voting-age black population had registered to vote. By 1969, that number had climbed to nearly 67 percent. The 17,000 black Mississippians who attempted to vote during the turbulent project helped achieve these numbers; so did the 1,600 who actually voted. This success rate contributed to the passage of the Voting Rights Act of 1965 (see the later section "The Voting Rights Act of 1965").

The Mississippi Freedom Democratic Party (MFDP)

With support from SNCC, the Mississippi Freedom Democratic Party (MFDP) launched in 1964 as an alternative to Mississippi's reigning Democratic party, which promoted white supremacy. MFDP elected its own delegates: Annie Devine, Victoria Gray, and the charismatic Fannie Lou Hamer, who had endured severe beatings in her quest to secure the freedom to vote for herself and her fellow Mississippians.

Fearing the backlash from Mississippi's "official" Democratic party, President Johnson tried to prevent the MFDP from attending the Democratic National Convention in Atlantic City, New Jersey. But MFDP delegates didn't back down and took their case to the credentials board where Hamer testified about the beatings she endured in Mississippi for trying to vote.

Still, MFDP was barred from entering the Convention, so members borrowed passes from sympathetic delegates. When their seats were removed the second day, they remained and sang freedom songs. Although disappointed by the chilly reception in 1964, the MFDP went on to attend the 1968 Democratic National Convention in Chicago.

Forty-one freedom schools helped educate black Mississippians about much more than learning how to vote. Likewise, black Mississippians taught the students and the world that hope could thrive in the direst circumstances. Most important, Freedom Summer demonstrated the positive impact that all Americans, be they white and privileged or black and poor, could have on the nation overall.

Oh Lord Selma: Back in Alabama

Alabama had been a bittersweet site for the King-led contributions to the civil rights movement. Although the successful Montgomery Bus Boycott made King a national figure (see Chapter 8), the deaths of Birmingham's four little girls and countless others had been tough to swallow. Yet King and others under his SCLC umbrella returned to the contentious state in January 1965 to begin Project Alabama, a campaign to secure federal protection for voting rights.

Project Alabama experienced some of the same challenges as the Albany Movement in Georgia, with tensions between SCLC and SNCC ranking supreme. As in Albany, SNCC had arrived in the area before SCLC. For months, SNCC battled the many obstacles preventing black voter registration such as educating black Alabamans about their voting rights. In addition, SNCC navigated bureaucracy such as voter registration offices only opening two days of the month and the endless paperwork. Many SNCC members felt that King and SCLC would receive credit for SNCC's hard work. Other prominent SNCC leaders like John Lewis continued to support King. Although these tensions were strong, neither side voiced them to the public.

Getting arrested again

To bring attention to Alabama's voting inequities, King needed authorities to arrest him and others. On February 1, he succeeded by leading a group of demonstrators in defiance of the July 1963 judgment banning all meetings and marches in Selma. When authorities, led by Sheriff Jim Clark, arrested him, local black students marched in defiance and police arrested them, which is what King anticipated. The national media captured the sequence of events.

From a jail cell on February 1, King, during his first arrest since Birmingham, wrote in a letter to the American public: "There are more Negroes in jail with me than there are on the voting rolls."

During a peaceful march on February 18, the situation became very dramatic when 26-year-old Jimmie Lee Jackson was shot and killed trying to protect his mother from the blows of a billy club. His death galvanized momentum for a federal voter registration law. Once again, the American public placed civil rights at the top of the nation's agenda.

Then on Sunday, March 7, a group of 600 people led by SNCC Chairman John Lewis and SCLC's Hosea Williams, defying the armed Alabama state troopers blocking their way, attempted to cross the Edmund Pettus Bridge. As the group marched, ignoring Major John Cloud's demand to turn around, officers charged them, in the process trampling them, whipping them, beating them, and tear-gassing them. Referred to as *Bloody Sunday,* the event was captured by the media and broadcast nationwide on the evening news. The ABC network even preempted its showing of the film *Judgment at Nuremberg* with coverage from Selma.

Marching from Selma to Montgomery

After Bloody Sunday, a court order banned King from leading a second march on March 9, so King took the group of protesters to the edge of the Edmund Pettus Bridge, knelt in prayer, and turned the group back. Emotions ran higher as that same night white men severely beat Reverend James Reeb. Two days later, the white minister from Boston died.

With court approval and the protection of armed forces, King led a third march from Selma to Montgomery on Sunday, March 21. King, with wife Coretta by his side as well as Rosa Parks and several other key civil rights leaders, reached the state capitol on March 25. Approximately 25,000 people attended the victory rally.

The Voting Rights Act of 1965

Without Freedom Summer and Selma, it's doubtful that the Voting Rights Act of 1965 would have ever passed. Although black men had received the right to vote with the Fifteenth Amendment and the Nineteenth amendment had extended voting rights to all women, Southern states actively hindered black voting, using several methods, the two most popular being the poll tax and literacy tests:

- **Poll tax:** Black voters, many of whom were poor, were charged fees to deter them from voting.

- **Literacy test:** In order to vote, black Southerners, many of them with little formal education, were given a myriad of tasks such as reciting parts of the Constitution to the administrator's satisfaction, transcribing passages from the Constitution, and answering obscure technical questions such as "how many people can testify against a person denying his guilt of treason?"

With Southern states actively stopping African Americans from voting, a practice that had gone on for decades, the federal government finally stepped in. On August 6, 1965, President Johnson signed the Voting Rights Act (VRA) into law. Key features of the law include

✔ **Federal supervision of voter registration in areas where less than 50 percent of the nonwhite population hadn't registered to vote:** Instead of waiting for grievances to be filed, the federal government became proactive in identifying areas where whites were intimidating blacks from voting.

✔ **Federal approval of change in local voting laws:** In areas with a history of disenfranchisement as well as less than 50 percent of the black population registered to vote, the federal government had to approve any changes in voting requirements.

✔ **Prohibition of literacy tests:** The federal government banned the use of literacy tests for all American voters.

✔ **Authorizing the U.S. attorney general to investigate the use of poll taxes.** Although the VRA itself didn't ban poll taxes, that change did come eventually. While the Twenty-fourth Amendment, passed in 1964, banned the use of poll taxes in federal elections, the Supreme Court banned the use of poll taxes in state elections in 1966, with *Harper v. Virginia Board of Elections*.

The VRA made it emphatically clear that the nation as a whole would no longer tolerate blatant voter discrimination. The law made an immediate impact. Within three weeks, more than 27,000 African Americans in Mississippi, Alabama, and Louisiana registered to vote. Renewed four times since its passage, the VRA received a 25-year extension in 2006.

Black Power Rising

Not all African Americans were committed to King's doctrine of nonviolence. As white supremacists became increasingly more violent, some black Americans were compelled to fight back. During the mounting tensions of the 1960s, messages of black empowerment became louder and louder. Prominent spokespersons such as Malcolm X and organizations like the Nation of Islam and the Black Panther Party began to command as much attention as King and civil rights organizations such as the NAACP, CORE, and SCLC. These developments directly affected SNCC, which began a metamorphosis.

As African Americans became more outspoken, conflicts erupted in both the North and the South. The days of patiently waiting for change were long gone. With direct nonviolent action (refer to Chapter 8) continuing in the South and rioting breaking out in the North, the nation found itself battling many wars.

The Nation of Islam

Until the 1960s, the Nation of Islam (NOI) was foreign to most Americans. Although its premise was religious, the NOI's strongest selling points for many black Americans became its endorsement of black nationalism and black self-sufficiency. Its emphasis on black separatism, including its insistence that white people were devils, greatly distinguished it from SCLC and other civil rights organizations that emphasized Christian love and forgiveness regardless of the transgression.

Unlike King and his followers, the NOI sanctioned violent retaliation. Based in Chicago, its aggressiveness appealed most to the nation's urban areas. Actively recruiting its membership from the prison system, the NOI found great success. NOI membership often gave prison converts the discipline they required to survive imprisonment. Once released, many found employment with the NOI, which operated several businesses.

Even though NOI leader Elijah Muhammad built the NOI into a formidable organization that exceeded its humble 1930 origins, Malcolm X propelled the NOI into mainstream awareness. (You can read more about the Nation of Islam in Chapter 12.)

Although not recognized by mainstream Islamic organizations until recently because of significant theological differences that have since been altered, NOI members followed certain aspects of mainstream Islam such as reading the Koran and observing Muslim practices such as the separation of the sexes during worship. Religious services as well as the NOI's schools emphasized the values of self-sufficiency and self-discipline.

Malcolm X

Although best known for slogans such as "By Any Means Necessary" as well as posters depicting him with a gun, Malcolm X, shown in Figure 9-1, was a very complex man. An ex-convict, Malcolm X's strength, charisma, and intelligence only underscored the potential the nation tucked away in its prison systems. *The Autobiography of Malcolm X,* published months after his death, offered insight into who he once was, who he became, and who he might have been.

His initial views proclaiming white people as devils, a view consistent with the Nation of Islam (NOI) and its leader Elijah Muhammad whom Malcolm X followed, propelled him to the attention of the news media — that and the tens of thousands who came to hear him speak. Ultimately, Malcolm X's break with the NOI, as well as his renunciation of equating white people to the devil, placed him in greater favor with many, black and white. Unfortunately, violence cut that new journey short but not his legacy as one of the 20th century's elite freedom fighters.

Figure 9-1:
Malcolm X.

© Michael Ochs Archives/Corbis

The rise of Malcolm X

As a child, Nebraska-born Malcolm Little's life was torn apart when a group of white extremists murdered his father. Forced to go on welfare, the Little household became unstable, and the children often lived in foster homes. Extremely bright, Little dropped out of school when a white teacher told him that becoming a lawyer "was no realistic goal for a nigger."

With limited opportunities available to him, Little ventured into a life of crime. While serving a ten-year sentence for burglary, he seriously explored the Nation of Islam and eventually dedicated himself to the group, even conversing with leader Elijah Muhammad.

By the time Little was released from prison in 1952, he had met Elijah Muhammad and officially joined the NOI, adopting the name Malcolm X to rid himself of what he characterized as his slave surname. He moved to Chicago and studied directly under Muhammad, who sent Malcolm X to spearhead a Harlem branch for the NOI as part of his plan to expand the organization's reach.

Malcolm's message

As a national NOI spokesperson, the handsome and articulate Malcolm X generated much media attention, particularly for his disagreements with King's nonviolent methods of protest as well as for the NOI's message of black self-sufficiency and separatism. Malcolm X's criticism landed him a public platform when he appeared in a weeklong television special titled "The Hate That Hate Produced" with TV journalist Mike Wallace.

Conflicts with the Nation of Islam

As Malcolm X's public stature grew, tensions developed within the NOI. Malcolm X, also known as El-Hajj Malik El-Shabazz, lived by a strict moral code. After becoming a Muslim, he remained celibate until he married Betty Shabazz in 1958. In addition, he didn't engage in extramarital affairs (as confirmed by the FBI agents who followed him). In 1963, he discovered that Elijah Muhammad had engaged in sexual relations with as many as six women in the NOI and that some of those affairs had produced children. Muhammad's moral failings greatly contributed to Malcolm X's eventual split from the NOI.

Around the same time, Malcolm X offended many with his response to President Kennedy's assassination. According to Malcolm X, Kennedy "never foresaw that the chickens would come home to roost so soon," meaning that white Americans or presidents weren't exempt from the violence that denied life and liberty to African Americans. Although Elijah Muhammad suspended and silenced Malcolm X for 90 days for his statements, Malcolm X suspected that Muhammad had other reasons for silencing him. In March 1964, Malcolm X left the NOI and formed the Muslim Mosque, Inc.

But he wasn't finished evolving. After traveling to Mecca, Saudi Arabia, in April 1964 and sharing his religious pilgrimage with Muslims of all races, Malcolm X returned to the U.S. and softened his stance on racial separatism. In May 1964, he founded the Organization of Afro-American Unity.

His death

By early 1965, it was clear that Malcolm X was marked for assassination. On February 14, someone firebombed his family's New York home, but the family escaped unharmed. On February 21, 1965, Malcolm X wasn't so lucky: During a speech at the Audubon Ballroom in Harlem, three men later revealed to be members of the NOI (a fact some people debate) fatally shot Malcolm X multiple times at close range. Many contend that the three men, convicted of first-degree murder in 1966, colluded with the FBI.

While it's impossible to know where Malcolm X would have directed his talents, many believe that he would have worked more closely with Martin Luther King, Jr. Despite depictions of the two as opponents, Malcolm X shared King's commitment to freedom and equality. Just before his death, he had corresponded with King about his efforts in Selma. In addition, Malcolm X had become increasingly more pan-Africanist in his view: Before his death, he began to draw great correlations between the American oppression of black Americans and the worldwide oppression of people of color in general. Without him, the Organization of Afro-American Unity ended.

The Black Panther Party

Like the Nation of Islam, the Black Panther Party for Self-Defense, founded in 1966 by Bobby Seale and Huey Newton, rejected assimilation and advocated black power and black liberation. The party's demands for full employment, decent education, and affordable housing in their Ten Point Plan didn't differ greatly from the goals of many mainstream civil rights organizations. The difference was mainly in their application. Two key points of the plan included

- ✔ **An immediate end to police brutality:** Although members of the Black Panthers often donned berets and sometimes brandished guns, the Black Panthers didn't necessarily advocate violence. Instead, they believed that black Americans could use their inalienable right guaranteed by the Bill of Rights to bear arms to protect themselves against police brutality.

- ✔ **Full employment:** The Black Panthers demanded that the government provide jobs for black Americans. Employment, they believed, would improve the standard of living in black neighborhoods.

On October 28, 1967, the arrest of Black Panther Party cofounder Huey Newton for allegedly killing white police officer John Frey became a turning point for the organization. Although the details are still sketchy, a jury convicted Newton of manslaughter, and he received a sentence of 2 to 15 years in prison. Convinced of Newton's innocence, the Black Panthers united in a "Free Huey" movement that turned Newton into a symbol of oppression and police brutality.

The transformation of SNCC

The appeal of black power and the Black Panther Party became apparent to SNCC's Stokely Carmichael, who had grown frustrated with the consequences of nonviolent tactics. A Freedom Summer veteran (see the earlier section "Targeting Mississippi for Voter Registration: Freedom Summer"), Carmichael's black power stirrings manifested itself during his participation in the James Meredith March Against Fear campaign.

James Meredith, who integrated Ole Miss in 1962 (refer to Chapter 8) with the assistance of federal forces, proposed a lone, 220-mile walk through Mississippi in June 1966 to encourage blacks to exercise their right to vote. Beginning his journey in Memphis, Meredith was barely a day into the march when a sniper, later revealed as a KKK member, shot him as he crossed the Mississippi-Tennessee border.

King, SNCC Chairman Carmichael, and CORE's new leader Fred McKissick flocked to Meredith's bedside to get his blessing to continue the march. Meredith agreed to their proposal. As the various civil rights groups prepared to continue the march, dissension emerged. CORE and SNCC participants denounced nonviolence, proclaiming that, if struck, they would strike back. SNCC's appeal to Louisiana's Deacons for Defense and Justice, a group of armed black men, many of them war veterans organized in 1964 to protect civil rights workers and activities, further demonstrated its more militant leanings. In addition, Carmichael wanted an all-black march.

Carmichael's insistence on an all-black march horrified the NAACP's Roy Wilkins; his arguments that nonviolent resistance had outgrown its usefulness disturbed Wilkins even more. Both Wilkins and the National Urban League's Whitney Young believed that marching without whites and abandoning nonviolence would mean suicide. Disgust for this new attitude among CORE and SNCC members prompted Wilkins and Young to leave Memphis. King stayed on the condition that CORE and SNCC participants adhere to his rule of nonviolence. Because King's presence guaranteed the media attention necessary to navigate Mississippi successfully, participants agreed.

In Greenwood, Mississippi, the nonviolent agenda changed when a SNCC member yelled "Black Power" to a crowd of black Mississippians, and they shouted back in approval. Arrested in a June 16 rally in Greenwood, Carmichael emerged from jail and publicly revealed his newly adopted militant attitude. "We been saying 'freedom' for six years," he quipped, "and we ain't got nothin. What we gonna start saying now is 'Black Power!'" Like before, the crowd responded approvingly.

Carmichael went on to coauthor a book entitled *Black Power* and briefly affiliated himself with the Black Panther Party in Oakland, California. Although blacks in both the North and the South had grown impatient with nonviolent resistance, race relations in the North began to take center stage.

Race Relations in the North

While the South seemed to move forward, race relations in the North were an enigma. Although free of signs segregating black from white, racial discrimination manifested itself in the North primarily through African American unemployment. Police brutality was also a problem in the North, but television cameras didn't capture these transgressions like they did in the South. In many ways, the Watts riots in Watts, California, shifted national attention from the obvious racial problems in the South to the less obvious, but just as virulent, problems in the North.

Rioting in Watts

On August 11, 1965, when a police officer stopped Marquette Frye in urban Watts, California, a riot was the farthest thing from his mind. As he and Frye bantered back and forth, a crowd gathered. Concerned, the officer called for backup. Matters intensified when Frye's mother showed up. Eventually police arrested the entire Frye family (Frye's brother had been in the car with him when he was stopped). Even with a crowd gathered, there were reports that the situation appeared to be resolved. As with most riots, however, definitive details leading up to the actual eruption of violence are sketchy. What's clear, however, is that the Watts riot surprised the nation.

For six days, homes and businesses burned or fell to looters. As the National Guard and police tried to contain the violence, some rioters retaliated with guns. After the smoke cleared, 34 people, mostly black, were dead. The injured list numbered another 1,000 with police arresting an estimated 4,000. Property damage ranged from $50 million to $100 million. Martin Luther King, Jr., took note and took the movement "up south."

The Chicago Freedom Movement

As the nation pondered the cause of the riots in Watts, Martin Luther King, Jr., decided that black America's urban centers also needed him, and he turned his attention to Chicago. Perhaps Chicago's appeal to King rested in its growing population of Southern blacks, its active black clergy, its strong political leadership, its organized unions, and its liberal white community.

In 1966, King, supported by other civil rights organizations, launched the Chicago Freedom Movement (CFM), which brought the civil rights movement north. King even moved himself and his family to a neighborhood on

Chicago's West Side. Discriminatory housing practices such as *redlining,* unfair economic practices based on race that included denying loans to African Americans to keep them from living in certain areas, served as the CFM's main target.

King attempted a strategy of marches, sit-ins, and boycotts in Chicago. Much like white Southerners, white Northerners also used violence such as throwing rocks in resistance to any efforts to end racial inequality. In addition, Chicago Mayor Richard Daley was as formidable a foe as any mayor or governor King had faced in the South. Added to the Watts riots, King's difficulties in Chicago forced him and the nation to acknowledge that racism wasn't just a Southern problem but a national problem. The difference in the North, however, was that no signs pointed out the lines.

Before King left Chicago, however, city officials signed the ten-point agreement intended to strengthen laws such as the city's 1963 open housing ordinance and other measures that addressed housing discrimination in Chicago. Realtors agreed to become more open-minded while lenders agreed to practice more equitable lending. Because the agreement was more self-policing and lacked an emphasis on outside enforcement, many considered King's and the CFM's efforts a failure. Those with a more realistic view of the national impact of racism, however, recognized that the battle was long-term.

The Poor People's March

Although King had once remarked that taking a broad approach to segregation in Albany during the Albany Movement contributed to his failure there (refer to Chapter 8), he ignored those earlier concerns with the launch of the Poor People's Campaign in 1967. A broad-based movement, the Poor People's campaign sought to address poverty in the U.S. Unlike the civil rights movement of the 1950s and early 1960s, the Poor People's Campaign wasn't black and white — it was all shades and colors. Economic inequality replaced racial inequality as the main culprit for unrest. To bring attention to the plight of America's poor, King proposed another march on Washington, dubbed *The Poor People's March.* This effort led to his fateful trip to Memphis in March of 1968.

At the behest of friend and colleague Rev. Billy Kyles, King led a march on March 28, 1968 in Memphis in support of striking sanitation workers. Unfortunately, not all the 6,000 demonstrators followed King's nonviolent tactics. When someone broke a window, violence erupted, with police using nightsticks, mace, tear gas, and gunfire to restore order. At the end of the scuffle, 16-year-old Larry Payne lay dead of a gunshot wound. With 60 people injured and another 280 arrested, the state legislature issued a 7 p.m. curfew.

Four thousand National Guardsmen also moved into Memphis as an added precaution.

On April 3, King returned to Memphis and delivered one of his most fiery speeches, in hindsight a foreshadowing of his own death. "We've got some difficult days ahead," he told the crowd. "But it doesn't matter with me now. Because I've been to the mountaintop. And I don't mind. Like anybody, I would like to live a long life. Longevity has its place. But I'm not concerned about that now. I just want to do God's will. And He's allowed me to go up to the mountain. And I've looked over. And I've seen the promised land. I may not get there with you. But I want you to know tonight, that we, as a people will get to the promised land."

Death of a King

Very few people doubt that Martin Luther King, Jr., knew that his days were numbered. The fates of other figureheads and leaders in the civil rights movement — particularly the murders of Medgar Evers and President John F. Kennedy in 1963 and Malcolm X in 1965 — greatly clarified the risk that accompanied King's work. Even after battling Alabama's notorious Bull Connor and enduring repeated jailings and assaults, King pressed on, lending his leadership and influence to efforts in Chicago and Memphis. He seemed unfazed by or perhaps resigned to the prospect of death.

The night of his death and the mourning after

On April 4, 1968, at the Lorraine Motel in Memphis, King stood alone on the second-floor balcony. At around 6 p.m., a single shot hit him in the neck. King's longtime friend Ralph David Abernathy was among the handful who immediately rushed to his side. At 7:05 p.m., not even a full hour later, doctors at St. Joseph's Hospital pronounced him dead. Before the night's end, President Johnson addressed the American public on all major networks and urged unity in this time of crisis. A national day of mourning followed.

For many Americans, especially African Americans, more than King died on that motel balcony that fateful night. In no less than 60 cities, including Chicago, Washington, D.C., and New York, African Americans lashed out in violence as the reality of King's assassination sank in. Civil disorder was so high that as many as 40,000 regular and National Guardsmen filtered throughout the nation. Some cities adopted curfews to curtail the violence.

Nationwide an estimated 46 died. Injuries were as high as 3,000, but authorities arrested many thousands more mostly for looting.

Instead of canceling his appearance before a black audience in Indianapolis, presidential hopeful Bobby Kennedy bravely informed the crowd of King's death. "We can do well in this country," he told the crowd, trying to restore hope. "We will have difficult times; we've had difficult times in the past; and we will have difficult times in the future. . . But the vast majority of white people and the vast majority of black people in this country want to live together, want to improve the quality of our life, and want justice for all human beings that abide in our land."

On April 9, Jacqueline Kennedy, Vice President Hubert Humphrey, U.S. Supreme Court Justice Thurgood Marshall, and other dignitaries descended on Atlanta to attend King's funeral. An estimated 100,000 people walked behind King's body during the funeral procession, and millions more watched the event on television.

Continuing his work

Those closest to King, despite their grief, bravely marched to tie up some of King's loose ends. On April 8, just days after King's assassination, Ralph David Abernathy and Coretta Scott King led a silent march of 20,000 through Memphis in support of the Memphis Sanitation Workers' Strike, the cause that brought King to Memphis in the first place. The 65-day strike ended with a bittersweet settlement just 8 days later.

That May, as the SCLC's new president, Abernathy tried to keep King's Poor People's Campaign alive by establishing Resurrection City, where more than 2,000 people of varying ages and races camped out near the Lincoln Mall. The optimism of Resurrection City ended with the news of Robert F. Kennedy's assassination on June 5.

Two days following King's funeral, Congress passed the Civil Rights Act of 1968. Most people know Title VIII of the act as the Fair Housing Act. It is significant because it prohibited discrimination based on "race, color, religion, or national origin" in selling or renting property. It also made designating any preference in advertising the rent or sale of a property based on race, color, religion, or national origin illegal.

Despite this victory, the civil rights movement was never the same. So many people had given their lives for freedom and equality. Black America was at a crossroads. King's assassination was a hard blow. Only time would tell if America's deepest scars would heal.

Chapter 10

Where Do We Go from Here? Post–Civil Rights and Beyond

*M*artin Luther King Jr.'s death, discussed in Chapter 9, put the civil rights movement in limbo. As the leadership struggled to regain its momentum, black power stepped up louder, with the Black Panther Party becoming the biggest beneficiary. However, its dominance wouldn't last long. It simply couldn't survive with its key leaders either behind bars or dead. At the same time, the Vietnam War presented other challenges.

If the 1960s were about dismantling the nation, for many, the 1970s were about trying to put it back together better than before. Like George Jefferson of the 1970s sitcom *The Jeffersons*, many African Americans were moving on up, with black elected officials heading cities and walking the halls of state legislatures and Congress, even in the midst of urban blight.

This chapter explores those changes plus the onslaught of crack cocaine in the 1980s, rising awareness of HIV/AIDS in the 1990s into the 2000s, and other challenges that continue to confront African Americans. It also reflects on the remarkable journey, heartbreaking and inspiring, that still fuels the drive to the final destination Martin Luther King, Jr., Malcolm X, Marcus Garvey, W.E.B. Du Bois, Ida B. Wells-Barnett, Booker T. Washington, Harriet Tubman, Frederick Douglass, and so many countless others fought so hard to achieve.

The Panthers Stumble

Black power rumblings began before King's death in 1968. During a march through Mississippi in 1966 with King, SNCC Chairman Stokely Carmichael announced his allegiance to a black power ideology. (Refer to Chapter 9 for details on Carmichael's rejection of nonviolence.) Carmichael, who later became Kwame Ture, formally affiliated with the Oakland-based Black Panther Party (BPP), an organization founded in 1967 by Bobby Seale and Huey Newton and linked to black power. In the late 1960s and early 1970s, the BPP, which coincidentally worked with many white activists, was the nation's most prominent representative of black power.

Huey Newton: A symbol of black oppression

The 1967 arrest of Huey Newton for allegedly killing a white police officer sparked a "Free Huey" campaign (flip back to Chapter 9 for more details). Newton and his impending trial came to represent the condition of black people everywhere. The truth of that belief wasn't lost on Newton; in his 1973 book *Revolutionary Suicide,* he wrote, "Every day they kept me there I grew as a symbol of the brutalization of the poor and Black as well as a living reproach to society's indifference to the inequities of the legal system."

Ample propaganda furthered the association. Newton's image and the "Free Huey" slogan showed up on flags, buttons, T-shirts, and posters. Curiously, Newton became a living martyr. King's death left a void that, in many ways, the fight to free Newton filled. Although there was no shortage of great causes to fight, there were few symbols to galvanize the public's interest. Newton became such a symbol.

The fall of the Black Panther Party

Ultimately, Huey Newton's incarceration and the notoriety of the Black Panthers became a detriment to the organization. Matters worsened when BPP cofounder Bobby Seale received an indictment as part of the Chicago 8, a group of activists accused of crossing state lines to incite rioting during the 1968 Democratic National Convention in Chicago. With both Newton and Seale out of the Panthers' active picture, the BPP began to change.

Soul on Ice

Although Eldridge Cleaver returned to the United States from exile in 1975 and renounced the Black Panther Party (BPP), most Americans remember him as a Black Panther because of his book *Soul on Ice,* released in March 1968. Cleaver's admission to raping black and white women helped fuel the many myths associated with the BPP. Other books such as *Seize the Time* (1970) by BPP founders Huey Newton and Bobby Seale, and former BPP president Elaine Brown's *A Taste of Power* (1992) offer more balanced insight into the BPP.

Eldridge Cleaver and the party's growing association with violence

Eldridge Cleaver, more radical than either Newton or Seale, seized control of the BPP. An ex-convict who joined the Panthers after spending time in jail, Cleaver advocated confrontations with the police and, in 1968, was involved in a shootout with police. When that incident threatened to put him back in jail, he fled to Algeria.

Even though self-defense was clearly the BPP's original intent, some unfortunate incidents suggested otherwise. When George Jackson, who established a BPP chapter at California's Soledad Prison, and two other prisoners were charged with murdering a prison guard in retaliation for the murder of a friend, Jackson and the case gained notoriety when his younger brother Jonathan snuck guns into a California courtroom. Jonathan, along with the two Soledad prisoners in the courtroom, took the judge and four others hostage before being gunned down later.

The case also brought national attention to Angela Davis, a college professor and member of the Communist Party. Registration for Jackson's guns traced back to Davis, a friend unaware of his plans. Still Davis spent 18 months in jail without bail and eventually received an acquittal in 1972. Guards at California's San Quentin Prison killed George Jackson in 1971 for allegedly trying to escape.

During the legal trials of Newton and Seale, the Black Liberation Army, a more violent group comprised of many ex-Panthers, emerged. They engaged in many confrontational and violent activities between 1970 and 1976. Unfortunately, many people associated this group's actions with those of the Black Panthers.

Fred Hampton, a murder in Chicago

Attracted mainly by the BPP's Ten Point Plan, a bill of rights–like manifesto you can read more about in Chapter 9, Fred Hampton joined the Panthers in

1968 and helped establish a successful Illinois chapter before the end of the year. Committed to community development, Hampton's key successes included:

- ✔ Spearheading the signature Black Panther Party Free Breakfast for School Children Program in Chicago. (The first program was established in January 1969 in Oakland to provide nutritious breakfasts to black schoolchildren.)

- ✔ Establishing a free medical center and implementing door-to-door sickle cell anemia (an inherited blood disorder largely affecting people of African ancestry) testing.

- ✔ Brokering a peace pact among Chicago's gangs to form what he called a *rainbow coalition,* a term that Jesse Jackson would later use for his own organization (see section "Making political strides in the '70s"). Because the BPP previously had numerous run-ins with the Blackstone Rangers, one of Chicago's biggest gangs, the pact was even more of an achievement.

Chicago police cut Hampton's good deeds short on December 4, 1969, during a special raid on the apartment (also a BPP headquarters) Hampton shared with Deborah Wilson (Akua Njeri), who was pregnant with his child. The murder of two Chicago policemen allegedly by the Black Panthers a month earlier prompted the raid, which left Hampton and fellow Black Panther Mark Clark dead.

Changing focus: Embracing nonviolence and women's rights

By the early 1970s, the BPP became a nonviolent organization that began to work within the system for social change. Seale, who had beat the charges against him, ran for mayor of Oakland in 1973. Although he lost, his strong showing was encouraging. Other BPP members also ran for office, and the BPP successfully supported the election of other African Americans to political offices.

In 1974, another murder accusation against Newton, who had been cleared of his earlier charges, prompted him to flee to Cuba, where he lived in exile for three years before eventually receiving an acquittal. Elaine Brown succeeded Newton to become the BPP's first female president that same year. Committing the party to women's rights initiatives (you can read more about the African American women's movement in the later section "Arn't I a Woman, Too?"), Brown led the BPP until 1977.

Throughout the 1980s and, in some instances, until the year 2000 when prominent attorney Johnnie Cochran finally succeeded in securing BPP political prisoner Geronimo Pratt's release, cases involving BPP activity dating back to the 1970s and 1960s continued. In 1989, Newton became a victim of urban crime and died of a gunshot wound in Oakland. Bobby Seale still works with youth. Although the BPP faltered in the late 1970s, its legacy and spirit lives on, especially in Oakland.

Further investigations and COINTELPRO

Police claimed that they killed Hampton and Clark in response to shots first fired by the Black Panthers. Since militant quotes by Hampton in the *Chicago Sun-Times* had already put white Chicago on guard, the police account only confirmed their perceptions of the Black Panthers as armed thugs. Yet subsequent investigations revealed that, of the 99 shots fired that day, only one came from the Panthers.

In 1975, the Church Committee (nicknamed for its leader, Idaho Senator Frank Church) uncovered information about the FBI's Counter Intelligence Program (COINTELPRO), confirming African American suspicions about FBI interference in the affairs of the Black Panthers, as well as those of civil rights leader Martin Luther King, Jr., among others.

Fighting Vietnam

Starting in the mid-1960s, the Vietnam War was a hot-button issue for many Americans. The conflict began when Vietnam split into two factions: communist and noncommunist. Although President John F. Kennedy first sent military advisors into Vietnam before his 1963 assassination, the number of American troops escalated during Lyndon B. Johnson's presidency, and their advisory role ended. With mounting fatalities, no exit strategy in place, and no visible American gain to the war's outcome, college campuses across the nation bustled with antiwar activity, which continued until the war finally ended.

In accordance with President Harry Truman's executive order desegregating the military, by the end of the Korean War in 1950 the military was almost completely desegregated. Consequently, more African Americans served in the Vietnam War than in any other war preceding it.

An unfair fight

Deferments for college attendance and certain civilian occupations favored privileged white Americans. Project 100,000, a Great Society program initiated in 1966 that offered more lenient entrance requirements to bolster military forces, only increased those disparities. An estimated 41 percent of the 350,000 new enlistees were African Americans, mainly from poverty-stricken areas. Even more disturbing, 40 percent of those enlistees drew combat assignments and suffered twice the casualty rates of other military enlistees.

Overall African American casualty rates constituted almost 20 percent of all combat deaths between 1961 and 1966; African Americans, however, only comprised 13 percent of the U.S. population and 9 to 10 percent of the military. The numbers were so high that the military worked hard to bring them down and, by the time the war finally ended in 1975, the 12.5 percent overall black casualty rate was a vast improvement. At the same time, African American military personnel had also increased significantly. In 1976, African Americans constituted 15 percent of the military.

Reacting to the war

The Black Panther Party (BPP) vehemently opposed war in Vietnam. Their Ten Point Plan demanded "an immediate end to all wars of aggression." Specifically, the BPP objected to African Americans serving and dying in disproportionate numbers (refer to the preceding section), especially since their own country treated them poorly. Not surprisingly, the Student Nonviolent Coordinating Committee (SNCC) and the Congress of Racial Equality (CORE) also opposed the Vietnam War. Martin Luther King, Jr.'s public opposition to the Vietnam War was surprising, however, and very unpopular among the civil rights mainstream.

King, who had won the Nobel Prize for Peace in 1964, shocked many when he linked his opposition of the Vietnam War to the civil rights movement and attacked President Lyndon Johnson's administration directly in an April 1967 speech entitled "Declaration of Independence from the War in Vietnam," also known as "A Time to Break Silence." For King, the resources used for the Vietnam War could be better used to fight poverty.

The New York Times denounced King, as did Bayard Rustin, Ralph Bunche, and Jackie Robinson, among others. The NAACP and National Urban League worried that opposing the Vietnam War would adversely affect funding for civil rights initiatives. When Johnson admonished King, telling him to stick to civil rights, King refused to alter his position, which won him respect with black power stalwarts even though they still disagreed with his nonviolent approach.

Coming home

Once at home, many black Vietnam veterans publicly supported the war and defended themselves against antiwar protestors, a lonely position given that, unlike in previous wars, discharges from Vietnam were staggered, so veterans couldn't defend themselves or the war in large numbers. It also didn't help that, in Vietnam, some soldiers became addicted to heroin while others became alcoholics — a sad scenario that resulted in a stereotype that many veterans resented.

Clarence Thomas hearings, 1991

Conflicts between black women's dual allegiance to race and gender came to a head in 1991 during the Senate confirmation hearings of Clarence Thomas for a seat on the Supreme Court.

During the hearings, black law professor Anita Hill, who worked under Thomas at the Equal Employment Opportunity Commission, was villified by many African Americans for testifying that Thomas made sexually inappropriate comments to her during their working relationship. Hill, who received considerable support from white women, was accused of being a pawn to block the ascension of a black man.

Arn't I a Woman, Too?

From the mid-1960s to the early 1970s, black women were in a difficult position. Between the civil rights and feminist movements, where did they fit in? They had been the backbone of the civil rights movement, but their contributions were deemphasized as black men, often emasculated by white society, felt compelled to adopt patriarchal roles. When black women flocked to the feminist movement, white women discriminated against them and devoted little attention to class issues that seriously affected black women, who tended to also be poor.

Historically, black women have chosen race over gender concerns, a choice that was especially poignant during Reconstruction when African American female leaders such as Frances Ellen Watkins Harper supported the Fifteenth Amendment giving black men the right to vote over the objections of white women suffragists.

Black women have a long feminist tradition dating back to 19th-century activists such as Maria W. Stewart and Sojourner Truth as well as organizations like the National Association of Colored Women's Clubs (NACWC) and the National Council of Negro Women founded in 1896 and 1935 respectively. The 1960s and 1970s, not to mention black men's changing attitudes regarding the role of black women, peaked awareness around new concerns such as race, gender, and class, and several organizations attempted to address these issues:

✔ **The ANC (Aid to Needy Children) Mothers Anonymous of Watts and the National Welfare Rights Organization (NWRO):** Johnnie Tillmon was an early pioneer of addressing the concerns of poor black women. A welfare mother living in Los Angeles's Nickerson Projects, Tillmon helped found ANC (Aid to Needy Children) Mothers Anonymous of Watts in 1963. She was later tapped to lead the National Welfare Rights Organization (NWRO), founded in 1966. Through these organizations, Tillmon addressed such issues as equal pay for women, child care, and voter registration.

✔ **Black Women's Liberation Committee (BWLC):** Student Nonviolent Coordinating Committee (SNCC) member Francis Beal was one of the founders of the Black Women's Liberation Committee (BWLC) in 1968. In 1969, Beal helped clarify the struggles of black women in the influential essay "Double Jeopardy: To Be Black and Female" that also appeared in the landmark 1970 anthology *The Black Woman,* which ushered in a new wave of black female writers (read more about this literary movement in Chapter 14). Beal identified capitalism as a key factor in the chasm between black men and women. During the early 1970s, the BWLC evolved into the Third World Women's Alliance.

✔ **National Organization for Women (NOW):** Reverend Dr. Anna Pauline (Pauli) Murray is a cofounder of the nation's most prominent feminist organization, the National Organization for Women (NOW), founded in 1966.

✔ **The National Black Feminist Organization:** While many black women remain active in mainstream feminist organizations only, other black women have created organizations aimed at addressing black women's unique concerns more effectively. The National Black Feminist Organization launched in 1973 with the specific goal of including black women of all ages, classes, and sexual orientation. Although it and similar organizations didn't outlive the 1970s, the legacy of black feminism lives on.

In 1983, Alice Walker coined the term *womanism,* a feminist ideology that addresses the black woman's unique history of racial and gender oppression. Women such as Angela Davis, law professor Kimberlé Crenshaw, academics Patricia Hill Collins, Beverly Guy Sheftall, and bell hooks, and historians Darlene Clark Hine, Paula Giddings, and Deborah Gray White have greatly expanded the context in which black women and their history and activism is discussed by underscoring black women's issues related to race, gender, and class.

A Race to Office

African Americans voted in unprecedented numbers after the passage of the 1965 Voting Rights Act, and African American politicians became the main beneficiaries. From the mid-1960s into the 1970s, black politicians became congressmen, state legislators, and mayors in record numbers. By the end of the 1980s, both Chicago and New York had elected black mayors. Jesse Jackson also made two historic presidential runs. Carol Mosley Braun, the nation's first black female senator, took office in 1993, but the 1990s, especially during Bill Clinton's presidency, became defined more by historic African American appointments, a trend that has largely continued into the 2000s. The following sections offer a few highlights of the political power that the legendary activist W.E.B. Du Bois advocated in the early 20th century.

The Congressional Black Caucus

In January 1969, African American members of the House of Representatives, including Shirley Chisholm, Louis Stokes, and William L. Clay, founded the Democratic Select Committee, which became the Congressional Black Caucus in 1971. Functioning primarily as a lobbying group to the larger Congressional Democratic Party, the caucus focuses on issues affecting African Americans. It launched with nine members; in 2005, that number had reached 43.

Registering black voters became an essential strategy for electing black officials. In addition, the success of black politicians — such as Oscar DePriest, the first black politician elected to serve in Congress in the 20th century, and New York's firebrand Congressman Adam Clayton Powell, Jr. — was significantly influenced by the Great Migration, the mass relocation of African Americans from the South to the North. Large black voter turnout helped these men secure victory, a lesson that wasn't lost on black politicians in the late 1960s and into the 1980s.

Getting a foot in the door in the '60s

In the late 1960s, black politicians got the ball rolling by winning a number of key elected positions.

- ✔ In 1966, Massachusetts's Edward W. Brooke III, a Republican, became the first black politician elected to the U.S. Senate since Reconstruction. Black female politicians Yvonne Braithwaite Burke in California and Barbara Jordan in Texas won offices within their respective state governments.

- ✔ In 1967, black mayors Richard B. Hatcher and Carl B. Stokes headed the Midwestern cities of Gary, Indiana, and Cleveland, Ohio.

- ✔ In 1968, more blacks than ever were elected to their state legislatures, and to top it off, Brooklyn's Shirley Chisholm became the first black woman elected to Congress. Nationwide, 370 black politicians won elections that year.

Making political strides in the '70s

In the 1970s, black elected officials flourished. Organizations such as the Black Panther Party embraced the political process as a significant agent of change for black America.

Wisely, African Americans cut their teeth on smaller offices before tackling bigger jobs. Because so many had participated in civil rights organizations, they were already familiar with government bureaucracy. Julian Bond, for example, went straight from SNCC to the Georgia legislature, and Andrew Young, a close aide of Martin Luther King, Jr., served as a congressman, the mayor of Atlanta, and a U.S. ambassador.

As important as serving in a federal office was, black politicians also exerted considerable power by leading major cities. The 1973 elections of Coleman Young and Maynard Jackson as the first black mayors of Detroit and Atlanta were important milestones. That same year, Thomas Bradley's election as mayor of Los Angeles offered more promise, because unlike Atlanta and Detroit which had sizeable black populations, Los Angeles was only 15 percent black. Bradley's win signaled that some white Americans were willing to elect black officials to major positions.

Eyeing a bigger prize in the '80s

With more African American mayors, state legislators, and congressmen in office, civil rights leader Jesse Jackson began eyeing the presidency. He also helped usher in a new concept in African American politics by building a coalition among African American, Latino, gay, and other voting groups. Although he was the second African American to mount a nationwide presidential campaign (Congresswoman Shirley Chisholm became the first in 1972), the Operation PUSH (People United to Save Humanity) founder surprised numerous political pundits when he placed third in the Democratic primaries in 1984.

During Jackson's second run in 1988, he won an unprecedented 11 primaries, and by the time he reached the Democratic National Convention in Atlanta, he was a serious candidate to win the nomination. Despite a stirring speech in which he commiserated with the nation's poor, he failed to capture the nomination; yet he brought much-needed dialogue to national politics.

Similar to King's Poor People's Campaign (refer to Chapter 9), the National Rainbow Coalition, which Jackson established in 1985, strives to bring all races together on a variety of issues, including employment, fair housing, and affirmative action. In 1997, Operation PUSH and the National Rainbow Coalition merged to form the RainbowPUSH Coalition.

Still thriving in the '90s and 2000s

President Bill Clinton, who received a large majority of the African American vote and is dubbed, by many, the nation's first black president, appointed five African Americans, including Ron Brown as secretary of commerce and

Hazel O'Leary as secretary of energy, to his cabinet in 1993. Despite an overall decrease in black presidential appointees during George W. Bush's administration, Colin Powell did become the nation's first African American secretary of state in 2001; Condoleezza Rice, who succeeded him, became the nation's first African American female secretary of state in 2005.

One issue that emerged among African Americans during the 2004 presidential campaign was the disenfranchisement of African American men. Due to felony convictions, which affect a disproportionate number of African American men, as many as 13 percent of the African American population have lost their right to vote. Still the political future looks bright for African American candidates. In 2006, Deval Patrick became Massachusetts's first black governor and only the second one elected in the nation's history. At the top of 2007, when Barack Obama, the only black senator in Congress, joined the presidential race for 2008, political pundits welcomed him as a Democratic candidate to watch.

Money, Money, Money

Well over a century ago, Booker T. Washington encouraged African Americans to concentrate on economic empowerment over political empowerment. Since the civil rights victories of the 1960s, however, it's not a question of gaining one at the expense of the other. Increasingly, African Americans have used political power to address the economic inequities racism has created. For almost fifty years, affirmative action has been one of the main strategies used to address those inequities. Undoing the long term effects of systematic racist practices such as *redlining,* charging African Americans more to live in certain areas or not granting them loans to live in others, hasn't been easy. Redlining has historically reduced African American homeownership, a proven determinant of wealth. Because African Americans possess less wealth individually and as a community, surviving economic hardships such as unemployment becomes more difficult.

In *The Hidden Cost of Being African American: How Wealth Perpetuates Inequality* (2004), sociology professor Thomas M. Shapiro found that economic inequities persist in the United States because white Americans tend to inherit and generate more wealth than African Americans. Discriminatory housing practices have prevented African American homeowners who live in largely African American neighborhoods from accumulating significant wealth in their homes; in recent years, as more white Americans have moved into traditionally black neighborhoods in cities all across the United States, home equity has soared. At the same time, higher prices have displaced African Americans, fueling rates of homelessness in some instances. Conditions such as these, argues Shapiro, create disparities that aren't easily solved through programs that increase African American income.

Working toward economic equality

Government has played a significant role in trying to reverse the adverse effects of racism on African American wealth in years past. Roy Innis, who took over the Congress of Racial Equality (CORE) in 1968, was one of the first civil rights activists to advocate government assistance, such as providing government loans to encourage black entrepreneurship. In the late 1960s and 1970s, Jesse Jackson led economic boycotts to increase black employment at businesses black consumers supported.

Eyeing a bigger slice of the pie for African Americans, Jackson turned his attention to corporate America in 1996 with the Wall Street Project. The project's two main goals are to increase the number of nonwhite executives working in corporate America and to expand contracting opportunities for nonwhite firms.

Black-owned businesses

Spurring African American businesses has become the theme for the 21st century. During the 1990s, companies such as Texaco, Coca-Cola, and Denny's Restaurants paid out huge settlements for mistreating African American consumers and/or employees. More recently, companies have created partnerships with African American businesses to reinvest in black neighborhoods. Former NBA star Magic Johnson, who has succeeded in partnerships with Loews Movie Theatres and Starbucks in particular, is a great example. *Empowerment zones,* areas (particularly in urban communities) that yield tax breaks and other incentives to companies and individuals that invest in them, have helped spark economic growth in once-depressed urban communities.

Historically, black-owned businesses have succeeded by filling a void ignored by mainstream businesses. Publications such as *Ebony, Black Enterprise,* and *Essence* exist precisely because white publications overlooked African American consumers. Similarly, Robert Johnson, credited as the nation's first black billionaire, launched Black Entertainment Television (BET) in 1980 to service black consumers. Radio One founder Cathy Hughes, along with her son Alfred Liggins, has built an African American media empire that includes 70 radio stations and the cable network TV One.

Today, many mainstream companies are buying into or swallowing companies that service the African American market. In the 1990s, cosmetic conglomerates such as L'Oreal bought into black-owned companies like Soft Sheen. Viacom purchased BET in 2000. Time Warner, which owns *Time Magazine,* became sole owner of *Essence* in 2005. Mainstream companies have also formed alliances with leading African American personalities to capture the black consumer market. Southwest and McDonald's are just two companies that have enjoyed a lengthy partnership with leading black radio personality Tom Joyner, who helms *The Tom Joyner Morning Show*. In the 21st century, both black entrepreneurs and mainstream companies respect African American buying power, estimated at $847 billion in 2007.

The Unforeseen Enemies

During the mid-1980s and 1990s, two unforeseen enemies — crack cocaine and HIV/AIDS — hit African American communities hard. Crack cocaine ravaged black neighborhoods in innumerable ways while the HIV/AIDS epidemic simply confounded African Americans. Following is a brief synopsis of these two formidable enemies.

Crack cocaine

Illicit activity has historically plagued poor African American communities. Until the 1980s and 1990s, however, such activity remained a significant subculture. Crack cocaine changed that. During the 1980s and early 1990s, crack cocaine devastated the African American community. Suddenly, crack addicts and crack pipes were household terms among African Americans. Drug dealers, in some communities, became more common than buses.

When street gangs began selling crack, conditions worsened as crack cocaine found a wider national network. Studies estimate that crack hit Detroit in 1985, New York and Los Angeles in 1986, and Chicago in 1988 before expanding to smaller cities in the 1990s.

Labeled "the poor man's cocaine," crack, a derivative of powder cocaine, could literally be mass-produced into rocks that created a powerful high when smoked. Because the drug could be cooked up in the kitchen and packaged for sale in large numbers, the number of drug dealers and crack users escalated very quickly. Highly addictive, crack usage resulted in broken homes as "crackheads" lost control and lost their jobs. This course of events greatly undermined the economic stability of many African American households and neighborhoods:

✔ **Neighborhoods under attack:** The Reagan administration's massive social service cuts and the demise of manufacturing jobs allowed crack cocaine distribution to grow. As unemployment rates surged, hitting African American men especially hard, greater distribution networks for crack cocaine generated unbelievably large sums of money. Soon enough, disputes over territory and other factors generated massive violence. Urban neighborhoods became war zones as homicide rates skyrocketed.

Dangerous accusations

Many in the black community have long insisted that, since African Americans don't own the planes and boats that ship cocaine into the country or manufacture guns, the government has to be involved in trafficking drugs to the inner city. In August 1996, the *San Jose Mercury* published "Dark Alliance," staff writer Gary Webb's three-part investigative series alleging that Nicaraguan drug traffickers supplied cocaine to Los Angeles drug dealers in the 1980s. Webb contended that the CIA knew that the profits from such activity helped fund the Nicaraguan Contras, which the Reagan administration supported in its fight against the Sandinistas, Nicaragua's ruling party and a Cuban ally. Numerous outlets, including *The Washington Post,* attacked Webb's claims. Webb published his book *Dark Alliance* in 1999 and included declassified documents related to the story. In 2004, Webb died from two gunshot wounds to the head.

According to one source, black males aged 14 to 24 comprised only 1 percent of the population in the mid-1990s but were 17 percent of homicide victims and 30 percent of homicide perpetrators.

✔ **Sad fate for many African American males:** As the drug trade grew, African American males became increasingly entangled in the legal system for drug possession, drug dealing, homicide, and a plethora of other offenses, many of them nonviolent. One study reports that, between 1979 and 1990, the percentage of African Americans admitted to state and federal prisons increased from 39 to 53 percent of all offenders. Probation tied another significant portion of black men to the legal system. While most black men worked or attended school and weren't engaged in illicit activity, the growing numbers of incarcerated black men were still alarming.

Prior to 1980, African American males, ages 18 to 24, in college greatly outnumbered African American males in the same age range in prison. In 2000, the ratio of black men in college was roughly 2.6 to every incarcerated black man in the same age group. The number for white males in the same age group was 28 to 1.

✔ **Effect on families:** Single-parent households in African American communities were already on the rise prior to the advent of crack cocaine, but crack cocaine added to the problem. High incarceration rates among black males and unbelievably high homicide rates increased the numbers of single-parent households. Teenage pregnancy rates complicated matters more. All these factors further stressed overall African American economic viability.

✔ **Class wars in the black community:** Often fleeing drug war zones, wealthier African Americans relocated to the suburbs. This move deepened class issues within the African American community, which was

> traditionally comprised of African Americans of all classes. At no other point in American history, however, had African Americans been so prosperous. Some have argued that the disappearance of these role models made drug dealing and drug use more appealing to black youth.

The tide is turning. Statistics show that outrage in the African American community, antiviolence campaigns, youth programs, and other initiatives have made a difference since the late 1990s. Homicide and other crimes, as well as crack cocaine use and drug dealing are down significantly.

HIV/AIDS

During its initial discovery in the 1980s, most viewed HIV/AIDS as a disease that afflicted white, gay men. Although an HIV/AIDS epidemic began hitting the African continent hard in the late 1980s, few suspected that the African American community was at great risk. For most, the 1993 AIDS-related death of tennis great Arthur Ashe, who contracted HIV through a blood transfusion, was an isolated incident. Two years earlier, however, NBA great Earvin "Magic" Johnson did generate some concern when he announced that he was HIV-positive. The 1995 death of West Coast rapper Eric "Eazy-E" Wright reportedly from AIDS-related complications was another indication that heterosexuals were also at risk of contracting HIV/AIDS.

Numbers for the 2000s are startling. According to the Centers for Disease Control and Prevention (CDC), African Americans accounted for 50 percent of all new HIV/AIDS cases in 2004. Seventy-three percent of the infants diagnosed with HIV/AIDS that year were African American. In 2002, HIV/AIDS was among the top three causes of death for African American men aged 25 to 54 and one of the top four causes of death for African American women aged 25 to 34. The HIV/AIDS epidemic has seen particular growth in the African American teen population.

Although unsafe sexual practices is a big reason African Americans have suffered high rates of HIV/AIDS infection, many have placed much of the blame on *down-low* (a term popularized by R&B artists in reference to furtive heterosexual relationships originally) men who appear heterosexual but engage in bisexual sex. Given the traditional homophobic attitudes in the black community (read more about this in Chapter 11) plus incidents of faithful wives and girlfriends who contracted HIV/AIDS from their "committed" partners, a mass hysteria developed among African Americans. The *Oprah Winfrey Show* even dedicated an episode to the down-low phenomenon and the HIV/AIDS crisis. J.L. King, the author of *On the Down Low: A Journey into the Lives of 'Straight' Men Who Sleep with Men,* was a primary guest.

Several organizations specifically addressing HIV/AIDS in the African American community exist. One of the oldest is the Los Angeles–based Black AIDS Institute founded by Phil Wilson, a gay man who has lived with HIV/AIDS for more than 25 years. The Black AIDS Institute mobilizes black media and black institutions such as churches to acknowledge the HIV/AIDS epidemic in order to prevent its spread. It also provides the latest information on treatment and government funding. BET's "Rap It Up" campaign enlists African American celebrities such as singer Mary J. Blige and rapper Common for public service announcements that encourage African Americans, especially teenagers, to take an HIV test.

The Racial Divide

Several events in the 1990s indicated that opinions held by black and white Americans on race differed greatly. Two of the most explosive events occurred in Los Angeles — the 1992 L.A. riots and the 1995 O.J. Simpson verdict. Riots in other cities such as Cincinnati in 2001 showed that L.A. wasn't an isolated incident. The 41 shots NYC police officers fired in the 1999 death of Amadou Diallo and the more recent 50 shots NYC police officers fired in the death of Sean Bell a day before his wedding are further evidence that police brutality still exists. In addition, the 1998 dragging death of James Byrd, Jr., in Texas proved that some Americans still harbor deep racial hatred. For many Americans, black and white, the local, state, and federal response to the many African Americans standing atop roofs following Hurricane Katrina had racial and class undertones unacceptable for the 21st century.

L.A. riots

Charges of police brutality in Los Angeles largely went unheard until the Rodney King incident. Rappers and political activists had long charged that the Los Angeles Police Department was out of control. Proof wasn't delivered, however, until a wayward video camera captured the brutal police beating of Rodney King by four LAPD officers (three white and one Hispanic) in March 1991.

As news programs around the nation broadcast the footage, few figured that any jury would acquit the four officers. In April 1992, when a mostly white jury in predominantly white Simi Valley did just that, the predominantly black area of South Central Los Angeles erupted in violence within hours. Two days later, the violence, which included rampant looting, reached its highest intensity but continued for almost a week before the California National Guard and federal troops quelled the disturbance.

Between 50 and 60 people lost their lives; as many as 2,000 suffered injuries. News cameras caught black youth brutally beating white truck driver Reginald Denny. Authorities arrested nearly 10,000 people, mostly African American and Hispanic. Property damage estimates ranged up to $1 billion with over

1,000 buildings destroyed. Korean merchants suffered greatly, but so did African American business owners.

Latasha Harlins's death also played a role in the riots. Two weeks after King's brutal beating, a security camera captured a Korean shop owner Soon Ja Du fatally shooting and killing Harlins for allegedly stealing. Du's suspended sentence, 400 hours of community service, and five-year probation angered African Americans. Therefore, black Los Angeles was responding to the overall judicial disregard for African American life.

The O.J. Simpson verdict

Perhaps few other incidents illuminated racial chasms better the O.J. Simpson verdict. One of the nation's most popular celebrities at the time, former pro athlete Simpson was charged with the murder of his ex-wife Nicole Brown Simpson and her friend Ron Goldman, both white, in June 1994. Simpson spent a reported $4 million on his legal team that included African American attorney Johnnie Cochran. Christopher Darden, another African American attorney, worked for the prosecution. The defense's accusation of the LAPD planting evidence gained credence when police office Mark Fuhrman testified under oath that he'd never used racial epithets yet was later heard on audiotapes doing otherwise. A glove found at the crime scene became another prominent feature of the case when it didn't fit Simpson's hand. In his closing argument, Johnnie Cochran told the jury, "If it doesn't fit, you must acquit," and that's exactly what happened on October 3, 1995.

Racial perceptions make Simpson's acquittal significant. White Americans felt Simpson was guilty but acquitted because of his money and celebrity status. While many African Americans didn't disagree with that conclusion, they weren't outraged by the verdict; instead, they felt that Simpson simply bought his acquittal as wealthy white men in similar positions had done for years. To this day, mainstream white circles ostracize Simpson; although there are African Americans who believe he is guilty, very few have ostracized him. Simpson, however, has been his own worst enemy in regards to dispelling any doubts that he committed the double murders. His proposed 2006 book *If I Did It* generated such a public outrage that the publisher's parent company refused to release the completed book.

A modern-day lynching

Unfortunately, random violence against African Americans persisted into the latter half of the 20th century. Perhaps most brutal was the 1998 dragging death of James Byrd, Jr., in Jasper, Texas. Byrd accepted a ride home from three white men who severely beat him, chained him to the back of their truck, and dragged him about 3 miles, severing his head.

Unlike decades before, however, justice was swift, as two men received the death penalty and one received life in prison. In response to the crime, some Texans pushed for the passage of hate crime legislation which then-Governor George W. Bush opposed. In 2001, the Texas legislature passed the James Byrd Jr. Hate Crimes Act. The bill underscored intolerance for crimes motivated by factors such as race and sexual orientation by enhancing penalties for these crimes. Again, this was a strong and positive change in race relations.

Hurricane Katrina

Most of the nation watched news broadcasts stunned as Hurricane Katrina, a Category 3 storm (downgraded from Category 5), ravaged New Orleans and the Mississippi Gulf Coast in August 2005. As television news crews and others entered New Orleans to cover the story, people began to question why the Federal Emergency Management Agency (FEMA) wasn't already on-site doing something. When the levees broke, most Americans couldn't believe their eyes as day after day fellow Americans, overwhelmingly black and impoverished, stood on rooftops seeking refuge from the high water.

During the first critical days, their cries for helped appeared largely ignored. Days later when help finally arrived, New Orleans's African American Mayor Ray Nagin and Louisiana's white female governor played the blame game. In the midst of all this, African Americans in particular began asking, "Where is Bush?" Rapper/producer Kanye West expressed the unspoken thoughts of many African Americans when he stated, "George Bush doesn't care about black people," during a live telethon.

Although more African Americans than white Americans believed that race and class motivated the government inaction on all levels, Hurricane Katrina did bring more mainstream attention to those issues. The media referencing of fleeing New Orleans residents as "refugees" instead of "evacuees" or in its portrayal of hungry African Americans as looters and white Americans as "finding food" opened up much-needed discussions about race and class in America. *The New York Times* even apologized for not addressing poverty in New Orleans during most of its coverage of the crescent city.

Black and white Americans responded to the needs of Hurricane Katrina survivors quickly. Ordinary American citizens have rallied around New Orleans in ways the government and insurance companies haven't. While race and wealth disparities persist, the United States has come a mighty long way from slavery. The journey has been rocky, but inspiring as well. Instead of seeing the glass as half-empty, we have to look at it as half-full, knowing that we are free to add more water at any time.

Part IV
Cultural
Foundations

The 5th Wave   By Rich Tennant

"When did we stop saying 'amen' and start
giving the 'wave?'"

In this part . . .

What it means to be African American is a complex issue. From family life and stereotypes to traditions, religion, and education, African American culture is wholly unique.

This part introduces you to various aspects of African American life as well as focuses on the faith and education, which have been the cornerstones of African American life both in slavery and in freedom. You discover that, before freedom officially came, African Americans had already begun establishing their own churches, and after emancipation, the black church rose to even greater prominence, standing at the forefront of many of black America's most transformative events.

Regarding education, this part explains how African Americans pursued it fiercely and relentlessly used their educations in the fight for freedom. You come to understand that education has proven a heated battlefield in recent years, with debate raging on the issues of affirmative action, how failing public schools affect the futures of African American children, and what the future holds for Historically Black Colleges and Universities.

Chapter 11

Something Borrowed, Something New: Becoming African American

In This Chapter

▶ Fostering family ties

▶ Examining the position of black women

▶ Breaking down stereotypes

▶ Influencing language and food

▶ Celebrating unique and traditional holidays

*T*wo schools of thought dominated the study of African American culture in the 20th century. African American sociologist E. Franklin Frazier argued in several works, including *The Negro Family in the United States* (1939), that slavery destroyed any vestiges of African culture and that African American culture mimicked European American culture. White anthropologist Melville Herskovits, with his influential *Myth of the Negro Past* (1941), countered Frazier's view, arguing that African American culture contained important retentions from West African culture. As the study of African American culture has expanded, more scholars have weighed in on the issue with most opinions falling between the two camps, acknowledging that African American culture is a tenuous hybrid with both African and European or Western influences.

This chapter presents general overviews of several aspects of African American culture, including family life and culture, gender roles and sexuality, and elements of broader American culture like language, food, and holidays. In examining these topics, I trace their roots and changes through the decades, in some cases from slavery to the present.

Black Families, from Past to Present

Two types of family structure existed in Africa: matrilineal and patrilineal.

- ✔ **In the matrilineal system,** men took on prominent roles but derived their leadership through the female lineage. In the clan system of government favored by many African societies, for example, a woman's eldest brother usually headed the community. Women didn't belong to their husbands' families but rather remained a part of their own; husbands had to ensure good treatment of their wives and were required to compensate the family in some form. Children belonged to the mother in this system, with the eldest brother, not the father, assuming responsibility for them. Also, it wasn't uncommon for women and their children to reside with their mothers, away from their husbands.

- ✔ **In the patrilineal system,** which traced power through the male's lineage, women traditionally had less power. Bearing male children, especially an heir, increased a woman's power, sometimes conferring on her the status of Queen Mother in those societies that had chiefs or kings.

Both matrilineal and patrilineal societies shared common characteristics:

- ✔ **Polygamy:** Although polygamy was found in both types of society, it wasn't a universal practice. Often a family helped finance a man's first marriage, but he had to bear the expense of taking on additional wives. Polygamy wasn't necessarily a sexual structure. Polygamous unions meant more adults and potentially more children to share the workload, which appealed greatly to agricultural societies. Marrying biological relatives wasn't an option; therefore, Africans rarely sought marriages within their own family group.

- ✔ **The importance of external kinship relationships:** Extended families were an important part of the African family structure. Marriage in many African cultures didn't result in a nuclear family. Even in polygamous relationships, an extended family existed beyond the structure of husband, wife or wives, and children. Parenting wasn't a solo affair, as extended family members cast a watchful eye over how children were raised. Biological mothers didn't necessarily have more authority over children than extended family members, exemplifying the African proverb, "It takes a village to raise a child," which inspired the title of Hillary Clinton's 1996 best seller. This structure also allowed for the care of the elderly, a highly respected population in African culture.

- ✔ **Egalitarian roles:** Even by contemporary Western standards, early African civilizations were very egalitarian, particularly in West Africa, the region from which many American slaves hailed. Men and women took on roles, especially in the household, that generally complemented one another. Unlike in Western cultures, it wasn't uncommon for some African men, particularly those who lived in the forest, to care for the children while the mothers hunted. In some African societies, women held important positions in government, science, and agriculture, and it wasn't unusual for women to step up militarily if needed. Queen Nzinga (1583–1663), for example, ruled a kingdom and led armies in what is now Angola. Female merchants also helped expand early African trade locally and internationally.

The slave trade disrupted these traditions of African culture and family. As African slaves were brought to the Americas, how well (or even whether) they were able to preserve parts of their African culture largely depended on where they ended up.

Family structure in Latin America and the Caribbean developed quite differently than it did in North America. Because large groups of Africans from the same or similar clans weren't uncommon in Latin America or the Caribbean, it was slightly easier for Africans to create a family structure more similar to what they had known previously. That was rarely the case for Africans in North America, where it was customary to separate Africans of similar cultural groups from the moment they arrived. In addition, enslaved Africans in North America rarely resided in one area or with one owner for a lifetime.

An exception was South Carolina, which had a black majority because of the need for slaves skilled in rice cultivation. Because the terrain was too harsh for whites, a black majority not heavily supervised by whites developed. This circumstance was more conducive to preserving old traditions as well as creating new ones, which resulted in *Gullah* culture prominent in coastal South Carolina and Georgia. Scholars in various disciplines have examined Gullah culture to understand the African influence on African American and general American culture better.

Marriage

Because the colonists required more brute force during slavery's early years, men greatly outnumbered women. As slavery grew, the gender balance improved. Enslaved Africans, as many scholars have demonstrated, valued family life. Initially, slaveholders didn't encourage slave marriages; this stance changed, however, when the slave trade became illegal. Slaveholders encouraged slave marriage not to address the companionship needs of their slaves but to replenish their slave supply. They also found that families often increased productivity while at the same time decreasing the chances of a slave running away.

HISTORICAL ROOTS

Jumping the broom

Although ample evidence, largely from former slaves, indicates that the practice of jumping the broom was common during slave weddings, the origins of the tradition are unclear. Both Danita Roundtree-Green, in her book *Broom Jumping: A Celebration of Love* (1992), and Hariette Cole, in her book *Jumping the Broom: The African-American Wedding Planner* (1993), link the slave ritual to Africa. Ghana is the African country frequently cited for the ritual's origins. Folklorist Alan Dundes, in his 1995 *Journal of American Folklore* article "Jumping the Broom: On the Origin and Meaning of an African American Wedding Custom," linked the practice to Gypsies in Scotland and England, suggesting that jumping over the broom, which is often a symbol of witchcraft, represented love conquering evil. Considering that European slaveholders likely attended ceremonies in which the practice was performed for that reason, it's possible they introduced the ritual to African Americans. Uncorroborated speculation claims that the Moors introduced the Scottish and English to the practice. Regardless of its origin, contemporary African Americans have embraced the tradition, often culminating their wedding ceremonies by jumping the broom.

The high number of marriages between slaves from different plantations, however, dismayed some slaveholders, presumably because of its potential threat to productivity. Many captured runaways, for example, were often visiting spouses on other plantations. To discourage this practice, slave owners encouraged marriage between their own slaves and even served as matchmakers. In addition, it wasn't uncommon for free blacks, particularly men, to marry slaves and later purchase their spouses' freedom.

Generally, slave marriages weren't legally recognized, but slaves honored them as did many owners. Frequently, slave marriage ceremonies ended with the couple *jumping the broom,* a practice in which the couple literally jumped over a broomstick (see the sidebar for more). Being married, however, didn't shield husbands and wives from being sold separately. Slave auctions frequently separated husbands from wives and parents from children (discussed in the next section).

During the Civil War and after, legal marriages became a priority for many former slaves. Some sought legality because of religious beliefs. Others simply wanted to make their unions uncontestable. Nonetheless, this practice showed how much former slaves valued matrimony. In the early 20th century, African Americans, like all Americans, continued to value marriage. Divorce, however, wasn't as stigmatized in the African American community as it was in the white community, especially for women.

Discipline

During slavery and afterward, African Americans, especially Southerners, typically disciplined their children more harshly than nonblack parents disciplined their children, mainly because the stakes for blacks were extremely high. A sharp word, any kind of slight, or almost any act against a white person of any age could result in bodily harm or death. Black parents practiced tough love in order to save their children's lives.

Although life in the North, in terms of racism, wasn't as rigid as it was in the South, African American children there faced restrictions as well. Parents had to communicate to their children many unspoken rules. African Americans typically addressed white men and women as either Mr. or Mrs., although it was perfectly acceptable for white people, even children, to call an elderly African American by his or her first name. Looking a white person directly in the eye or addressing any white person first carried harsh penalties in certain areas that could even lead to death. As in slavery, parenting black children was akin to walking a tightrope. That tenuousness only continued into the 1960s and beyond.

Parenting

Neither slave mothers nor fathers exerted complete control over their own lives or the lives of their children. Because the law viewed them and their children as property, slaveholders held ultimate authority over them all.

With the constant threat of a slave auction separating families, slave mothers were particularly sensitive to the fate of their children, especially their sons since male slaves were more valuable than females. Members of the slave community tried to comfort mothers who lost their children through auctions. Whenever slaveholders sold mothers, adopted "aunts" and extended family cared for the children left behind.

After emancipation, reuniting with separated loved ones was top priority for most African Americans. Runaway slaves returned South hoping to find their family members. Those who could read and write posted ads in black newspapers for lost family members. Those who couldn't read or write often paid others to post ads for them. Many African Americans adopted orphans as their own as well as cared for older people who couldn't care for themselves and didn't have family to help them. Interestingly, since Mississippi was the final destination for many slaves, it had particularly strong slave families.

Motherhood

During slavery, motherhood was hard for black women in many ways. Pregnancy didn't necessarily yield any breaks. Pregnant women still worked in the fields, with some giving birth there. Forced to endure hard physical labor during pregnancy, many slave women suffered miscarriages. Stillbirths were also pervasive. Pregnancy didn't prevent slaves from being whipped if their pace slowed.

Although some women received time to recuperate from childbirth, few slave women spent substantial time with their children. In the eyes of the law, a slave's duty to her master took precedence over her responsibility to her own children. If a child was born sickly, a slave mother frequently couldn't care for him or her. Still worse, slave masters forced many slave women to nurse white children with milk intended for their own children. Many children denied the care of their mothers died. Infant mortality rates were at least twice that of white babies. Enslaved mothers took motherhood very seriously and were far less likely than men or childless women to escape to freedom and leave their children behind.

Mothers spent as much time as they could with their children. Some women picked cotton with their babies strapped to them. As the children became older, it wasn't uncommon for children to work alongside their mothers in the field or in the main house. Slave children with present mothers frequently spent a considerable amount of time with their mothers in spite of slavery's many restrictions, but as in Africa, raising children was a communal enterprise, especially on large plantations.

After emancipation, black women spent more time with their children but considerably less than white women. Many black women, as free black women had during slavery, worked as domestics, often caring for their family and their employers' family. Still mothers took charge of their children's education and moral instruction.

Fatherhood

If being a slave mother was hard, slave fathers fared little better. They spent even less time with their children, even if the same slave master owned them. Fathers living on different plantations from their families saw their children even more infrequently. Slave records rarely acknowledged the slave father. Only the mother and child's name appeared, presumably to hide the numbers of slaveholders who fathered children with their slaves.

There's plenty of evidence that black men made great strides to parent, even with extreme limitations. Slave narratives written by men often reference children, frequently describing the heartbreak of either leaving them behind or having them sold away from them. Just as enslaved women stepped in as surrogate mother figures, enslaved men also stepped up as father figures.

Parenting during slavery was challenging. Slave fathers couldn't protect their children from whippings. They couldn't shield their daughters from sexual assault. Those realities, however, didn't prevent many of them from trying. Sometimes slaveholders shipped fathers off to avoid such confrontations. Except in instances where male slaves served as studs to father the children of several women, there's little evidence to suggest that enslaved black men didn't take fatherhood seriously. That sense of responsibility was even stronger among free black men.

Numerous accounts exist of men purchasing their wives, children, and mothers out of slavery. Many of these men worked diligently for years to save enough money to do so. Some statistics referencing African Americans as slave owners (and there were a few) don't distinguish between actual slave owners and those who purchased family members and freed them.

During Reconstruction, men assumed a greater role in their children's lives. Many even stepped up and cared for children they didn't father. Economic opportunities for black men were still sparse. Many times black men had to leave their families in order to provide for them. As in slavery, a large number of black men demonstrated their willingness to care for their children and others.

Childhood

Slaves had very short childhoods because simple chores such as bringing water to the fields or serving as a playmate to the master's children began at an early age. Mothers, in particular, tried to prepare their children for slave life as much as they could, and knowing the inevitable, many parents attempted to free their children. When the Fugitive Slave Act of 1850 passed and slaveholders intensified their efforts to return runaway slaves, some mothers such as Margaret Garner, the inspiration behind Sethe in Toni Morrison's *Beloved* (1987), chose to kill their children rather than return them to slavery.

Typically, between ages 8 and 10, enslaved children became aware of their status as mere property. For some who had spent a considerable amount of their childhood serving as playmates to their slaveholder's children, this realization was especially shocking. Others with cruel playmates weren't as overwhelmed. It wasn't unusual for slave owners who once handed out sweets to begin treating older slave children more cruelly. Even for children who received consistent warning, this change had to be unsettling. Most distressing, perhaps, was the fact that it was unlikely to change.

After emancipation, conditions did improve for African American children, but they were still far from ideal. Unlike in slavery, however, black kids could receive some schooling. Unfortunately, because of Jim Crow, that schooling was very limited. In Northern areas, though, black children had greater opportunities to further their education. For children in the South, particularly in rural areas, they were lucky to make it to the fifth grade.

Considering the great levels of poverty many African Americans experienced, children often found jobs as early as they could. While this wasn't an uncommon practice for many Americans, regardless of race, African American childhoods were still overwhelmingly short in comparison. As African Americans initiated the process of leaving the country for the city, the South for the North, black childhoods and black life in general became increasingly divergent.

Country or city?

In his pioneering study, *The Philadelphia Negro* (1899), W.E.B. Du Bois revealed that cities weren't as conducive to African American families as rural areas. Because rent was high and wages were low, Du Bois determined that African American city dwellers married later in life and, as a result, had fewer children. Many African Americans living in cities were lodgers. A large number lived alone. Parents often left their children behind in rural areas with family members, usually grandparents, until the parents could afford to move the children to the cities and care for them. Du Bois also found that more women in cities never married as opposed to rural areas.

During the Great Migration, as African Americans moved North in increasingly large numbers, the trends Du Bois noted about African American family life only worsened. Ironically, under Jim Crow, black families were common, mainly because agricultural work usually required large families. Although cities offered higher wages and promised greater opportunities, they took a disastrous toll on African American families that has reached into the 21st century. In many respects, the American concept of the welfare queen as well as fatherless homes is rooted in slavery as well as early urbanization.

Challenges for the modern black family

For a time, the migration North to industrialized cities such as Detroit, Chicago, Cleveland, Philadelphia, and New York yielded favorable results, contributing to the middle class model that emerged in many of those cities. Yet, from the late 1960s to the 1980s, city life became especially harsh for African American families, and the promise of the North disintegrated. Some contributing factors include the following:

- Factory jobs were lost in once-booming auto and steel towns.
- The number of two-parent families began to decline, and the number of single-parent households increased.
- High death rates and incarceration rates contributed to decreased family participation among black men.

As black families struggled to keep their heads above water financially, the government programs designed to assist families included regulations that denied help to intact families (that is, those with a male head of household). The problem became even more notable after the government released *The Moynihan Report*, which resulted in stereotypes about the black family that haven't gone away. Few can deny, however, that drastic changes have taken place with the black family and that the consequences have been dire. Declining marriage rates and the dwindling numbers of black fathers in the home go hand in hand.

The Moynihan Report and media response

Named for then Assistant Secretary of Labor Daniel Patrick Moynihan, *The Moynihan Report* was the federal government's attempt to examine the causes behind the rapid decline of black lower-income families, especially in the nation's urban areas. Although its intentions were good, after it appeared for public consumption in 1965, the welfare queen became the predominant stereotype of black women. Black and white media began focusing attention on the high number of single-parent households in the African American community, even before that type of household became a leading trend among all American households. In addition, white and some black media ignored the extended family relationships in African American communities. Two-parent households, especially among the African American middle class, which has expanded since the 1960s, and many Southern families aren't extinct, but they haven't received as much media attention.

Where's the ring?

Since the late 1960s, marriage rates for black women have steadily declined, with many never marrying. Marriage rates have also declined among African American men but not at the same rate as those of black women. More black men are unmarried by choice, while many African American women cite unacceptable or unavailable mates as the reason they didn't marry.

High incarceration rates among black men coupled with the lower numbers of black men seeking college and professional education are the two main reasons cited for the large percentage of unmarried black, female professionals. Although traditionally there are many examples of black women marrying black men with less education as well as lower earnings than themselves, recent opinion suggests that such men are unacceptable mates for professional black women, thus creating more tension between black men and women.

The higher numbers of black men married to non-black women also contribute to the problem, according to some perspectives. From 1960 to 2000, black men who interracially married increased sevenfold. Traditionally, black women, however, have been less likely to marry non-black men, but that has changed in recent years. Historically, moving past the sexual assaults many black women endured during slavery and Jim Crow has been one of the main taboos limiting marriage between black women and white men. In recent years, more black women have married outside their race, but the numbers are still relatively small.

Where's daddy?

One of the biggest points of contention in recent years for African Americans is the dearth of black fathers and other positive black male role models for African American children. Between 1970 and 1979, two-parent black households dropped by 25 percent. That trend continued into the 1980s and 1990s as unusually high murder and incarceration rates among black men have left a record number of black children fatherless.

While households with present fathers still exist and a number of black fathers not married to their children's mothers are active in their children's lives, their numbers are alarmingly low. These conditions have been especially dire for African American boys who drop out of school and are arrested, incarcerated, and murdered more than any other group of adolescents in the nation. Writer, activist, and educator Jawanza Kunjufu has been particularly active concerning this issue, publishing books such as the *Countering the Conspiracy to Destroy Black Boys* series and *Keeping Black Boys Out of Special Education,* but he isn't alone. Many black men have tried to remedy the situation through organizations such as 100 Black Men and Big Brothers/Big Sisters, in addition to becoming better fathers. Such efforts have made a difference, encouraging others to join and continue the cause for positive change.

The Role of Women

Black women have made great contributions to their own communities and beyond, but it hasn't been easy. Sexism and racism, along with poverty, has compounded black women's struggles. Yet despite a history mired by sexual exploitation and other injustices, few can debate the tremendous role black women have played in the foundation of African American life and culture.

Sexual exploitation and mores

Even before reaching American shores, black women endured sexual assault. On many slave ships, sailors forced female captives into sex. Black women frequently stood on auction blocks naked while prospective buyers freely fondled their breasts. Overseers and slaveholders molested female fieldworkers, but those working within the intimate confines of the master's household were at even greater risk. While the older black woman is the common image of the prototypical female house slave, the truth is many young women worked in plantation households, serving as playmates to the slaveholder's little girls before learning the domestic duties of cooking, sewing, and other household tasks. Such close proximity meant these young women were especially vulnerable to their masters' or other white men's advances.

"Slavery is terrible for men," wrote Harriet Jacobs in *Incidents in the Life of a Slave Girl,* "but it is far more terrible for women." Published in 1861, Jacobs's slave narrative was the first to address in grave detail the atrocities slave women endured. Because a number of men were products of rape, their slave narratives often mention this widespread travesty but lack the detail and perspective found in Jacobs's narrative. Unfortunately, Jacobs published her book too late for such atrocities to serve as primary motivators to abolish slavery.

Not all black women reconciled themselves to such treatment. Although it's hard to prove that black women were heavily involved in some of the more famous slave rebellions, it's reasonable to assume that they assisted those efforts. Some women aborted children fathered by their masters, and some slave women murdered their masters for unwanted sexual advances. Poisoning was common enough for South Carolina and Georgia, in particular, to pass laws issuing harsh punishments against such acts.

Black women couldn't legally defend themselves from rape of any kind, and white women rarely offered their sympathy. Some white women even blamed slave women for their husbands' actions, portraying black women as exotic temptresses with animalistic sexual desires that white men were powerless to resist. Some white women divorced their husbands on the grounds of their illicit activity with slave women. Still, Southern white women, arguably little better than slaves themselves, generally remained quiet. Ironically, while many white women questioned the moral standards of black women, black women — influenced by generations of fervent church involvement and in response to damaging white stereotypes — tended to be more sexually conservative than white women.

Even after emancipation, black women couldn't escape sexual exploitation. Those who remained mistresses to white men were not the norm; extremely active in the church, most black women fought hard to achieve "true womanhood," the moral standard of the day. The threat of sexual exploitation prompted many black women, who still worked in white households after slavery ended, to leave the South. Well into the mid–20th century, white men raped black women with very little recourse. As in slavery, black women possessed very few legal options.

Fighting for civil rights

After Reconstruction, black women became especially critical in civil rights efforts. Ida B. Wells-Barnett, Mary McLeod Bethune, and Mary Church Terrell were just three of the very powerful female leaders in the African American community at the end of the 19th century and into the early 20th century.

- ✔ **Ida B. Wells-Barnett** ignited the ire of Southern white men with her investigations of lynchings, revealing that white women were often the sexual predators of black men. (Read more about Wells-Barnett in Chapter 7.)

- ✔ **Mary McLeod Bethune,** who founded the National Council of Negro Women and a school that eventually became Bethune-Cookman College, was extremely active in African American affairs, calling national conferences and frequently visiting the White House during Theodore Roosevelt's presidency.

- **Mary Church Terrell,** an Oberlin graduate, educator, and prominent speaker and writer against segregation, fought for civil rights to the end of her life: At the age of 89, she participated in efforts to desegregate Washington, D.C., businesses.

- **Ella Baker,** during the civil rights movement of the 1960s, was a principal force in the Southern Christian Leadership Conference (SCLC) and later the Student Nonviolent Coordinating Committee (SNCC), which she nurtured.

- **Daisy Bates,** as an NAACP activist and newspaper publisher, was a pivotal figure in integrating Central High School in Little Rock, Arkansas, in 1957. (Find more information on the contributions of Ella Baker and Daisy Bates in particular in Chapter 8).

- **Pauli Murray,** civil rights activist and cofounder of the National Organization for Women (NOW), was one of the country's pioneering feminists.

Gender roles and black feminism

Even among those rare free black families where black women didn't have to work during the 19th and early 20th centuries, many still did. When African American men couldn't find employment, black women worked to help start businesses for their men in addition to establishing their own. After the Civil War, some black men insisted their women not work in an effort to duplicate the white patriarchal structure, but economic necessity quickly took over. Often, when black men couldn't secure employment, black women at the very least could work as laundresses.

In the early 20th century, black households still needed the extra income generated from black women working, making few black women homemakers only. While some black women worked as teachers, nurses, and business owners, many more worked as domestics and in other menial jobs. Despite the long history of black women working and playing an active role in black households and other institutions, however, black men during and following the civil rights movement in the 1960s increasingly demanded a more patriarchal family structure. These demands created considerable rifts between black men and women.

Black women who cast their lot with black men in the late 19th century didn't always find sisterhood among the white women in the revived feminist movement of the late 1960s and early 1970s. Their differing realities contributed heavily to that rift. Black women, for example, had always worked while many white women were still embracing working outside the home. For a number of black women, feminism didn't address their unique reality. Therefore, *womanism,* a feminist view associated with Alice Walker that incorporated black women's unique experiences and history, developed.

The fight for (and about) voting rights

Giving black men the right to vote through the passage of the Fifteenth Amendment in 1870 angered not only white Southerners but white women as well because they still didn't have the vote. Most black women, including prominent writer Frances Ellen Watkins Harper, cast their lot with their men and refused to agitate with white women for women's suffrage because they didn't want to risk the amendment not passing. But Sojourner Truth was different; she long maintained that black women needed the vote as much as black men.

At an 1867 meeting for the American Equal Rights Association (AERA), an organization founded by Susan B. Anthony, Elizabeth Cady Stanton, and Frederick Douglass, Truth said she feared that, if black men received the vote but black women didn't, the men would also be free to dominate black women. Douglass didn't disagree with women's suffrage; he just felt that securing the right for black men to vote was more vital. At an 1869 AERA convention, Douglass cited numerous examples of racial discrimination that made suffrage for black men more pressing. When someone noted that black women also endured such horrible indignities, he replied "Not because she is a woman, but because she is black."

Society's Two Strikes: Race and (Homo)sexuality

As it is in mainstream American culture, homosexuality is a hot topic in the African American community. Despite the great accomplishments of well-known African American homosexuals such as Langston Hughes, James Baldwin, and civil rights activist Bayard Rustin, African American homosexuals aren't fully embraced in the African American community.

The black church, according to many experts, has played a key role in shaping these attitudes. It's no secret that homosexuality's harshest critics frequently cite the Bible as justification for their condemnation of homosexuality. With much of African American culture based in the church, there's bound to be tension, even though Christianity itself is a doctrine based on love and acceptance. The alarming HIV/AIDS rates in the African American community are changing the discussion, as are leading black gay/lesbian activists Keith Boykin and Jasmyne Cannick who frequently challenge the black church and its leading voices about the condemnation of black homosexuals.

Although risky sexual practices (for example, not using condoms) is the primary cause of rising HIV/AIDS in the African American community, many have elected to blame the "down-low" phenomenon, where African American men who appear heterosexual purportedly engage in homosexual behavior, for the rising HIV/AIDS rates among African American women. This has created a greater divide between the African American community and black gay men in particular. Hip-hop, some argue, is the main culprit. Black men, as perpetuated in hip-hop music, project themselves as warriors, unable to show any weakness, especially in a society that seems to thrive on breaking them. Therefore, many in the black community associate homosexuality with softness and heterosexuality with hardness. As a result, homosexuality in itself becomes an attack on one's manhood instead of an alternative sexual reality.

Curiously, hip-hop, which disdains black male homosexuality, has embraced bisexuality among African American females in its many videos and rap lyrics. The African American community at large has historically rejected African American women who consider themselves lesbians. When Alice Walker published *The Color Purple* in 1982, she took a lot of heat for presenting images of lesbianism. Awareness of lesbianism or bisexuality in the African American community, particularly in entertainment, isn't uncommon; for example, female lovers have been associated with Ma Rainey, Bessie Smith, and Billie Holiday. Still, despite all the evidence of the great contributions African American homosexuals have made to African Americans in various arenas, there are very few prominent, openly gay African Americans, even in the 21st century.

The African American Image

The African American image has rarely been positive in the dominant American culture. Racist physical representations of African Americans such as blackface and exaggerated lips from the minstrel and vaudeville circuits were transferred into products and advertising during Jim Crow. As in slavery, white society relegated African Americans to childlike status, frequently calling them "boy" or "girl," especially in the South. Images of criminality continue to dog black men. The following sections briefly examine these stereotypes.

Black men: Lazy or dangerous

During and after slavery, white men in particular accused black men of laziness and perpetuated that stereotype, mainly through minstrel shows, literature, and film. White supremacists justified lynchings by portraying the African American man as incapable of controlling his sexual desires for white women.

Early film and television reinforced the lazy black man stereotype. Film star Stepin Fetchit, whose career height spanned from the late 1920s into the early 1950s, became the poster child for lazy black men. Since the 1960s, black men have become perennial criminals in popular culture. During the 1970s, for example, black men played pimps with alarming frequency. Some African Americans are dismayed that so many black men, especially rappers, have encouraged such images by embracing the pimp and hustler stereotypes found in the blaxploitation films of the 1970s (refer to Chapter 17). For them, that endorsement directly correlates to the number of black men frequently shown as criminals by the news media.

Although roles as black male professionals have increased in television and, most importantly, in real life, with prominent black men such as Richard Parsons and Kenneth Chenault leading esteemed companies such as Time Warner and American Express, the thug image predominates; some argue it's because of hip-hop, which seems to thrive on America's criminal stereotypes of black men. (For more on hip-hop, turn to Chapter 16.) As a result, stereotypes about the black male criminal are just as viable today as they were over century ago.

Black women: Mammy or sexpot, but not beautiful

During and after slavery, images of black women painted them as unattractive: from the sexless, forever nurturing, overweight mammy to the smoldering, promiscuous sexpot who seduced white men. Yet even as a sexpot, the black woman has not been considered beautiful by American popular culture.

A complex (ion) issue

Frequently society erected white women as the ideal beauty in contrast to black women. Prior to the civil rights and black power movements, black women with lighter complexions, who appeared closer to white, served as the standard for black beauty. Even as slogans such as "Black is beautiful" reigned and afros became more common, black women's beauty, especially for dark-skinned women, wasn't always reaffirmed.

The white community alone hasn't been guilty of these attitudes. African Americans themselves haven't always embraced black as beautiful. Black and white people frequently laud women resembling Halle Berry, who is biracial, as the epitome of beauty. Although music artist Lauryn Hill, who wore her hair in dreadlocks in the late 1990s, also received praise for her beauty from both the black and white community, her experience is still rare.

Most black women, however, don't receive similar reinforcement. *Essence* created a stir within the black community when Sudanese model Alek Wek graced its cover in 2000. Many African Americans charged that the jet-black Wek who wears short, natural hair, a bona fide supermodel, wasn't beautiful enough to grace the cover. In addition, several groups of black women have criticized rappers for not only exploiting black women's bodies but also perpetuating the stereotype of black women with light complexions and long hair (along with nonblack women) as the beauty ideal in their videos.

Hair story

Outside of skin color, hair has been black women's biggest beauty issue. Madam C.J. Walker, whom many erroneously credit for inventing the pressing comb to straighten black women's hair, frequently corrected people that hair care, not straight hair, was her main goal. Still, there's no denying that straight hair or "good hair," as many once called it, has been highly coveted in the black community. Black men even sported conks during the Jazz Age and, during the 1970s, pressed hairdos such as the one Ron O'Neal wears in the film *Superfly*.

The black hair-care industry, which includes products, salons, and real and synthetic hair, is a billion-dollar industry, and straight hair, whether achieved through perms, or long hair, usually accomplished through weaving, a process by which synthetic or real hair is woven into or attached to one's natural hair, is the industry's driving force. Lengthy discussions within the black community on this topic have yielded positive results, as the acceptance of natural hairstyles for women has increased in and outside the black community, with some black women in corporate America even embracing natural styles.

Countering stereotypes

African Americans have been extremely active in countering stereotypes, especially in regards to style and beauty.

Defining style

African American men and women have continually countered the frequent portrayal of them as poorly dressed by developing their own styles. Even during slavery, black people saved their best clothes for Sunday, their day off, a practice that continued in freedom. Frequently the black community praised those who dressed well, especially from the 1920s to 1950s, when male and female black entertainers, gospel singers included, dressed elegantly. During the 1960s and 1970s, black people created their own aesthetic with afros and brightly colored ensembles. Meanwhile black designers such as the late Patrick Kelly, Byron Lars, and Tracy Reese made tremendous inroads within the mainstream fashion industry during the 1980s and 1990s

The advent of hip-hop, with its signature baggy jeans, revolutionized popular culture by scoring with mainstream youth culture. Still, not everyone has accepted the hip-hop aesthetic. In recent years, the NBA instituted a "business casual" dress code in 2005, presumably to counter hip-hop's anti-corporate and "thug" image that players such as Allen Iverson helped popularize. Many argue that this code represents an effort to appease the NBA's rich, white, corporate fan base. Still, older African Americans such as Bill Cosby have also been outspoken opponents of hip-hop style and dress.

Reclaiming beauty

Black female writers such as Toni Morrison (with her 1970 novel *The Bluest Eye*) questioned black standards for beauty, including light skin and so-called good hair, and explored how they affected black women's self-esteem. Those and other questions also bolstered *Essence* magazine, which launched in 1970.

Unlike white women, black women haven't obsessed over becoming model thin. Full-figure comedian Mo'Nique, the force behind the show/pageant *Mo'Nique's F.A.T. Chance* for full-figured women, is a good example. While white Americans largely adopted 19th-century Europe's disdain for the large buttocks of the so-named Hottentot Venus, for example, African American men didn't. Rapper Sir Mix-a-Lot expressed this sentiment not-so-eloquently in his song "Baby Got Back" in 1991, and black men everywhere celebrated tennis champion Serena William's 2002 "cat suit" highlighting her assets.

Making a Mark on the English Language

Africans who arrived in what became the U.S. didn't have a standardized language; they hailed from various cultural and ethnic groups and consequently spoke various languages. That cultural gumbo peppered various English words and expressions with African roots, such as "tote" (from the Kikongo word "tota"), "banana" (from the Wolof word "banana"), and "cola" (from the Temne word "kola"). More important than African-derived words that appear in the English language are African-influenced speech patterns.

When the school board in Oakland, California, voted in 1996 to allow for the use of Ebonics in the school system to help African American children perform better in school, a nationwide controversy erupted. Coined by black clinical psychologist Dr. Robert Williams in 1973, *Ebonics,* derived from the words "ebony" and "phonics," includes various idioms and social dialects of black people. Lorenzo Dow Turner's *Africanisms in the Gullah Dialect* (1949) and the work of others revealed that African American speech was more than broken English and, like standard English, possessed discernible rules and patterns. More than slang, *Black English,* as some refer to it, contains consistent linguistic features, such as the following:

- **Dropped "r's" and the ending "ing":** For example, "summertime" may sound like "summahtime," and "tripping" becomes "trippin."

- **Stressed first syllables:** For example, "De-*troit*" becomes "*De*-troit."

- **Liberal use of the verb "to be":** For example, one may say "He been had that job," meaning, "He has had that job for a while."

The influence of jazz and hip-hop on language

Historically, African Americans have spiced up their speech and that has carried over. For example, 1970s "jive" owes a lot to the jazz lingo that preceded it. Expressions such as "bad" meaning "good" and "fly" meaning "great" are also found in the jazz lexicon. Hip-hop, whose once-popular "homeboy" and "homegirl" derived from references migrating Southerners applied to folks they encountered outside their hometowns, has pushed the boundaries even further; for example, the phrase "fa shizzle," which is associated with the rapper Snoop Dogg and means "for sure," has become a part of overall American culture. "Bling," from the 1999 rap song "Bling, Bling" by New Orleans rappers B.G. and the Hot Boys, appeared in the *Oxford English Dictionary* in 2003. Today, it's widely used to refer to luxury items such as diamonds and expensive cars.

Hip-hop has made language variety among African Americans more acceptable, and commercial media has helped disseminate that language. It's so pervasive that even politicians have been known to lift a few words and phrases! This is a dramatic turnaround from decades ago when African Americans suffered greatly for their speech. Today, more Americans accept that African Americans speak in a variety of ways. African American comedians, in particular, often peg those differences in their routines.

Much of what scholars know about African American speech patterns stems from research initiated in the 1940s of the Gullah/Geechee people located mainly in coastal South Carolina, where African Americans outnumbered white Americans. The strong cultural retention in this area has offered insight into African American culture overall, but has proved invaluable for tracking the language which many, including African Americans, have labeled "poor English."

Mixing Up Traditional American Food

Southern cuisine reveals the fact that Southern culture is highly influenced by African Americans. During slavery, African American women, not their mistresses, manned the kitchen. In their own modest quarters, they used spices to turn scraps into inviting meals and prepared similar dishes for their master's households. Subsequently, slaves, as well as poor and well-to-do whites, enjoyed similar preparations of collard greens, black-eyed peas, cornbread, and hominy (grits). To this day, for example, black and white Southerners start their New Year's with black-eyed peas and greens, two dishes intended to bring good luck and prosperity.

Some dishes trace their roots directly back to Africa. African slaves (specifically those from Ghana) in Louisiana introduced a thin fish stew with okra that evolved into gumbo. There's evidence that Africans, prior to coming to the Americas, fried some dishes in palm oil. Okra and yams are just two foods Africans are credited with bringing to North America.

Creating food empires

African Americans who migrated from the country to the city or from the South to the North during Reconstruction and beyond often longed for the food of their past. That desire birthed some of the black community's first strong businesses. In Harlem, Chicago, Philadelphia, Detroit, and other cities, gifted cooks parlayed their talents into formidable businesses that often attracted blacks and whites. Here's a sampling:

✔ **Sylvia's (New York):** For years, tours of Harlem were incomplete without a visit to Sylvia's for pork chops, collard greens, and macaroni and cheese, among other traditional soul food/Southern fare.

✔ **Harold's Chicken Shack (Chicago):** One of the nation's few African American–owned fast food chains, Harold's is best known for its fried chicken and distinctive barbecue sauce.

✔ **Roscoe's House of Chicken N' Waffles (Los Angeles):** The West Coast's most famous black-owned eatery, Roscoe's, as most call it, has served its legendary chicken wings and waffles combo since the 1970s to a variety of people that include politicians, singers, and actors.

✔ **Michele's Foods:** Michele Hoskins took a syrup recipe handed down to the women of her family from her great-great grandmother, who had been a slave, and built a multimillion-dollar business.

✔ **Glory Foods:** Before his unexpected death in 2001, William (Bill) Williams, along with cofounders Iris Cooper, Daniel Charna, and the late Garth Henley, captured the essence of African American–style cuisine in cans and bags with Glory Foods products, sold by various supermarket chains.

✔ **TLC Beatrice:** One of the biggest food coups in history was Reginald Lewis's buyout of Beatrice International in 1987 to form TLC Beatrice, a snack food, beverage, and grocery store conglomerate with sales sometimes exceeding $1 billion.

✔ **Barbara Smith:** A former model better known as B. Smith, Smith has built a lifestyle empire. Often dubbed the black Martha Stewart, Smith has restaurants in New York and Washington, D.C., the syndicated television show *B. Smith with Style*, and several cookbooks, including *B. Smith's Entertaining and Cooking for Friends* (1995).

With meat at a premium, slaves often used the few pieces they were allotted to flavor their vegetables, the cornerstone of the slave diet. Because food was scarce, slaves wasted almost nothing. Using scraps of slaughtered pigs, slaves turned chitterlings or chitlins, the pig's intestines, into a delicacy. Pot liquor, the liquid left in the pot from cooking vegetables and meat, became gravy. Stale bread became bread pudding. Very resourceful, a cook's skill in the kitchen placed her high in demand, so much so that whenever she fell ill, her owner got her immediate medical attention.

The term *soul food* refers to comfort food traditionally associated with African Americans, such as baked macaroni and cheese and fried chicken. In the 1960s, people used "soul" to reference almost everything related to African Americans, so the idea of soul food evolved from there. Soul food is usually an important part of family reunions, Thanksgiving, Christmas, and Easter.

Holidays and Special Gatherings

Holidays were few for enslaved Africans, but even within those confines, they created memorable celebrations. Some distinctive ones include the Pinkster Festival, Election Day, Juneteenth, Emancipation Day, and others.

Although many people have heard of Juneteenth, they are less familiar with the Emancipation Day celebrations many black communities held commemorating the day they learned of emancipation. In a few Midwestern towns that no longer have significant black populations, their state fairs evolved from such celebrations.

Celebrations during slavery

Because slavery was less restrictive in the North than in the South, slaves there enjoyed greater freedom. Two of the main celebrations for Northern slaves were the Pinkster Festival and Election Day.

✔ **Pinkster Festival:** Although it began as a Dutch religious holiday celebrating the Pentecost, Pinkster festivities evolved into considerably more for African Americans in New York. One of the few times enslaved Africans could feel independent, Pinkster, which typically occurred about a week after Easter, not only reaffirmed African Americans' cultural ties but also allowed them to reconnect with family and friends. Originally, King Charles, a slave who had been a prince in his country, supervised the expert dancing and merriment. Pinkster was so popular that the Albany, New York, government passed ordinances diminishing its importance.

Today, the state capitol of New York in Albany sits on the site that once hosted Pinkster celebrations. Philipsburg Manor in Sleepy Hollow, New York, continues the Pinkster tradition, with participants donning period garb.

✔ **Election Day:** A replica of colonial elections, Election Day, which also spread to outside areas such as Massachusetts, began in Connecticut around 1750 and continued in some areas for at least a century. African Americans took the opportunity to elect their own officials who governed the slave community, primarily settling disputes. Both serious and fun-filled, festivities culminated in an impressive parade. Historian William Piersen has argued that such celebrations helped shape the American parade tradition.

Those enslaved in the South had fewer opportunities to engage in formal celebrations. Because Christmas and Easter were consistently the only times Southern slave families could truly spend together, they became very big holidays among African Americans and continue to remain two of the most important family celebrations. Watch Night Services and Juneteenth are two communal celebrations associated with the South.

- ✔ **Watch Night Services:** The popular tradition of African Americans attending church on New Year's Eve has two historical inspirations. Prior to the end of slavery, slave owners tallied up their accounts for the coming year on New Year's Eve. If they came up short, they often sold off slaves. Consequently, New Year's Eve was often the last time some families spent together. This night took on added significance when African Americans gathered in churches primarily in the North December 31, 1862, to pray for President Lincoln's delivery of the Emancipation Proclamation (see Chapter 6).

- ✔ **Juneteenth:** Named for June 19, 1865, the day when slaves in Texas finally learned of the Emancipation Proclamation, festivals celebrating freedom's arrival sprouted almost immediately. Other festivals known as Emancipation Day Celebrations were also popular, but followed the same principle. Therefore, some were celebrated on May 8, others on August 8. Many of these celebrations discontinued around 1920. As African Americans migrated to bigger cities, argue some scholars, they rejected such freedom festivals as a reminder of the rural lives they wanted to escape. Today, Juneteenth festivals have once again become popular in various parts of the country.

Bud Billiken Day Parade

Some observers argue that both the Pinkster and Election Day spirit is present in Chicago's long-running Bud Billiken Day Parade. In 1923, Bud Billiken appeared in the pages of the black newspaper the *Chicago Defender* to communicate middle class values to the city's many Southern migrants. By 1933, the Bud Billiken Day Parade began electing "the Mayor of Bronzeville," Chicago's historic black community. Today, the Bud Billiken Day Parade, which has attracted stars ranging from Duke Ellington and Lena Horne to Muhammad Ali and LL Cool J, still features high-stepping bands and eye-catching costumes as well as some of Chicago's and the nation's most prominent African Americans in fields ranging from politics and business to music and film.

Creating new traditions

On March 23, 2000, Washington, D.C., Mayor Anthony A. Williams signed a bill making the District of Columbia Emancipation Day (which commemorates the April 16, 1862, bill that freed slaves in Washington, D.C.) a legal paid holiday for Washington, D.C., residents. While the District of Columbia Emancipation Day doesn't extend to all, the two biggest African American celebrations in the 20th century, Black History Month and the Martin Luther King, Jr., Day, went national a few decades back. Kwanzaa, a holiday celebrated from December 26 to January 1, has also grown in popularity.

✔ **Kwanzaa:** Created in 1966 by Maulana Karenga, a black studies professor at California State University, Long Beach, to counter the growing commercialism of Christmas, Kwanzaa derives its name from the Swahili phrase "matunda ya kwanza," meaning "first fruits." Kwanzaa is marked by seven principles: Unity, Self-determination, Collective Work and Responsibility, Cooperative Economics, Purpose, Creativity, and Faith. There are also seven basic symbols as well as a candelabrum that holds a candle for each day in the colors of red, black, and green, which come from the Pan-African flag created by Marcus Garvey's Universal Negro Improvement Association in 1920.

Celebrants stress that Kwanzaa isn't a substitute for Christmas but rather an affirmation of African American culture and values.

✔ **Black History Month:** Celebrated in February, Black History Month began as Negro History Week in 1926. Known as the Father of Black History, Carter G. Woodson wanted to bring attention to the African American contribution to American history. Woodson selected the second week of February for his celebration because both Frederick Douglass and Abraham Lincoln were born then. The holiday became Black History Week in the 1960s when the word "Negro" was no longer in fashion. In 1976, as the nation celebrated its bicentennial, Black History Week became Black History Month and has remained so since then.

✔ **Martin Luther King, Jr., Federal Holiday:** Michigan Congressman John Conyers originally proposed the King Holiday to Congress in 1968, just days after King's assassination. Spearheaded by King's widow, Coretta Scott King, the King Center began observing King's birthday in 1969. In 1973, Illinois became the first state to recognize and celebrate the holiday. President Ronald Reagan signed the bill, passed by an overwhelming majority of Congress, to make the Martin Luther King, Jr., holiday official in 1983, but formal recognition by the federal government didn't officially kick in until 1986. Still, some states like Arizona refused to recognize the holiday. By 1999, however, all states celebrated the national holiday, held on the third Monday in January.

Chapter 12

Somebody Say "Amen": The Black Church

In This Chapter

▶ Converting African slaves to Christianity

▶ Developing the black church tradition

▶ Blurring the line between politics and religion

▶ Exploring African American involvement in other religions

*E*arly African slaves weren't overwhelmingly Christian, but converting to Christianity didn't change African Americans as much as African Americans changed Christianity. As the first uniquely black institution in American culture, the black church is unparalleled in its impact on the overall development of African American culture. Historically, the black church has been more than a place of worship; it's also served as a community center, a relief society, and a political think tank, among other things.

This chapter traces the development of the black church back to the politics of Christian conversion and explores the church's emergence, its social impact and influence, its political backbone, and its shortcomings. It also acknowledges that while Christianity has ruled much of black America for centuries, not all African Americans were (or are) Protestant Christians. There's a reason black Americans have been solidly religious for centuries, and this chapter explains why.

Converting to Christianity

Differences between how white and black Americans worship haven't gone unnoted. The black church's divergence from European-based Christianity reflects the early religious differences between Europeans and Africans and the contrasting realities of life for black and white Americans, as well as the enduring legacy of retained characteristics of African religious practices.

Religion in Africa

Religiously, Africa has never been an inactive continent. Because religion is a focal point of most cultures, invading forces promoted their own religious beliefs. Initially, Muslims made the biggest impact on the African continent, particularly in West Africa, where a large percentage of African slaves to America came from. Islam, however, coexisted alongside distinctly West African religious practices. Coinciding with the onset of the transatlantic slave trade, Christian forces also made headway.

In the Caribbean and Latin America, religious practices such as Voudou (or Voodoo), Obeah, Santeria, and Candomblè prominently feature African deities and spiritual forces. Additionally, religious scholars have noted that Africans in Latin America and the Caribbean were able to accept Catholicism by substituting Catholic patron saints for their own African deities. Ultimately, these religious practices emphasize a personal connection to a guiding spiritual force (or forces). This sense of personal connection, many historians argue, is what drew Africans to Christianity in large numbers. Others have argued, however, that Africans had little choice but to convert to Christianity.

Early objections, early conversions

During the 1660s in New England, Puritan minister John Eliot argued that slave owners had a duty to provide religious instruction to their slaves. Eliot believed that teaching slaves to read the Bible expedited their Christian conversion. Slaveholders hesitated at the prospect, probably because slavery itself was a relatively new and unstable practice. Later, slave masters greatly feared that teaching slaves to read and interpret the Bible would incite rebellions. Nat Turner, the leader of one of America's most notorious slave rebellions, for example, was deeply religious (see Chapter 4 for more about him). Because many slaves achieved literacy through religious organizations, slaveholders associated slave insurrections with religious instruction.

Some baptized slaves successfully gained their freedom by challenging the lifetime enslavement of Christians, prompting some white religious leaders, like Rev. James Blair, a representative of the bishop of London in Virginia, to suspect that some slaves converted to Christianity purely in hopes of gaining freedom. "I doubt not," he wrote his superior in 1729, "some of the Negroes are sincere Converts, but the far greater part of them little mind the serious part, only are in hopes that they will meet with so much the more respect, and that some time or other Christianity will help them to their freedom."

To alleviate slaveholders' worries that conversion to Christianity could result in their slaves gaining freedom, colonial legislators passed laws stating that Christian baptism didn't alter one's slave status. By 1706, at least six colonial legislatures had passed such laws. Because African heathenism had once been one of the main justifications for African enslavement, such legislation was a major shift. Gradually, race alone became the backbone of American slavery.

Eliot continued his mission to convert slaves through religious education by promising slave masters that he would only teach slaves scriptures. Cotton Mather, his successor, appeased slave owners further with his 1693 leaflet, "Rules for the Society of Negroes." Working with slaves in Massachusetts, Mather used religion as a form of social control by twisting the Ten Commandments into a doctrine that demanded slaves accord their masters the same respect as God.

Still, many slaveholders objected, for purely capitalistic reasons, to the religious instruction of their slaves. To appeal to their profit-minded motives, some missionaries stressed that converted slaves worked more efficiently and therefore yielded greater profits. Tax incentives sometimes enticed slaveholders to allow spiritual instruction to their slaves.

Of course, slaves weren't always receptive to conversion attempts, preferring their own religious practices to those of their slaveholders'. It wasn't until the Great Awakenings that African conversion to Christianity gained momentum.

The Great Awakenings: Called to convert

The First Great Awakening, a religious movement in the 1730s and 1740s that began in New England, radicalized religion by making it more personalized. Suddenly individuals could exert some control over their own salvation. They were also encouraged to express their emotions. The Second Great Awakening occurred during the 1820s and 1830s.

Distinguished by their revival style, a very novel concept at the time, the Great Awakenings, especially the first one, had a lasting impact on African Americans even though the movement's main messengers, Jonathan Edwards, George Whitefield, and Gilbert Tennent, were white. These leaders noticed almost immediately the impact their meetings, often held outside to accommodate large numbers of attendees, had on African Americans. Leaders such as Samuel Davies, a minister who became president of the College of New Jersey (Princeton), actively evangelized blacks.

Historians have argued that the Great Awakenings had such a profound effect because their fervent worship style and emphasis on a personal relationship with God meshed with core African religious beliefs. Despite the multitude of languages and cultures that existed among enslaved Africans, common threads allowed them to bond with one another. When the First Great Awakening emerged, they were able to embed their existing beliefs into a form of religious expression that was acceptable to whites.

The rise of plantation missions coincided with the Second Great Awakening. Advocates such as Charles Colcock Jones contended that rural slaves weren't receiving proper religious instruction and appealed to various religious and secular parties, including slaveholders, to remedy the situation with plantation missions. As abolitionism gained momentum, plantation missions became a complicated proposition. Slaveholders worried about slaves receiving the same religious instruction as whites. They also feared that religious instruction encouraged rebellions. To ease their concerns, plantation missions ministered to slaves orally. Its advocates also reminded plantation owners that religious instruction could teach slaves discipline and encourage obedience. Southern Methodists made the biggest inroads with plantation missions.

Christianity, African American–style

Culturally, African American Christianity has distinctive features. Like Europeans, West Africans in particular believed in an ultimate supreme being, but, unlike Europeans, lesser deities aided their supreme being. Scholars believe that, in Latin America and the Caribbean, Catholicism's patron saints replaced African deities. Christianity, scholars argue, resonated with African Americans for a variety of reasons. Already the concept of a supreme being correlated with similar African religious beliefs.

Black liberation theology

Although some argue that the concept of the Trinity — God, Jesus Christ, and the Holy Ghost — attracted African Americans to Christianity, others believe that the Bible's biggest selling point became the many circumstances that approximated the African American experience of slavery. C. Eric Lincoln, one of the foremost authorities on the black church, observed in his seminal work with Lawrence H. Mamiya, *The Black Church in the African American Experience,* that African American Christianity places a "symbolic importance" on the concept of freedom. It wasn't hard for African Americans to believe that they were God's chosen people who would be led out of bondage. Very few African Americans, enslaved or free, accepted slavery as the natural order. Just because death assured freedom didn't mean that one couldn't achieve it while living.

During the 1970s, James H. Cone, author of the groundbreaking *Black Theology and Black Power,* formalized this concept of freedom and became a leading proponent of *black liberation theology.* Cone argued that, for black people, Christianity should reflect their unique experience of oppression. Cone advocated a communal approach to Christianity for African Americans, rejecting a focus on the individual. He also encouraged African Americans to view God in their own image. In many ways, Cone just reconfirmed how African American Christianity had functioned for a few centuries.

Viewing God as African American wasn't an entirely new concept. Speaking before the turn of the 20th century, African Methodist Episcopal Bishop Henry McNeil Turner made it clear that African Americans "have as much right biblically and otherwise to believe that God is Negro." Certainly, there had been others before him, as well as those like Marcus Garvey and others after him, who expressed similar sentiments.

Music for the soul

Music is one of the most distinguishable aspects of African American Christianity. Many historians trace African American music and dance back to the *ring shout,* a religious ritual that is the oldest documented African performance style in this country. Typically performed after formal worship, the ring shout, which includes two groups, shouters (or dancers) and singers, organized in a circle, exemplifies two key characteristics of the black church and black music:

- ✔ **Call-and-response:** The leader sings (or calls) and the group responds. African American preachers often perform the same function with their congregations during sermons. They also tend to speak rhythmically, using their voice in ways similar to vocalists that many scholars cite as a precursor to rap.

- ✔ **Use of rhythm:** Slaveholders banned drums after the Stono Rebellion in 1739 (see Chapter 4), so clapping and foot tapping provided the rhythm considered essential to African music. Often performed in unison, songs themselves embodied the communal nature of many African cultures, especially since freedom served as a major theme in early spirituals. (Read more about African American music in Chapter 16.)

Building and Sustaining the Black Church

The African Baptist (or "Bluestone") Church, founded on the William Byrd plantation near the Bluestone River in Mecklenburg, Virginia, in 1758, could be the first established black church in America, but that distinction frequently goes to the Silver Bluff Baptist Church in Beech Island, South Carolina. Silver Bluff's offshoots, the Springfield Baptist Church in Augusta, Georgia, and the First African Baptist Church in Savannah, Georgia, are also included among the oldest black churches in the United States. While these early black churches existed in the South, the North, which tended to have more documentation, especially surrounding the important creation of the African Methodist Episcopal (AME) and African Methodist Episcopal Zion (AMEZ) orders, dominates early African American church history.

Silver Bluff Baptist Church

Located on the estate of slaveholder George Galphin, Silver Bluff Baptist Church got its start between 1773 and 1775 through the work of white minister Gait Palmer, who baptized Galphin's slaves, including David George and Jesse Peters (also known as Jesse Peters Galphin). Georgia-based black preacher George Liele, a childhood friend of George's, also preached at Silver Bluff.

During the Revolutionary War, the congregation of about 30 sought the protection of the British in Savannah, who promised freedom to slaves who sided with them. After the British defeat, George relocated to Nova Scotia, where he established a church, before continuing his ministry in Sierra Leone. Liele left America in 1782 for Jamaica and established a church there. Before leaving, he converted a slave named Andrew Bryan, who went on to lead the First African Baptist Church of Savannah, which predates the white Baptist church there.

Peters didn't flee following the Revolutionary War. Instead, he returned to Silver Bluff and eventually gained his freedom. Around 1787, he established the Springfield Baptist Church, located in Augusta, Georgia. Morehouse College traces its roots back to this historic church. Today, Silver Bluff, Springfield, and First African are still active churches.

Black churches in the North

Racial mistreatment within churches produced the independent black church movement in the North. Two important orders, the African Methodist Episcopal (AME) and the African Methodist Episcopal Zion (AMEZ), didn't necessarily set out to become independent black churches. Both of these orders began with parishioners who were content to worship with white people of faith. Generally, white parishioners didn't feel the same.

The African Methodist Episcopal (AME) Church

At St. George's Methodist Episcopal Church in Philadelphia, the congregation included blacks and whites. When the white membership decided to segregate worship and force the black membership to the back of the church in 1787, two black members, Absalom Jones and Richard Allen, made plans to establish their own church. Historians believe that Jones and Allen left St. George's several months after they formed the Free African Society (see Chapter 3) that same year. By 1794, the two men had successfully spearheaded the St. Thomas's African Episcopal Church (also the African Episcopal Church of St. Thomas).

Plans changed when the Methodist Church refused to supply the church a minister. A majority of St. Thomas's congregation voted to affiliate with the Episcopal Church, so Allen, a die-hard Methodist, detached himself from the church and Jones, credited as the first black ordained Episcopal priest, led the congregation. Allen began a congregation within the official confines of Methodism but by 1816 united African American congregations in Philadelphia, New York, New Jersey, Delaware, and Maryland to form the African Methodist Episcopal (AME) Church, a uniquely African American organization operated by African Americans. Allen, a former slave who purchased his freedom at age 38, became the AME Church's first bishop. His Philadelphia church, Bethel AME, frequently referred to as "Mother Bethel," served as the order's anchor.

Allen explained his refusal to abandon Methodism with the observation: "I was confident that no religious sect or denominations would suit the capacity of the colored people so well as Methodists, for the plain simple gospel suits best for any people, for the unlearned can understand, and the learned are sure to understand."

The African Methodist Episcopal Zion (AMEZ) Church

Despite their similar names, the AME and AME Zion Church aren't the same. The AME Zion Church traces its roots back to 1796, to the John Street Methodist Church of New York City. Although the Methodist Church, in keeping with founder John Wesley, opposed slavery, it refused to ordain black ministers, among other things. So, in 1796, black members broke off and, by 1801, had their own church, the African Methodist Episcopal Church of the City of New York, also known as Zion.

Although separate, Zion and its affiliate churches operated under the guidance of the white-controlled Methodist Episcopal Church (MEC) for a number of years. Once they decided to make a clean break, they teetered with joining forces with the AME Church, headed by Allen, but formed their own order, AME Zion or AMEZ, instead.

James Varick assumed leadership around 1820 and became sanctioned by the general Methodist Episcopal Church in 1822. They didn't completely break from the MEC until 1824, however. High profile abolitionist members such as Frederick Douglass, Harriet Tubman, and Sojourner Truth earned the AMEZ Church the label "the Freedom Church."

The black church in the antebellum South

African Americans found worshiping in the South more precarious. Southern laws generally prohibited literacy, which was practically synonymous with religious instruction. Even before the increase in converted slaves, laws prevented slaves from gathering in large numbers. As the Christian conversion of slaves became more common, some Southern states prohibited blacks from ministering to each other and punished such acts with whippings, among other things.

As a result, many black preachers conducted ministries in secret. Meeting in the woods, black people weren't only free to worship but, more importantly, able to worship freely. Those who could read the Bible didn't have to hide that fact in these gatherings. Even the most learned, however, kept the gospel simple to appeal to everyone. One of Christianity's biggest draws for those enslaved was the reaffirmation of their humanity.

Threats of violent consequences didn't deter some preachers who maintained that, if Jesus died on the cross for their sins, they could withstand beatings for ministering God's word. Surprisingly, however, many slave owners didn't object to their slaves holding worship services as long as it didn't interfere with their work. During times of rebellion or on suspicion of insurrection, slaveholders were more restrictive. Perhaps some slaveholders acquiesced to separate worship services because proving that the Bible sanctioned black enslavement was a cornerstone of early conversion efforts, particularly in the South. Nonetheless, some scholars refer to these meetings, secret and open, as the *invisible church.*

Not all black churches in the South were unorganized, however. Pockets of the South such as Richmond, Virginia; Charleston, South Carolina; and New Orleans, Louisiana, had free black communities which established churches that drew black people who were enslaved and free. Baptists and Methodists were the predominant denominations of Southern blacks, mostly because of the Great Awakenings (refer to the earlier section "The Great Awakenings: Called to convert"). The South had an estimated 468,000 black church members in 1859.

Baptist churches in the South

The earliest known black churches in the South were largely Baptist. In the midst of slavery, there were still black churches such as the African Huntsville Church in Alabama and the Rose Hill Church in Natchez, Mississippi, that white religious orders recognized. Churches such as the Grand Gulf Church in Mississippi and Mount Lebanon Church in Louisiana, though technically integrated, had relatively few white members. Borders states such as Kentucky also boasted independent black churches prior to the Civil War.

These churches weren't necessarily white-controlled either. Sir Charles Lyell, in his book *A Second Visit to the United States of North America,* marveled at the First African [Baptist] Church of Savannah in 1846. Noting that he was the only white man out of about 600 black people, Lyell commented favorably on not just the excellent singing; the competent preaching also impressed him. He noted that the minister, who preached without notes, used surprisingly good English. On top of that, Lyell felt the preaching style was very imaginative and held the congregation's attention. Overall Lyell wrote that his experiences at First African marked "an astonishing step in civilization."

Gowan Pamphlet

Gowan Pamphlet, the property of a female tavern owner, began preaching in Williamsburg, Virginia, in the 1770s. Undeterred by the local Baptist organization's decision that "no person of color should be allowed to preach," Pamphlet persisted and negotiated time away with his owner to attend to his ministry. By 1781, his congregation was possibly as large as 200.

When Pamphlet's owner relocated her business, he didn't abandon his ministry. With a new owner, he returned to Williamsburg In 1791. Confident in his congregation of about 500 and faithful that he could evade the law prohibiting slaves from preaching, Pamphlet applied to the Dover Baptist Association for official recognition and received it after a two-year inspection period.

During the antebellum period, after Pamphlet was long gone, his church weathered many storms, including being shut down for a year due to Nat Turner's Rebellion (see Chapter 4). In 1843, decades after Pamphlet's death, forced reorganization subordinated the church's black pastors, but black leadership resumed after the Civil War. A testament to Pamphlet's legacy, First Baptist Church, which preceded white Baptist churches in Williamsburg, is still standing.

The Methodist Church in the South

While the AME church grew very slowly in the South, there were AME churches in Baltimore, Charleston, and New Orleans. Through the efforts of Daniel Coker, black Methodists in Maryland, a critical border state during the Civil War, were among the original AME founders in 1816. Morris Brown led the African Church of Charleston until local authorities uncovered Denmark Vesey's plots for rebellion (see Chapter 4). Barely escaping death, Brown made it north, but black Methodism didn't return to Charleston until after the Civil War.

New Orleans, well-known for its large black Catholic population, had four black Methodist churches, three led by slave preachers supervised by white ministers, before the Civil War. The exception was St. James AME led by Charles Doughty. In Missouri, two free black men led black Methodists there.

White Methodists, however, usually ministered to black Methodists, largely slaves, in the South, a curiosity since Methodism's founder John Wesley opposed slavery. Such ministries, however, were directly born out of early slave conversion attempts. During the early 1800s, the Methodist Episcopal Church (MEC) softened its stance on slavery. Interestingly, its ministry to slaves accounted for a significant portion of its growth in the 19th century.

Even with a softened stance on slavery, it was generally unacceptable for Methodist clergy to own slaves. When Rev. James Andrews of Georgia inherited a female slave in 1840, conflict erupted, but he wasn't expelled. When he later married a woman who also owned a slave, he had a choice to either free the slaves or leave the church, which created a rift among Methodists. In 1844, Southern Methodists broke away and formed the Methodist Episcopal Church, South. Up until the Civil War, the black Methodist population, largely enslaved, continued to grow.

Post–Civil War and Reconstruction

After gaining freedom at the Civil War's end, black Southerners wanted to seize control over their own spiritual needs, and black churches of all denominations flourished in the postwar South. Both the AME and AMEZ church made considerable inroads outside the Northeast.

New denominations that emerged included the Colored Methodist Episcopal Church (renamed the Christian Methodist Episcopal Church in the 1950s), when, with the blessings of their white Methodist counterparts, 41 men gathered in Jackson, Tennessee, in December 1870 to form the church. At least three-fourths of the South's estimated 200,000 black Methodists joined the CME, taking $1.5 million in buildings and properties with them.

As more Baptist churches emerged, they began to assert their racial heritage more. They also began forming more complex, African American–led Baptist organizations. Prior to the Civil War, black Baptists in the North had already attempted to form greater affiliations. On the brink of Civil War, black Baptists in Illinois and Ohio were among the first to form successful, all-black Baptist organizations on a larger scale. Nearly two million former slaves helped bolster the Baptist membership rolls, increasing the need to organize.

Of the many organizations that emerged, the National Baptist Convention, U.S.A., formed in 1895 at Friendship Baptist Church in Atlanta, is one of the most significant. Although several Baptist organizations merged to create the National Baptist Convention, U.S.A., key splits in 1915 and 1961 splintered the organization into the National Baptist Convention of America and the Progressive National Baptist Convention, whose original membership included Martin Luther King, Jr. In 1988, the National Missionary Baptist Convention also joined those ranks. Disputes involving publishing concerns were the reason for some of the splits, but differing opinions regarding the black church's role in the civil rights movement were also at play (read more about this later in the chapter).

Worship in the early 20th century

In the 20th century, the biggest shift for black Christians became the advent of the Church of God in Christ (COGIC). Emerging around the turn of the 20th century, the Church of God in Christ, a Pentecostal offshoot, mainly traces its roots back to Rev. Charles Harrison Mason. After being expelled from one Baptist college and dropping out of another, Mason found kindred spirits in Arkansas minister J.A. Jeter and Mississippi ministers Charles Price Jones and W.S. Pleasant.

Relieved of his duties at a Baptist church in Arkansas over his beliefs in sanctification, Mason, along with his newfound colleagues, hosted a revival for black Baptists in Jackson, Mississippi, in 1896. Filled with the spirit, the revival, while a success, alienated even more-traditional black Baptists who considered Mason and his cohorts' behavior extreme.

According to Mason, he and his group "only wanted to exalt Jesus and put down man-made traditions." When the local Baptist association ostracized Mason and Jones for their adherence to the doctrine of sanctification, they felt they had no choice but to create something new. In 1897, Mason, who claimed that the name came to him as he walked down a street in Little Rock, Arkansas, birthed COGIC. His journey, however, wasn't complete.

William Joseph Seymour

An important catalyst to the global Pentecostal movement and considered by some the father of Pentecostalism, William Joseph Seymour was born to freed slaves in Louisiana. As a child, Seymour, who was raised Baptist, had visions. His holiness teachings began when he relocated to Cincinnati in 1901 and joined the "reformation" Church of God. Around 1903, he joined a Houston church pastored by Lucy Farrow, a black woman, who connected him with Charles Fox Parham, whose students spoke in tongues.

With the aid of Farrow and Parham, Seymour relocated to Los Angeles and eventually found a home for his Pentecostal message. To accommodate the large number of people drawn to him and his teachings, he held services in a warehouse on Azusa Street. His main message was one of "love, faith, and unity," but Los Angeles newspapers concentrated more on the congregation's practice of speaking in tongues. Negative press actually drew more people to Seymour's Azusa Street Revival, which peaked between 1906 and 1909.

Although Seymour inspired many, including COGIC founder Charles Harrison Mason, his movement collapsed. Some attribute Seymour's failure to a jealous female member taking his mailing list. Others believe his rift with his Chicago leader William Durham diluted his movement's white membership. Regardless, Seymour, who died in 1922, made great contributions to the modern Pentecostal movement.

HISTORICAL ROOTS

A musical foundation

Music was another major turning point in the church during the 20th century. After the Civil War, many outside of the black community learned of spirituals. Despite the fact that spirituals contributed greatly to the creation of secular musical genres such as blues and jazz, most churches rejected those genres. Still, the church wasn't unaffected by the rise of black secular music. During the 1930s Thomas Andrew Dorsey, a former blues piano player, began mingling the blues with sacred music. Eventually that resulted in gospel music, which injected more instrumentation and individuality into black church music. It's noteworthy that Pentecostal/Holiness churches often had full bands that included drums and other instruments, a huge contrast to the organ-based music of many Northern churches. In this way, music was one of the main ways COGIC and other Pentecostal/Holiness churches distinguished themselves from the more traditional black churches.

By the 1950s, gospel music, thanks in large part to Sister Rosetta Tharpe and Mahalia Jackson, was a widely known byproduct of the black church. Gospel singers such as Sam Cooke brought greater attention to the music of the black church. During civil rights marches and other protest efforts, songs of the church were commonplace. Music was and is an important component of the African American church (see Chapter 16 for more details on black music).

Looking for an even more meaningful and complete experience, Mason, after encountering Pentecostal pioneer William Joseph Seymour (see the sidebar), later changed COGIC's direction. In line with the Holiness Movement, which focused on restoring the personal holiness and connection originally taught by John Wesley, COGIC began placing special emphasis on the resurrection of Christ. COGIC followers believe in the Trinity (the Father, the Son, and the Holy Ghost). They believe that God grants repentance and salvation to all Christian believers who ask for it. In addition, they're known to speak in tongues; as a result, their services are usually spirited. Although they believe in divine healing, they don't eschew modern medical services. Jeter and Jones rejected Mason's Pentecostal message, and the three men split.

COGIC continued to grow, especially as blacks migrated to the cities, largely because Mason sent evangelists to urban centers such as Detroit and Chicago to help migrants, who responded to the more fervent style of worship many of them knew from their rural communities. So although COGIC, headquartered in Memphis, began as a more rural religion, by the time Mason died in 1961, its membership was largely urban.

The modern era: Megachurches

In recent years, megachurches have become the most noteworthy development in African American religion. Overall church membership may be down (refer to the later section "Challenges to the Black Church"), but so are the numbers of small churches. Instead they've been replaced by churches with very large congregations that range from 5,000 to 20,000 members and upward. These megachurches offer everything from schools and small business instruction to personal financial management and lending services.

One example is Potter's House, a megachurch in Dallas whose minister T.D. Jakes has been featured on the cover of *Time Magazine*. Jakes's "Woman, Thou Art Loosed" mission to reclaim black women who have been sexually abused has become an international movement. Other black megachurches include West Angeles Church of God in Christ in Los Angeles and New Birth Missionary Baptist Church in Atlanta.

The black ministers who head many of these megachurches have built their own multimedia empires. By and large, they're successful televangelists who spread their messages via sales of audiotapes, CDs, and DVDs. They sponsor hugely successful conventions, and some, like Jakes, also have successful publishing careers. Although targeted black TV channels regularly feature gospel programming, mainstream Christian channels such as the Trinity Broadcasting Network also welcome larger-than-life black ministers. The breadth of their exposure has made black ministers and their congregations even more desirable political partners on several fronts.

Challenges to the Black Church

Throughout much of slavery, Reconstruction, and post-Reconstruction, the black church served as the focal point of the African American community, and it retained that distinction for much of the 20th century. In a world marked by Jim Crow (see Chapter 7) where African Americans suffered indignities on a daily basis, black churches, in keeping with Christianity's function during slavery, reaffirmed the humanity of its black congregations.

For many African Americans who moved North during the Great Migration, the church served the important function of acculturating them to their new surroundings. Churches were also critical information centers and did everything from reuniting migrants to helping them secure housing and employment.

In most communities, black churches served important functions from the time of slavery into the 1960s and 1970s mainly. They were schools, relief societies, social clubs, and political think tanks. Therefore, black churches were important social buffers. Yet despite its central role in the African American community, the black church today faces a variety of challenges.

Class tensions

Historically, even in the face of class tensions, African Americans still worshiped together in great numbers. As more well-to-do African Americans began leaving the city for the suburbs in the 1980s, that was no longer true. Sometimes poor congregations couldn't sustain a church. Others argue that the church failed to address the direct needs of its significant poorer communities.

Some argue that the black church itself has become a middle-class phenomenon, reflected most poignantly in the church's increasing emphasis on prosperity and the individual, instead of the overall community. Gone were the days, some lamented, when congregations sacrificed themselves and their wants for the greater good of all black people.

Waning church membership

Trends show that the more prosperous many African Americans become, the less relevant church is. Additionally, in many homes, church attracts individuals, not entire families. Growing numbers of African American children have never attended church regularly, a phenomenon unheard of just three decades ago. Increasingly, African American youth, like children of other races, are disinterested in church. In an age dominated by rap music and hip-hop culture, church, in many instances, has lost its edge, especially among young boys and men, who are less apt to attend church.

To reverse this trend, some churches are experimenting with new methods of appealing to men and young people. It isn't uncommon to find men-only ministries in many black churches, for example. Former rappers such as MC Hammer, Run from Run-D.M.C., Curtis Blow, and Mase have become ministers themselves. Some churches have also begun incorporating elements of hip-hop in their services to appeal to the younger generation. There are even "holy" rappers who perform Christian hip-hop with the blessing of some churches.

While the membership rolls of Baptist and Methodist churches have declined, African American membership in Pentecostal and Apostolic churches has spiked without reaching out to the hip-hop generation. Apparently, more spirit-filled institutions with clearly defined spiritual agendas, coupled with more dynamic preaching and more lively musical selections, have greater appeal. In contrast with older denominations such as the AME Church, especially in more urban areas, the worship styles of

Pentecostal and Apostolic orders greatly diverge from the more European-style worship of some denominations. To survive, several traditional Baptist and Methodist churches have adopted neo-Pentecostalism methods.

The role of women

Following the civil rights and black power movements, not to mention the advent of a stronger feminist movement, reconciling the role of women in the church became a major issue. Historically, black women assumed key leadership roles: Born a slave in 1797, Sojourner Truth is perhaps the earliest known black female preacher. In 1819, Richard Allen authorized Jarena Lee to preach eight years after her initial request. Lee, however, found it difficult to sustain a ministry and became an itinerant preacher. Rebecca Cox Jackson, who had a significant black female following, led her own Shaker (a female-founded religious order) community.

In the 20th century, however, sexism kept black women out of the pulpit. Black men generally viewed the church as one of the few arenas where they could exert power. Quietly, however, black women were the heart and soul of the church, running everything from church-based schools to church fundraisers. This was particularly evident during the civil rights era. When many ministers tried to close the church's doors to civil rights workers, black female church leaders opened them.

During the 1970s, more black women, to the dismay of others, began clamoring for official leadership roles, particularly in the pulpit traditionally reserved for men. Prior to this push, a few black women held leadership roles, exceptions that didn't all date back to the 19th century. Ordained in the 1950s, Reverend Dr. Johnnie Coleman, for example, the founding minister of Christ Universal Temple in Chicago, led a large church during a time when the highest leadership positions available to most black women included church secretary and the minister's wife. In recent years, black women such as Dr. Vashti Murphy McKenzie, the AME Church's first female bishop, have made additional strides, but black church ministers remain largely male even though most congregations are overwhelmingly female.

Politics and the Church

The black church is no stranger to politics. Even before its formal inception, politics dictated the African American church. From debates regarding whether or not to convert African Americans to the role the black church played in eliminating slavery, building schools, and supplying the civil rights movement with its army, religion has been a powerful political force in the lives of African Americans — so much so that some black religious leaders have assumed national positions of power outside the church.

Getting more political

During the mid-1950s and 1960s, black churches actively battled Jim Crow. White supremacists burned countless churches in recognition of the power the black church wielded among African Americans. More conservative black church leaders, especially those whom local white politicians controlled, didn't embrace the civil rights movement, but Martin Luther King, Jr., became a leading national figure (see Chapters 8 and 9 for more details). During the 1970s and 1980s, black churches became more active in the political process, mainly through voter registration drives, to help elect black politicians and others.

On the heels of the black power movement, younger African Americans began to view the black church as a place where black people, as Malcolm X once charged, worshiped the "white man's god" and followed "the white man's religion." Countering that charge, some churches embraced black power. James H. Cone termed this new philosophy *black liberation theology* (refer to the earlier section "Christianity, African American–style"). Potential members, in other cases, embraced alternative religious organizations such as the Nation of Islam.

Minister-politicians: Pulling double duty

Some ministers directly mixed formal politics with the pulpit. Ordained AME minister Hiram Revels, who ironically replaced Jefferson Davis, the Confederate president, became the first African American member in the Senate during Reconstruction. Adam Clayton Powell, Jr., pastor of New York's legendary Abyssinian Baptist Church, was arguably the most prominent minister-politician.

Using the power of Abyssinian, Powell became a prominent civil rights leader during the Great Depression. Through mass meetings, rent strikes, and public campaigns, Powell forced companies and utilities, including Harlem Hospital, to hire or promote black employees. In 1941, he became New York City's first black councilman and then, in 1945, he began service as New York's first black congressman. Congress attempted to remove Powell, who had served on several important committees, in 1967 on charges of misappropriating funds for personal use. Charles Rangel defeated him in 1970.

On the national level, former congressman Floyd Flake has been the most prominent black minister to serve in the federal government in recent years. Jesse Jackson and Al Sharpton have sought big offices such as the presidency of the United States.

Jesse Jackson and Al Sharpton

One of the chief beneficiaries of the King legacy, Rev. Jesse Jackson made two credible runs for the presidency of the United States using a Christian foundation as his base. A proponent of economic rights, Jackson has led many successful boycotts as well as advocated that African Americans cultivate wealth, mainly through Wall Street. Active internationally, Jackson has successfully negotiated the release of American prisoners and hostages from hot spots around the world (read more about Jackson in Chapter 10).

Rev. Al Sharpton, who acknowledges Jackson as a mentor, has created a career similar to Jackson's. Ordained at age 10, as a teenager

Sharpton served as youth director of Jackson's Operation Breadbasket and founded the National Youth Movement. Through the National Action Network, founded in 1991, Sharpton has expanded his political and social activism. Yet his support in 1987 of Tawana Brawley, a New York teen whose claim of rape by several white men was ruled unfounded, damaged his credibility in many circles. Sharpton, often ridiculed for the signature processed hairstyle he wears to honor musical legend James Brown for whom he once worked, has failed to win his bids for a U.S. Senate seat, New York City mayor, and the U.S. presidency in 2004.

Fighting for civil rights: Minister-activists

The majority of black ministers have been active on the issue of civil rights and equality without ever holding an elective office. Martin Luther King, Jr., for example, brought national and international attention to the prominent role the black church played in politics and issues of moral righteousness. Far from the first Christian minister to involve his congregation in the fight for civil rights, King has proven the most successful one. Through the Southern Christian Leadership Conference (SCLC), King and his colleagues spurred other ministers to greater political action.

Thirty-three delegates, including King, representing 14 states formed the Progressive National Baptist Convention (PNBC) in 1961. The PNBC gladly supported the efforts of the NAACP Legal Defense Fund, the March on Washington, the Civil Rights Act of 1964, and the Voting Rights Act of 1965. With the tagline "A people of faith and action," the PNBC, whose membership includes Jesse Jackson and Benjamin Hooks, continues to uphold an activist tradition.

Continuing the struggle

The black church remains the single-most influential institution in the African American community, and that power hasn't gone unnoticed in the battle to addresses many issues critical to African Americans. In recent years, the black church has become critical in the battle plan to fight HIV/AIDS. Black churches have also battled against diabetes, high blood pressure, and other diseases that disproportionately affect African Americans.

Many religious leaders have denounced the complacency that set in with many black churches in the late 1970s, 1980s, and 1990s and returned to more activist stances. They have become leaders in providing affordable housing as well as in creating childcare services. "It takes a church to raise a people," Dr. Clarence G. Newsome, the longtime former dean of Howard University's Divinity School who heads Shaw University, once stated. Historically, it's been the black church that's provided that leadership, and that legacy hasn't been lost.

Worshiping Outside the Black Christian Mainstream

Although Baptists, Methodists, and Pentecostals dominate the African American religious experience, African Americans have considerable roots outside the black Christian mainstream. While the black religious net is wide, Muslims, Catholics, Jehovah Witnesses, and Seventh-day Adventists constitute the majority of those outside the black Christian mainstream. Religious leaders, considered demagogues, have also played major roles in the black community, especially in the 20th century.

Muslims and the Nation of Islam

Muslims made tremendous inroads into Africa prior to the transatlantic slave trade and comprised as much as 20 percent of the slave population of some plantations. Yet the African Islamic influence didn't survive slavery in large numbers. In the 20th century, however, universally recognized Islamic traditions haven't attracted as much media attention as prototypical Islamic organizations such as the Moorish Science Temple and the Nation of Islam, which emphasized black nationalism despite the fact that Islam doesn't generally make racial distinctions.

The Moorish Science Temple

Founded in Newark, New Jersey, in 1913 by the Prophet Noble Drew Ali (born Timothy Drew), the Moorish Science Temple began as the Canaanite Temple and contended that African Americans were of Asiatic descent and thus were originally Islamic. Ali, who relocated his movement to Chicago in 1925, admired Marcus Garvey and considered him a prophet (refer to Chapter 7).

Like Garvey, Ali supported black power but insisted on referring to black people as "Moorish Americans." Trademarks of the Moorish Science Temple include fezzes, turbans, membership cards, the star and crescent, and adding an "El" or "Bey" to one's surname. Its main teachings come from the *Holy Koran of the Moorish Science Temple of America.*

The Nation of Islam

The Nation of Islam is perhaps the most well-known alternative to the traditional black church in the African American community. Influenced by Noble Drew Ali and Marcus Garvey, W.D. Fard infused the Allah Temple of Islam, a precursor to the Nation of Islam (NOI) he founded in 1930, with elements of black nationalism, Islam, and Christianity.

Working in various professions such as door-to-door salesman and a street vendor in Detroit, Fard attracted several thousand followers. Black separatism was at the core of Fard's teaching, and so was the belief that white people were inherently evil. Elijah Muhammad, born Elijah Poole in Georgia, discovered Fard's teachings in Detroit and seized control of the NOI in Chicago. Muhammad's many improvements included the introduction of the newspaper *The Final Call to Islam* in 1934 (which evolved into *Muhammad Speaks* in the 1960s and later as *The Final Call*). Muhammad also created a NOI school. Under Muhammad's leadership, the NOI's strict moral code against drinking, smoking, and premarital and extramarital sex provided well-received discipline to the many ex-convicts the organization targeted for membership.

The NOI's most legendary member was Malcolm X (whom you can read about in Chapter 9). After his departure and murder, the NOI lost its momentum. Muhammad's death in 1975 divided the organization into two factions; an estimated 100,000 members followed Muhammad's son Imam Warith Deen Muhammad, now Warith Deen Mohammed, who favored Islam in its more traditional form. Displeased with Warith Deen Mohammed's vision, Louis Farrakhan assumed leadership of the NOI in 1978 but reportedly restored the organization closer to its original form in 1981, continuing the organization's black separatist tradition.

A controversial leader, Farrakhan, despite frequent accusations of anti-Semitism, is highly regarded among many African Americans, even those who find it difficult to accept the NOI's philosophical beliefs, primarily because of his willingness to challenge white authority. Others respect its policing of tough, urban areas and its continued outreach to ex-convicts. The hip-hop community, especially in its early years, embraced the NOI's aggressive efforts to fight urban decay. For many African Americans, 1995's Million Man March remains Farrakhan's crowning achievement.

It can't go unnoted, however, that most black Muslims don't belong to the NOI. Significant numbers of ex-NOI members belong to more universally respected Islamic organizations, but the NOI still garners more media attention.

Patrick Francis Healy

Born in Macon, Georgia, to a white, Irish-American father and a mulatto slave mother, Patrick Francis Healy, along with his siblings, attended a Jesuit school in the North to escape the South's racial limitations. When discovery of Patrick Francis Healy's race threatened to disrupt his studies, his father sent him to a university in Belgium where he received his PhD. Ordained as a priest in 1864, Healy returned to the U.S. in 1866 and began teaching philosophy at Georgetown University where he eventually became president. Often referred to as Georgetown's "second founder," Healy Hall was named for him, and he's buried on university grounds. His brother James Augustine Healy became bishop of Portland, Maine. Some additional Healy siblings served as priests and nuns.

Black Catholics

Catholicism claims a greater percentage of people of color worldwide than any other Christian religion, but in the United States, black Catholics have traditionally been a small group. Black Catholics were present, however, in areas such as St. Augustine (Florida), Los Angeles, Chicago, and Baltimore that would later form the United States. Following the Louisiana Purchase in 1803, New Orleans became the predominant black Catholic haven. New Orleans and pockets of Mobile, Alabama, where the religion is more closely associated with Creoles or mixed-race African Americans, have retained strong Catholic identities over the years.

The Black Catholic population in the U.S. increased significantly after the Civil War. Unlike other religious denominations, there's little evidence that Catholics of any race spoke out strongly for or against slavery, but white Catholics did discriminate against African Americans. Patrick Francis Healy and his brother James Augustine Healy succeeded in the Jesuit order, but their race was unknown. Father Augustus Tolton, on the other hand, had to be ordained in Rome in 1886 before his installment as pastor over St. Joseph Church's black congregation.

Boosting black Catholicism, Daniel Rudd, born to enslaved Catholic parents, spearheaded the National Black Catholic Congress, the first mass meeting of black Catholics, in 1889. For reasons unknown, the group stopped meeting in 1894 but resumed activities in 1987. Over the years, other black Catholic organizations have included the Federated Colored Catholics, the National Office of Black Catholics, and the National Black Catholic Clergy Caucus.

Today, large cities such as New York, Chicago, Miami, and Los Angeles boast considerable numbers of African American Catholics. Stellar secondary educational institutions have attracted many of them. In Chicago, the dominant

Irish Catholic political structure contributed to the rise in black Catholics, manifested particularly in several historic black Catholic elementary and high schools. New York's and Miami's large Haitian populations and growing Afro-Latino populations come with a long-standing Catholic tradition. New Orleans, however, remains the bastion of black Catholicism in the U.S. where its Xavier University is the only predominantly black Catholic university in the United States.

On the leadership level, Archbishop Wilton D. Gregory, the first African American to head the U.S. Conference of Catholic Bishops (2001–2004), was a leading voice during the Catholic Church's sex abuse scandal. Many credit him for quickly denouncing priests guilty of child molestation, a move critical in restoring faith in Catholicism in general. Gregory's historic position also reinforced the Catholic Church's commitment to serve all its members.

Jehovah's Witnesses

Jehovah's Witnesses trace their origins back to the Bible Students, a group organized by Charles T. Russell in the 1870s. Once influenced by Nelson H. Barbour's predictions that Christ would visibly return to earth, Russell broke from Barbour in 1879 over substitutionary atonement, the belief that Jesus died for all people's sins. In 1881, Russell established the Watch Tower Bible and Tract Society in Pennsylvania. He also founded the International Bible Students Association in the United Kingdom.

Followers adopted 1914 as the beginning of Christ's presence (albeit invisibly) on earth and his enthronement as king, thus kicking off the last days. By 1922, the organization, believing that God selected them as his people, began to emphasize preaching house to house. Although they began calling themselves Jehovah's Witnesses in 1931, the organization thrived after Nathan Horner Knorr took over in 1942. During his leadership, membership rose from just over 100,000 to over 2 million in 1975. That number was over 6.6 million worldwide in 2005.

Jehovah's Witnesses dress very moderately, with women often required to wear skirts and dresses over pants, and abstain from many popular activities. They don't celebrate holidays or birthdays. They don't believe in whole-blood transfusions and oppose political involvement.

Seventh-day Adventists

Less restrictive than Jehovah's Witnesses, Seventh-day Adventists trace their roots back to followers of the Baptist lay leader William Miller of the early 19th century, who believed that the Bible contained coded language regarding the end of the world and the second coming of Jesus. Miller is credited for inspiring the Second Great Awakening (refer to the earlier section "The Great

Awakenings: Called to convert" for details on how this event contributed to the Christian conversion of early African Americans). Black Seventh-day Adventists constitute around 27 percent of the estimated 14 million members worldwide. Alabama's Oakwood College is a predominantly black Seventh-day Adventist institution.

Seventh-day Adventists celebrate the Sabbath on Saturday. They also believe in higher education and have a special concern for health issues. Religious tenets such as original sin and the resurrection of Christ are in line with conservative Christian beliefs. While Seventh-day Adventists contend that Christ's return is imminent, they don't necessarily believe in spiritual immortality.

African American demagogues

Father Divine, Sweet Daddy Grace, and Rev. Ike are three of the most well-known black demagogues, with all three of these so-called religious leaders boasting considerable numbers of followers that include blacks and whites.

- **Father Divine:** According to *The New York Times,* Father Divine's International Peace Mission Movement had 50,000 members in the 1930s. Father Divine, who claimed himself as God, had an admirable social agenda that fought lynching and opposed school segregation. After his death in 1965, his widow carried on his movement. When Jim Jones, who claimed to follow Father Divine, led a mass suicide in Guyana in 1974 that claimed 914 lives, momentum for the movement dramatically slowed. Today the movement, which draws largely from Father Divine's sermons and writings, maintains several domestic and international branches despite decreasing membership.

- **Sweet Daddy Grace:** Born in Brava, Cape Verde Islands, Charles "Sweet Daddy" Grace immigrated to the U.S. in the early 1900s. He built his United Houses of Prayer for All People in Massachusetts, North Carolina, Washington, D.C., and Egypt. Unlike Father Divine, Sweet Daddy Grace used the Bible as his main text. A flamboyant dresser frequently accused of exploiting poor people, Grace and his followers did perform community services. Although Grace died in 1960, the United House of Prayer still boasts over 3 million members.

- **Rev. Ike:** A pioneer of "the gospel of prosperity," Dr. Frederick Eikerenkoetter, or Rev. Ike, peaked in the 1970s when some 1,700 television and radio stations broadcast his message from his Christ Community United Church. Quoted as saying, "The lack of money is the root of all evil," the once-flamboyant Rev. Ike now stresses "Thinkonomics," which encourages followers to reject thoughts of limitation and lack to create abundance, a message consistent with many popular New Age teachings against scarcity. For years now, Rev. Ike has continued operating a mail campaign and Web site.

Chapter 13

More Than Reading and Writing: Education

• •

In This Chapter

▶ Following the progression of early education

▶ Moving up to higher education

▶ Recognizing the impact of Historically Black Colleges and Universities (HBCUs)

▶ Examining the uniqueness of the black Greek system

• •

*P*erhaps no other group of Americans has had its access to education blocked more than African Americans. During slavery, learning to read was punishable by beatings, fines, and even death. Yet African Americans persevered, eventually building formidable educational institutions of their own in addition to excelling in America's most prestigious schools.

Triumph over Jim Crow and its grossly inadequate schools (see Chapter 7) didn't end education-related struggles; busing and affirmative action brought new challenges. This chapter walks you through key periods and events in the history of both early and higher African American education. It also examines some important education-related institutions — the black Greek system, the United Negro College Fund, and Historically Black Colleges and Universities (HBCUs) — that have had pivotal roles in the progression of African American education.

A Brief History of Early African American Education

Slave narratives, written and oral, indicate that African Americans in bondage and in freedom valued literacy. Yet prior to the Civil War, the majority of African Americans were illiterate, and, with few exceptions, no educational system was in place to remedy that fact. African Americans who could read at all were largely self-taught.

Cotton Mather, the Bible, and slavery

As early as the 17th century, intense debate raged as to whether slaves should learn to read the Bible. Massachusetts colonist and Puritan minister Cotton Mather solved the dilemma by twisting religious instruction to slaves into a justification of slavery. Mather interpreted the Ten Commandments to give slaveholders the same respect as God. Thus, Christian conversion of slaves became a means of reinforcing the slave status of Africans, shifting the justification of slavery from *heathenism* (not believing in Christianity) to race.

After the Civil War, education was made more accessible to black Americans, but it was vastly inferior to the education that white Americans received, and students and teachers alike continued to face harassment and fines. Making matters worse was the Supreme Court ruling in *Plessy v. Ferguson* (1896), which said that separate facilities for black and white were acceptable as long as they were equal. In many Southern states, however, "equal" was simply having a building available to African Americans. (Refer to Chapter 7 for details on the *Plessy* decision.)

Revolting education

Like enslaved Africans, many slaveholders equated education with empowerment. For them, illiteracy was essential to keeping the slave system intact because literate slaves were more likely to run away. The line of thinking was that slaves who knew how to read and write could forge the papers free blacks were required to carry in some areas or could map their way to freedom, as many did.

Overwhelmingly, revolts were the most feared consequence of educating slaves, and when rebellions did occur, abolishing access to education was often a response. Reactions to the Stono Rebellion in Charleston in 1739, for example, included the passage of the Negro Act, which prohibited the education of all slaves in South Carolina. Following Nat Turner's Rebellion in 1831, Virginia passed even more legislation reinforcing punishments for African American literacy. (To find out more about these and other significant slave rebellions, go to Chapter 4.)

After the American Revolution ended in 1783, Massachusetts led many Northern states in abolishing slavery. In the midst of the growing chasm that formed between North and South regarding the slavery issue, educating slaves quickly became a highly contested issue.

In the South

As antislavery activity intensified in the 1800s, Southern states held tightly to slavery and resurrected old laws as well as passed new ones known as the *Slave Codes* (refer to Chapter 4). Among other things, these laws increased the penalties for teaching slaves to read and write. The punishments reflected one's status in society:

- ✔ **Free blacks:** Free blacks could be beaten, fined, jailed, and even enslaved.

- ✔ **Slaves:** To deter other slaves, slave owners punished slaves severely, sometimes killing them for daring to educate themselves.

- ✔ **Whites:** In Georgia, in 1829, the law fined whites $500 in addition to possible imprisonment for teaching slaves or free blacks to read. More often, in many of the colonies, other whites ran them out of town.

Not even the threat of death quelled African Americans' thirst for knowledge. But because of the laws prohibiting literacy, slave education was mostly unorganized and supervised:

- ✔ **By other slaves in secret meetings:** Slaves who could read and write, even at the most rudimentary levels, were compelled to teach others. In the South, *camp meetings,* similar to secret meetings held in West Africa to discuss important issues, were held in the woods. In more urban areas, *Sabbath school* lessons were conducted in secret in a house or a church, usually on a Sunday or whenever slaves could steal some free time.

- ✔ **By slave owners:** Curiously, some slaves learned how to read with the help of their owners, some of whom had experienced religious conversions and thus believed in the religious value of African American literacy.

- ✔ **By luck:** Slaves who accompanied their masters' children sometimes lucked out and were educated simply by being in the right place at the right time.

Frederick Douglass pointedly expressed the thirst for education in his *Narrative of the Life of Frederick Douglass, an American Slave Written by Himself* (1845) when he wrote, "These dear souls came not to Sabbath school because it was popular to do so, nor did I teach them because it was reputable to be thus engaged. Every moment they spent in that school, they were liable to be taken up, and given thirty-nine lashes. They came because they wished to learn."

Underground schooling ruled much of the South, with churches often shouldering that responsibility. But even they weren't safe. When a Richmond newspaper commented on black children carrying books on Sundays, local law enforcement raided the church. Laws restricting African American education persisted in the South, even after the Civil War.

Just because free blacks couldn't legally attend schools in the South didn't mean they didn't pay for them. Free blacks in Baltimore (then considered a part of the South), for example, were forced to pay taxes for schools they weren't allowed to attend.

In the North

Leading up to the Civil War, educational opportunities for free blacks improved considerably in the North. In 1758, the Anglican-affiliated Associates of Dr. Bray opened a school for free blacks in Philadelphia. By 1770, Frenchman Anthony Benezet, a teacher who educated slave children in his home, had established the Negro School of Philadelphia with the help of his Quaker peers. In addition to private education efforts, public education for African Americans developed in a number of Northern cities, including:

- **Boston:** In 1820, the city established a black public school, and in 1855, Boston became the first school system in the country to integrate public school education.

- **Philadelphia:** The city's first public school for African Americans began in 1822, and by 1850, there were eight such schools.

- **New York City:** The first Free African School opened in 1787 followed by another school in 1820, which housed 500 boys. By the early 1830s, there were four other such schools in the city, and African Americans took full control of them in 1832 until a public school system emerged in 1834.

Even with the rise of education among free blacks, resistance continued to simmer in the North and parts of the Midwest. New York, Connecticut, Rhode Island, and Ohio began developing policies, sometimes informal, of segregated education, and white taxpayers were known to object to funding public schools for blacks and effectively delay the construction of schools intended for them.

Reconstructing: Education post–Civil War

During Reconstruction, education for African Americans changed significantly. For the first time in American history, educating African Americans became a national public policy issue of major concern. Prompted by secular aid societies and prominent philanthropists who later felt that only the government could handle the tremendous educational demands of recently freed slaves, the Bureau of Refugees, Freedmen and Abandoned Lands, more popularly known as the Freedmen's Bureau, shouldered the responsibility of educating African Americans. By 1867, the Freedmen's Bureau had opened almost 4,500 schools, many of them free. An estimated 250,000 students had enrolled by the 1870s.

Many Southern whites weren't moved by this passion to educate African Americans, so they burned schools for blacks and taunted and beat white teachers who taught black students. As a means of maintaining a system of white supremacy, Southern whites who acquiesced to educating African Americans often insisted upon elementary education only. Interestingly, efforts to educate recently freed slaves helped create a nationwide public school system that also benefited poor whites. When Reconstruction ended in 1877, however, the federal government didn't become actively involved in educating African Americans again until the Supreme Court's landmark 1954 *Brown v. Board of Education* decision that legally desegregated public schools (see Chapter 8).

Emboldened by the end of Reconstruction and the landmark Supreme Court *Plessy v. Ferguson* decision in 1896 proclaiming that separate institutions for blacks and whites were acceptable if they were equal, Southern whites showed no pity in regards to African American education. A year before the *Plessy* ruling, South Carolina spent $3.11 per white pupil compared to a paltry $1.05 per black pupil. By 1930, that gap had widened to an unbelievable $52.89 per white pupil and just $5.20 per black pupil. In addition, black teachers received a third of the salary that white teachers received. With these realities, it's no surprise that, in 1915, there were more privately owned black schools than county-owned ones in Georgia, for example.

Even with great numbers of African Americans migrating North, schools for blacks in the South were still in high demand. By the 1930s, black school attendance equaled that of whites. Black students, however, attended school in shorter terms, mainly because of the *sharecropping* system in which families worked land they didn't own in exchange for a wage or portion of the land's crop profits; parents often needed their children's help.

Curiously, the Great Depression (from the late 1920s through the 1930s) increased educational opportunities for black children. With less cotton to pick, there was more time for school. Black high school enrollment, for example, was five times greater during this period than in 1920. Lack of facilities, however, tempered much of that growth. Separate schools required funds, and with funds low due to the Depression, there simply weren't enough schools to accommodate the demand.

20th Century Educational Milestones

Although additional progress is still needed, there have been amazing improvements in the education of school-age black children who, once upon a time, were punished for learning to read. Contemporary public school education has advanced considerably, especially if you consider that the idea of a nationwide public school system isn't even two centuries old and that a fully equitable school system not legally determined by race is less than a century old!

Re-segregating?

One study of the nation's largest school systems during the 1997–1998 school year revealed that cities like New York, Chicago, Los Angeles, and Dallas had public school enrollments that were less than 20 percent white, even though public school enrollment for predominantly white neighborhoods remained quite high nationwide suggesting that

✔ In areas with substantial minority populations, white parents don't send their kids to public schools at the same rate as parents in predominantly white neighborhoods.

✔ Since public school attendance continues to reflect the complexion of the neighborhoods in which the schools are located, American whites, even in the 21st century, may still elect to live in predominantly white areas, even when more-diverse areas are an option.

Mixing it up with the Brown case

On a national level, legal cases challenging school segregation largely focused on higher education. Various protests were mounted but, in the North and in some Southern cities, blacks focused their energies on improving school facilities, building new schools, and securing more black teachers, among other issues. Then, with *Brown v. Board of Education* (1954), the Supreme Court ruled in favor of integration in public schools, essentially overturning *Plessy v. Ferguson* (see Chapter 8 for the details of the *Brown* case).

In the South

White Southerners vehemently resented the federal intervention of the *Brown* ruling. In 1957, an angry white mob greeted the nine black students who attempted to integrate Central High School in Little Rock, Arkansas. To force compliance with the Supreme Court's decision, President Eisenhower sent federal troops to escort the students (see Chapter 8 for more details). In 1960, six-year-old Ruby Bridges attended a New Orleans public school for a year by herself with one white teacher because white parents and school officials spurned integration. Other efforts to integrate also met with resistance and required the presence of federal troops to enforce the law. In fact, many Southern schools didn't desegregate until the early 1970s.

In the North

Prior to the 1930s, many Northern schools could be deemed integrated, when in reality they really weren't. Although the North didn't have a formal policy of segregation in place, as the South did, African Americans, already relegated to all-black neighborhoods, were conveniently forced into all-black schools. Thus, segregation in the North was more informal and, therefore, harder to challenge than in the South.

The 1971 Supreme Court decision in the case of *Swann v. Charlotte-Mecklenburg Board of Education* helped change that. Although the case specifically addressed conditions in North Carolina, the ruling also affected the North. The Supreme Court upheld a judge's decision to achieve desegregation through busing black students to white schools. It rejected de facto (unofficially sanctioned) racial segregation and cleared the way for similar desegregating strategies in Northern school systems.

In the 1973 case *Keyes v. Denver School District No. 1,* Denver became the first major city outside of the South to have its school policies in respect to desegregation challenged before the Supreme Court. This case is significant for two primary reasons:

- ✔ It turned school desegregation into a national and not just Southern problem.

- ✔ It established that schools with substantial numbers of African American and Hispanic students weren't desegregated because the two groups suffered similar conditions.

The Supreme Court gave Denver instructions to use school busing to achieve school desegregation. Throughout the 1970s and into the 1980s, busing was a key strategy in ongoing efforts to desegregate the nation's public schools in both the North and South.

Turning back the clock?

More than 50 years after *Brown v. Board of Education*, some activists claim that the United States is returning to segregated education. Others ask whether school desegregation should still be the goal. The *Brown* decision made clear that separate, by its very nature, is not equal; therefore, the only way to equalize the quality of education was to integrate schools. Civil rights activists contend that two 2006 cases *(Meredith v. Jefferson County [Kentucky] Board of Education* and *Community Schools v. Seattle School District No. 1)* challenging the use of race to achieve school diversity may reverse the historic *Brown* decision. With the absence of retired Justice Sandra Day O'Connor and the addition of conservatives Justice Samuel Alito and Chief Justice John G. Roberts, Jr., an end to *Brown* isn't inconceivable. It would take a few years, however, to decipher what a reversal would truly mean for future affirmative action initiatives in elementary, secondary, and higher education.

Vouchers and school choice

Because where a student lives determines where a student attends public school, African American parents, especially those who are poor, have had relatively fewer choices regarding where they can send their children if their neighborhood school is inadequate. Therefore, *public vouchers,* government-funded tax credits that allow poorer students to attend private schools, and *public charter schools,* publicly funded schools exempted from certain local and state regulations to allow for more creative education solutions, have become viable educational alternatives for many African Americans.

Supporters of voucher programs and charter schools argue that these initiatives provide alternatives to lower-income families while also challenging public schools to improve or lose students. Those opposed to the initiatives warn that voucher programs and charter schools can only help a handful of students and fail to address how public schools can work for all students.

Many African Americans support voucher programs and charter schools. In a public opinion poll conducted in 2000 in Milwaukee and Cleveland, where public voucher programs exist, 57 percent of African Americans favored public vouchers. Despite constituting 17 percent of the nationwide public school population during the 2000–2001 school year, African Americans comprised an estimated 33 percent of the charter school population. What's not completely clear is how big a difference these initiatives have made and whether African American children are benefiting significantly.

Leaving no child behind? Maybe

Congress's approval of the No Child Left Behind Act (NCLB) in 2001 has created more nationwide dialogue around elementary school reform than any other legislation in at least two decades. The cornerstone of NCLB is creating accountability for the nation's failing public schools. Some key provisions include

✔ Allowing parents to transfer their children to better-performing schools

✔ Providing financial assistance for tutoring and summer programs

✔ Making reading a mandate for every child

✔ Improving teaching quality

✔ Expanding federal support for charter schools

Critics of NCLB, which passed Congress with bipartisan support, have charged that, because the program was severely underfunded, schools can't meet the benchmarks that NCLB mandates.

Most African Americans appear to support NCLB in theory but feel that it needs strengthening. Many seem to like the idea of a national report card presenting student performances categorized by race, while some activists believe that NCLB can help identify and eliminate core racial problems in public education.

While it's still too early to assess NCLB's effectiveness, according to the U.S. Department of Education, reading and math scores for African American 9-year-olds are at all-time highs, as are math scores for African American 13-year-olds. In addition, NCLB appears to be closing the achievement gap between white and black students. Overall, urban schools are reportedly performing better. Some charge that these numbers are misleading because not all school systems operate by the same standards.

Higher Learning

In the 19th century, higher education was rare for the majority of Americans — black or white. College was reserved for the wealthy. Still, African Americans strongly believed that their fate as a race depended on education. With the majority of African Americans enslaved, education was viewed as a prerequisite for achieving universal freedom for all African Americans. Before the Civil War, developments including the founding of the following colleges and universities laid the foundation for the higher education of African Americans:

- ✔ **Cheyney University:** Richard Humphreys originally established this Pennsylvania institution in 1837 as the Institute for Colored Youth. Today, it's the oldest of all Historically Black Colleges and Universities (HBCUs) in the United States.

- ✔ **Oberlin Collegiate Institute:** This Ohio institution, nudged along by a conditional donation from Arthur Tappan, a 19th-century abolitionist and wealthy businessman, became the first in the nation to adopt an open policy with respect to all qualified black students rather than accept them on a case-by-case basis.

- ✔ **Berea College:** Conceived as an institution for blacks and whites, Berea College, located in Kentucky, began its troubled history in 1855. In 1865, it closed before reopening as a segregated institution from 1904 until 1954.

- ✔ **Wilberforce University:** Founded in 1856 by the African Methodist Episcopal (AME) Church, an important force in establishing black higher education, Ohio African University changed its name to Wilberforce in honor of William Wilberforce, the Englishman instrumental in outlawing the slave trade in Britain, when it merged with Union Seminary in 1863. It was the first college owned and operated by African Americans. Former congressman Floyd Flake became the school's 19th president in 2002.

- ✔ **Lincoln University:** Renamed for Abraham Lincoln in 1866, Lincoln University began as Ashmun Institute, named after Jehudi Ashmun, a white emigrationist who served as Liberia's first president.

In spite of the inroads made by some higher education institutions in the years leading up to the Civil War, by the time the war began, only an estimated 28 African Americans possessed bachelor's degrees.

Launching higher education for the African American masses

The Civil War was a pivotal boon to African American education. Between 1861 and 1890, Northern churches and missionary groups created more than 200 black private schools in the South. The Freedmen's Bureau (refer to Chapter 6) later joined that effort.

Most of these schools, public and private, didn't start out as full-fledged colleges and universities but rather as *normal* (an archaic term for teacher's college) schools and institutes, many with an emphasis on agricultural and industrial education. Because of the high illiteracy rate among African Americans, the more-advanced institutions initially functioned as high schools. In keeping with the early beginnings of African American education, these institutions produced preachers and teachers whose mission was to teach and prepare others. By 1872, institutions such as Atlanta University began granting baccalaureate degrees, and two institutions ventured into medicine:

- ✔ **Howard University** in Washington, D.C., chartered by an act of Congress in 1867, enjoyed close ties with the Freedmen's Bureau. That relationship resulted in the establishment of the Freedmen's Hospital in 1868 and Howard University College of Medicine in 1869.

- ✔ **Meharry Medical College** in Nashville, founded under the auspices of the Freedman's Aid Society of the Methodist Episcopal Church in 1876, is the nation's largest and second-oldest historically black medical school.

The fall of Noyes Academy

Some members of the New England Anti-Slavery Society and the American Anti-Slavery Society (both established in the early 1830s) took a practical approach to higher education for African Americans. From 1832 to 1834, they collected funds for what was known as the Manual Labor School, a college preparatory high school open to white and black students.

Canaan, New Hampshire, was the location for what later became the Noyes Academy. In March 1835, 28 white students and 14 black students, including Alexander Crummell, who would go on to become a noted African American intellectual, began classes at Noyes Academy. The school was short-lived, however. After Noyes Academy's own antislavery society president, a black student, delivered a fiery, public antislavery speech on the Fourth of July to thunderous applause, some of Canaan's white residents gave the school a month to close. When the school didn't comply, Canaan's white residents and residents of neighboring towns used 100 oxen to remove the school from its foundation and reportedly dump it in a nearby swamp.

The role of whites in black colleges

With the end of Reconstruction and the Supreme Court sanction of separate but equal in *Plessy v. Ferguson* in 1896, African American colleges were in a precarious position. Ill-meaning whites who controlled black public colleges in some Southern states withheld needed funds. Some well-intentioned whites exhibited paternalistic attitudes that reinforced plantation values despite their mission to educate and uplift black students.

White leadership dominated many African American colleges simply because initially there weren't enough African Americans qualified for such positions. (Well into the 1960s, some black colleges never had nonwhite presidents.) Without white support, many black colleges wouldn't have survived.

When the Freedmen's Bureau closed in 1872, Northern missionary organizations didn't abandon their original missions. One such organization was the all-important American Missionary Association, which was created in 1846 specifically to educate and prepare African Americans to lead themselves. Aid from missionary and benevolent aid societies as well as donations from blacks kept black colleges afloat. After 1900, *Negro colleges,* as they were called, benefited greatly from the expansion of aid from secular foundations, particularly those created by Northern philanthropists. Funding from organizations such as the General Education Board of the Rockefeller Foundation, the Southern Education Board, the Julius Rosenwald Fund, the Phelps-Stokes Fund, and the Carnegie Foundation, helped black colleges thrive.

Until the 1970s, Meharry and Howard trained nearly 80 percent of the nation's African American physicians. Even today, the two institutions, along with the Morehouse School of Medicine in Atlanta and the Charles R. Drew University of Medicine and Science, which operates a college of medicine in conjunction with UCLA, train a high percentage of the nation's black doctors.

The Morrill Acts: Making it stick

The Morrill Acts are some of the most important pieces of legislation for higher education in the United States. Proposing that the government set aside land for each state to create at least one "land-grant college" to educate those who worked the land, Vermont representative Justin Morrill introduced the bill to the House of Representatives in 1857. Morrill's system would provide liberal and practical education to farmers and laborers, among others, especially in the agricultural and mechanical arts (hence, the A&M moniker in the name of many land-grant colleges). Originally vetoed by President Buchanan, the Morrill Act, under President Lincoln in the midst of the Civil War, was reintroduced and passed by Congress. A second Morrill Act in 1890 demanded that states either distribute equal funding to black land-grant colleges or admit blacks to the existing, predominantly white institutions.

Although Southern states in particular continued to underfund comparable black institutions and bar black students from attending predominantly white institutions, the Morrill Acts set important precedents in higher education that the NAACP Legal Defense Fund used in later decades in its attempts to desegregate higher education (refer to Chapter 8 for more).

Determining goal of higher education

An intense intellectual debate divided African American intellectuals for nearly half a century. Booker T. Washington, the elder statesman, and W.E.B. Du Bois, an emerging leader, differed on the most beneficial kind of education for African Americans. Washington was in the industrial education camp; Du Bois favored liberal arts education.

While historically Du Bois and Washington, whom you can read more about in the political realm in Chapter 7, have been portrayed as polar opposites, the truth is that they weren't diametrically opposed to one another. Given the fact that Washington often said one thing while secretly doing another and that Tuskegee offered courses in what are traditionally considered liberal arts areas, Washington and Du Bois may have had more middle ground than the academic community at large suspected. Ultimately, both men were deeply concerned with the overall well-being of black people and each worked tirelessly to uplift the race. Although black educators bitterly debated their arguments long after Washington's death in 1915, each man's argument has some truth to it. In hindsight, the right answer for African American higher education may be a combination of both philosophies.

Booker T. Washington's position

At the turn of the 20th century, Booker T. Washington, shown in Figure 13-1, was the most powerful black man in the United States and one of the nation's most powerful men of any color. Born in Virginia in slavery's last days, Washington studied to become a teacher at Hampton Normal and Agriculture Institute. Inspired by Hampton's white principal's emphasis on industrial education, moral fortitude, and manual labor, Washington eventually headed the newly formed Tuskegee Normal and Industrial Institute in Alabama and built a formidable institution steeped in the values he had learned at Hampton.

Washington influenced countless other institutions, big and small. Known as "the Wizard" for all his complex maneuvering, his ability to relate to various audiences aided him well. Careful not to offend Southern white planters, Washington managed to "stay in his place" while attracting large amounts of money from Northern philanthropists.

Washington's emphasis on trade or industrial education addressed the realities of the recently freed masses. In the late 19th and early 20th centuries, Washington knew that African Americans had a strong connection to agriculture and used Tuskegee to address those immediate needs. Thanks to the work of scholar George Washington Carver, an important agricultural science pioneer, Tuskegee taught local farmers new techniques that allowed them to get the most from the land. The Tuskegee model empowered students to become self-sufficient and to spread that message to other black people by teaching and serving as examples, in addition to founding their own schools.

Figure 13-1:
Booker T.
Washington.

© Corbis

W.E.B. Du Bois's position

Born in 1868 in Great Barrington, Massachusetts, where he was one of just 50 blacks, W.E.B. Du Bois's experience differed from most African Americans. Unable to afford Harvard, Du Bois attended Fisk College in Nashville, where he encountered the plight of black Southerners for the first time. After graduating from Fisk, Du Bois entered Harvard and eventually completed a PhD. He also spent a year of study in Berlin.

Du Bois was an influential faculty member at Atlanta University, the leading institution in the Atlanta University system. During his lifetime, he authored several pioneering scholarly works including *The Suppression of the African Slave Trade* and *The Philadelphia Negro*.

George Washington Carver

Tuskegee's George Washington Carver favored fields and labs to the spotlight. An agricultural genius, Carver's outstanding work is still relevant today. Born during slavery's later years, Carver spent much of his early life with his one-time slave owners Moses and Susan Carver, who also raised his brother.

A sickly child, Carver showed an early aptitude for horticulture. Susan Carver encouraged his education, and Carver, who wasn't permitted to attend school in his hometown, set out for high school in Kansas at age 13. Rejected by several colleges because of his race, Carver eventually attended Simpson College in Iowa, where he excelled in art and music before transferring to Iowa State Agricultural College. Asked to pursue graduate studies, Carter received national recognition as a botanist for his work in plant pathology and mycology.

In 1896, Booker T. Washington recruited Carver to Tuskegee Normal and Industrial Institute in Alabama, where Carver remained until his death in 1943. At Tuskegee, Carver tackled the plight of black farmers; to solve the problem of soil depletion, he suggested they alternate planting cotton crops with legumes such as peanuts or sweet potatoes to restore depleted nutrients to the soil. He also created new uses for crops, especially peanuts, to make them more profitable. Even President Teddy Roosevelt praised Carver's work. Even today, Carver's innovations in regards to multiple uses for peanuts and soy continue to set the tone for agricultural study.

Highly educated and an impeccable scholar, Du Bois applied a scientific approach to the so-called "Negro Problem." Unlike Washington, whose educational approach favored the black masses, Du Bois believed in educating a *Talented Tenth,* the best and brightest members of the race who would then lead the black masses. Although Du Bois acknowledged a need for industrial education, he didn't view industrial education as a means of elevating the race overall. Du Bois believed that only the exceptional men of the race could save it and that black colleges had a responsibility to train this Talented Tenth to become "leaders of thought" and "missionaries of culture." Therefore, he advocated a classical education steeped in languages, such as Latin and French, and texts by Aristotle and Plato.

Du Bois's emphasis on a classical education didn't exclude black culture. As the author of numerous books, many scientific and sociological in scope, Du Bois pioneered early African American–focused education. Nor did Du Bois believe in excluding the black woman from receiving a classical education. When citing men who embodied his ideals of the Talented Tenth, Du Bois often mentioned that their wives read Homer or other venerable works.

Desegregating higher education

African American attendance at predominantly white universities dates as far back as the 18th century, with a number of black students graduating from mainstream universities in the 19th century. The bulk of black students, however, entered white colleges in significant numbers in the 1960s and 1970s on the heels of *Brown v. Board of Education*. Today, black students continue to attend and graduate from predominantly white institutions in significant numbers.

To ensure diversity on college campuses, many schools instituted affirmative action programs in the 1970s. Because some of these programs utilized racial quotas to meet their diversity goals, legal challenges contesting this practice began. The most notable was *Bakke v. California Board of Regents* in 1978. Although the Supreme Court ruled against the use of racial quotas as the main criterion for admitting a student, it decided that a college or university could consider race as one of its criteria in admission policies.

In recent decades, attacks on affirmative action have increased and become more successful. In 1996, California voters passed Proposition 209, which effectively eliminated affirmative action in public school admissions and government hiring. Civil rights activists contend that, as a direct result of Proposition 209, black and Latino enrollments in California colleges have dropped to all-time lows. States such as Michigan and Florida have adopted similar measures.

The United Negro College Fund

Private black colleges faced serious financial challenges in the 1940s. Although they were educating an estimated half of the South's black students, the Great Depression and World War II complicated fundraising efforts. Faced with this financial crisis, Tuskegee Institute's third president, Dr. Frederick D. Patterson, published an open letter in *The Pittsburgh Courier* urging other presidents of black private colleges and universities to pool their resources and raise funds cooperatively. The next year, with 27 colleges and universities on board, the United Negro College Fund (UNCF) raised nearly $800,000.

Pending school desegregation threatened to undermine the UNCF's efforts: With white institutions theoretically opened to black students, the UNCF had to work harder to convince donors to give to black institutions. Always full of surprises,

the UNCF kicked off its second capital campaign in 1963 at the White House; the event was hosted by President John F. Kennedy, who donated the Pulitzer Prize money he received for his book *Profiles in Courage*. Other notable individual contributions to the UNCF include $50 million from billionaire Walter Annenberg and $1 billion from Bill and Melinda Gates.

In 1972, the UNCF adopted the slogan "A Mind Is a Terrible Thing to Waste," which was destined to become one of the most recognizable slogans in American advertising history. First televised in 1979, the star-studded telethon, *The Lou Rawls Parade of Stars*, now *An Evening of Stars*, has contributed over $200 million to the UNCF. For more on the UNCF, check out its Web site at www.uncf.org.

HBCUs: National treasures

The Higher Education Act of 1965, which introduced the label "HBCU," declared such institutions national treasures. While increased African American enrollment at predominantly white colleges and declining numbers at some HBCUs (in addition to some permanent closings) have raised concerns about the viability of HBCUs in the 21st century, there have been efforts to strengthen HCBUs.

Presidents from Jimmy Carter to George W. Bush have signed executive orders intended to enhance HBCUs, and there's evidence that, despite the closing of some HBCUs, state and federal funding for these educational institutions has increased considerably since 1965. Inequities in funding for predominantly black and white universities, as charged in the 30-year court case of *Ayers v. Fordice* involving predominantly black

public institutions such as Jackson State University, haven't disappeared, however. Private institutions such as Atlanta's Spelman College began sidestepping those limitations with aggressive individual fundraising efforts in the 1990s. Under the leadership of then president Dr. Johnnetta B. Cole, Spelman raked in over $100 million during that time.

As Latino and white enrollment in HBCUs also increases, hope grows that perhaps one day Americans will judge all colleges on academic excellence, student-teacher ratios, campus life, and other important factors that measure institutional quality and not racial climate. HBCUs have maintained a tradition of excellence against tremendous odds and that legacy is of vital importance to the nation as a whole.

Extremely competitive colleges and universities in particular use a number of factors when considering enrollment, including region, community service, and socioeconomic status, in addition to test scores and academic performance, which remain the strongest requirements for entry. Challenging admission policies based on race ignores the reality of the admissions process as a whole and reinforces the erroneous perception that higher education is still a "white only" privilege. In addition, by insisting that African American and other minority students have been admitted to some of the nation's most prestigious institutions solely based on race, affirmative action challengers (many of them white and male) have created the perception of black intellectual inferiority.

John Singleton's 1995 film *Higher Learning* took on the various challenges of contemporary college life, particularly for African American students, at a predominantly white university.

School daze: The black Greek system

Marshaling the spirit of racial uplift with a commitment to academic excellence, community service, and brotherhood/sisterhood, Black Greek Letter Organizations (BGLOs) are one of the few institutions uniting black students of both mainstream universities and HBCUs. Outside of African American collegiate circles, knowledge of the *Divine Nine,* the nine fraternities and sororities that comprise the National Pan-Hellenic Council (NPHC), the governing body of African American Greek organizations, is rare. Yet they remain an important force in the overall black community.

BGLOs' historical relevance is profound. Particularly during the early 20th century, BGLO membership at mainstream universities provided a social network to students often isolated because of race. In some cases, funding from BGLOs provided housing in close proximity to schools during a time when black students couldn't live in dorms and often traveled long distances to pursue their educations at predominantly white institutions. Aspiring members must meet acceptance criteria that includes a designated grade-point average, letters of recommendation, and a commitment to community service.

Five fraternities and four sororities make up the Divine Nine; five of these organizations trace their origins to Howard University. Each BGLO is an intense network that connects students and alumni of undergraduate and graduate colleges and universities across the nation and even across the globe for a lifetime, not just the school years. In addition to chapter meetings, BGLOs have regional meetings and annual national conventions. Table 13-1 lists the nine organizations.

Table 13-1			The Divine Nine	
Organization	**Date Founded**	**Founding College**	**Colors**	**Prominent Members**
Fraternities				
Alpha Phi Alpha	1906	Cornell University	Black and gold	W.E.B. Du Bois, Martin Luther King, Jr., former Atlanta mayor Andrew Young, Supreme Court Justice Thurgood Marshall, actor Paul Robeson
Kappa Alpha Psi	1911	Indiana University	Red and white	Talk show host Tavis Smiley, BET Founder Bob Johnson, former Los Angeles Mayor Tom Bradley, tennis legend Arthur Ashe
Omega Psi Phi	1911	Howard University	Purple and gold	Carter G. Woodson, Jesse Jackson, Shaquille O'Neal, Bill Cosby
Phi Beta Sigma	1913	Howard University	Blue and white	Black Panther cofounder Huey P. Newton, Ghanaian President Kwame Nkrumah, NFL great Emmitt Smith, gospel music legend Bobby Jones

(continued)

Table 13-1 *(continued)*

Organization	Date Founded	Founding College	Colors	Prominent Members
Iota Phi Theta	1963	Morgan State University	Brown and gold	*Good Morning America* weatherman Spencer Christian, journalist Michael Frisby, Baltimore Commissioner of Housing Daniel Henson
Sororities				
Alpha Kappa Alpha	1908	Howard University	Pink and green	Coretta Scott King, Phylicia Rashad, astronaut Dr. Mae Jemison, WNBA player Chamique Holdsclaw, Miss America 1990 Debbye Turner
Delta Sigma Theta	1913	Howard University	Red and white	Ida B. Wells-Barnett, Carol Moseley Braun, Olympic gold medalist Wilma Rudolph, AME Bishop Vashti Murphy McKenzie
Zeta Phi Beta	1920	Howard University	Blue and white	Writer/folklorist Zora Neale Hurston, opera singer Grace Bumbry, comedian Sheryl Underwood, poet Gwendolyn Brooks
Sigma Gamma Rho	1922	Butler University	Blue and gold	Finance author Cheryl Broussard, actress Hattie McDaniel, gospel singer Vanessa Bell Armstrong, artist Ruth Russell Williams

Step shows, one of the BGLOs' most recognized activities, are elaborate productions in which opposing Greek organizations or chapters of the same organization demonstrate coordinated body and dance moves that feature rhythmic stomping and clapping accompanied by boastful chanting. Many historians have noted the African retentions in these rituals. Most recently, the 2007 film *Stomp the Yard* brought awareness of stepping and step shows to a broader audience. Stepping was an element of Spike Lee's critical look at black college life, including the black Greek system, in the 1988 film *School Daze.* Although the 2002 film *Drumline* centered on the grand African American marching band tradition, glimpses of black Greek life were also evident.

Part V
A Touch of Genius: Arts, Entertainment, and Sports

The 5th Wave   By Rich Tennant

"I don't get it. I'm playing a legendary jazz musician and the director keeps telling me to stick to the script and stop improvising."

In this part . . .

Rags to riches stories don't happen everyday. Yet, in African American history, especially in arts and entertainment, examples abound.

Talent really does conquer all, and African Americans have rarely squandered their gifts. This part breaks down the history of African Americans in the arts and entertainment world by genre: literature (including slave narratives, the Harlem Renaissance, and award-winning black female writers of the late 20th century); theatre and dance (including blackface, musicals, dramatic theatre, and expanding dance forms); music (including slave spirituals, jazz, pop, and rap); film and TV; and sports.

Chapter 14

Writing Down the Bones: African American Literature

*N*ot allowed to read or write for much of the nation's early years, the majority of African Americans were illiterate until after the Civil War. Yet despite the fact that African Americans were denied basic literacy in many parts of the growing United States, some African Americans, like Phillis Wheatley, created works of great literary merit. As with music (which you can read more about in Chapter 16), African Americans' literary roots are traceable back to Africa.

This chapter explores those roots, from African Americans' rich oral tradition to early novels by such writers as William Wells Brown. I move on to the literary high points of the 20th century, such as the Harlem Renaissance, and the explosion of black women writers in the 1970s and 1980s.

Troubled Beginnings

English wasn't the native tongue of the Africans who arrived in what would become the United States. The first enslaved Africans hailed from different parts of Africa, with some arriving in the colonies by way of the Caribbean. Consequently, slaves didn't share a common African language. They did share several similar traits, including the all-important oral tradition, however. Eventually they melded those similarities with their new European-inspired environment as well as adapted to America's unique characteristics.

Other early works about and by African Americans

The designation of African American poets Lucy Terry and Jupiter Hammon as the first published African American writers in this nation isn't controversy-free. Books about African Americans, including some credited to African Americans, preceded these works. Typically, however, these early African American works were "as told to" stories. Examples include

✔ *Adam Negro's Tryall,* which appeared in 1703, arose from a case in which slave Adam Negro sued his master John Saffin for not honoring his promises to free Negro. Negro eventually won the case, mainly through the aid of Samuel Sewell, who disdained Saffin. Because *Adam Negro's Tryall* contains an amalgamation of documents surrounding the case and lacks one

clear author, many scholars have decided that it isn't a true slave narrative.

✔ *The Declaration and Confession of Jeffrey, a Negro, who was executed at Worchester, October 17, 1745, for the murder of Mrs. Tabitha Sanford, at Mendon, the 12th of September Preceding* is a criminal narrative with questionable black authorship.

✔ *Some Memoirs of the Life of Job, the Son of Solomon, the High Priest of Boonda in Africa,* a 1734 book by white author Thomas Bluett, tells the story of ex-slave Job ben Solomon, who was reputed to be the son of the high priest of Bondu. (For more on this former slave's story, refer to Chapter 3.)

Africans valued orality, and that continued in the new world, especially given the many barriers preventing them from learning to read and write English. In Africa, official storytellers known as *griots* were responsible for keeping the history of their respective villages or areas. They also passed on morality tales, better known as *folktales.* Although some of the details changed to reflect American realities, these tales remained essentially the same as their African predecessors. Folklore became an important means of transferring essential information, particularly survival mechanisms and key African American values such as the importance of community.

As African American literature developed, folktales were the first stories of African American culture and among the first for the broader American culture. The *griot's* role as a historian proved to be a vital one as the oral history tradition became the method by which many African Americans preserved their collective and individual histories. Early published works by African Americans, however, didn't directly reflect black folk traditions. Actually, many such works rarely contained any indications of race.

Early poets

There's very little evidence that any enslaved Africans learned English formally. Separated from those who spoke their language, African slaves had to find a way to communicate with each other as well as their white slaveholders. In the early 18th century, American literature was still developing and African American literature generally didn't exist. Yet despite these limitations, some African Americans beat the odds to lay the foundation for future African American writers. First among them are the poets:

- **Lucy Terry:** Although published a little over 100 years after it was composed in 1746, Lucy Terry's only surviving poem "Bars Fight," about the Indian massacre of two white families in Deerfield, Massachusetts, makes her, for many scholars, the first published black writer in the United States. In the poem, Terry's race is undetectable even though she was born in Africa and kidnapped into slavery.

- **Jupiter Hammon:** Frequently credited as the first published black writer, American-born slave and devout Christian Jupiter Hammon composed "An Evening Thought. Salvation By Christ with Penitential Cries," in 1760. Owned by several generations of the Lloyd family in Long Island, New York, Hammon was formally educated.

- **Phillis Wheatley:** Phillis Wheatley, who was captured into slavery at age 7 from her native Senegal in West Africa and had mastered English by the age of 13, is the most famous of the early black poets. Wheatley's owners cultivated her intellectual abilities by permitting her to study Greek, Latin, mythology, and history. By 1767, the 13-year-old published her first poem. Many sources cite Wheatley's work in poetry as the genesis of African American literature.

Since asserting that the intellectual inferiority of enslaved Africans was a cornerstone of American slavery (see Chapters 4 and 5 for more details), some colonists, including Thomas Jefferson, questioned Wheatley's authorship, forcing Wheatley to prove her authenticity in court in 1772; Boston luminaries like John Hancock certified Wheatley as genuine. When a London publisher published Wheatley's *Poems on Various Subjects, Religious and Moral* a year later, it included a certificate of authenticity. Because of Wheatley's race, Boston publishers had refused to publish the book. (NBA player Chris Webber owns a first edition copy of that 1773 book of poetry.)

In later decades, religious conversion to Christianity became the primary context in which African Americans learned to read. Under that circumstance, the Bible became increasingly more important to African American writers. (Flip to Chapter 12 for more on religious conversion and literacy during slavery.)

Slave narratives

After the American Revolution, the North and South began to divide themselves as antislavery and proslavery. Unlike the work of early African American writers, race was a primary concern of black writers during this period. As a result, a new genre known as the *slave narrative* emerged. While these narratives were autobiographies to an extent, they served a greater abolitionist function (read more about slavery and abolitionism during the 1800s in Chapters 4 and 5). Slave narratives share certain key characteristics:

- ✔ **Claim of authorship:** Proslavery factions often accused those opposed to slavery of making up horrific stories about slavery. Therefore, it was critical for slave narratives to establish the authenticity of the individual telling the story. As the slave narrative developed, many were written by the former slaves themselves, but some were dictated to others.

- ✔ **Testimonial from respected white abolitionist or editor:** Few slave narratives went unauthenticated. The words of both William Lloyd Garrison and Wendell Phillips, two of the nation's most prominent abolitionists, appeared at the beginning of Frederick Douglass's 1845 slave narrative.

- ✔ **Tales of bondage:** "I was born" begins the first sentence of many slave narratives as authors (usually male since fewer women penned slave narratives) shared the early details of their lives. Quite often, the author's father was white or unknown. Recognition of one's status as a slave was critical in the early part of the narrative. Meanwhile, the bulk of the narrative discussed the actual bondage experience, with the author frequently including details about Christian conversion and learning to read. Whippings that they themselves or others received was another prominent feature, as were tales of separated family members and failed escape attempts by themselves or others.

- ✔ **Escape and freedom:** Typically, considerable planning went into successful escapes and, in the narratives, the authors disclosed enough details without being too specific, because of the fear that too many details would prevent others from also escaping. Becoming free was the ultimate goal of the slave narrative, so slave narratives ended with the author's freedom.

Although proslavery factions frequently accused the authors of slave narratives of exaggerating the horrors of slavery, more often than not, the authors hadn't exaggerated the incidents but, rather, humanized them. Since slavery functioned on a belief in the inhumanity of African Americans, slave narratives rebuked this thinking by asserting and affirming that humanity.

Before 1865, an estimated 100 slave narratives were published, with the bulk of them published between 1830 and 1860. Given the high illiteracy rates among both whites and blacks in early America, the number of published narratives is quite high. Scholars frequently cite *The Interesting Life of Olaudah Equiano or Gustavus Vassa* as the first published slave narrative.

Narrative of the Life of Frederick Douglass, an American Slave

Slave narratives became an important tool to advance abolitionism and few were as influential as Frederick Douglass's *Narrative of the Life of Frederick Douglass, an American Slave,* published in 1845. A skilled orator, Douglass already had quite an abolitionist following prior to the publication of his *Narrative.* Although simple and full of the slave narrative tropes discussed earlier, Douglass's writing possessed an uncommon eloquence.

More than contributing eloquence, Douglass brought attention to the hidden messages in slave or *sorrow* songs, suggesting that African Americans developed subversive strategies to manage slavery. As later generations discovered, Douglass's work revealed that African Americans possessed a unique culture that was distinctly different from that of white Americans. That reality fueled African American literature for generations.

Incidents in the Life of a Slave Girl

Orators such as Maria Stewart and Sojourner Truth discussed sex and sexuality before Harriet Jacobs, but their prose lacked the emotional and sustained punch of Jacobs's slave narrative, *Incidents in the Life of a Slave Girl,* published in 1861.

Because *Incidents in the Life of a Slave Girl* came out in the same year the Civil War began, it made a greater impact in the 20th century as a direct testimony of the sexual exploitation experienced by slave women. You can find more coverage of gender issues in Chapter 11.

A novel journey

By providing the first portraits of African American heroes, slave narratives played a key role in the development of the African American novel. Readers of slave narratives learned that African Americans possessed great intellect and tremendous courage, remarkable qualities for fictional characters. Therefore, it's little surprise that slavery figured so prominently in *Clotel; or The President's Daughter,* the first African American novel. After all, its author, William Wells Brown, published his successful slave narrative, *Narrative of William W. Brown, a Fugitive Slave,* in 1847.

Published in London in 1853 and inspired by Thomas Jefferson's rumored relationship with his slave Sally Hemings, *Clotel* traces several generations of racially mixed women linked to Thomas Jefferson. Brown, whose father and grandfather were white, established the *tragic mulatto* as a key literary archetype in African American literature. Historically, the tragic mulatto has been a female tormented by being neither black nor white. *Clotel* was so successful that it went through several editions.

Other key early novels include

✔ ***Our Nig,*** by Harriet E. Wilson (published in 1859). Like Brown, Wilson used the tragic mulatto theme but went a step further by also presenting an interracial marriage. Much of *Our Nig* mirrored Wilson's life.

Our Nig is both the first novel by an African American published in the United States *and* the first by an African American female writer. Until Harvard's Henry Louis Gates rediscovered *Our Nig* in the early 1980s, however, it was a forgotten text.

✔ ***The Garies and Their Friends*** (published in London in 1857), by Frank J. Webb: Interestingly, this rarely studied novel, published in London, was the first to feature free blacks as well as a lynch mob. It was also among the first works to discuss the concept of passing for white in detail.

✔ ***Blake,*** by Martin Delany (serialized in two African American publications in 1859 and 1860): *Blake* is noteworthy for its trailblazing black national-ist and Pan-Africanist sensibilities. Unlike *Clotel* or *Our Nig,* Delany's pro-tagonist isn't biracial. In addition, *Blake* is largely about a rebellious plot to liberate both black Americans and black Cubans. First published in book form in 1970, the novel advocates black self-reliance over white benevolence and boldly references white oppression of blacks.

After the Civil War, racial inequality replaced slavery as the hot-button issue, and literary works by African Americans reflected that. Because black liter-acy rates increased, black writers could no longer assume that their audience was almost exclusively white. Two key developments during this period include *racial uplift* and the *black folk tradition.*

Racial uplift

The concept of racial uplift prevalent in African American works from the late 19th and early 20th centuries acknowledged the challenges of racial inequal-ity but remained hopeful that African Americans could rise above them. Therefore, many of the early protagonists in these works were model charac-ters, often suppressing their individual wants for the greater good of the larger black community while also communicating the middle-class values whites found acceptable. The work of Pauline E. Hopkins and others reflected these tensions. The most popular texts embodying the "racial uplift" mantra, however, include

✔ ***Iola Leroy*** **by Frances Ellen Watkins Harper:** Although better known as a poet, Harper published the novel *Iola Leroy* in 1892. Set at the close of the Civil War and at the onset of Reconstruction, the novel covers some important historical events such as reuniting with family after the war. Ultimately, the biracial heroine, though raised as white, chooses not to marry a white suitor who insists that she never reveal her race. Instead, she marries a biracial black doctor, and they dedicate themselves to uplifting the race.

✔ ***Up From Slavery*** **by Booker T. Washington:** Tracing Washington's life from his birth and experience of slavery to his journey to educate him-self before becoming Tuskegee's renowned leader, *Up From Slavery* champions middle-class values, emphasizing education and hard work as key qualities to help black people overcome racial inequality. Read more about *Up From Slavery* in Chapter 20.

Considered by some the last of the great slave narratives because Washington was born in slavery, more often, *Up From Slavery* (1901) is acknowledged as the first great African American autobiography.

✔ *The Souls of Black Folk* **by W.E.B. Du Bois:** W.E.B. Du Bois's seminal work, *The Souls of Black Folk* (1903), is a myriad of things: social commentary, history, poetry, and sociological treatise. Du Bois's essays consider the challenges African Americans face, in particular the "twoness" of African American culture, or simply the reality of being black in a white world. In *The Souls of Black Folk,* Du Bois advocates the idea of a *Talented Tenth,* in which the best and brightest of the black community would bear the responsibility of advancing the whole race. This concept fueled many debates during the Harlem Renaissance. See the next section for more information on the Harlem Renaissance and turn to Chapter 20 for more information about *The Souls of Black Folk.*

Black folk tradition

A few black writers began incorporating African American vernacular and folk culture in their work. This development didn't occur in a vacuum, however. White writers, most notably Mark Twain, were also embracing "common" folk and speech. Others such as Thomas Nelson Page, Joel Chandler Harris, and George Washington Cable were writing tales where the plantation played a prominent role. Two early pioneers of the black folk tradition are

✔ **Paul Laurence Dunbar:** With his book, *Lyrics of a Lowly Life* (1896), which combined two previously published volumes, Dunbar became the first black poet since Phillis Wheatley to enjoy widespread popularity. The Dayton, Ohio, native's expert mixture of English and dialect brought African American folk traditions into African American literature. His two notable works of fiction include *The Strength of Gideon and Other Stories* (1900), which deals with the plantation and features only African Americans as the primary characters, and *The Sport of the Gods* (1902), one of the first novels set in Harlem as well as one of the first to deal with the negative aspects of city life.

✔ **Charles Chesnutt:** Considered the first major African American fiction writer, Chesnutt consciously employed the black folk tradition to counter the proslavery spin that white authors, such as Joel Chandler Harris who penned the popular Uncle Remus series, put on African American folklore. Chesnutt's Uncle Julius in *The Conjure Woman, and Other Stories* (1899), his most popular work of fiction, outsmarts a transplanted white Northerner. African American folklore served as tales of both morality and survival, a function not always communicated by Harris and others. Chesnutt went beyond simply using the black folk tradition; he also placed emphasis on the positive aspects of that tradition, which Harlem Renaissance writer Zora Neale Hurston later expanded.

In the face of racial uplift, the creative choices of using black folk tradition appeared counterproductive, especially to those who felt that literature could show that African Americans possessed the same values that the white population treasured. Other African Americans felt that emphasizing and embracing black folk culture and speech could empower black Americans.

Writers' Party: The Harlem Renaissance

No period of African American literary history receives as much attention as the Harlem Renaissance, which ranged roughly from the beginning of World War I to the Great Depression. For the first time, African American artists from various realms — literature, art, and music — formed a collective movement. Although Harlem still gets most of the credit, Washington, D.C., specifically Howard University, was another important site, mainly because of the significant role Howard University professor Alain Locke played in the movement.

Influenced heavily by his studies abroad, when he explored the African influence on Western civilization, Locke, the nation's first African American Rhodes scholar, encouraged black artists in America to look to Africa for inspiration and apply that influence to their own work. Lack of culture was one of the reasons cited to justify the enslavement of black people. Locke felt that disproving that theory would affect both black and white people positively. In addition to identifying artists and hosting discussions among them, Locke published the important anthology *The New Negro,* a collection of essays about African American contributions to the arts as well as a sampling of fiction and poetry by emerging black artists, in 1925.

Even though he received much of the attention, Locke wasn't the only one who recognized the impact black artists could have in improving race relations. Both the National Urban League (NUL) and the NAACP, the nation's two leading civil rights organizations, played significant roles in cultivating writers in particular. From 1923 to 1928, the NUL's Charles S. Johnson fostered the careers of many artists by organizing dinners that allowed writers to network with book publishers, magazine editors, and other writers as well as establishing literary contests with monetary prizes. Jessie Redmon Fauset, a noted Harlem Renaissance writer in her own right, also nurtured new talent by publishing their works in the pages of the NAACP magazine, *The Crisis.*

Why Harlem?

Several factors outside of New York serving as the headquarters for both the NAACP and the NUL contributed to Harlem serving as the mecca for this movement:

- **Harlem as a cultural center for black Americans:** The black Broadway invasion, which you can read more about in Chapter 15, generated more interest in black culture among whites. White dramatists such as Eugene O' Neill took an interest in black life and culture. In 1920, O'Neill's play *The Emperor Jones* placed an African American in a leading role. The next year the black Broadway musical, *Shuffle Along,* captivated both black and white audiences. All this coincided with the increasing popularity of jazz, and Harlem was a major nucleus for it all. Several clubs such as the Cotton Club purposely catered to white patrons intrigued by black culture.

✔ **Harlem as one of the primary destinations for the Great Migration.**
The Great Migration refers to the mass exodus of black people from the South that began in 1914 (flip to Chapter 7 to read more about the Great Migration). As a result, Harlem artists hailed from various parts of the United States, creating an atmosphere full of new ideas. At the same time, Harlem wasn't shielded from the migration's negative effects, such as overcrowding, segregated housing, and race riots, either. Therefore, many of the works created by the artists who lived in Harlem or, at least, visited it regularly, reflected a national black identity.

The movement wasn't originally dubbed the Harlem Renaissance. Alain Locke and others referred to it as the *New Negro Movement,* which reflected the sweeping changes African Americans all over the nation were experiencing. Jacksonville, Florida, native James Weldon Johnson, a writer who became a leader of the NAACP, actually coined the movement the "Harlem Renaissance" and the moniker stuck.

Key Renaissance artists and themes

A large number of artists representing various parts of the country participated in the Harlem Renaissance. The overwhelming majority were highly educated, hailing from some of the most prestigious black and mainstream universities in the nation. Many were very accomplished in other professions. For example, writer Rudolph Fisher, noted for *City of Refuge,* was also a medical doctor.

Harlem Renaissance writers embraced a myriad of themes, but middle-class black America figured prominently in many of the works, as did the theme of *passing,* an expansion of the tragic mulatto theme first introduced in the mid–19th century (refer to the earlier section "A novel journey"). Nella Larsen's *Passing* (1929), about a chance encounter that reunites two childhood female friends, one who is passing for white and another living as a black person, is a seminal work. Another highly regarded book on the subject is James Weldon Johnson's *The Autobiography of an Ex-Coloured Man* (1912). The book, written as a fictional autobiography about a man who ultimately chooses to pass as white to free himself from the mistreatment black people receive, achieved popularity when it was reissued in 1927.

Ultimately, class tensions created a sizable rift among many Harlem Renaissance writers, with Langston Hughes and Zora Neale Hurston becoming the most famous advocates of the black folk. Both Hughes and Hurston rebuffed arguments that writing about the black middle class would improve race relations by showing white readers that many African Americans were like them. Critics of Hurston and Hughes felt that embracing the black folk would reinforce primitive stereotypes about black people instead of setting the record straight. Others had simply internalized feelings that African American life and culture was inferior to that of white Americans.

Jean Toomer

Jean Toomer's background was racially mixed, and he didn't identify himself as African American until time spent in Sparta, Georgia, brought him into intimate contact with black rural life. As much a reflection of Toomer's own search for identity, his mixture of poems, short stories, and drama, *Cane* (1923) presents black Southern culture as well as the black Southerner's adaptation to the urban North before reconciling those two realities in the black South.

In critical ways, *Cane* encapsulated the massive search for black identity that underscored the key debates of the Harlem Renaissance. Many artists and leaders, even those who embraced their racial heritage, weren't quite sure how to incorporate their past into their present. While this tension wasn't a new concern, rendering it in a distinctly artistic mode was unique. *Cane* demonstrated the artistic potential and merit of these tensions as grounding forces for great literary work.

Contemporary scholars include Jean Toomer's *Cane* in both the Harlem Renaissance and the Lost Generation, a group of World War I–era American writers that included F. Scott Fitzgerald, Ernest Hemingway, and T.S. Eliot.

Langston Hughes

One of the Harlem Renaissance's first published writers, Hughes's poem "The Negro Speaks of Rivers" appeared in the NAACP magazine *The Crisis* in 1921. Even though Harlem Renaissance artists were encouraged to depict black life, some advisors championed black middle-class life and values over those of the working class. Hughes disagreed, and in his influential 1926 essay "The Negro Artist and the Racial Mountaintop," he asserted that the black artist who ran away from himself couldn't be great. Hughes championed black art that reflected black life, not just appropriate black life. Hughes was later known for his seminal 1951 poem "Harlem," often erroneously labeled "A Dream Deferred" for its famous line of "what happens to a dream deferred?" and other works.

Zora Neale Hurston

Zora Neale Hurston never outgrew her Harlem Renaissance fame. A student of anthropology who studied with Columbia University's Franz Boas, Hurston also worked for noted black historian Carter G. Woodson and accompanied Alan Lomax on some of his most celebrated folklore missions. Raised in the all-black town of Eatonville, Florida, Hurston was an outspoken supporter of rural African Americans and black folk traditions. Hurston's white patronage did trouble many of her black contemporaries who accused her of pandering to whites. Despite winning several contests for impressive short stories like "Spunk" and writing for a number of noted publications during the height of the Harlem Renaissance, Hurston published most of her acclaimed works in the

1930s during the Harlem Renaissance's decline. After Alice Walker's rediscovery of *Their Eyes Were Watching God* (1937) in the 1970s, the novel became an important text in the African American literary canon and in many Southern literature classes as well. (For more on this work, check out Chapter 20.)

Other noteworthy artists

Other important Harlem Renaissance figures include Wallace Thurman, best known for *The Blacker the Berry* (1929); poet Countee Cullen, noted for his poem, "Heritage"; and poet Claude McKay, known for his poem "If We Must Die" and the novel *Home to Harlem* (1928).

Supporting the arts

Alain Locke, Charles S. Johnson, and Jessie Redmon Fauset may have been intimately involved in fostering black artists, but these artists still required financial support and additional exposure. Therefore, several patrons, white and black, including a few key white organizations, facilitated that process. Some of the more prominent included

✓ **Charlotte Osgood Mason:** The influential Charlotte Osgood Mason, a financial patron to both Langston Hughes and Zora Neale Hurston, became involved in the Harlem Renaissance after hearing Alain Locke lecture on black artists in 1927. Extremely meddlesome, Mason, who hosted many gatherings for black artists in her Park Avenue apartment, tried to dictate Hughes's whereabouts and reportedly had Hurston sign an agreement not to publish anything without her approval. Both writers had fallen out with her by 1932. Soon after, she withdrew all financial support from the Harlem Renaissance.

✓ **Carl Van Vechten:** A writer himself, Carl Van Vechten was fascinated with Harlem's vices and frequently commented on the "exoticism" and "primitivism" of black culture, which bothered many. His 1926 novel titled *Nigger Heaven* didn't alleviate those concerns. Still, he brought a lot of mainstream attention to Harlem and black artists in various genres. A photographer as well, Van Vechten included a number of prominent black artists among his famous portraits.

✓ **The Harmon Foundation:** Although more noted for its contributions to African American artists, the Harmon Foundation, endowed by real estate tycoon William E. Harmon, also provided financial awards to writers. While its influence extended beyond the Harlem Renaissance years, it first established its reputation as a premier supporter of African American fine arts during the Harlem Renaissance.

✓ **A'Lelia Walker:** One of the few black patrons, A'Lelia Walker, the only daughter of Madame C.J. Walker, who became a millionaire in the black hair-care industry, was notorious for her well-attended Harlem parties, but not for any outright monetary gifts to Harlem Renaissance artists.

To the dismay of artists such as Claude McKay, these patrons sometimes had their own creative ideas and dictated them to the artists. Faced with the threat of withdrawal of funds, some artists acquiesced to their demanding patrons.

Post–World War II, Civil Rights–era Literature

Literary scholars are often at a loss in clearly defining the literary period following the Harlem Renaissance. Although Richard Wright began his writing career during the last years of the Harlem Renaissance, he became the predominating African American literary voice in the 1940s. He was such a literary titan that critics frequently dubbed male writers who followed him as "sons of Richard Wright." Both Ralph Ellison and James Baldwin wrote in the shadow of Richard Wright.

Naturalism, realism, and modernism became the predominant literary styles of this period. Much of Richard Wright's early work follows the rules of *naturalism,* where an author attempts to apply scientific principles to human behavior. *Realism,* as its name suggests, is a realistic rendering of life even in fiction. Therefore, many black writers embraced the common black man and woman, specifically tying the unrealized potential of African Americans to racism.

Rejection of previous traditions is a key component of *modernism,* and a number of black writers embraced this concept as well. They broke with the Harlem Renaissance theme of using literature for the purpose of social acceptance but didn't unconditionally embrace all things "folk." In addition to experimentation with form, the incorporation of African American myth and ritual became important elements that would later resurface in works by Toni Morrison and Gloria Naylor in particular. Black writers during this period continued to grapple with the effects of the Great Migration, which ebbed and flowed. Although the city took center stage in these new works, vestiges of rural Southern life remained, often resulting in underlying tensions relating to class and culture.

While a number of very good writers such as Ann Petry, Pulitzer Prize–winning poet Gwendolyn Brooks, William Attaway, Chester Himes, and Dorothy West (who is lumped with Harlem Renaissance writers), emerged in the post-Renaissance, pre–Black Arts era of African American literature, Richard Wright, Ralph Ellison, and James Baldwin dominated.

Richard Wright

A legend in his lifetime, the Mississippi-born Richard Wright became the benchmark for African American writers. Black writers, especially male writers, either embraced him or spurned him, but they couldn't ignore him.

Although he followed other black artists such as Josephine Baker by relocating to Paris to escape American racism in 1946, Richard Wright remained an American literary titan, even after his death in 1960. A few of Wright's most notable literary achievements include

- ✔ *Uncle Tom's Children* **(1938):** Wright first attracted attention with this collection of four novellas exploring the brutal reality of surviving racism in the American South. Trying to find dignity and a realization of self within the systematic oppression of Jim Crow was a unifying theme for the collection. In "Big Boy Leaves Home," for example, white mob violence mars an innocent outing to the swimming hole, prompting Big Boy to flee the South. Another edition of *Uncle Tom's Children,* with a couple of new stories, appeared in 1940.

- ✔ *Native Son* **(1940):** In this novel, Bigger Thomas, poor and uneducated, takes a menial job with a rich white family. When the daughter ignores the social taboos dictating proper contact between a white woman and black man, Thomas becomes fearful to the point that he accidentally kills her. During his trial, where the main objective becomes saving Thomas from the death penalty, Wright emphasizes that American racism turns many well-meaning black men into Bigger Thomas on a routine basis. Although Bigger is guilty, Wright makes a strong argument that forces beyond his control have crippled his life by severely limiting his choices.

Influenced by Communism and the *Chicago School* (a group of social scientists, black and white, who pioneered race relations by studying the impact of urbanization and other forces on ethnic communities), Wright's *Native Son* sold 250,000 copies in its first run. It was also the first Book of the Month Club recommendation from a black author.

- ✔ *12 Million Black Voices: A Folk History of the Negro in the United States* **(1941):** Like Wright's autobiography *Black Boy* (1945), *12 Million Black Voices* addresses the Great Migration, among other seminal events. In this work, Wright's poetic words match the powerful images of black American history.

Frank Yerby

Successful writer Frank Yerby enjoyed quiet success with best-selling novels like *The Foxes of Harrow* (1946), which became an Oscar-nominated film starring Rex Harrison and Maureen O'Hara. A thorough researcher, the Augusta, Georgia, native often footnoted his historical novels. Before he died in 1991, Yerby published 33 novels, including *The Dahomean* (1971), later published as *The Man from Dahomey.*

Ralph Ellison

Unlike Richard Wright and James Baldwin, Ralph Ellison produced few works (*Juneteenth,* his second novel, was published posthumously). Ellison's novel *Invisible Man* (1952) is such a crowning achievement, however, that it alone has solidified his place not only in African American literature but also in the broader category of American literature. In *Invisible Man*, an unnamed black protagonist born, raised, and partially educated in the South, tracks his 20-year journey of social invisibility from the South to New York City, documenting his transformation from racial naiveté to enlightenment. He also documents his journey from subscribing to the belief that the American dream is a possibility for African Americans to the ultimate realization that that belief is untrue. In the North, he finds that, while the color line isn't as firmly fixed as in the South, it still exists. Yet he holds on to his grandfather's deathbed advice to, in essence, keep living.

Unlike protagonists in novels of the past, however, Ellison's unnamed protagonist doesn't seek the social acceptance of white America nor is he uncritical of black America. Prominent African Americans such as Booker T. Washington and Marcus Garvey, albeit fictionally rendered, aren't safe from his social critiques. *Invisible Man* draws from a broad historical context but doesn't reject the black folk past either. The novel embraces jazz and blues, uniquely American art forms created out of African Americans' status as second-class citizens as well as slaves. Although the history that produces them is heartbreaking, their existence is hopeful.

James Baldwin

Primarily with the novel *Another Country* (1962), James Baldwin stretched conversations regarding personal and racial identity issues further by adding homosexuality and consensual interracial relationships to the African American literary discussion. The Harlem native was also among the first to criticize the black church beyond a black-white dynamic; in his largely autobiographical first novel, *Go Tell It on the Mountain* (1955), Baldwin, a former child-preacher tormented by his preacher stepfather, places the black church under a microscope, examining its historical function as well as its repressive effects. While it's clearly understood that the black church disdains homosexuality, there's an unstated homoerotic tension within the novel. An outspoken civil rights supporter, Baldwin's essays *Notes of a Native Son* (1955) and *The Fire Next Time* (1963) proved as popular as his works of fiction, some of which didn't feature any black characters.

The Breakthrough: The Black Arts Movement

By the late 1960s and early 1970s, black writers had become more secure with their own identities and no longer felt obligated to speak to white audiences directly. Instead, they turned inward, bringing their literary journey full circle to embrace the values advocated by the Black Arts Movement.

Unlike the Harlem Renaissance, the Black Arts Movement was free of white patronage and black middle-class restraints; essentially, it was far more self-contained. According to Larry Neal, one of the movement's chief architects, "The Black Arts Movement is radically opposed to any concept of the artist that alienates him from his community. Black arts is the aesthetic and the spiritual sister of the Black Power concept. As such, it envisions an art that speaks directly to the needs and aspirations of Black Americans."

The beginning of the movement

Acknowledged as a leading force of the Black Arts Movement, LeRoi Jones (also known as Amiri Baraka) enjoyed considerable mainstream success before embracing black nationalism. His critically acclaimed tome *Blues People* (1963) tied African American music to various social and political developments. His 1964 play *Dutchman,* which uses the flirtation between a black man and white woman to attack the white racist power structure, won an Obie (the Off-Broadway theatre award). Yet despite these successes and his position as an influential Beat poet, Jones severed his ties to the white community, including his white wife Hettie Cohen Jones.

Prompted by Malcolm X's assassination in 1965, Jones left Manhattan's Lower East Side to establish the Black Arts Repertory Theatre/School (BARTS) with a group of other artists in Harlem. For many, this marked the formal beginning of the Black Arts Movement. Although BARTS was short-lived, its formation inspired others in Chicago, Detroit, the Bay Area, and other urban centers. More importantly, artists in these areas embraced the Black Arts ideology as national publications such as the *Negro Digest* (later known as *Black World*) kept the Black Arts concept in the public eye.

Welcoming new voices

Many new African American voices, particularly poets, emerged during the Black Arts Movement. In Detroit, Dudley Randall's Broadside Press published a slew of new poets, including Nikki Giovanni, Sonia Sanchez, Etheridge Knight, and Don L. Lee (also known as Haki Madhubuti). Acclaimed poet Gwendolyn Brooks, who, in 1950, became the first black writer to win the coveted Pulitzer Prize, served as a treasured advisor and member of the Chicago-Detroit arm of the Black Arts Movement. Other popular Black Arts affiliates included spoken word artists The Last Poets and Gil Scott-Heron.

Theatre was also a major component of the Black Arts Movement, with Barbara Ann Teer's National Black Theatre in New York and Val Gray Ward's Kuumba Theatre in Chicago serving as hallmarks. On the university level, Nathan Hare led the charge for universities to establish black studies programs. Dismissed by Howard University in 1967 for his black power activities, including his demand that Howard become an institution more responsive to the black community, Hare, who coined the term "ethnic studies," established the first black studies program at San Francisco State in 1968. He and Robert Chrisman also established *The Black Scholar,* the first journal of black studies and research in the country.

Its legacy

By the mid-1970s, the Black Arts Movement, along with other organizations tied to the black power movement, began to disappear. Its legacy of creating art for and about black people lived on in an entirely new generation of black artists who refused to compromise their identities, however. Ultimately, the movement, as Langston Hughes suggested in his 1926 essay "The Negro Artist and the Racial Mountaintop," recognized that the new black artist had to step away from Du Bois's notion of double consciousness as well as resist dialoguing with the white reading public at the expense of communicating with black people about black people.

Anthologies from the Black Arts Movement

Key publications representative of the Black Arts Movement include these anthologies:

- ✔ *Black Fire,* **edited by Amiri Baraka and Larry Neal (1968):** A signature work with over 180 selections, including essays, poetry, and short stories, from 75 writers.

- ✔ *Black Voices,* **edited by Abraham Chapman (1968):** An impressive collection drawing from black voices such as Frederick Douglass, Richard Wright, Malcolm X, Mari Evans, and historian John Henrik Clarke that span over a century.

Women's Work

Historically, African American literature has been male-dominated. Before the 1970s, only a handful of black women writers had created what many scholars considered important work. Toni Cade Bambara's 1970 anthology *The Black Woman* helped launch an entirely new literary movement. This momentous work celebrating the unique voices of black women was unprecedented and helped change the core of African American literature, taking it to new heights both creatively and commercially.

As black women writers like Toni Cade Bambara, Alice Walker, Toni Morrison, Maya Angelou, and a host of others focused on black women in their work, a fuller sense of the black community emerged. Not just consumed with racial equality, black women writers contemplated questions of self-love, motherhood, and sexuality. They tackled serious explorations of how women related to men and, just as important, how women related to each other.

Unlike other literary movements, there's little debate over when the black women writers' explosion began. With the publication of Bambara's anthology *The Black Woman*, Alice Walker's *The Third Life of Grange Copeland,* and Toni Morrison's *The Bluest Eye,* 1970 was a watershed year for black women's literature. Although many excellent writers emerged during this time, Alice Walker and Toni Morrison became the most important and universally well-known.

With Walker and Morrison leading the charge as literary innovators, black women writers ushered in a new generation of women writers; the Brooklyn-born Gloria Naylor, author of *The Women of Brewster Place* (1982) and *Mama Day* (1988), stood out from the bunch. African American women dominated the period so completely that, aside from Ernest Gaines, few black male writers received considerable attention.

Black women writers before 1970

Black women writers began building a literary tradition long before 1970. Writers such as Harriet Jacobs, Harriet E. Wilson, and Frances Ellen Watkins Harper, among others, from the slavery and Reconstruction eras were early pioneers of the African American female literary tradition. The less well-known Alice Dunbar-Nelson drew from her New Orleans Creole upbringing for her unique stories before the more well-known writers Jessie Redmon Fauset, Nella Larsen, and Zora Neale Hurston emerged.

Gwendolyn Brooks, Ann Petry, and Dorothy West were the prominent female writers of the 1940s and 1950s. In 1959, Paule Marshall published her groundbreaking *Brown Girl, Brownstones,* which injected the black female immigrant voice into the American literary landscape. Margaret Walker Alexander, best known for her acclaimed collection of poetry, *For My People,* contributed the novel, *Jubilee,* in 1966, which showed the literary possibilities of the neo–slave narrative from a female perspective.

Ernest Gaines and *The Autobiography of Miss Jane Pittman*

Louisiana native and celebrated Southern writer Ernest Gaines earned his stripes with the 1971 novel *The Autobiography of Miss Jane Pittman*, the story of a 100-year-old black woman whose life spans the Civil War, Reconstruction, Jim Crow, and the civil rights movement. While Gaines also lived in California as a child, his Southern heritage inspires his outstanding work, which includes *A Gathering of Old Men* (1984) and *A Lesson Before Dying* (1993), which like *Miss Jane Pittman* have both been television movies.

Alice Walker

Born to sharecroppers in 1944 in Eatonton, Georgia, and active in the predominantly white feminist movement, Alice Walker pushed the literary boundaries of black female characters. Her most enduring work, *The Color Purple* (1982), which discussed the rape and sexual exploitation of black women by black men, angered some black men and women who accused her of airing the black community's dirty laundry. Her depiction of black lesbianism also generated criticism.

A former civil rights worker, Walker, mainly in her novel *Meridian* (1976), was among the first writers to use fiction to explore the complexities of that movement, especially from the perspective of an African American woman. Aware of black women's displacement in both African American and women's literature, Walker restored Zora Neale Hurston's literary legacy when she discovered her work in the 1970s.

Recognizing feminism's limitations regarding black women, Walker proposed a new context for black women's experiences that she labeled *womanism* in her book of essays *In Search of Our Mothers' Gardens* (1983). Derived from the black Southern term "womanish," usually applied to little girls who act older than their years, womanism is a feminist view that addresses the black woman's unique experience of double oppression as both black and female.

Octavia Butler

The first major black science fiction writer, the California-born Octavia Butler's popular works include *Kindred* (1979), *Parable of the Sower* (1993), and its sequel, *Parable of the Talents* (1998). Butler, who died in 2006, infused science fiction with the African American experience. In *Kindred*, for example, a black woman travels to the 19th century and meets her ancestors: a white slaveholder and a free black woman forced into slavery.

Other successful black science fiction writers include Samuel R. Delany and Steven Barnes. The black science fiction anthology series *Dark Matter*, edited by writer Sheree R. Thomas, has introduced new voices that include Nalo Hopkinson.

Toni Morrison

Toni Morrison, born in Lorain, Ohio, in 1931, didn't pursue writing until later in life. A graduate of Howard and Cornell universities, Morrison taught at the college level for several years before becoming a book editor. As an editor at Random House, she shepherded black writers such as her friend Toni Cade Bambara and Gayl Jones. Morrison also edited *The Black Book* (1974), an overview of African American history. While working on that book, Morrison encountered the story of a fugitive slave who killed her children instead of returning them to a life of slavery, and event that became the seed for Morrison's Pulitzer Prize–winning novel *Beloved* (1987).

Rich in ritual, fable, and folklore, Morrison's Gothic approach to African American literature distinguishes her as not only a great black writer, but one of the greatest American writers of the 20th century. In 1993, she received the Nobel Prize for Literature, making her the first black female Nobel winner. Her tremendous body of work also includes *Sula* (1973), *Song of Solomon* (1977), and *Jazz* (1992). Packed with African American history, Morrison's work explores the complexity of black culture, racism, and sexism in a manner that's both individual and collective. The Middle Passage, where countless Africans lost their lives making the journey from Africa to the United States, slavery, the Great Migration, and Jim Crow are just a few of the topics she explores in depth.

African American popular lit

African American literature continued its considerable strides into the 1990s, hitting *The New York Times* Best Seller list with regularity, a major departure from the one or two at a time in years past. Authors of these best sellers didn't necessarily become spokespersons for all African Americans either and few of the books were hailed as definitive platforms for improving the nation's race relations even though most of them significantly featured African American life and culture. In recent years, African Americans have created their own best sellers list such as Blackboard.

Los Angeles native Walter Mosley, who published his first novel in 1990, scored big with his Easy Rawlins mysteries (even claiming former President Bill Clinton as a fan), which include *Devil in a Blue Dress*. Some best selling African American authors self-published before a major publisher picked them up. E. Lynn Harris's unlikely best seller, *Invisible Life* (1991), in which the lead male character takes readers into a world where seemingly heterosexual black men secretly engage in homosexual behavior, is a good example of a self-published novel that attracted a major publisher. However, no contemporary African American author tops Terry McMillan.

Seizing on a formula that has dominated women's commercial fiction for decades, Michigan-born Terry McMillan's novel *Waiting to Exhale* (1992) engaged white and black readers with the standard tale of four female friends who maintain their friendship throughout their individual trials and tribulations. It was so successful that it hit its tenth printing only three weeks after its release! A subsequent film starring Whitney Houston and Angela Bassett made McMillan one of the first African American writers to achieve multimillionaire status.

Looking for the next big black writer, publishers signed up African American authors in unprecedented numbers. In addition to *black chick lit,* which largely refers to the work of female African American writers who duplicate Terry McMillan's style, other commercial genres have sprouted. Zane, the author of *Addicted* (2001) and *The Sex Chronicles* (2001), pioneered the black erotica genre, and hip-hop literature has become popular.

Taking inspiration from the late 1960s and early 1970s *street literature* of Donald Goines and Iceberg Slim, the momentum for the contemporary street literature movement began with Teri Woods's self-published novel *True to the Game* (1998) and activist Sister Souljah's *The Coldest Winter Ever* (1999). Since then, Carl Weber, author of *Baby Momma Drama* (2003), and Vickie Stringer, a former drug dealer who wrote *Let That Be the Reason* (2002), have published other writers in the genre through their respective publishing companies, Urban Books and Triple Crown Publications.

Chapter 15

The Great Black Way: Theatre and Dance

As unbelievable as it sounds today, there was a time when African Americans weren't even allowed to portray themselves on stage. Eighteenth-century performances of Shakespeare's *Othello,* about a Moor who kills his white wife Desdemona, for example, almost never featured a black actor as Othello. In the 18th-century English comic opera *Padlock,* a white actor in blackface typically played the drunken West Indian slave named Mungo who speaks in dialect. In addition, early American plays such as *The Fall of British Tyranny* faithfully included black characters but never black actors.

In time, African American theatre took root, starting with black musicals. As African American dancers wowed Broadway, American society began co-opting popular black dances. This chapter traces African American theatre from its early beginnings to the more recent triumphs of George C. Wolfe and the late, great August Wilson. It also touches upon African American dance history, celebrating masters like Katherine Dunham, Alvin Ailey, and Arthur Mitchell.

Making an Early Statement

In 1821, after being denied an opportunity to participate in mainstream theatre (even when productions called for African Americans), James Henry Brown and James Hewlett founded the African Grove Theatre, the first known black theatre in the United States. The African Grove Theatre grew out of gatherings that began around 1816 and were held in Brown's backyard. After hiring a group of actors, the theatre company's performances included Shakespeare's *Richard III* and *Othello.* There's also evidence that the company staged *King Shotaway,* a play Brown penned about a 1796 uprising of black Caribs on the island of Saint Vincent; it's believed to be the first full-length African American play.

Ira Aldridge

A graduate of New York's African Free School, Ira Aldridge launched his acting career at the African Grove Theatre. Frustrated by American racism, Aldridge relocated to England to further his acting career. He served as a dresser to a British actor before taking to the stage. Eventually, Aldridge's talent, especially his portrayal of Othello, overwhelmed British audiences, and by 1825, Aldridge had top billing at London's prestigious Royal Coburg Theatre as Oroonoko in *The Revolt of Surinam, or A Slave's Revenge.* Aldridge used his talent in many antislavery productions. He also played white characters, donning whiteface for the title role in Shakespeare's *Richard III* and Shylock in *The Merchant of Venice.*

As Aldridge's reputation grew, he toured Europe and Russia. Aldridge died in 1867 in Poland, before a planned trip back to the United States. Of the 33 actors of the English stage who have bronze plaques at the Shakespeare Memorial Theater at Stratford-upon-Avon, Aldridge is the only African American.

White patrons weren't excluded from African Grove Theatre performances or relegated to the balcony, but their typically unruly behavior relegated them to seats in the back of the theatre. Because of disturbances by white patrons and the police, the African Grove Theatre relocated several times. In 1823, the African Grove Theatre burned down, but its demise didn't squash the African American desire to master the stage.

Minstrelsy: Performing in Blackface

Almost like a sad, cruel joke, the origins of minstrelsy are traceable to the many talented slave dancers, comedians, and musicians who performed, often for their owners, on their respective plantations. In the early 1800s, white performers in America and England darkened their faces with burnt cork and either imitated those performances or simply performed the popular English and Irish dances of the day.

Performing in *blackface* wasn't new — even for dramatic performers — but duplicating the rhythms of black performers was. As the antislavery movement heated up in the 1850s, minstrel shows became decidedly proslavery.

White minstrels

Minstrelsy as an American institution began around 1830 when white performer Thomas Rice, more popularly known as Daddy Rice, observed an old black man singing and dancing. Rice found the performance hilarious, co-opted it, and began performing a song and dance number, "Jump Jim Crow"; Rice's performance spawned many imitators.

By the 1880s, the term "Jim Crow" had moved beyond its minstrel roots and become synonymous with racial segregation. You can read more about Jim Crow and life in the segregated South in Chapter 7.

Ethiopian minstrelsy was the label some used to describe the practice of white performers consciously imitating African American songs, dances, and humor. It wasn't until 1843, however, at New York's Bowery Amphitheatre that four actors calling themselves the Virginia Minstrels ushered in the *minstrel show* by performing comic skits and songs in blackface continuously. Until the Virginia Minstrels, minstrel performances supported a main show, such as the circus; they weren't the main show themselves.

Proslavery factions twisted Harriet Beecher Stowe's antislavery treatise *Uncle Tom's Cabin* through unauthorized stage adaptations. These adaptations contributed to the portrayal of Uncle Tom, for example, as a harmless yes-man eager to please his white slave owner — a misinterpretation that continues today.

Black minstrels

Around 1855, minstrel shows with black performers emerged. Despite being billed as more authentic than their white counterparts, black minstrels still followed the same conventions as white minstrels: They blackened their faces and painted their lips white and outlined them in red to exaggerate their size. They also perpetuated the two common stereotypes: the plantation darky, who had a happy and nostalgic view of slavery, and the Northern dandy, who was typically a lazy and overdressed city boy concerned with having a good time. As scholars such as Robert Toll have noted, these were the conventions black minstrels inherited, not what they created.

AFRICAN AMERICAN FACES

William Henry Lane

William Henry Lane, better known as Master Juba, helped pave the way for other black performers. Tutored by "Uncle" Jim Lowe, an older black dancer and named after the *juba,* the African dance he mastered, Lane became so popular that he and John Diamond, the reigning white dance champion, squared off several times. Although both Lane and Diamond declared themselves victorious, the contests bolstered Lane's career. Until Lane, minstrel shows were a white-only affair. Lane was such a masterful talent that he began receiving top billing at white minstrel shows in 1845. Far from just an American sensation, Lane took London by storm in 1848. He remained there and died in 1852 at age 27. Frequently credited as the creator of modern tap dance, Lane is among America's first great black performers.

In addition to attracting white audiences, black minstrel shows appealed to black audiences in spite of the shows' many proslavery conventions. Scholars have suggested that black minstrel shows contained a subversive element that escaped the attention of white audiences. Perhaps black audiences simply enjoyed seeing black performers. As their form of entertainment grew in popularity, black minstrels quickly incorporated new dances into their shows, created new jokes, and introduced a new kind of music now known as *ragtime* (flip to Chapter 16 for more on ragtime).

REMEMBER

Black minstrel shows were the first large-scale opportunity for African Americans to enter show business. Overall, the minstrel show formalized the incorporation of African American culture into general American entertainment.

Moving toward Broadway: Black Musical Theatre

As black musical theatre developed, the conventions of the minstrel show slowly began to fade. The change was gradual, however, and was influenced by the following artists and their productions, which helped move the black minstrel show closer to the modern musical format:

> ✔ **Sisters Anna Madah and Emmie Louis Hyers and *Out of Bondage*:** Better known as the Hyers Sisters, these women played a frequently uncredited role in the development of black musical theatre. Born free in California in the 1850s, the Hyers Sisters were trained opera singers and

performed outside the general minstrel tradition. In 1876, they began performing a musical play initially called *Out of the Wilderness* but changed to *Out of Bondage* because the general story traced African Americans from slavery until after the Civil War. Before they disbanded in the 1890s, the Hyers Sisters staged other similar productions.

✔ **Pauline Elizabeth Hopkins and *Slaves' Escape*:** Hopkins was the first African American to write a musical, *Slaves' Escape* (another version was entitled *Peculiar Sam; or the Underground Railroad*). *Slaves' Escape* ran in Boston from 1879 to 1881 and dealt with the themes of slavery and freedom. It also subtly criticized the minstrel show format by presenting the requisite plantation slaves as unhappy. Hopkins, herself a performer with her family's singing group, the Hopkins' Colored Troubadours, also performed in productions of the play.

✔ **Sam T. Jack and the *Creole Show*:** This 1890 production changed African American entertainment the most. In *The Creole Show*, the white Sam T. Jack added a chorus of 16 beautiful black female performers to the all-male black minstrel show formula, greatly expanding opportunities for black female performers. It also embraced contemporary costumes, a significant departure from the plantation gear featured in previous shows.

✔ **John W. Isham and *The Octoroons* and *Oriental America*:** With the 1895 production of *The Octoroons,* Isham pushed the envelope by including more female talent and boasting a continuous plot. His 1896 production of *Oriental America,* credited as the first black show on Broadway, distanced itself even further from the minstrel show by replacing the customary minstrel finale with a medley of operatic-style solos and choral numbers. Led by acclaimed singer Sissieretta Jones, dubbed the Black Patti after reigning opera diva Adelina Patti, the *Black Patti Troubadours,* continued this innovation.

More than minstrels

Considered the first true black musical, *A Trip to Coontown* (1897), composer Bob Cole and Billy Johnson's take on the white Broadway hit *A Trip to Chinatown*, was the first major show conceived, written, produced, performed, and managed by African Americans. Despite its frequent use of the term "coon" and other such words (which were common at the time), the production was revolutionary, especially its finale song, "No Coons Allowed," which dramatized a man's inability to treat his girl to a night out at the city's "finest" restaurant because "no coons were allowed." There was no recourse either, because coons weren't allowed in the courthouse. Such parody wasn't lost on the African American audience. Cole, along with Rosamond Johnson (civil rights activist James Weldon Johnson's brother) also created *The Shoo-Fly Regiment* (1906) and *Red Moon* (1909).

Clorindy, the Origin of the Cakewalk, which opened in 1898, mixed comedy, songs, and dances. Presented by composer Will Marion Cook, *Clorindy* marked the first time a Broadway cast danced and sang simultaneously. Thrilling audiences, *Clorindy* ushered in a new creative force, making the black musical a Broadway staple.

Williams and Walker on Broadway

Bert Williams and George Walker started out as a minstrel duo before becoming one of Broadway's most successful teams. Partnering with Will Marion Cook and celebrated poet Paul Laurence Dunbar, Williams and Walker created *In Dahomey* (1902).

Williams and Walker were known for the cakewalk. In fact, Will Marion Cook had created *Clorindy, the Origin of the Cakewalk* with the duo in mind, but a successful engagement on the West Coast prevented them from starring in *Clorindy.*

Unlike other black musicals, *In Dahomey* positively incorporated African themes. The song, "Evah Dahkey is a King," translated today as "every black person is a king," is just one example. Well-received, the show toured England. Williams and Walker became more ambitious with African themes in *Abyssinia* (1906), but that play didn't match the success of *In Dahomey.* For *Bandana Land* (1908), they focused on the South.

While touring with *Bandana Land* in 1909, Walker fell ill and died in 1911. After Walker's death, it became more difficult for African Americans to appear in groups on Broadway. One factor was the tense atmosphere following New York's 1910 race riot in response to black heavyweight Jack Johnson's defeat of boxing's "great white hope" Jim Jeffries (see Chapter 18). Williams, however, continued to perform to critical acclaim, primarily as a member of the *Ziegfeld Follies,* which he joined in 1910. Performing in blackface obscured his talent so much that he became a poster child for all African American blackface performers.

From 1913 to 1917, Williams was the only black artist on Broadway. His loyalty to the race was so great that, though frustrated by the limited but acclaimed work he did with the *Ziegfeld Follies,* he remained with the group for ten years. Without him, he feared that there would be no black artists on Broadway. "We've got our foot in the door," Williams said. "We mustn't let it close again."

Marlon Riggs's classic 1978 documentary *Ethnic Notions* used Bert Williams as an anchor to examine the deeply rooted, antiblack stereotypes in American culture. Spike Lee also linked his lead characters to Bert Williams in his 2000 film *Bamboozled,* which tackled the perpetuation of the minstrel show tradition.

The rumblings of serious black theatre

Outside of minstrel work, 19th-century stage roles for African Americans were those of servants and slaves. George Aiken's 1852 stage adaptation of *Uncle Tom's Cabin* allowed black actors, especially in the role of Uncle Tom, the dutiful slave, and Topsy, the unruly slave girl transformed by love, to demonstrate their acting skills. Perhaps the lost *King Shotaway*, written by African Grove Theatre cofounder James Henry Brown and assumed to be the first play by an African American (see the earlier section, "Making an Early Statement") had richer roles. It wasn't until 1858 that another play by an African American appeared. Yet that play — William Wells Brown's *The Escape; or, A Leap of Freedom*, which tells the story of two slaves from different plantations who marry and try to escape to freedom via the Underground Railroad — was never produced. Instead, Brown, who published the novel *Clotel* in 1853, frequently read the play at antislavery gatherings.

While musicals such as *Out of Bondage* and *Slaves' Escape* provided a transitional point between the black musical and the black drama, several dramatic associations also existed in various locations, particularly in the 1880s. Washington, D.C., had the Lawrence Barrett Dramatic Club (1882); Baltimore had the Our Boys Dramatic Club (1888); and there was the Aldridge Dramatic Association (1889) in New Haven, Connecticut.

African American theatre became a more serious enterprise in the 20th century. Playwright Loften Mitchell, who wrote *Black Drama: The Story of the American Negro in the Theater* (1967), referred to the period between 1909 and 1917 as the First Harlem Theatre Movement, even though Harlem wasn't the only city active in cultivating serious black actors and black drama.

Prompted primarily by the 1915 release of the antiblack film, *The Birth of a Nation*, the NAACP's Washington, D.C., branch organized the Drama Committee, which successfully presented Angelina Weld Grimke's *Rachel*, a play about the impact that witnessing lynching and other forms of racial violence has on the choices the black female lead makes. It was the first drama written, performed, and produced by African Americans.

Early black theatre companies

Although early black theatre companies didn't embrace material by African Americans initially, they did play important roles in cultivating African American actors. Chicago's Pekin Stock Company and New York's Lafayette Stock Company were among the most influential:

- **Pekin Stock Company:** This Chicago-based company, also known as the Pekin Players, was the first high-profile African American theatre company to make a foray into serious drama. Organized in 1906, the Pekin Players produced several "white" plays such as well-known dramatist Bronson Howard's *Young Mrs. Winthrop*, about a husband and wife bound by their child. These productions showed white critics, in particular, that African American actors were more than the caricatures infused in the minstrel show format.

In its "serious" format, the Pekin Players championed mainstream (read "white") productions. When it committed itself to musicals, however, it vowed to present those written by African Americans. One standout was *The Mayor of Dixie,* an early work by the successful writing team of Flournoy Miller and Aubrey Lyles, who later took Broadway by storm with *Shuffle Along* (read more in the section "Shuffling ahead").

✔ **The Lafayette Players:** The Lafayette Players, the most famous of the early black theatre companies, shared the Pekin Players' original mission to feature black actors in productions that usually excluded them. To demonstrate that African Americans could play any role, the Lafayette Stock Company performed Shakespeare, *Dr. Jekyll and Mr. Hyde* (with Clarence Muse, known for his butler roles in film, performing in whiteface), and *The Three Musketeers,* among others.

Hitting the larger stage

As black theatre companies provided new opportunities for African American actors, white playwrights were discovering black life and culture. During the Harlem Renaissance, there were several key productions created by white playwrights. Ridgely Torrence made the first big splash in 1917 with his three one-act plays written for black performers:

✔ ***The Rider of Dreams:*** A story centered around a husband and wife who possess different ideas about spending and saving money.

✔ ***Granny Maumee:*** The story of a grandmother who'd gone blind after a lynch mob viciously killed her innocent son and anxiously awaits another elusive male heir before her death.

✔ ***Simon the Cyrenian:*** A story based on the biblical account of Simon from Cyrene, who played a key role during the crucifixion of Jesus.

White critics and the largely white audience were very receptive to Torrence's presentation of black actors in dramatic roles, a first for Broadway.

Eugene O'Neill kept the momentum going with *The Emperor Jones,* first staged in 1920. Charles Gilpin, a former member of both the Lafayette and Pekin Players, played the lead to critical acclaim. Harlem audiences weren't bowled over by the story of a prison escapee who establishes himself as a king in a Caribbean island; white audiences loved it. In contrast, O'Neill's 1924 play *All God's Chillun Got Wings,* a story about an interracial marriage starring Paul Robeson and white actress Mary Blair, generated bomb threats in addition to vilification from the press for its interracial casting and subject matter.

Other notable productions by white playwrights featuring black actors included:

- ✔ *In Abraham's Bosom* **(1926):** Paul Green won the Pulitzer Prize for his play about a black Southerner's tragic attempt to start a school for black children in North Carolina.

- ✔ *Porgy* **(1927):** Set in Charleston, South Carolina, on fictitious Catfish Row, *Porgy*, a story about a beggar, achieved critical acclaim for its unique presentation of Southern black life and use of Gullah language, a creolized form of English with significant Africanisms. Husband-and-wife team Dorothy and DuBose Heyward created the play from DuBose Heyward's 1925 novel.

- ✔ *The Green Pastures* **(1930):** Adapted from a folk novel by Roark Bradford, Marc Connelly's *The Green Pastures,* about a child who sees the Bible through her own eyes, won the Pulitzer Prize in 1930.

- ✔ *Porgy and Bess* **(1935):** Intrigued by the original *Porgy*, Gershwin collaborated with its creator DuBose Heyward to create a folk opera about black Southern life in Catfish Row. Problematic from the start, many black actors and black audiences in general viewed *Porgy and Bess* as stereotypical, especially for its attempts at Southern black dialect and its focus on poverty and violence. Although criticized musically as well for approximating jazz and other forms of African American music, *Porgy and Bess* did produce the classic American song "Summertime."

Shuffling ahead

As influential as some of the dramas by white playwrights featuring black actors became, the black musical *Shuffling Along* generated the most excitement about African American talent and, in many eyes, officially ushered in the Harlem Renaissance.

Known as the Dixie Duo, Noble Sissle and Eubie Blake were one of the first black acts to perform without blackface and in elegant dress on the white vaudeville circuit. At a NAACP benefit, the duo met Flournoy Miller and Aubrey Lyles, showbiz veterans who once had a blackface comedy-dancing act. Together the four created the musical revue *Shuffle Along,* which became a surprising hit when it opened in 1921.

The breathtaking choreography and energetic songs overwhelmed Broadway's white audiences. Barriers were broken when, during the run of *Shuffle Along,* black audiences, though still segregated, were allowed to sit beyond the balcony, and white audiences, which had previously rejected presentations of romantic love scenes, applauded the song "Love Will Find a Way" and its accompanying love scene. "I'm Wild About Harry," also became a popular song. Dance, which you can read about in "Black Dance in America," was another important contribution from *Shuffle Along*. *Shuffle Along*'s success spawned many similar shows, including *Runnin' Wild,* another Flournoy Miller and Aubrey Lyles collaboration.

Encouraging more serious fare

Civil rights leaders such as W.E.B. Du Bois weren't content with having just white dramatists and black musical phenoms represent the African American experience. During this time, the NAACP and the National Urban League, primarily via the Opportunity awards, stepped up to reward and encourage black creative development with more serious fare. The following theatre companies were also critical in nurturing that talent:

✔ **Krigwa Players:** In 1925, inspired by the NAACP Drama Committee, Du Bois cofounded with Regina Anderson (also Regina Andrews) the New York–based Krigwa Players to encourage the creation of serious stage work by and for African Americans that spoke to the political issues of the day. Two plays — *Climbing Jacob's Ladder* about a lynching and *Underground* about the Underground Railroad — written by Anderson were among the plays produced.

✔ **Howard University Players:** Reorganized in 1923 by Howard University professors Alain Locke, a leading voice in the New Negro/Harlem Renaissance Movement, and Montgomery Gregory, the Howard University Players diverged from Du Bois's vision of black drama to focus not so much on the message and the political propaganda but the artistic development of African American actors and, later, playwrights. In 1923, Jean Toomer's *Balo, A Sketch of Negro Life,* about a black peasant in Georgia, became among the first plays by an African American the group produced. Ruby Dee, Ossie Davis, Phylicia Rashad, and Isaiah Washington, among other actors, later honed their craft with the Howard University Players.

✔ **Karamu Players:** Launched by husband and wife Russell and Rowena Jelliffe in Cleveland in 1915, the Playhouse Settlement evolved into a movement that attracted African American theatre talent, including actors and playwrights. Karamu welcomed early on African American plays such as *Joy to My Soul,* a comedy about the Cleveland underworld by celebrated writer Langston Hughes.

Early noteworthy dramas

Plays about African American life written by white dramatists dominated early Broadway, but some plays by African Americans did break through. In 1923, pioneering African American dramatist Willis Richardson's one-act play, *The Chip Woman's Fortune,* about a younger man conspiring to rob an older woman of her hidden fortune, was the first serious, nonmusical play by an African American to have a Broadway run. Former bellhop Garland Anderson's *Appearances,* about the incidents in the life of a bellboy, followed Richardson's in 1925 and has the distinction of being the first full-length, nonmusical play on Broadway by an African American. The show created quite a stir for its mixed-race casting, which was illegal at the time.

In 1929, *Harlem,* the play Wallace Thurman (best known for the book *The Blacker the Berry* about intraracial prejudices within the black community) co-wrote with a white writer about the struggles of a black family that migrated from the South, received mixed reviews and limited success. Technically, the 1935 Broadway production of Langston Hughes's *Mulatto,* believed to be auto-biographical for its story about a white father's rejection of his mulatto son, was the first hit play written by an African American. Hughes, however, was displeased because the show's white producer added a rape scene and made other changes without his knowledge.

The Harlem Renaissance period would only crack Broadway's doors to African American actors and playwrights; it would take continued pushing to open them. Plays such as Zora Neale Hurston's *Color Struck* and Georgia Douglass Johnson's *Blue Blood* exploring intraracial and interracial strife, along with the continued development of African American theatre companies to train black actors, generated excitement for African American theatre overall.

Black Theatre Comes of Age

Musicals, black and white, declined when the Great Depression took root in the 1930s. Hollywood absorbed a considerable amount of Broadway's white talent but black performers, with the primary exception of dancers, had little recourse. Hope for black dramatic productions, in particular, came from the most unlikely of sources — the Negro Theatre Unit of the Works Progress Administration's Federal Theatre Program (FTP). Although the FTP lasted only a short four years before the House Committee on Un-American Activities (HCUA) ended it in 1939, it had a tremendous decades-long impact on black theatre and drama. As black theatre moved into the 1940s, the need for black artists and their communities to cultivate their talents remained, and other theatre companies, most notably the American Negro Theatre, stepped up to fill the void.

The Federal Theatre Program and black drama

Headed by Hallie Flanagan, previously a drama professor at Vassar, the FTP operated in various regions throughout the country, with the Harlem and Chicago units being among the most popular. Unlike Broadway, the FTP favored dramatic productions featuring African Americans that not only enabled black actors to develop their craft, prepared black actors for more mainstream Broadway fare, and encouraged black-oriented productions.

In addition to all-black versions of mainstream plays, such as Shakespeare's *Macbeth,* the classic tale of power and betrayal, and George Bernard Shaw's

Androcles and the Lion, about a slave saved by a lion, other key performances by FTP included new plays written by African Americans:

- **Walk Together Chillun,** by Frank Wilson, about the trials of Georgia laborers who migrated to New York after World War I and the division migration created within the Northern black community

- **Conjur Man Dies,** by Rudolph Fisher, a Harlem murder mystery featuring a black Sherlock Holmes-inspired detective adapted from his novel, *The Conjure Man Dies*

- **Big White Fog,** by Theodore Ward, about a father who invests his family's money in Marcus Garvey's UNIA Movement while Garvey sits in prison (see Chapter 7 for more details on Marcus Garvey)

Artistic disagreements between white administrators and black talent, coupled with censorship from government and other entities, played a role in the slow production of plays by African American dramatists. Another factor was the expectation of the audience — both black and white — to see singing and dancing popularized by the black musical and vaudeville acts. Nonetheless, the FTP helped prepare actors, dramatists, other black theatre professionals, and, equally important, audiences, black and white, for the bolder black theatre that emerged during the civil rights era.

The American Negro Theatre (ANT)

One of the most influential institutions that emerged during the 1940s was the American Negro Theatre (ANT). Spearheaded by playwright Abram Hill and actor Frederick O'Neal, the ANT launched in Harlem in 1940 as an artist cooperative, with the artists agreeing to work as a collective and to donate 2 percent of any income they made back to the ANT. Hill's *On Striver Row,* a satire of black middle-class social climbing, became the ANT's first successful production. By 1942, the ANT added the Studio Theatre, a training program for actors that both Sidney Poitier and Harry Belafonte attended.

Civil rights theatre: The Free Southern Theater

The Free Southern Theater (FST), founded in 1963 by Student Nonviolent Coordinating Committee (SNCC) field directors Doris Derby and John O'Neal, along with *Mississippi Free Press* writer Gilbert Moses, was an offshoot of the civil rights movement. Well-supported by established actors, both black and white, of the time, the FST took theatre productions to areas throughout Mississippi that had never been exposed to live theatre. Continual harassment in Jackson forced the FST to relocate to New Orleans. Debates about direction and form, among other issues, resulted in the company disbanding in 1971.

Anna Lucasta, a Polish drama about a prostitute and her family dynamic adapted for an African American cast, became such a success that it opened on Broadway in 1944 and ran continuously until 1946. Broadway success, however, undermined the ANT, moving it away from its community roots to achieving Broadway acclaim. By 1949, the ANT was no more, but its legacy paved the way for more dramatic success. ANT alums included playwrights such as Alice Childress, best known for her 1970s play and film *A Hero Ain't Nothin' But a Sandwich* about a young, black boy caught up in the urban trap of drugs and crime.

A place to call home

With more black theatrical talent than there were available roles or plays in mainstream theatre, African Americans once again turned inward. Several influential dramatic enterprises began in the late 1960s and the early 1970s that remain today:

- ✓ **The Negro Ensemble Company (NEC):** Douglas Turner Ward and Robert Hooks officially founded the Negro Ensemble Company in 1967 to nurture actors and playwrights. In addition to esteemed NEC participants such as Esther Rolle and Roscoe Lee Browne, the NEC also welcomed talented playwright Charles Fuller, noted most for his Pulitzer Prize–winning *A Soldier's Play* about the murder of a black soldier on a Southern army base. Ward's own *A Day of Absence,* a play performed in whiteface about a town whose black population disappears, and Joseph A. Walker's *The River Niger,* about a Harlem family's struggles in the 1970s, were among the first plays the NEC produced.

- ✓ **The New Federal Theatre:** Unlike other theatres that struggled to survive from the beginning, the New Federal Theatre, founded in 1970 by Woodie King, Jr., scored early with classics such as Ntozake Shange's *For Colored Girls Who Have Considered Suicide/When the Rainbow Is Enuf* and actors such as Denzel Washington.

- ✓ **Frank Silvera Writers' Workshop:** Counting Morgan Freeman among its early founders, the Frank Silvera Writers' Workshop (FSWW), spearheaded by stage manager Garland Lee Thompson, set up shop in Harlem in 1973. Named for the Jamaican-born actor Frank Silvera, who nurtured black theatre talent out of his own pocket, talent the FSWW supported early on included Richard Wesley, who served as screenwriter for the Sidney Poitier/Bill Cosby films *Let's Do It Again* and *Uptown Saturday Night.*

Lorraine Hansberry

Lorraine Hansberry became the first African American and youngest playwright to win the New York Drama Critics Circle Award with her play *A Raisin in the Sun,* which opened on Broadway in 1959. Inspired by her own family's experience integrating a white neighborhood in Chicago, Hansberry's play presented a complex portrait of a working-class black family's human struggle with one of the most complex issues of the day. The play starred Sidney Poitier, Ruby Dee, and Louis Gossett, and was the first play on Broadway directed by an African American (Lloyd Richards).

Phylicia Rashad, best known from *The Cosby Show,* became the first African American actress to win the Tony Award for Best Performance by a Leading Actress in a Play for the 2004 Broadway revival of *A Raisin in the Sun,* which also starred rapper/producer Sean "Diddy" Combs, Hollywood actress Sanaa Lathan, and respected theatre actress Audra McDonald.

Alive and kickin': Black musicals, 1940s and beyond

During the 1940s, *Carmen Jones,* the black version of the Georges Bizet opera *Carmen,* hit big, but shows such as *St. Louis Woman,* set among the black horse-racing set, flopped. Despite Lena Horne's successful Broadway debut in *Jamaica* and a revival of *Porgy and Bess,* black performers were largely absent from Broadway in the 1950s. The 1960s were slightly improved. In addition, musicals drew a social edge influenced by the success of *A Raisin in the Sun* and the turbulent times. Diahann Carroll starred in the 1962 musical *No Strings* as the black model girlfriend of a white expatriate writer living in Paris. *Golden Boy,* the 1964 musical starring Sammy Davis, Jr., infused the musical with the civil rights struggle as Davis played a boxer from Harlem whose brother works for the Congress of Racial Equality.

Purlie, the musical version of *Purlie Victorious,* the 1961 comedy written by veteran actor Ossie Davis and set on a cotton plantation in Georgia, made Melba Moore a star and kicked off the 1970s black musical revival. In the 1970s, *The Wiz,* a black version of the *Wizard of Oz,* literally averted financial ruin by appealing directly to black audiences and welcomed a new theatre-goer to Broadway. Other musicals like *Ain't Misbehavin,* which used the music of Fats Waller, and *Sophisticated Ladies,* based on the music of Duke Ellington, were also Broadway hits. Nothing compared to the 1981 debut of *Dreamgirls,* as the Supremes-inspired musical enthralled audiences, making stars of Sheryl Lee Ralph and Loretta Devine, and a legend of Jennifer Holiday and her big song "And I'm Tellin' You," which jumped straight to classic status. At the Tony Awards, *Dreamgirls* won an impressive 6 of its 13 Tony Award nominations.

Dance-heavy musicals such as *Black and Blue* and *Jelly's Last Jam* (read more about some of Broadway's best dancers and choreographers in the section "Black Dance in America") dominated the end of the 1980s and 1990s. Also in the 1980s, *Mama I Want To Sing,* a gospel stage play about a shy, church-honed singer who ventures into secular music, ushered in an entire movement that, in recent years, helped propel the Christian-inspired plays of Tyler Perry, best known for his role as the sassy older woman Madea. *Diary of a Mad Black Woman* and *Woman Thou Art Loosed,* his dramatic adaptation of Bishop T.D. Jakes's best-selling self-help book for women who've survived sexual abuse, are two of Perry's well-known stage plays.

David E. Talbert's stage plays, while largely Christian in theme, scored big by dealing more directly with romantic relationships and, in recent years, embracing R&B-tinged songs more. Shelley Garrett, best-known for his popular relationship-gone-wrong *Beauty Shop,* set in a beauty shop during the late 1980s, inspired Talbert, whose best-known plays include *The Fabric of A Man,* involving a love triangle between a successful fashion designer, her disgruntled husband, and a sexy tailor.

Two Visionaries

Beginning in the 1980s, two African American visionaries—August Wilson and George C. Wolfe—emerged, representing different spectrums but both bringing a fuller and more textured portrait of African American life and culture. Together they, more than any other individuals in the 1980s and 1990s, challenged the theatre's cultural gatekeepers and audiences to delve deeper into the African American experience and to see music, in particular, as an extension, not simply a product, of that experience. Quite often, they didn't choose, as many had before them, to elevate music over drama or vice versa. Instead, they celebrated that richness in all its glory, bringing the beauty and pathos of jazz and blues to life in ways never before imagined.

August Wilson

Easily among the greatest American playwrights of the 20th century, August Wilson almost single-handedly reshaped the American theatre's perception of African American life. Meshing drama with music and laughter with tears, Wilson proposed and delivered his astounding ten-play cycle, one for each decade, documenting African American life in the 20th century.

Using his native Pittsburgh as his primary canvas, Wilson painted majestic characters and situations of everyday people and everyday life. *Fences,* a complex story of a former Negro Leagues baseball player-turned-garbage man at odds with his athletically gifted son in the 1950s, won the Pulitzer Prize. The Pulitzer Prize winning *The Piano Lesson* is a story about a sister and brother from Mississippi at odds over the ancestral piano. In this work, Wilson used the piano as a metaphor for the tug between discarding the past and its pain in order to begin anew, and maintaining a balance in order to inherit and maintain the strength that's made survival possible.

Through his frequent collaborations with Yale School of Drama dean Lloyd Richards, who directed *A Raisin in the Sun* on Broadway, Wilson's plays featured such top Yale talent as Angela Bassett, Charles Dutton, and Courtney B. Vance. The first and last installment of The Pittsburgh Cycle, *Gem of the Ocean* for the 1900s and *Radio Golf* for the 1990s, were staged in 2003 and 2005 respectively. Sadly, Wilson died of liver cancer in 2005.

George C. Wolfe

Raised in segregated Kentucky in the 1950s and 1960s, playwright and director George C. Wolfe opened the theatre up to African Americans and other underrepresented populations in his role as artistic director and producer of the New York Shakespeare Festival/Public Theater from 1993 to 2004. After cutting his teeth at Los Angeles's black Inner City Cultural Center, Wolfe made noise off-Broadway with his satirical look at slavery and other events in African American culture in *The Colored Museum*. He took the black Broadway musical to new heights with *Jelly's Last Jam,* which combined great music and dance numbers with an introspective story of jazz's self-proclaimed founder, Jelly Roll Morton.

In a departure from black-themed material, the openly gay Wolfe directed Tony Kushner's groundbreaking AIDS drama *Angels in America* to critical acclaim. He also directed Suzan-Lori Parks's *Topdog/Underdog,* a contemporary story of two brothers grappling with their lives past and present, that won the 2002 Pulitzer Prize. Wolfe conceived and directed *Bring in Da Noise, Bring in Da Funk,* tap dancer Savion Glover's star-turning vehicle; he directed playwright/actress Anna Deavere Smith in her solo rendition of the L.A. riots in 1994's *Twilight: Los Angeles 1992.* More recently, Wolfe took his directing talents to the small screen with the HBO film *Lackawanna Blues,* a project that began on the stage.

National Black Theatre Festival

Held biennially in Winston-Salem, North Carolina, Larry Leon Hamlin, founder of the North Carolina Black Repertory Company, created the National Black Theater Festival (NBTF) in 1989 to unite black theatres, actors, and other stage professionals from across the nation. Maya Angelou served as the NBTF's first chairperson. The 2005 NBTF boasted over 100 performances.

Black Dance in America

Unlike dance in the Caribbean, which retained a more pronounced African influence, black dance in America almost immediately combined African and European influences. Africans dancing didn't bother the Catholic Church, so the French and Spanish rarely prohibited slaves in their Latin American and Caribbean colonies from dancing. In America, however, the Protestant church strongly disapproved of dancing. Slaveholders and other Europeans didn't understand the strong link between music and dance that enslaved Africans cherished.

Early dances

Protestant restrictions notwithstanding, many plantation owners had no objection to slave dance competitions. One of the early dances to emerge from this activity was the *cakewalk,* in which black dancers parodied white dancers by combining their stiff upper-body movements with the fancy foot-work common in many African dances.

Still, professional dance was the province of whites. In the 1830s, the white minstrel performer Thomas Rice traveled extensively performing the song-and-dance number "Jump Jim Crow" he'd lifted from black culture (refer to the section "White minstrels" earlier in the chapter for information on minstrel shows). African American William Henry Lane was unusual for his time. He wasn't just allowed to dance; he was acknowledged for it. Lane was said to be the first performer to add syncopation and improvisation to his dancing, making him a strong candidate as an early tap dance innovator.

By the 1900s, African American dance found a wider audience. Black composers wrote songs that described how dances were performed, and black vernacular dance slowly crept into white society events. The musical *Darktown Follies* at the Lafayette Theatre in Harlem in 1911 featured dances including the cakewalk, Ballin' the Jack, and the Texas Tommy, a forerunner to the Lindy; the show changed how white producers approached all-white shows in that they began borrowing heavily from black musicals. Broadway impresario Florenz Ziegfeld even purchased a circle dance from *Darktown Follies* for his own Broadway show.

Tap dance

Quite possibly, tap dance grew out of a ban on drums by slave owners following the Stono Rebellion (see Chapter 4 for more details); because they couldn't use drums, slaves often created rhythms with their feet and sometimes by clapping their hands. Although flamenco, clogging, and other dance forms were also influential, tap dance still bears a strong African influence.

The 1921 musical *Shuffle Along* really injected black dance into popular American dance, introducing both the Charleston and tap dancing to white audiences. The Charleston reached frenzied heights after being featured in the 1923 musical *Runnin' Wild*. *Runnin' Wild* made dancer Florence Mills, who thrilled audiences with her high kicks, a star. Josephine Baker, whose unique style made her a star in France, made an impression in the chorus line.

Throughout the 1920s, dance accompanied the jazz craze; tap dance, in particular, came into its own during the swing jazz era. Tap dancers accompanied some of the biggest names in jazz and added even more finesse to those musical performances with their elegant dance moves, often achieved while wearing a tuxedo with tails. Those smooth and thrilling routines full of jumps and synchronized moves landed some of the best of the best tap dancers onto the big screen.

Famous African American tap dancers include

- **Bill "Bojangles" Robinson:** One of the first African Americans to become a tap star, Robinson, best known for his role as the docile servant who often danced with Shirley Temple in films from the 1930s, didn't become a star until the age of 50 when he landed a breakout role in the Broadway musical *Blackbirds of 1928*. An innovative dancer, Robinson wore wooden-soled shoes and could duplicate any rhythmic sound from a drum.

- **The Nicholas Brothers:** Known for their high acrobatic moves, the Philadelphia-raised Fayard and Harold Nicholas worked at the famed Cotton Club along with Duke Ellington, Cab Calloway, and other luminaries. They also worked on Broadway in productions like *The Ziegfeld Follies of 1936*. Their extensive film career, which includes *Stormy Weather*, began in 1934 and spanned several decades.

- **Charles Atkinson:** Better known as Cholly Atkins, Atkinson earned fame as the man behind the smooth Motown moves. As the in-house Motown choreographer, Atkins worked with many groups, most notably the Temptations. While the Temptations didn't tap dance, they did emit a collected cool typically associated with the best tap dancers of the time. In 1988, Atkinson, Fayard Nicholas, and a few others choreographed the Broadway musical *Black and Blue,* which won a Tony Award.

- **Sammy Davis, Jr.:** He began his career as a dancer in the Will Mastin Trio, with his father Sammy Davis, Sr., and "uncle" Will Mastin. An all-around entertainer, Sammy Davis, Jr., inspired Gregory Hines, one of tap's most noted dancers in the late 20th century.

✔ **Gregory Hines:** Tony winner Hines helped keep tap alive. He began his career at an early age as one-third of the family trio Hines, with his father and brother. When he later moved into film and television, he worked hard to bring the spotlight back to tap dancing in films like *Tap* (1989) and *Bojangles* (2001) about the life of Bill "Bojangles" Robinson. Hines enjoyed a Tony Award–winning turn in *Jelly's Last Jam,* which he also helped choreograph. He passed the tap dance baton to the young Savion Glover, with whom he worked in *Jelly's Last Jam.*

✔ **Savion Glover:** In 1996, Glover helped create the groundbreaking *Bring in Da Noise, Bring in Da Funk,* which tells African American history through tap dance. Glover, who won a Tony for his choreography of that show, also appeared in *Bamboozled* (2000), a film that explores the legacy of racism on film and TV. Glover continued to push the boundaries of tap dance with edgy collaborations, such as with the band IF TRANE WUZ HERE, in which a poet, dancer, and saxophonist all interpret the music of jazz great John Coltrane.

Break dancing

Like other popular dance crazes, break dancing and other forms of hip-hop dance took the country by storm in the 1970s and 1980s. A recognizable element of hip-hop culture developed alongside rap music in the South Bronx in the 1970s, break dancing eventually evolved an identity of its own. Signature moves that include the head-spin and the *windmill,* in which the dancer rotates his or her body on the ground using one arm, also developed. Break dancing, which contains many moves that bear a striking resemblance to the Brazilian martial art form Capoeria developed by enslaved Africans, broke into the mainstream in 1983 when Michael Jackson featured it in his groundbreaking video for the song "Beat It." From then, *breaking,* as it's also called, benefited from greater exposure in films such as *Beat Street* (1984) and *Breakin'* (1984) in addition to many rap videos.

Classical dance forms

African Americans didn't distinguish themselves only in popular dance. Masters such as Katherine Dunham, Pearl Primus, Alvin Ailey, and Arthur Mitchell contributed to the transformation of modern dance in America. Numerous other dancers and choreographers, such as Bill T. Jones, Donald McKayle, and Debbie Allen, are also integral parts of African American dance history.

Whereas the few African American dancers preceding them took cues from white dancers, early pioneers Dunham and Primus were both trained anthropologists, and both women imbued their work with a cultural backbone that hadn't existed before.

- ✔ **Katherine Dunham** insisted that her dancers understand the cultural significance of her choreography before they danced it; she was so serious about unearthing those connections that she studied dance in the Caribbean, most notably in Haiti. Although Dunham appeared in several films and Broadway productions, she blazed her own trails. In 1945, she opened the Dunham School of Dance in New York, and the following year she received critical acclaim for *Bal Negre,* a dance revue. The New York Metropolitan Opera commissioned Dunham to choreograph its 1963 production of *Aida.* Until her death in 2006, Dunham, who also wrote several books, lived in East St. Louis, Illinois, where she used the arts to combat poverty.

- ✔ **Pearl Primus** drew inspiration directly from Africa. Her intention wasn't to dance as a black dancer but rather as a dancer who had African roots. She favored imbuing her work with strong social commentary; for example, her Broadway debut in 1944 featured the piece "Strange Fruit," in which a woman reacts to a lynching. Her 1952 show *Dark Rhythm* reflected her travels to Africa; she incorporated dances from Liberia, Sierra Leone, and other countries.

Alvin Ailey and Arthur Mitchell stepped up in later decades to provide formal instructional institutions for African American dancers.

- ✔ **Alvin Ailey** was inspired to dance by Katherine Dunham. A former athlete, he made his debut in 1953 with the Lester Horton Dance Theatre in *Bal Caribe.* An instant star, Ailey danced in the film *Carmen Jones* (1954) and appeared on Broadway with noted dancer Carmen de Lavallade in *House of Flowers.* A diligent student, Ailey continued his dance training and studied with masters like Martha Graham. By 1962, Ailey had formed the Alvin Ailey American Dance Theater (AAADT), an integrated company of dancers committed to presenting new works along with older works, both black and white. Artistic director Judith Jamison, one of Ailey's star dancers, took over the AAADT after his death in 1989 and continued Ailey's pioneering efforts.

- ✔ **Arthur Mitchell** was the first African American to become a principal dancer at the prestigious New York City Ballet. Classically trained, Mitchell rarely danced specifically black parts; for example, he won acclaim for his role as Puck in *A Midsummer Night's Dream.* Knowing firsthand the limited opportunities available for African Americans to train in classical ballet, Mitchell cofounded the Dance Theatre of Harlem (DTH) in 1969 and has trained dancers in some of the most prestigious companies in the U.S. and the world.

Chapter 16

Give Me a Beat: African American Music

Music is the most widely acknowledged African American contribution to American culture. Enslaved Africans melded their traditional musical styles with the influences and realities of their new surroundings to create even more innovative sounds. Recognized and cherished the world over, African American musical genres include blues, jazz, gospel, R&B, and hip-hop, as well as their many variations.

This chapter explores those roots and traces today's sounds back to the views early Africans held about music and how they manifested those views during slavery. It also explores jazz, blues, gospel, and R&B as well as hip-hop's path from humble beginnings to global exposure.

African Roots

Every African village had musicians. Some worked directly for kings or chiefs, and many such positions were hereditary. In some African cultures, musicians sat near the king or chief during various ceremonies to indicate their exalted status. Africans used several types of instruments, but drums such as the snare, congas, and bongos were the most common. Frequently, the drum served as a royal or sacred instrument. Idiophones, most typically represented by bells, gong-gongs, and xylophones, were also popular. Early European travelers, who noted that Africans highly valued music, also wrote about *chordophones,* string instruments that resembled fiddles. The human voice was another important instrument.

During 18th-century slave voyages, slave traders intentionally separated Africans from their own cultural groups to prevent slave revolts. So when the Africans sang aboard slave ships, slave traders never imagined they were forming new alliances. Perhaps Africans, themselves, didn't initially know that music would become one of their defining cultural links.

Ironically, slave owners also valued the musical ability of their slaves and sometimes included it as an attractive feature in slave sale announcements. Slaves performed at slave auctions, and notices for runaway slaves even referenced musical talents. Enterprising masters hired musicians out, spawning the tradition of blacks entertaining whites.

African American Music Fundamentals

To illustrate the basic fundamentals found in African American music overall, scholars often point to the *ring shout,* a religious ritual performed in a circle comprised of shouters (or dancers) and singers. The ring shout is the oldest known African American performance style. Its common features are

- ✔ **Call-and-response:** Also known as *antiphony,* the leader sings a line and the other participants answer in unison.

  Music wasn't a solitary act; observers were encouraged to participate by clapping, dancing, and joining in the refrain. This call-and-response format is an important feature of all African-based music, especially African American music.

- ✔ **Vocality:** Includes cries, calls, hollers, and moans, among other expressions. In addition, singers display an intense emotionality as well as vocal versatility.

- ✔ **Rhythm:** *Polyrhythm,* the existence of two contrasting rhythms, as well as improvisation and *syncopation,* the stressing of a normally unstressed beat, are typical in African American music.

- ✔ **Texture:** Includes harmony and the simultaneous performance of the same melodic line with individual variations. In the absence of drums and other instrumental accompaniment, clapping and foot patting enhance the texture of the voice.

Although the ring shout has typically been attributed to the South, it existed among Northern blacks as well. Until the discovery of the McIntosh County Shouters in Georgia in 1980, however, the ring shout was believed to be extinct.

Feeling the Spirit: The Spirituals

Spirituals represent the greatest body of African American songs created before the Civil War. Distinguished American folklorist and musicologist Alan Lomax noted that the repetition, relaxed vocalization, and polyrhythmic accompaniment common in spirituals was consistent with the performance style found throughout Africa. Some spirituals even contain African melodies. Although all traditional spirituals feature the call-and-response element routinely found in African American music, thematic content makes them uniquely African American. Freedom, faith, struggle, hope, and patience are themes born directly from slavery.

Drawing inspiration from the Bible, slave spirituals often highlighted Jacob, Daniel, Moses, and Gabriel, among other biblical figures. Death was particularly prominent, and heaven differed greatly from the real-life degradation of slavery. Slaves envisioned an afterlife with no white people or work. Also, spirituals were assigned different purposes. Certain songs accompanied funeral services, the ring shout, and everyday life as well as formal worship services.

Most white people were completely unaware of spirituals until after the 1867 publication of *Slave Songs of the United States*. This collection represented the first systematic effort to collect and preserve these songs. Lead editor William Francis Allen, a Harvard graduate, began collecting the songs from former slaves while working on St. Helena Island in South Carolina as part of the Freedmen's Aid Commission. The book categorizes the songs by state and includes other notations.

The Fisk Jubilee Singers

Beginning in 1871, the Fisk Jubilee singers of Fisk University helped spread the spirituals to a larger audience through touring. University treasurer and music professor George L. White borrowed money and took nine students — seven former slaves and two children of former slaves — on the road. In high demand, the Fisk Jubilee Singers traveled throughout the United States and Europe popularizing the spirituals.

Most important, however, is that the Fisk Jubilee Singers, who inspired the formation of similar groups at other black colleges, set a precedent for African Americans to perform African American–oriented material abroad and break down barriers domestically. Undoubtedly, the Fisk Jubilee Singers' success contributed to the later spread of ragtime, jazz, and other forms of black music globally.

Spirituals were much more than songs of worship. Certain songs contained messages regarding secret meetings, as well as clues about escape routes for runaway slaves. Flip to Chapter 5 fore more information about the role music played for those trying to escape slavery.

Ragtime

Toward the end of the 19th century, popular or secular black music emerged in the form of *ragtime,* also known as *jig piano* because it's played on a piano. Named for its signature syncopation, ragtime is the first truly American musical genre. Because ragtime developed among black audiences, the exact date it emerged is unknown. There's evidence, however, that Philadelphia musician "Old Man" Sam Moore performed ragtime before 1875.

An important milestone in African American music, ragtime marked a departure from the fiddles and banjos that characterized antebellum black music. After slavery, many black families purchased small organs on installment plans that lasted a lifetime. Those organs, as well as pianos, were pivotal to the development of ragtime.

Ragtime's popularity increased during the 1890s. To even get songs published or performed, usually on the minstrel stage, African Americans had to write "coon songs," a term popular for the times. One particular song, "All the Coons Look Alike to Me" (1896) by African American songwriter Ernest Hogan was such a mammoth hit that semifinalists in the Ragtime Championship of the World Competition in 1900 were asked to rag it.

Minstrelsy

African Americans influenced white American's musical tastes before ragtime. Minstrelsy, a popular form of 19th-century American entertainment where whites performing in blackface largely ridiculed African American culture, relied on songs often influenced by enslaved African Americans living on plantations. Celebrated 19th-century songwriter Stephen Foster, who wrote "Oh! Susana" and "Camptown Races," visited Kentucky plantations to hear African American slaves sing. To his credit, Foster did ask white minstrels who performed his songs not to mock African Americans. As African Americans performed in minstrel shows more, the African American–dominated minstrel show evolved. These shows, especially in the 20th century, became a legitimate disseminator of African American music. Read more about minstrelsy in Chapter 15.

Scott Joplin became ragtime's most famous figure. Although music publishers rejected his most famous composition, "Maple Leaf Rag," in 1898, Joplin made it popular by playing it constantly at the Maple Leaf Cafe in Sedalia, Missouri, where he worked as a pianist. When a small publisher released the work in 1899, "Maple Leaf Rag" quickly became the model for classic ragtime. Later in his career, Joplin taught in New York and even published a ragtime manual for musicians titled *The School of Ragtime* (1908). In addition to creating ragtime classics, including the 1902 rag "The Entertainer" that appeared in the 1974 classic film *The Sting,* Joplin created the folk opera *Treemonisha* (1911), which extolled the value of education for African Americans, and *The Ragtime Dance,* a ballet performed in Sedalia in 1899. Despite his tremendous influence, Joplin wasn't wealthy when he died in 1917.

Singing the Blues

The blues grew out of backbreaking work conditions. Cotton plantations sprouted in Mississippi, Alabama, Tennessee, Louisiana, and Texas as a direct result of the invention of the cotton gin in 1793 and the Louisiana Purchase in 1803. Singing made the work tolerable, so slaves sang spirituals and work songs. The rhythm of work songs, in particular, established a steady work pace. The blues, broken down in its simplest form, is a merging of the saddest spirituals with work songs.

Born out of the American experience of slavery and Jim Crow, the blues also comes from the African American oral tradition (refer to Chapter 14) and tells a unique story of hardship and heartache. Although considered sad music, Southern writer Albert Murray, author of "bluesy" novels like *Train Whistle Guitar,* has argued that the blues identifies life's harshest realities but is also a coping mechanism for transcending them.

Blues basics

Blues lyrics typically follow an AAB form: A different third line follows two identical lines. In Bessie Smith's "Lost Your Head Blues," for example, she sings "I was with you baby when you didn't have a dime" twice before singing "Now since you've got plenty of money you have throwed your good gal down." In addition, many early blues songs reference the supernatural, which some have argued reflects an African cosmology. The devil is also prominent but bears a greater resemblance to the trickster figures of African folktales than to the Christian concept of an evil being.

African origins of the banjo

Descriptions of banjo-like African instruments made of drinking gourds with strings attached appear in Richard Jobson's *The Golden Trade* (1623) as well as works by other Europeans. Banjos may have been present on slave ships as well since traveler Adrien Dessalles described the *banza,* a banjo-like instrument used in musical celebrations in Martinique, in 1654.

On American plantations, the banjo, known as a *bandore* or *banjer,* was quite common among slave musicians. In the 19th century, the banjo became a fixture in minstrel shows, which may explain why African Americans abandoned the banjo in the early 20th century. White musicians, particularly in the Southern Appalachia region, embraced the banjo, which is still a prominent instrument in bluegrass music.

Like the wandering verses of spirituals, blues verses freely float from one song to another, especially in early songs. The guitar is the most commonly used instrument, probably because it's a close cousin to the banjo, which was relatively easy to make and was welcomed on plantations (see the sidebar "African origins of the banjo"). Early blues artists used various guitar techniques, such as sliding a knife or other device along the strings to achieve a particular sound.

Generally regarded as the Father of the Blues, W.C. Handy popularized the blues, particularly the 12-bar blues structure, which typically has four beats in every measure and a chord progression that rises and falls. Always intrigued by the work songs and spirituals he heard growing up in Alabama, Handy really learned about the blues while working as a bandmaster and director of dance orchestras in the Mississippi Delta region, around Clarksdale, Mississippi. A better blues composer than player, Handy, who relocated to Memphis, attempted to publish blues music several times. Finally, in 1912, he self-financed the publication of "Memphis Blues," which became hugely popular. His 1914 composition, "St. Louis Blues," became a classic.

Blues genres

The blues flourished and spawned several genres, including classic blues, Delta blues, and urban blues:

> ✓ **Classic blues:** Today, blues is largely associated with men, but as blues rose to prominence during the 1920s, women were the stars and songs about no-good men were extremely popular. Classic blues singers

Gertrude "Ma" Rainey and Bessie Smith were two of the most popular African Americans singers of their time. Both women honed their talents on the minstrel and vaudeville circuits.

✔ **The Delta blues:** Texas-born Blind Lemon Jefferson became the first popular male blues artist, but Mississippi-born bluesmen dominated the genre, even creating a subgenre known as the Delta blues. Characterized by hardships such as imprisonment at Mississippi's notorious Parchman Penitentiary, unemployment, jealous women and husbands, and raunchy good times in juke joints, the Delta blues has become one of the most popular forms of blues, with stars such as Charley Patton and Robert Johnson.

✔ **The urban blues:** Before African Americans migrated to Northern cities like Chicago during the Great Migration (see Chapter 7), they went to Southern cities like Memphis, known for its famed Beale Street, which became an important hub for the blues and later rhythm and blues and rock-and-roll. Beginning in the 1940s, Chicago became another important home for the blues, with Maxwell Street occupying a similar importance to Memphis's Beale Street. Chicago was home to many transplanted black Southerners, a significant number of them from Mississippi. A genre called urban or Chicago blues, characterized by electric guitars and a fuller band sound, sprouted there. Muddy Waters is arguably the genre's most successful artist.

Famous blues musicians

There were countless successful blues artists, many of whom recorded 150 songs or more. Yet many artists, even those who were stars, died broke. Below is just a sampling of some of the many influential blues artists:

✔ **Gertrude "Ma" Rainey:** Billed as the "Mother of the Blues," Rainey began singing in the blues style as early as 1902, some years before her first recording in 1923. Touring the Theater Owners Booking Association (T.O.B.A.) circuit helped Ma Rainey's career peak in the 1920s as she sold an impressive number of records.

T.O.B.A. was an organization of clubs, throughout the South mainly, where black acts performed for black audiences dating from roughly 1909 to its height in the 1920s.

✔ **Bessie Smith:** Bessie Smith, known as the "Empress of the Blues," recorded mainly for Columbia Records. Her recording career lasted from 1923 until around 1933. Unsung blues pioneer Alberta Hunter wrote "Down Hearted Blues," one of Smith's many hits. Credited with creating a demand for a grittier blues style, artists Smith influenced include Billie Holiday and Mahalia Jackson.

✔ **Charley Patton:** Often called the "King of the Delta Blues," Charley Patton, who recorded his first record in 1929, was a great influence on Delta blues artists like Willie Brown, with whom he often performed, Son House, and the legendary Robert Johnson.

✔ **Robert Johnson:** Johnson is the most legendary Delta blues figure. In his short lifetime (he died at age 27), Johnson wasn't an overwhelming blues success, but his distinctive guitar style, coupled with the tale that he sold his soul to the devil in exchange for his much-improved guitar skills, have fueled his legend.

✔ **Muddy Waters:** Born on a Mississippi plantation, Muddy Waters was the most successful urban blues artist. By 1947, Waters, who had upgraded to using an amplified guitar, was recording for Chess Records in Chicago. Waters used the slide guitar technique and the traditional AAB blues form. Artists he influenced include Junior Wells and Buddy Guy, who played for him, and the Rolling Stones, who took their name from the Waters song "Rollin' Stone."

✔ **B.B. King:** Born in the Mississippi Delta in 1925, B.B. King sang gospel as a child but hit his stride singing about everyday life, particularly romantic relationships. Combining his smooth vocals with guitar expertise, B.B. King has recorded no less than 50 albums. Together, he and Lucille (the name he gives to all his guitars as a reminder of the night he ran into a burning building in Arkansas to save his precious instrument) have taken blues, particularly his signature song "The Thrill Is Gone," all around the globe.

Race records

Music recording wasn't widely open to black musicians until Perry Bradford, a seasoned vaudeville and minstrel show performer and musician, convinced Okeh Records to record Mamie Smith when white singer Sophie Tucker became too ill to record. The two songs Smith cut in February 1920 ("That Thing Called Love" and "You Can't Keep A Good Man Down") performed well enough that Okeh allowed Smith to record "Crazy Blues" that summer. Okeh promoted Smith, and "Crazy Blues" sold 1 million copies, alerting white companies to the potential of the African American market. Other companies such as Columbia also entered the business to record black artists to sell specifically to black people.

In 1921, the black-owned Pace Phonograph Company founded by W.C. Handy's former partner Harry Pace began recording artists on Black Swan Records, named in honor of the Black Swan Elizabeth Taylor Greenfield. Initially the company floundered, but fortunes changed when Black Swan signed Bessie Smith. The recording scored big with the public. White-owned companies took note and entered the black music market with a fury. By 1923, Paramount had purchased Black Swan Records.

It's nearly impossible to list all the other influential blues artists. Those born in Mississippi alone include Eddie James "Son" House, Jr., Chester "Howlin' Wolf" Burnett, Sonny Boy Williamson II, Willie Dixon (known as the "Granddaddy of Chicago Blues"), Skip James, Mississippi John Hurt, Bukka White, John Lee Hooker, and R.L. Burnside. Innovators of the Piedmont blues, a style from the Carolinas and Georgia, include Tampa Red. Louisiana has contributed Huddie "Leadbelly" Ledbetter and Lonnie Johnson. Lightnin' Hopkins and T-Bone Walker hailed from Texas. The Tennessee-born vocalist Bobby Blue Bland straddled the fence between blues and soul. Today's blues artists include Taj Mahal, Bobby Rush, and Robert Cray. Of the female blues singers, long-gone legends like Memphis Minnie and Big Mama Thornton come to mind. Today, Chicago blues legend Koko Taylor has no equal.

Let the Good Times Roll: Jazz

In simple terms, jazz is a fusion of blues and ragtime with brass-band music and syncopated dance music. Common features are *blue notes* (notes played or sung below the major scale), polyrhythm, and improvisation, along with other aspects of African American music.

Several theories on the origins of the word "jazz" abound. Some have traced it back to an itinerant black musician in the Mississippi River Valley region named Jazbo Brown. Others claim it emanated from the musician Boisey James, who became known as "Old Jas" and played "Jas's music." In 1910, a Chicago sign painter wrote that "Music will be furnished by Jas.' Band." White New Orleans bands such as the Original Dixieland Jass Band were the first to introduce jazz to the public through recordings. By 1918, "jazz" was a common term.

The evolution of jazz styles

Like blues and ragtime, pinpointing when or where jazz started is hard. New Orleans jazz great Jelly Roll Morton, an early jazz innovator, untruthfully boasted that he invented jazz. (In 1915, "Jelly Roll's Blues" became the first published jazz arrangement, however.) Ragtime and its offshoot, boogie woogie, were pivotal to jazz's early development, and Morton was a top ragtime pianist. Eventually Morton, like many of his peers, began playing jazz, particularly in Storyville, a red-light district known for prostitution and hot music near New Orleans's French Quarter.

Jazz didn't begin in Storyville, but Storyville was important to jazz's overall development. New Orleans thrived as a major port city, thereby creating an environment in which great musicians like ragtime pianist Tony Jackson, who greatly influenced Morton, honed their craft.

Scholars have linked New Orleans's innovation in black music to the African-based musical heritage nurtured in Congo Square. Dating back to the 18th century when the French ruled New Orleans, slaves from the Tremé plantation gathered in Congo Square near the French Quarter on Sundays and held a market where they played music, sang, and danced, a practice that declined in the mid–19th century. Located at the southern corner of Louis Armstrong Park, Congo Square is on the National Register of Historic Places for its pivotal role in New Orleans's noted musical history.

Cornetist Charles "Buddy" Bolden, in particular, had a tremendous impact on New Orleans and jazz overall. Making a living through music alone was hard. By 1904, Morton, like other musicians, began traveling to other cities for work. When the federal government shut down Storyville in 1917, many New Orleans musicians migrated to Chicago.

Jazzing up the North with red hot jazz

In Chicago, New Orleans musicians ushered in an era of jazz that has several names, including red hot, Dixieland, and classic jazz. Common features included a rhythm section, group and collective improvisation, cornet or trumpet as lead instrument, an infusion of emotion, and an overall jazz swing feel.

Arriving in Chicago in 1917 during the first phase of the Great Migration (the mass relocation of black Southerners to the North; see Chapter 7), Bill Johnson was one of the earliest New Orleans musicians to establish himself. By 1919, Joseph "King" Oliver, one of New Orleans's most respected musicians of the time, had joined Johnson's band in Chicago; by 1920, he was leading his own band, King Oliver's Creole Jazz Band. Louis Armstrong, whom Oliver mentored in New Orleans, joined Oliver in Chicago in 1922. Other notable New Orleans musicians who lived in Chicago included Freddie Keppard, trombonist Kid Ory (his Kid Ory's Creole Jazz Band was the first black New Orleans band to record in 1922), clarinetist Sidney Bechet, and Jelly Roll Morton.

Big band jazz

Taking a lead from red hot jazz, big bands emerged during the 1920s. Unlike previous bands where there was a greater degree of improvisation, big bands had arrangers that structured the music more but allowed for more breakout solo improvisation. Suddenly bandleaders like Fletcher Henderson, Cab Calloway, Duke Ellington (see Figure 16-1), and Chick Webb flourished at places like Club Alabam and the Savoy Ballroom in Harlem and on the road. Fatha Hines and Count Basie led the Midwest's biggest big bands in Chicago and Kansas City, respectively. (Lionel Hampton kept the big band tradition alive well into the 1980s.)

Swing jazz

In the 1930s, Kansas City musicians were among the first to adopt the swing style of jazz, which stressed all the beats equally, thus producing a smooth-flowing rhythm. Typically, in swing jazz, a large number of musicians, backed by an especially strong rhythm section, played in a medium to fast tempo. Duke Ellington's 1932 hit "It Don't Mean A Thing If It Ain't Got That Swing" provided a name for this new style of jazz, which was very danceable.

Bebop: More than dancing

During the 1940s, jazz began changing, and the Harlem nightclub Minton's Playhouse was at the forefront of that change. Minton's luminaries included pianist Thelonious Monk, drummers Kenny Clarke and Max Roach, guitarist Charlie Christian, trumpeter Dizzy Gillespie, and saxophonists Charlie "Bird" Parker and Lester "the Prez" Young.

Out of this gathering of talent, bebop emerged. Characterized by complex polyrhythms, dissonant harmonies, and irregular phrases, bebop broke away from the more regimented style of jazz playing. Typically two horns — trumpet and saxophone — began in unison followed by a series of improvisations before the horns concluded the song by repeating the first sequence in unison. Bebop discarded the melodies of standard pieces such as "Stomping at the Savoy" and created new melodies over the old harmonic progressions. By emphasizing technical skill, bebop demanded that audiences really listen to the music. Thelonious Monk is credited as saying, "We wanted a music that they couldn't play"; "they" referred to white musicians.

"When we borrowed from a standard," Gillespie once explained, "we added and substituted so many chords that most people didn't know what song we were playing."

Figure 16-1:
Duke
Ellington
with Ella
Fitzgerald.

© Bettmann/Corbis

Hard bop

Bebop gave way to hard bop, a more rhythmically driven sound associated with drummers like Art Blakey and saxophonist Cannonball Adderley. Musicians such as Miles Davis and saxophonist Sonny Rollins who cut their teeth on bebop also participated. Bassist Charles Mingus even developed a funkier side to hard bop by incorporating popular black music like soul.

Avant garde, or free, jazz

Jazz continued to evolve throughout the 1960s. Saxophonists Ornette Coleman and John Coltrane were harbingers of the free jazz era. Coleman emphasized harmonic freedom, as showcased in the albums *The Shape of Jazz to Come* and *Free Jazz*. Incorporating elements of African, Arabic, and Indian music, Coltrane infused his music with a deep spirituality, captured by albums like *A Love Supreme* and *Meditation*. Pianist Charles Mingus revived the art of collective improvisation, reigning in the trend of solo improvisation.

Jazz singers

As jazz progressed, skillful singers adopted a scatting technique in which the voice functioned more like an instrument.

- ✔ **Billie "Lady Day" Holiday:** Born to teenage parents in 1915, the troubled Billie Holiday's first record, made in 1933, didn't sell well. A performance at Harlem's Apollo Theater in 1935, however, launched the Baltimore native's legendary career. Touring the South with white jazz musician Artie Shaw introduced Holiday's distinctive voice, punctuated by unique phrasings and a heart-wrenching delivery, to a wider audience. Repeated performances of the antilynching song, "Strange Fruit," at New York's integrated Cafe Society in 1939, secured her legend, but drug and alcohol abuse cut her life short in 1959.

- ✔ **Sarah Vaughan:** Newark's Sarah Vaughan, whose roots dated back to swing, was one of the few singers of the bebop era. Like bebop instrumentalists, Vaughan, along with her friend and colleague Billy Eckstine, improvised melodic lines based on the chord progressions of standard songs.

- ✔ **Ella Fitzgerald:** One of jazz's few female bandleaders, Ella Fitzgerald (refer to Figure 16-1) rose to fame with Chick Webb's band and hit with songs such as "A-Tisket, A-Tasket." After Webb died, she changed the group's name and toured as Ella Fitzgerald and her Orchestra. In 1941, she went solo and became most noted for her *Great American Songbook* series with Verve, in which she sang Cole Porter, Duke Ellington, and Irving Berlin standards.

Great jazz instrumentalists

The following jazz artists did more than excel individually; they either nurtured the genre in its formative stages or took it to greater heights:

- **Charles "Buddy" Bolden:** Emulated by later greats such as Louis Armstrong and King Oliver, Bolden was the first New Orleans cornetist and bandleader to play jazz music. By 1901, he was the most well-known musician in New Orleans. Unfortunately, Bolden predates jazz recordings, but his music still fuels New Orleans legends. Bolden, who died in 1931, is known for the songs "Buddy Bolden's Blues" and "Make Me A Pallet on the Floor."

- **James Reese Europe:** Credited with prepping Europe for jazz, the appropriately named James Reese Europe gave World War I soldiers a lift with his Harlem Hellfighters' band, drawn from New York's all-black 369th Infantry. Europe's recordings demonstrated the transition from ragtime and blues to jazz. By the time of his death (he was stabbed by a band member), Europe was the most prominent African American bandleader.

- **Louis Armstrong:** Satchmo, as many knew him, was one of jazz's first stars. Before mastering the trumpet, Armstrong began his musical career singing for pennies as a boy. At the Colored Waifs' Home for Boys, he learned to play several instruments and eventually led the home's brass band. After leaving the home, he got various gigs in New Orleans nightclubs and bars. He put his trumpet and voice to good use in the 1967 classic "What a Wonderful World."

- **Edward Kennedy "Duke" Ellington:** Known for his smartly dressed orchestra of precise musicians who performed in perfect unison, Ellington, born in Washington, D.C., in 1899, was one of America's greatest composers, leaving a catalog of more than 2,000 compositions when he died in 1974. He and frequent collaborator Billy Strayhorn, with whom he composed the classic "Take the A Train," were so in sync they often didn't know who contributed what.

- **Charlie Parker:** Noted as bebop's coarchitect, along with Dizzy Gillespie, Charlie "Bird" Parker, born in 1920, came from Kansas City's entrenched jazz tradition. A master of the saxophone, he took many musical risks, such as recording with strings, which resulted in the best-selling album, *Charlie Parker with Strings*. Unfortunately, drugs cut Parker's genius short in 1955.

- **Miles Davis:** A key member of Charlie Parker's quintet (refer to the earlier section "Bebop: More than dancing"), Davis led his own group of nine musicians by 1948. Using unconventional instrumentation such as the French horn and tuba, Davis charted new territory. He followed his well-received 1957 album *Birth of the Cool* with the platinum-selling *Kind of Blue* two years later. Over his long career, Davis infused jazz, soul, rock, and rhythm and blues in his music, a spirit he captured in his highly regarded 1970 album, *Bitches Brew*. Davis, who won a Grammy in 1987, remained a respected jazz innovator until his death in 1991.

Although men have dominated much of jazz's history, women instrumentalists weren't uncommon: Pianist Lil Hardin Armstrong, wife of Louis Armstrong, played with King Oliver; Mary Lou Williams, another pianist, contributed swing band scores to Benny Goodman and Earl Hines; Louis Armstrong tagged Valaida Snow the best trumpeter after himself; and the Grammy Award–winning Shirley Horn frequently accompanied herself on the piano.

Keeping the tradition alive

In the 1970s, jazz continued to be a free-for-all stylistically, but pianists including McCoy Tyner, Ramsey Lewis, and Keith Jarrett led the field. Pianist Herbie Hancock pioneered the use of synthesized instruments as well as absorbed funk elements into jazz. New Orleans–born, Julliard-trained trumpeter Wynton Marsalis, who emerged in the 1980s, objected to these deviations and called for a reinstatement of "classic" jazz style. To that end, Marsalis has supplemented his recordings with his work with Jazz at Lincoln Center, which has elevated jazz to American classical music.

Traditional or not, jazz artists like singers Nancy Wilson, Cassandra Wilson, and Dianne Reeves and musicians such as pianist Marcus Roberts, trumpeters Roy Hargrove, Russell Gunn, and Terence Blanchard, as well as saxophonist Joshua Redmon have kept the genre moving forward.

Spreading the Gospel

Thomas Andrew Dorsey, known as Georgia Tom in the world of blues and jazz, changed religious music for African Americans in 1930 when he meshed elements of blues and jazz with black sacred music, creating gospel. To spread this new music to black churches, Dorsey established a gospel music publishing house. He also tapped Sallie Martin, a gospel pioneer in her own right, to organize the National Convention of Gospel Choirs and Choruses.

Mahalia Jackson

New Orleans–born Mahalia Jackson moved to Chicago in 1927 to join the Johnson Brothers but pursued a solo career when they broke up. "Move On Up A Little Higher," released in 1948, catapulted her to international stardom, making her the world's most recognizable gospel star. By 1954, she had her own CBS radio series. A great friend and supporter of Martin Luther King, Jr., Jackson sang at the March on Washington as well as at King's funeral. Jackson, who was born in 1911, died in Chicago in 1972.

A prolific songwriter, Dorsey wrote over 1,000 gospel songs in his lifetime. Created out of the tragedy of losing his wife and son in childbirth, Dorsey wrote "Precious Lord" in 1932 to cope with his grief. In 1937, he penned "Peace in the Valley" for Mahalia Jackson, who would become the world's most famous gospel singer.

Gospel music has many unsung pioneers. Following are just a few individuals and groups who made significant contributions to the evolution of gospel music:

- **Sister Rosetta Tharpe:** As both a guitarist and singer, Tharpe mixed the sacred with the secular. She appeared on the pop charts with "This Train," played the Apollo Theater, and enjoyed success with hit songs such as "Up Above My Head."

- **Clara Ward:** A great influence on Aretha Franklin, Ward's group, the Famous Ward Singers, pushed the boundaries of gospel artists even further. From the 1940s into the 1960s, they appeared at the Newport Jazz Festival and sang at Radio City Music Hall. They also injected glamour into gospel with their jewelry and more-contemporary clothing.

- **Willie Mae Ford Smith:** A gospel purist, Smith emphasized the ministerial role of gospel singing and introduced the style of *song and sermonette,* singing coupled with testimony.

- **Reverend James Cleveland:** The man behind the modern gospel sound, James Cleveland paired jazz and pop influences with complex arrangements to create intricate harmonies specifically for the mass choir. To teach this new style, he created the Gospel Singers Workshop Convention (GSWC) within the Gospel Workshop of America, which he founded with mentor Albertina Walker. Kirk Franklin and John P. Kee are just two GSWC alums.

- **The Soul Stirrers:** Sam Cooke's former group set the standard of the lead singer supported by four-part harmony.

- **The Winans:** Originally, the Winans were brothers Marvin, Carvin, Michael, and Ronald. The Detroit family of ten, however, has also contributed duo BeBe and CeCe Winans, who both have successful solo careers, and younger sisters Angie and Debbie Winans, along with Marvin's former wife Vickie Winans.

Contemporary gospel stars such as Yolanda Adams, Donnie McClurkin, and Kirk Franklin have successfully reached out to secular circles, but secular acceptance of gospel isn't new. Edwin Hawkins and his Edwin Hawkins Singers enjoyed considerable success with "Oh, Happy Day," as did the Clark Sisters with the 1980s hit "You Brought the Sunshine." Both Mariah Carey and Beyoncé have cited Karen Clark Sheard as a major musical influence.

Mainstreaming Black Music

New genres of black music emerged in the mid–20th century, taking black music to even greater heights. Race music gave way to rhythm and blues (R&B). Not much later, R&B led to the creation of rock-and-roll. As rock-and-roll began to exclude African Americans, soul music took over.

R&B

Drawing heavily from blues and gospel, R&B meshed rhythm with blues. Consistent with other forms of African American music, early R&B incorporated the call-and-response pattern and improvisation into its performance style. Black pop quartets, such as the Ink Spots and the Mills Brothers, also played a role in R&B's development. Their mainstream sound, as well as that of singers Nat King Cole and Billy Eckstine, lost its appeal with many African Americans. Eventually R&B became the bridge between that sound and soul.

Although forgotten today, Louis Jordan, known for hits such as "Is You Is Or Is You Ain't My Baby?" and "Caldonia," was one of the first artists to demonstrate the crossover appeal that early R&B could have without adjusting it for white audiences. In 1943, Jordan, whose music inspired the 1992 Broadway hit *Five Guys Named Moe,* topped both the black and white charts with "Ration Blues." Jordan's early experimentation with *soundies,* short pictures with sound, anticipated the music video.

Rocking and rolling

Rock-and-roll has black roots, a fact that may seem surprising given the relative scarcity of African American rock artists and rock bands today. Ike Turner's 1951 recording "Rocket 88," the first boasting a distorted guitar, contained the driving backbeat and electric guitar that became commonplace in rock-and-roll. "Sh-boom," the first acknowledged rock-and-roll song, was recorded by the R&B group the Chords. Other black artists contributed to the new genre.

Despite rock's early ties to African American musicians, white artists covered early rock-and-roll songs by African Americans: The Crew Cuts, a white group from Canada, took "Sh-boom" straight to number one on the Billboardcharts in 1954. Bill Haley and the Comets scored with Joe Turner's "Shake, Rattle, and Roll," and Pat Boone covered Fats Domino's "Ain't That A Shame" and Little Richard's "Tutti Frutti."

Jimi Hendrix

Despite a heavy R&B tutelage that included playing with the Isley Brothers, 1960s guitarist Jimi Hendrix became a rock legend. (Hendrix's reputation on the guitar is akin to that of bluesman Robert Johnson.) Given the times, Hendrix's talent may have gone unrecognized had he not recorded in England. Known for the hits "Purple Haze" and "Voodoo Child (Slight Return)," Hendrix received his due during his lifetime, but his sudden death in 1970, at age 27, elevated him to cult status.

Historian Carl Belz, who wrote *The Story of Rock* (1969), observed that white audiences felt more comfortable with how white artists softened the new exotic sound of rock-and-roll. As landmark decisions dismantling segregation became more common, white America's racial gatekeepers didn't overlook rock-and-roll's black origins. Taunts of "white nigger" directed toward Elvis, who recorded at Sun Studios in Memphis, the first home for many black artists, were in response to rock-and-roll's black roots.

Some black artists broke through the racial matrix, however. Guitarist Chuck Berry had a hit with "Maybelline," blues pianist Fats Domino scored big with "Blueberry Hill," and Little Richard had "Good Golly, Miss Molly." British groups like the Beatles and the Rolling Stones had no problems commending black artists for their talents, particularly Muddy Waters and Bo Diddley, who's often cited as a key figure in the transition of R&B to rock-and-roll. T-Bone Walker, who fits into blues and R&B, pioneered the electric guitar sound. Although classified as R&B during the 1960s and 1970s, Ike and Tina Turner's style, in retrospect, was more rock-oriented, as evidenced on "Proud Mary." Jimi Hendrix wasn't only accepted; he was exalted.

Hendrix wasn't alone as a contemporary rock titan. Sly Stone, along with his brother and two sisters, exerted considerable influence with his group Sly and the Family Stone. From 1967 to 1975, the rock group, whose members were predominantly black, created the hits "Everyday People," "Hot Fun in the Summertime," and "Thank You (Falettinme Be Mice Elf Agin)." Mixing funk, soul, and the psychedelic culture of Bay Area hippies, Sly and the Family Stone created a rock sound and look that still distinguishes them. Black rock group Living Colour and Tina Turner, in her solo turn, continued that rock-and-roll legacy into the 1980s.

The Supremes

Launched as the Primettes, Diana Ross, Mary Wilson, and Florence Ballard, who became the Supremes, weren't hitmakers at first. They finally topped the charts In 1964 with "Where Did Our Love Go." Berry Gordy's controversial decision to replace the more soulful Ballard with the more crossover-friendly voice and look of Diana Ross (a move loosely chronicled in the hit Broadway musical and 2006 film *Dreamgirls*) was a difference-maker. With their 1966 album *Supremes A' Go-Go,* the Supremes became the first female group in history to have a number one album. Fully accepted by white audiences, the Supremes were among the first black artists to appear on such iconic programs as *The Ed Sullivan Show.* The Supremes also topped international charts. Their success opened the doors for many artists, not just their Motown peers.

Motown

As rock-and-roll took hold in the 1950s, Berry Gordy, songwriter and record shop owner, created a winning formula that combined the best of R&B, pop, gospel, and big band. Within a year of its launch, Gordy's label, popularly known as Motown, produced the top R&B single "Shop Around" from Smokey Robinson and the Miracles. Black-owned record labels such as Chicago-based Vee-Jay Records, home of the Dells, Impressions, and solo artists Jerry Butler and Gene Chandler, also existed, but Motown truly earned its "Hitsville, U.S.A." label.

The hits kept coming: 1961 to 1963 brought the Marvelettes' "Please, Mr. Postman," the Contours' "Do You Love Me," the teenaged Stevie Wonder's "Fingertips," and Martha and the Vandellas "(Love is Like a) Heat Wave." In 1964, the Supremes began their historic journey at the top of the charts. In its heyday, Motown was packed with some of music's biggest stars of the time, such as Marvin Gaye, the Four Tops, and the Temptations. Gladys Knight and the Pips even recorded with Motown.

More than just a label, Motown had its own finishing school and insisted that most of its artists present a refined and sophisticated image. Later in the 1960s, as the civil rights movement gave way to the black power movement (refer to Chapters 9 and 10), Motown's controlled image was not aggressive enough for many black Americans. Consequently, the grittier sound of soul music became more alluring.

Giving America soul

By today's standards, Ray Charles's 1955 number one hit "I Got A Woman" is tame. At that time, however, adapting a gospel song or sound for secular purposes — the basis of soul music — was controversial, especially within the gospel community. Charles continued to convert gospel songs to secular subject matter. "This Little Girl of Mine" and "Hallelujah, I Love Her So," among others, also became hits.

Charles's success encouraged Sam Cooke, a member of the legendary Soul Stirrers and one of gospel's brightest stars, to record secular records in 1957. Cooke became one of the biggest gospel stars to crossover to both the R&B and pop charts. The business-minded Cooke, who produced and wrote songs, also co-owned record label SAR. Following his untimely death in 1964, Cooke hit with "A Change Is Gonna Come," an instant classic addressing the turbulent 1960s.

The Godfather and Queen of Soul: James Brown and Aretha Franklin

Despite their very different backgrounds — she has the gospel background befitting soul royalty; he was born poor and spent time in prison — Aretha Franklin and James Brown were soul music's biggest stars.

James Brown: Born extremely poor in South Carolina during the Depression era, abandoned by his parents, and raised by an aunt in Augusta, Georgia, James Brown overcame huge obstacles. He achieved some early success with his group James Brown and the Famous Flames (formed with Bobby Byrd, whom he met in prison), when their song "Please, Please, Please" secured the group a record deal and reached number five on the Billboard charts. The group had other Billboard hits, including the number one "Try Me," in the late 1950s. Brown, known for his live performance antics, eventually dropped the Flames, and using his own money, recorded *Live at the Apollo* in October 1962 over his record label's objections. The album's success (it hit number two on Billboard) demonstrated the general viability of the soul album. (Previously, many black artists only cut singles.) Ultimately, James Brown' emphasis on rhythm meshed with the rebellious tension of the times, providing the soundtrack to black America's transition from the civil rights movement to the black power

movement. His 1968 hit "Say It Loud — I'm Black and I'm Proud" served as the perfect anthem. Brown's hits slowed around 1976, but he resurfaced in the 1980s, when hip-hop artists used his sounds to spark another black music revolution. At the time of his death in 2006, Brown was still the Godfather of Soul.

Aretha Franklin: The daughter of noted preacher C.L. Franklin, who recorded his sermons with the Chicago-based Chess (the label behind Muddy Waters and Chuck Berry), Aretha Franklin, as a teenager, released a gospel album and had recorded with Columbia Records. Despite these successes, she truly came into her own when she signed with Atlantic Records, where she was encouraged to be herself, exert the full power of her voice, and use all her talents. When her album *I Never Loved A Man The Way I Loved You* hit in 1967, Franklin instantly became the Queen of Soul as her songs topped both the R&B and pop charts. Between 1967 and 1992, Franklin had 89 Top 40 entries, 17 of which hit number one. Although shy and soft-spoken, Franklin never wavered in her support for the civil rights movement, lending her voice whenever needed. Interestingly, her "soul sister" status within the black community bolstered her popularity among white music lovers.

Solomon Burke's vocal techniques such as rhythmically stuttering words influenced the style of many subsequent soul singers, but Stax Records, an independent, Memphis-based label, gave soul music its biggest boost. Artists such as Otis Redding, Rufus Thomas, and Thomas's daughter Carla firmly established Stax and soul music. Otis Redding put a smooth spin on soul: His hits like "Try a Little Tenderness" and "I've Been Loving You Too Long (To Stop Now)," though secular, are reminiscent of gospel songs in feeling, if not content. Stax also had Sam & Dave, known for the hits "Soul Man" and "Hold On! I'm A Comin," co-written with Isaac Hayes, who became a star in his own right.

Other influential soul artists included Wilson Pickett, best known for "In the Midnight Hour"; Percy Sledge of "When A Man Loves A Woman" fame; and Etta James, who hit it big with "At Last." James Brown, dubbed "soul brother number one," among other names, and Aretha Franklin, the Queen of Soul, became soul music's biggest stars.

Post-soul black music

Black music underwent more changes in the 1970s, as artists began to move beyond the Motown sound, which favored material concerned with relationships, to include social issues like war and poverty. *What's Going On,* Marvin Gaye's 1971 album addressing the Vietnam War, became his most successful album to date. *Let's Get It On,* his sexy follow-up, was also a major success. Gaye resurfaced in the 1980s with "Sexual Healing" before his own tragic death at the hands of his father in 1984. Stevie Wonder hit big with "Superstition" and "Living for the City" and eventually won several Grammy awards, especially for his 1976 double album *Songs in the Key of Life.*

Kenneth Gamble and Leon Huff

Philadelphia created a name for itself in soul in the early 1970s when songwriters and producers Kenneth Gamble and Leon Huff formed Philadelphia International Records in 1971. Songs such as Harold Melvin and the Blue Notes's "If You Don't Know Me By Now," the O'Jays's "Back Stabbers," and the Grammy winner "Me and Mrs. Jones" by Billy Paul injected a new sound into black music. For the most part, Philadelphia International matched its male artists' strong, masculine voices with thumping bass lines and other new music techniques. The featured bass lines, also found in funk and hip-hop, later resurfaced in a new genre called disco. In the late 1970s and 1980s, Gamble and Huff collaborated to produce the classics "Close the Door" and "Somebody Loves You Back" for Teddy Pendergrass as well as Patti LaBelle's classic album *I'm in Love Again* with the hits "Love, Need, and Want You Baby" and "If Only You Knew." Gamble also played a pivotal role in President Jimmy Carter designating June as Black Music Month in 1979.

But Wonder and Gaye weren't the only soul artists from the 1960s flexing their expanded creative visions in the 1970s. More than anyone, Curtis Mayfield, the former member of the Impressions who penned the memorable civil rights songs "Keep On Pushin'" and "People Get Ready," literally created the soundtrack for ghetto life. *Superfly,* which accompanied the film of the same name in 1972, included "Freddie's Dead" and "Pusherman," songs that spoke to drug use and trafficking in urban communities. He duplicated that magic for the films *Claudine* (1974) and *Sparkle* (1975), which yielded the Aretha Franklin hit "Something He Can Feel."

Getting funky and popping off

Rhythm-heavy and instrumentally driven, *funk,* an off-shoot of R&B and soul, came into its own during the 1970s, aided by the George Clinton Parliament Funkadelic movement, which included brothers Bootsy and Catfish Collins. George Clinton's brand of funk hit its stride in 1978 with *One Nation Under A Groove.* Clinton began recording in the 1980s as George Clinton and the P-Funk All-Stars. Other pivotal funk groups included the Ohio Players, Graham Central Station, and the Bar-Kays.

Overall, bands were big in the 1970s and the early 1980s. The most popular include Earth, Wind & Fire, Rufus featuring Chaka Khan, the Commodores, Morris Day and the Time, and Cameo. Each of these groups mixed elements of R&B and soul with funk and incorporated their own signature styles into their recordings. Zapp, which included four brothers, most notably Roger Troutman, was a bridge between disco and funk in the 1980s. Troutman pioneered the "talk box," synthesized vocals resembling a robot.

Michael Jackson, the youngest of the Jackson Five (a group that included his brothers Tito, Marlon, Jermaine, and Jackie), was one of the 1970s' most promising crossover stars. The 1970s hits "ABC," "I'll Be There," and "Never Can Say Goodbye" set Jackson up for global pop success. Selling over 20 million records worldwide, *Off the Wall,* with the hit "Rock With You," marked the solo Jackson's first collaboration with renowned trumpeter and composer Quincy Jones. Their 1983 collaboration, *Thriller,* sold a then-unprecedented 51 million copies worldwide, spawned seven hit singles, including "Billie Jean," MTV's first video by a black artist, and won seven Grammys. More important, Jackson's movie-like video for "Thriller" changed the music video format, almost instantly elevating it. Black America's first undisputed international pop superstar, Michael Jackson opened the door for his sister Janet, Whitney Houston, Mariah Carey, Destiny's Child, Beyoncé, and Usher, among other more recent African American pop stars. Curiously, R&B singer, R. Kelly, has enjoyed platinum success without substantial crossover success.

Taking the Rap

In the mid-1970s, *hip-hop,* a brash mixture of rhythm and boastful talking, took hold in New York City. Out of nowhere, the Sugarhill Gang's "Rapper's Delight," rhymed over CHIC's "Good Times" and cut in 1979, became a commercial hit on the R&B, pop, and U.K. charts. By the early 1980s, hip-hop pioneers such as Grandmaster Flash and the Furious Five, Kurtis Blow (the first rapper signed to a major label, Mercury Records), the Funky Four Plus One, and Run-D.M.C. were changing the music scene. Run-D.M.C.'s 1986 album *Raising Hell,* which became the first rap album in the Billboard Top 10, along with their rock collaboration with white rock band Aerosmith on "Walk This Way," paved the way for hip-hop's subsequent dominance.

Hip-hop matures

Grandmaster Flash and the Furious Five had shown rap's political potential with 1982's "The Message," which detailed the horrendous conditions of ghetto life, but Public Enemy completely embodied it. Signed to Def Jam Records, Public Enemy, marked by lead rapper Chuck D's preacher-like presentation, directly politicized rap in the late 1980s and beyond with hits like "Fight the Power."

Hip-hop also came into its own artistically. The Bomb Squad, Public Enemy's producers, took hip-hop production to another level with multitextured layering and customized beats. Artists such as Rakim from Eric B & Rakim and KRS-One placed a greater emphasis on lyricism, as metaphors became a hip-hop staple. Others such as X-Clan, the Jungle Brothers, and A Tribe Called Quest comfortably flexed their Afrocentric views. During the late 1980s into the early 1990s, a variety of hip-hop styles flourished. Def Jam's first artist, LL Cool J, even emerged as a sex symbol.

The West Coast opens rap up

The West Coast was the first area to expand hip-hop beyond the East Coast. Initially, Too Short, Ice T, and N.W.A. were the artists that shined the brightest. Too Short injected the pimp game into rap lyrics, and Ice T incorporated themes of pimping and hustling into his rhymes. N.W.A., however, had the biggest impact.

The brainchild of Eric "Eazy-E" Wright, N.W.A. core members included Dr. Dre, Ice Cube, MC Ren, and Eazy-E. Although "Boyz-N-the-Hood" was their first hit, the group headed in a bolder direction with their second album, *Straight Outta Compton,* released in 1988. Guns, women, liquor, and other aspects of urban life weren't new to hip-hop, but those things viewed from the perspective of a gangster were. Ironically, N.W.A. uncovered both the hopelessness and resiliency borne out of oppressed conditions. "F*** Tha Police," a response to police brutality, placed N.W.A. on the FBI's official radar and labeled hip-hop, and gangsta rap in particular, America's real public enemy number one.

After leaving N.W.A., Ice Cube successfully established a solo career as a lyricist from the West Coast with his 1990 debut, *AmeriKKKa's Most Wanted.* Meanwhile, Dr. Dre's 1992 multi-platinum solo debut, *The Chronic,* officially ended the East Coast's rap dominance. It also formalized a new sound, G-Funk, inspired by the music of finkateers Roger Troutmand (and Zapp) and George Clinton, and established Snoop Doggy Dogg, whose 1993 debut *Doggystyle* entered the charts at number one, as a star. Heavily influenced by his family's Mississippi roots, Snoop's rap style arguably made the Southern drawl more acceptable to the rap masses.

Tupac's legacy

An international cult figure, Tupac Shakur has remained influential, even in death, with no less than five posthumous albums. Some of the nation's top universities have designed courses that deal with his "thuglife" philosophy, which applied to anyone who had survived the hood. Academics such as Michael Eric Dyson and Jamal Joseph have written books addressing his legacy. Shakur's posthumous documentary *Tupac: Resurrection* (2003), narrated by him through his many interviews, even received an Oscar nomination. His impact has been so strong that there are few rappers who don't cite him as an influence. To keep his memory alive and expand his vision, his mother established the Tupac Amaru Shakur Center for the Arts in Stone Mountain, Georgia, just outside Atlanta, in 2005.

Personal arguments and misunderstandings between the West and East Coast rap communities, most notably label owners Suge Knight and Sean Combs, better known as Puffy then, and their rappers Tupac Shakur and the Notorious B.I.G. (also known as Biggie), culminated in the violent, unsolved murders of Tupac in 1995 and Biggie in 1996. Stunned by the tragic lost of two hip-hop titans, the rap community took steps to mend the rift between the coasts. Violence, however, has remained an issue. In 2002, Run-D.M.C.'s Jam Master Jay became another victim of violence. Equally as frustrating to the rap community has been the police's inability to make arrests in any of these murders.

Women and the state of rap

Rap has continually battled allegations of misrepresenting women. Miami-based 2 Live Crew and its more well-known Luther Campbell, fueled those objections with its signature Miami Bass music, featuring pulsating rhythms and sexually explicit lyrics such as those on the 1989 hit "Me So Horny" off the *Nasty As They Wanna Be* album. In addition, the mostly naked women featured on the group's album covers and in their videos generated more outrage.

Some women, however, have grabbed the mic to represent for themselves. Rap's most visible female pioneers have been Salt-N-Pepa, MC Lyte, Queen Latifah, and Yo Yo. Guided by Atlanta-based hip-hop producer Jermaine Dupri, Chicago native Da Brat became the first female rapper to go platinum with 1994's *Funkdafied*. Beginning in the mid-1990s, Lauryn Hill made a big splash, first as a member of the Fugees and then as a solo artist, with her hip-hop infused *The Miseducation of Lauryn Hill,* her 1998 album that won five Grammys. Lil Kim, Foxy Brown, Missy Elliott, Eve, and Trina created a second wave of female rappers, with all but Missy Elliott and Eve adopting sexually provocative images and lyrics. Mary J. Blige, known as the queen of hip-hop soul, mastered the fusion of hip-hop with R&B, especially with her 1992 debut *What's the 411?,* to give the everyday young urban woman a voice within the hard-edged genre.

In recent years, rap has opened up to include various genres and various areas. Rappers who kept the genre moving forward in the 1990s include New York's Nas, Jay-Z,Busta Rhymes, the Wu-Tang Clan, and DMX. Texas's the Geto Boys, Scarface, and UGK, Atlanta's OutKast and GOODIE MOb, Louisiana's Master P (with his No Limit Soldiers) and the Cash Money Millionaires, Memphis's Eightball &MJG and Three 6 Mafia, and Chicago's Common. California's The Game and the Black Eyed Peas, Miami's Trick Daddy, New York's Ja Rule, Fabolous, and 50, Chicago's Kanye West and Atlanta's Lil Jon, Ludacrisand T.I. are among the newer rappers who've had platinum albums in the 2000s.

Chapter 17

Black Hollywood: Film and TV

In This Chapter

▶ Tracking the genesis of the black film genre

▶ Following the rise of popular black actors

▶ Connecting with audiences through comedy

▶ Making strides on the small screen

*J*ust as early minstrel shows conspired to keep African Americans in their place (refer to Chapter 15), so did early Hollywood, relegating African American actors to playing mammies, maids, and butlers. Some early black actors actually got their big break working as servants to Hollywood's white stars and industry brass. A great deal has changed since those early days.

This chapter explores African Americans' humble beginnings in early Hollywood, touching on race movies as well as African American contributions behind the camera — showing the skill and talent that prompted the creation of the NAACP Image Awards in 1969. In addition, it examines the African American presence in television, noting turning points like *Roots* and the media empires created by BET founder Robert Johnson and Oprah Winfrey.

Making Movies Black

The Birth of a Nation (1915), originally titled *The Clansman*, was the movie industry's first feature-length film. Director D.W. Griffith's creation was such a national hit that President Woodrow Wilson privately screened it at the White House. Adapted by Thomas Dixon from his novel *The Clansman: An Historical Romance of the Ku Klux Klan*, *The Birth of a Nation* was so decidedly antiblack and prosegregationist that the NAACP protested it.

In contrast to the depiction of and attitude toward African Americans in *The Birth of a Nation,* African American film got a boon through *race movies,* films with all-black casts. These films — over 500 were produced from 1910 to 1950 — expanded the roles of black actors, many of whom were seasoned vaudeville performers, beyond maids, butlers, and other roles that whites deemed suitable for them. By 1918, eight independent companies produced all-black films, a number that ebbed and flowed over the years. Some of the more noteworthy include

- ✔ **Foster Photoplay Company:** Founded by former vaudeville publicity and booking agent William Foster, the Foster Photoplay Company produced several well-received comical shorts like *The Railroad Porter* (1912) that white audiences also saw. The company folded in 1916.

- ✔ **Micheaux Film Corporation:** The topical films of Midwestern writer and homesteader Oscar Micheaux tackled everything from crooked preachers (one such film, *Body and Soul* (1925), served as Paul Robeson's film debut) and residential segregation to separatism versus assimilation and inter-racial marriage. Initially black audiences applauded Micheaux's work; after several years, however, black audiences expected more, and some black newspapers even took Micheaux to task for dedicating too much attention to gambling and other seedy elements.

- ✔ **Million Dollar Productions:** Ralph Cooper, better known as the creator of the Apollo Theater's world-famous Amateur Night, partnered with the white Popkin brothers to form Million Dollar Productions. Dubbed the Dark Gable, Cooper, who often starred in the company's productions, contributed entertaining, if not groundbreaking, films to the mix. One of Cooper's greatest contributions was the casting of a then-unknown Lena Horne in 1938's *The Duke Is Tops.* The movie business proved too taxing, however, and Million Dollar Productions folded.

- ✔ **Herb Jeffries, various projects:** Detroit native Herb Jeffries (sometimes Jeffrey) wanted to make movies and persuaded white producer Jed Buell to take a chance on him. The two created *Harlem on the Prairie* (1937) starring the fair-skinned, wavy-haired Jeffries as a singing cowboy. Encouraged by the film's success and favorable reviews, another independent producer, Richard Khan, tapped Jeffries to star in additional films such as *Harlem Rides the Range* (1939).

While combating the negative stereotypes in mainstream films, race movies created some of their own. In many race movies, light-skinned leading men and women were often good and beautiful, while the characters played by dark-skinned actors were low-class and uncultured. In addition, critics accused race movies of focusing too much attention on crime.

In spite of the African American casting, race movies had few credited black film writers, directors, and other behind-the-scenes personnel. In fact, only 33 percent of the companies behind race movies were completely black-owned. During the 1930s and 1940s especially, whites financed, directed, and produced most of these films. Oscar Micheaux is a well-known exception. Another, less well-known, exception is Spencer Williams, who appeared in the controversial 1950s TV series *The Amos 'n Andy Show*. Between 1929 and 1947, Williams directed eight films (including *The Blood of Jesus* [1941], which he also wrote and produced) and took a key if not a leading role in many of his films.

Theatres catering to white audiences showed race movies during matinee or *midnight ramble* hours (the term used for segregation-era midnight showings for black audiences).

Early black roles in white films

By 1929, Hollywood studios such as MGM were making films with African American casts. Despite having black casts and greater resources, many of these major studio films still perpetuated African American stereotypes and cast black actors in stereotypical roles. Many black actors portrayed servants, for example. Of these, the two best known are the multitalented Clarence Muse and Hattie McDaniel. Muse was a lawyer, director, writer, and composer, as well as an actor, and appeared in over 150 films from his debut in 1921 to his death in 1979. McDaniel, who became the first African American to win a Best Supporting Actress Academy Award (or any Academy Award for that matter) for her role of "Mammy" in *Gone with the Wind*.

The key characters Gummy and Zeke in the films *Hearts in Dixie* (1929) and *Hallelujah!* (1929) reinforced the stereotype of the lazy black man, avidly avoiding work. *Hearts in Dixie* was a major film for Stepin Fetchit, one of Hollywood's first black stars who became the symbol of Hollywood stereotypes (see the sidebar "Stepin Fetchit"). Dramatic films such as *Imitation of Life* (1934), about a young black girl who can pass for white, and the film version of Eugene O'Neill's play *The Emperor Jones* (1933), starring Paul Robeson, did offer some hope.

Escaping stereotypical roles was difficult for those who wanted to work in an industry pervaded by racism. Even when the studios adapted proven Broadway hits that contained more subtle stereotypes, film magnified them. Because the theatre was a more intimate affair that gave actors a greater degree of flexibility, a skillful actor could sometimes diffuse a stereotypical character. In film, even talented actors like Paul Robeson found it difficult to make a bad character better. For example, black critics lauded Robeson's acting and singing as Joe, the shiftless black male character in Universal

Stepin Fetchit

Stepin Fechit's many comedic appearances in mainstream films like *Judge Priest* (1934) and all-black films like *Miracle in Harlem* (1948) opened doors for other African American actors. But because he played *Sambo* roles, characters who were lazy and shiftless, he became vilified as the poster child for Hollywood's black stereotypes, even though these were largely the only roles available to African American actors of his day.

Despite a decent education and an interest in classical music, Stepin Fetchit, a name he earned on the vaudeville circuit, allowed the studio machine to paint him as an authentic "darky." By pretending to be illiterate, Stepin Fetchit played upon studio executives' notions and ignorance of black people. Consequently, he became one of the first African American movie stars, appearing in over 50 films and earning over $1 million. His lavish lifestyle, however, plunged him into bankruptcy. Eventually, protests by civil rights organizations against black stereotypes in films effectively sank his career.

Pictures 1936 film *Show Boat,* but still found the character itself stereotypical. That was also true of *The Green Pastures,* an award-winning play that reenacted stories from the Old Testament with a black cast speaking in African American vernacular.

Although mainstream Hollywood embraced black actors slowly, top black entertainers, known as *specialty acts,* were frequently included in top white films in the 1940s, usually in nightclub settings. Count Basie, Duke Ellington, Louis Armstrong, Hazel Scott, and others appeared in films like *Stage Door Canteen* (1943), *Atlantic City* (1944), *Reveille with Beverly* (1943), *Hit Parade of 1943* (1943), and *Rhapsody in Blue* (1945). African American dancers such as Katherine Dunham and the famed Nicholas brothers, Fayard and Harold, also scored screen time. At various points before the 1960s, Hollywood got behind several all-black musicals, with the most famous being *Cabin in the Sky* (1943), *Stormy Weather* (1943), *Carmen Jones* (1954), *St. Louis Blues* (1958), and *Porgy and Bess* (1959).

Moving in a different direction

Responding to protests from the NAACP and other civil rights groups, in addition to the nation's ongoing changes in race relations, Hollywood began including black characters, usually one or two, in nontraditional roles. For example, war movies, beginning in 1949 with the groundbreaking casting of

James Edwards in *Home of the Brave,* began prominently featuring at least one black soldier, a move cultural critic Gerald Early has suggested was prompted by President Truman integrating the military in 1948. Following are themes that some films of this era began to explore:

- ✔ **Racism:** Racism became the driving theme. Edwards's character in *Home of the Brave* was one of Hollywood's early attempts to communicate to white Americans how racism affected black Americans. In *No Way Out* (1950), a racist blames the black prison doctor for his brother's death. Sidney Poitier, the most famous actor from this period, played the doctor.

- ✔ **Racist taboos:** Films such as *Intruder in the Dust* (1949), adapted from William Faulkner's best-selling novel, and *To Kill A Mockingbird* (1962), based on Harper Lee's Pulitzer Prize–winning novel, were courtroom dramas about innocent black men facing death because of racist taboos. Although black characters didn't dominate screen time, films such as these attempted to analyze racism from a moral perspective. In some ways, these are the precursors to Hollywood films where white characters frequently save black characters from social ills.

- ✔ **"Passing":** Although early Hollywood films addressed the theme of "passing for white," films such as *Show Boat (*in which a "white" character's true black heritage is discovered), *Lost Boundaries* (1949), *Pinky* (1949) and the remake of *Imitation of Life* (1959) are the most famous of this later era.

  Interestingly, in all of these films, white, not black, actors portrayed the "passing" characters.

- ✔ **Interracial relationships:** Although *Guess Who's Coming to Dinner* (1967) starring Sidney Poitier and Katherine Hepburn is the more famous film, *One Potato, Two Potato* (1964) starring the lesser known Bernie Hamilton took a more serious look at societal restrictions against interracial relationships. Poiter's 1965 film *A Patch of Blue,* in which he and a blind white woman fall in love, actively reminded audiences that "love is blind."

- ✔ **Love stories involving black protagonists:** Although African American screen couples were rare in general, especially in serious Hollywood films, two films in particular are outstanding exceptions. Romance isn't the main story in *Bright Road* (1953) about a dedicated schoolteacher (played by Dorothy Dandridge) trying to reach one of her students, but Harry Belafonte's character doesn't hide his tender feelings for the schoolteacher. Directed by Michael Roemer and starring Ivan Dixon and Abbey Lincoln, *Nothing But a Man* is distinctive for its more realistic portrayal of a black couple's trials and tribulations in the Jim Crow South, with the civil rights movement serving as a backdrop.

Blaxploitation films

By the 1960s, African Americans were just 15 percent of the national population but accounted for 30 percent of moviegoers. During this time, black characters in mainstream films became increasingly more aggressive, a marked difference from early servant roles and Poitier's many model minorities (discussed in the later section "Sidney Poitier"). With several movie roles, particularly in the films *The Dirty Dozen* (1967), *The Split* (1968), and *100 Rifles* (1969), retired NFL player Jim Brown contributed to the depiction of this newly aggressive black male that also coincided with the rising black power movement. Although many black characters died following outbursts against "the man" (a reference to the white power structure), black audiences still applauded.

Melvin Van Peebles's 1971 film *Sweet Sweetback's Baadasssss Song* (1971) marked the official birth of *blaxploitation*. In this film, the black male protagonist, an embodiment of several stereotypes including the "sexual Mandingo" and the "buck," becomes the hero. Made on a shoestring budget, *Sweet Sweetback* grossed over $10 million. Equally impressive box office receipts from *Shaft* (1971), starring Richard Roundtree as a black detective who battles the community's bad guys, solidified the movement.

The combined success of *Sweet Sweetback's Baadasssss Song* and *Shaft* opened a floodgate for a barrage of titles to emerge during the 1970s. *Superfly* (1972), *The Mack* (1973), *Blacula* (1972), *Three the Hard Way* (1974), *Black Caesar* (1973), and *Truck Turner* (1974) are a few of the standouts.

Pam Grier

One of the very few women to reach iconic status during the blaxploitation film period, Pam Grier starred in the cult classics *Foxy Brown* (1974), *Coffy* (1973), and *Sheba Baby* (1975). The North Carolina–born beauty got her big break while working as a receptionist for a film company when film producer Roger Corman noticed her and cast her in *The Big Dollhouse* (1971). Her unique beauty and imposing physique struck a chord with moviegoers. Grier continued to act when blaxploitation's heyday ended but remained in the shadows until she starred in Quentin Tarantino's *Jackie Brown* (1997), which paid homage to blaxploitation films. In *Jackie Brown,* Grier stars as a flight attendant coerced into bringing down an arms dealer. Since then, she's made numerous television and film appearances.

America's urban ghettos were the main settings for blaxploitation films, with pimps and gangsters serving as major characters. Sex, violence, and opposition to the white power structure were also constant elements in the films. Some argue that blaxploitation films, many of them financed, produced, and even directed by whites, only reinforced negative stereotypes that justified the casting of black actors as prostitutes, pimps, and other criminals in mainstream films. Others defend them, arguing that the genre served as escapist fare for black audiences frustrated by racism.

During this same period, however, films that most African Americans embraced did emerge. *Lady Sings the Blues* (1972), a Billie Holiday biopic, and *Mahogany* (1975), about a black woman from urban Chicago striving to become a top fashion designer, are notable for the romantic pairing of Billy Dee Williams and Diana Ross. *Cooley High* (1975), helmed by black director Michael Shultz, who also directed *Car Wash* (1976), is one of the most beloved urban coming-of-age stories of all-time. Musical films such as *Sparkle* (1976), about three sisters trying to make it in the music industry, and *The Wiz* (1978), an urban version of *The Wizard of Oz* starring Diana Ross and Michael Jackson, stood out if only for the music.

Spike Lee and the Urban Film Renaissance

Several black directors stepped forward during the 1970s, but they didn't define themselves as just black directors. That changed when Spike Lee came on the scene. Prior to Lee's emergence, African American–oriented films of the 1980s were largely music-driven, such as *Purple Rain* (1984), which starred Prince and was loosely based on his life. Lee, however, almost single-handedly resurrected black film during his career; he also inspired a bold new black film movement.

Lee's first feature film was *She's Gotta Have It* (1986), about a woman juggling three lovers. The film's phenomenal success (made on a shoestring budget, it grossed about $7 million) gave the outspoken Lee a national platform. Never one to shy away from controversy, Lee used his early work in particular to address issues such as *colorism,* a preference for lighter skin over dark skin within the African American community, and black fraternities and sororities on black college campuses in *School Daze* (1988). In *Do the Right Thing* (1989), Lee examined the tenuous nature of race relations between Italians and African Americans in Brooklyn. The 1992 film *Malcolm X,* starring Denzel Washington, was an epic triumph for Lee.

These films with primarily black casts served as platforms for breakout performances by many black actors, including Wesley Snipes and Denzel Washington in *Mo' Better Blues* (1990), Samuel L. Jackson in *Jungle Fever* (1991), and Mekhi Phifer in *Clockers* (1995). In 2006, Lee, who prefers to generate his own projects, helmed a rare studio film, *Inside Man,* starring Denzel Washington, Jodie Foster, and Clive Owen that, at roughly $88 million, became the highest grossing film of his career.

Spike Lee has also helmed provocative documentaries like the Academy Award–nominated *4 Little Girls* (1997), which chronicles the murder of four girls in the Birmingham church bombing in 1963 (refer to Chapter 9), and *When the Levees Broke: A Requiem in Four Acts* (2006), his highly acclaimed exploration of post-Hurricane Katrina New Orleans, featuring survivors.

Hood films

In the early 1990s, USC film graduate John Singleton, inspired by Spike Lee, looked to his native Los Angeles to enhance his craft. His debut film, *Boyz n the Hood* (1991), garnered him an Academy Award nomination for Best Director, a first for an African American. Whereas Lee's films pose theoretical questions in regards to African Americans and race in the U.S., Singleton's debut grappled with the contemporary issues of single-parent homes and escalating gang violence against young black males in inner-city communities.

Violence is also a potent theme in *New Jack City* (1991), set in Harlem. Directed by Mario Van Peebles (whose father Melvin Van Peebles helmed *Sweet Sweetback's Baadasssss Song*), *New Jack City* presents the black drug empire in a manner never before seen on the big screen. Films like *Boyz* and *New Jack City* brought the realities of the drug world into the black urban sphere, with much of the action on screen centered in individual neighborhoods. At the same time, brothers Reginald and Warrington Hudlin were exploring a lighter side of urban neighborhoods by directing and producing the *House Party* franchise, which began in 1990.

Both *Boyz N the Hood* and *New Jack City* attempted a creative translation of the realities of contemporary urban life to screen and paved the way for a colossal wave of *hood films.* With the exception of a few films, however, including *Menace II Society,* directed by the Hughes Brothers, and the F. Gary Gray–helmed *Set It Off,* about four young black women trying to escape the hood through bank robberies, hood films became stagnant and clichéd. In recent years, African American audiences have embraced these films less and less, preferring to consume them in the direct-to-video market and not the movie theatre.

Urban film directors also graduated to mainstream studio films. In 2000, with *Scary Movie*, a spoof of Hollywood horror films, Keenen Ivory Wayans became the first African American to direct a mainstream film grossing over $150 million. Previously, Sidney Poitier reached the $100 million mark with *Stir Crazy* in 1980. F. Gary Gray and John Singleton also reached the $100 million mark with the mainstream films, *The Italian Job* and *2Fast 2Furious,* in 2003.

Stepping out of the hood genre

Atlanta-based filmmaker Tyler Perry, well-known for his character Madea, a cantankerous grandmother developed through his numerous traveling stage plays (flip to Chapter 15 for more details), has scored big with lighthearted films that grapple with drug abuse, juvenile delinquency, infidelity, and other serious issues through laughter and an underlying Christian theme. His first film *Diary of a Mad Black Woman* (2005) and his follow-up film *Madea's Family Reunion* (2006), each made for under $7 million, grossed over $50 million each at the box office. He released his third film *Daddy's Little Girls* in February 2007.

Likewise, Atlanta-based independent film production company Rainforest Films has done surprisingly well with sexually-tinged films such as *Trois* (2002) and *Pandora's Box* (2002) featuring more upwardly mobile black characters. In recent years, the company has embraced less racy films and scored big in January 2007 with *Stomp the Yard*, a film set at a black college about black fraternities and step shows that grossed over $38 million at the box office in two weeks.

Black Film Stars

African American actors have come a long way since Hollywood's beginnings, widening the range of roles available to them far beyond the maid and the butler. Secret agents, dignitaries, music legends, and any other imaginable characters are all within reach. During the mid–20th century, black entertainers (most notably musicians and comedians) sometimes had a leg up — a fact that was still relatively true in the latter part of the 20th century as rappers and comedians became the latest crop of black performers tapped for the big screen. Still, the backbone to black Hollywood, as it has been for Hollywood in general, is the serious actor, and those ranks have grown stronger as well.

From song to celluloid

Hollywood has long considered black musicians as prime candidates for film. Following is a sampling of a few notable entertainers, past and present, who've made an impact in Tinseltown:

- **Female singers-turned-actors:** Considered two of the most beautiful singers of their time, Lena Horne and Dorothy Dandridge never realized their full potential but left a legacy nonetheless. Horne, one of the first black actors to sign a long-term studio contract, broke many of Hollywood's social customs by eating in the studio's commissary and appearing in mainstream magazines; she was also the first black actor to land the cover of a fan publication. Dandridge became the first African American nominated for an Oscar for Best Actress (for her role in *Carmen Jones,* a black version of the classic opera).

- **Male singers-turned-actors:** Paul Robeson, Harry Belafonte, and Sammy Davis, Jr., are perhaps the more prominent men fitting this category. Athletic and intellectual with a pleasing singing voice and impressive acting ability, Paul Robeson's career was very short, with *The Emperor Jones* (1933) serving as his most memorable role. Likewise, Harry Belafonte, who popularized calypso music, left strong impressions with *Carmen Jones* and *Island in the Sun.* The multi-talented Sammy Davis, Jr.'s film credits include the films *Porgy and Bess* (1959), *Anna Lucasta* (1959), and the original *Ocean's Eleven* (1960).

- **Rappers-turned-actors:** Will Smith, with Oscar nominations for *The Pursuit of Happyness* (2006) and *Ali* (2001), leads the pack of "raptors." Another prominent rapper-turned-actor is Queen Latifah; her Oscar-nominated performance as Mama Morton in *Chicago* (2002) showed that she had come a long way since her debut film role as a waitress in *Jungle Fever.* Other rap artists who are successful as actors include Ice Cube, who has gone from a reluctant actor in John Singleton's *Boyz n the Hood* (1991) to an accomplished actor/producer with films such as *Friday* (1995), *Are We There Yet?* (2005), and the *Barbershop* films, and LL Cool J whose many roles include "Julian Washington" in *Any Given Sunday* (1999) and "Dwayne Gittens/God" in *In Too Deep* (1999).

Kings (and queens) of comedy

Comedy has long proved a good segue into television and film for African American men in particular. Before Redd Foxx, Flip Wilson, and Bill Cosby became television stars, they were successful comedians, with several hit comedy albums to their credit. For most urban stand-up comedians working their way up on comedy stages across the country, Richard Pryor, followed by Eddie Murphy, are the standards. As for black female comedians, no one has surpassed Whoopi Goldberg in influence.

Richard Pryor

Given the drama of Richard Pryor's personal life, including his notorious 1980 freebasing incident in which he set himself on fire, it's easy to forget how wide he opened Hollywood's doors for African American performers. Initially, Pryor found comedy success copying the clean-cut style of Bill Cosby. Later, he infused his comedy with personal experiences and stinging social commentary. Frequently, he is credited with changing American stand-up comedy. *That Nigger's Crazy* and *Is It Something I Said?* comprise just two of his five Grammy wins for his classic comedy albums.

Pryor's influence extends well beyond the black community; among black comedians, however, Pryor has no equals. Many divide the genre of black comedy into two categories: before Richard Pryor and after Richard Pryor.

Pryor flipped his success as a comedian into film roles. He won acclaim for his nuanced performance as a drug-addicted piano player in *Lady Sings the Blues* (1972), a Billie Holiday biopic; he played an impressive three characters in the comedy *Which Way Is Up?*(1977); and he starred as Wendell Pierce, the nation's first black stock racing champion, in *Greased Lightning* (1977). Still, most audiences remember him for his films with Gene Wilder: *Silver Streak* (1976), *Stir Crazy* (1980), and *See No Evil, Hear No Evil* (1989). A gifted writer, Pryor contributed to Mel Brooks's *Blazing Saddles* (1974) and television projects like *Sanford and Son,* his own short-lived series *The Richard Pryor Show,* and Lily Tomlin's Emmy Award–winning *Lily.*

Eddie Murphy

Eddie Murphy got his start at age 19 on television's *Saturday Night Live* (SNL), where he created memorable characters such as Buckwheat and Gumby. Before leaving the show in 1984, Murphy tested the movie waters opposite Nick Nolte in *48 Hours* (1982), a comedy about a cop who's paired with a convict to track down a killer. Murphy followed that film with a successful cable comedy special *Delirious* as well as box office hits *Trading Places* (1983) with fellow SNL alum Dan Aykroyd and the *Beverly Hills Cop* franchise.

Murphy's concert film *Raw* (1987), in addition to *Coming to America* (1988) and *Boomerang* (1992), remain favorites among black audiences. His few box office snags, such as *Harlem Nights,* which he directed, pale in comparison to his many successes, which include the *Nutty Professor* and *Dr. Doolittle* franchises from the 1990s and 2000s. Lending his voice to the *Shrek* animated franchise has been one of his biggest box office successes ever. For the 2006 film adaptation of the legendary Broadway hit musical *Dreamgirls,* Murphy tackled a rare dramatic role and received a Best Supporting Actor Oscar nomination and other honors for his efforts. A film veteran with over 20 years of experience, Murphy still claims some of the highest grossing films of any actor, and, like his idol Richard Pryor, he has inspired a new generation of comics.

Others who followed Pryor and Murphy

Following is a sampling of comedians/actors who might have found breaking into film and television much harder without the success of Richard Pryor and Eddie Murphy:

- ✔ **Jamie Foxx:** Even before winning the Best Actor Oscar for his turn as Ray Charles in the docudrama *Ray* (2004), Jamie Foxx fared better than other black comedians at the box office in noncomedic roles.

- ✔ **Martin Lawrence:** Since his humble beginnings in *House Party* (1990), Martin Lawrence has scored big in the hit franchise, *Big Momma's House,* as well as the buddy cop franchise *Bad Boys* with Will Smith.

- ✔ **Chris Rock:** Despite appearing in a slew of films, Chris Rock has enjoyed greater success on stage, with his comedy specials, and the small screen, with his breakout series *Everybody Hates Chris*, based loosely on his own childhood growing up in a black neighborhood and attending a predominantly white school.

- ✔ **Chris Tucker:** Although starring in *Friday,* opposite Ice Cube, was his big break, Chris Tucker's greatest success has come with the profitable *Rush Hour* franchise alongside Jackie Chan.

Whoopi Goldberg and the comediennes

A legend in her own time, New York native Whoopi Goldberg is still the nation's most successful black female comedian. While Moms Mabley, a vaudeville veteran who was especially successful in the 1960s, did well with black and non-black audiences, Goldberg is in a league by herself. She's excelled outside the comedy clubs, primarily in the film industry where she's scored big with the *Sister Act* franchise. She's also flexed her dramatic chops with *The Color Purple* (1985), *Ghosts of Mississippi* (1996), and *Ghost* (1990), for which she won an Oscar. She has also received a Tony, a Grammy, and an Emmy in addition to delighting audiences a number of times as the host of the Academy Awards.

Def Comedy Jam

From 1992 to 1997, *Russell Simmons' Def Comedy Jam* introduced HBO audiences to some of the rawest African American comedians in the nation. Boldly mixing hip-hop with comedy, the 30-minute shows created instant celebrities and revolutionized American comedy. Chris Tucker, Bernie Mac, Bill Bellamy, Adele Givens, and Eddie Griffin are just a few of the comedians who appeared on *Def Comedy Jam.* Martin Lawrence hosted the shows and New York DJ Kid Capri provided the music.

With only a handful of black, female comedians working, Mo'Nique and Wanda Sykes are among the few post-Goldberg female comedians who have made names for themselves. Sykes, who got her big break on *The Chris Rock Show,* has built a steady career that includes comedy clubs, television series, one-hour specials, and films. Best known as Nikki Parker from UPN's *The Parkers,* Mo'Nique has also scored with *The Queens of Comedy,* a stand-up comedy special, and *Mo'Nique's F.A.T. Chance,* a plus-size beauty pageant. Others include Kim Coles, Kim Wayans, former SNL player Ellen Cleghorne, Maya Rudolph, Adele Givens, Sheryl Underwood, Sherri Shepherd, Aisha Tyler, Kym Whitley, and Thea Vidale. In time, hopefully, more black women will embrace comedy as a career.

Enter stage left: Serious actors

Early African American film actors such as Lena Horne, Sammy Davis, Jr., and Harry Belafonte built their acting careers from their musical gifts, but toward the middle of the 20th century, dedicated African American actors began to emerge. The following sections introduce a few of the many venerable African American actors.

Sidney Poitier

Defying Hollywood typecasting, Poitier received plum roles from the beginning of his career, playing a doctor in his first film, *No Way Out* (1950), and a reverend in *Cry, the Beloved Country* (1951). He exuded dignity even when playing a convict in *The Defiant Ones* (1958), for which he received an Oscar nomination. In 1961, he revived his powerful stage role as Walter Lee Younger in the film version of the Broadway hit *A Raisin in the Sun.* He also became the first African American to win an Academy Award for Best Actor for his starring role in *Lilies of the Field* (1963), in which his character unwillingly aids impoverished nuns.

Raised in the Bahamas, Sidney Poitier came to New York as a teenager. Initially rejected by the American Negro Theater (ANT; see Chapter 15) because of his thick accent, Poitier worked hard to lose it. Determined to become an actor, Poitier worked as a janitor at the ANT in exchange for acting lessons.

Yet his career has not been without controversy. Black critics have charged that Poitier, whom they characterize as non-threatening to white audiences, ushered in a new stereotype of the ebony saint. Others noted that Poitier rarely enjoyed the on-screen romantic associations of other leading men. Today, however, Poitier's legendary status is never a question.

Denzel Washington

Like his idol Poitier, Denzel Washington has distinguished himself in one spectacular role after the next. Although Washington appeared in several films and won an Oscar in 1989 for his role in *Glory,* many believe that his Oscar-nominated performance in *Malcolm X* (1992) established him as one of Hollywood's top stars. In 2002, Washington, having been nominated in 2000 for *The Hurricane* (1999), finally won a Best Actor Oscar for his role as a crooked cop in *Training Day* (2001), helmed by African American director Antoine Fuqua.

Morgan Freeman

Few people whose careers include being a regular on the PBS children's show *The Electric Company* become Oscar winners. Mississippi native Morgan Freeman isn't most people. Freeman's New York theatre training shows in his many noteworthy performances, including his Oscar-nominated roles in *Street Smart, Driving Miss Daisy,* and *The Shawshank Redemption.* Finally, in 2005, Freeman won an Oscar for his supporting role in *Million Dollar Baby* (2004). Despite his many accomplished roles, many still cherish him as the tough high school principal Joe Clark in *Lean on Me* (1989).

Halle Berry

The same year that Denzel Washington won an Oscar, Halle Berry did as well for her role as Leticia in the independent film *Monster's Ball* (2001). A former beauty pageant contestant, Berry's breakthrough role was as a crackhead opposite Samuel L. Jackson in Spike Lee's *Jungle Fever* (1991). Recently, she's become better known as Storm from the highly profitable *X-Men* franchise.

The Revolution Is Televised

Most Americans can't imagine a time when African Americans appeared on television so rarely that black viewers often alerted others whenever they saw them. African Americans on television may not be as plentiful as some would like now, but there's no question that African Americans have come a long way since television's early days.

Black Hollywood scholar Donald Bogle traces the beginnings of African Americans on television to the one-night-only broadcast of *The Ethel Waters Show* by NBC in 1939, when television was still in its experimental stage. Bogle notes other shows like *The Bob Howard Show* on CBS in 1948; *Sugar Hill Times* (1949), a short-lived variety show starring Harry Belafonte; *The Hazel Scott Show* (1950), starring the beautiful pianist Hazel Scott; and the *Nat*

"King" Cole Show (1956). When these shows went off the air, African Americans showed up on television through guest appearances, mainly as entertainers, on programs like *The Ed Sullivan Show* until 1965. The actors who appeared in the comedies *Beulah* and *The Amos 'n Andy Show* were exceptions.

That changed in 1965, when Bill Cosby revolutionized weekly television as agent Alexander Scott in the espionage drama series *I Spy*. Others like Greg Morris in *Mission Impossible,* Nichelle Nichols in *Star Trek,* and Clarence Williams III in *The Mod Squad* quickly followed. There was even an integrated high school drama, *Room 222,* chronicling the experiences of a black male teacher. Then, as now, comedy ruled as the primary vehicle for African American talent.

Early black comedies

As early as the 1950s, two TV comedies prominently featured African American characters: *Beulah* and *The Amos 'n Andy Show*. Both series had beginnings in radio in which, interestingly, white actors voiced the black characters. When *Beulah* was adapted from radio to television, it was clear that, although the black maid was technically the star, her role was to cater to the white family she served.

The fact that Amos and Andy, played by Alvin Childress and Spencer Williams, were intended to be buffoonish didn't sit well with many African Americans, who objected mainly to the poor English the characters spoke as well as the incompetence of the show's black characters. Despite flashes of genuine humor, CBS pulled the show after two years but syndicated it until 1966. From that time until the late 1960s, African Americans were largely absent from television comedies on a routine basis.

Opening the doors wider

During the late 1960s into the 1970s, television underwent major changes. Although Bill Cosby secured his first solo comedy series with 1969's *The Bill Cosby Show,* two other shows from that period had a bigger impact:

✔ **Julia:** Diahann Carroll's 1968 series *Julia,* in which she starred as a widowed mother working as a nurse, was a rare glimpse into the life of a professional, black single mother, especially for a comedy. But many critics charged that, although it was nice, it wasn't groundbreaking. With the black power movement on the rise, for some black and white critics, Carroll wasn't "black enough," perhaps because her character was so likeable. The series ran from 1968 to 1971.

✔ *The Flip Wilson Show:* Variety shows were a staple of early television, and several African Americans, including Sammy Davis, Jr., starred in their own shows. None, however, had the impact of Flip Wilson in the early 1970s. Characters like Reverend LeRoy of the Church of What's Happening Now, Sonny the White House janitor, and, of course, Wilson's alter ego Geraldine Jones made the show a hit. *Time Magazine* even heralded Wilson as "TV's First Black Superstar" on its cover in 1972. Television executives took note of Wilson's popularity, whereas black intellectuals criticized Wilson for his comedy routines, which they felt reveled in the same stereotypes apparent in shows like *The Amos 'n Andy Show.*

Getting an edge

As TV became slightly edgier in the 1970s, so did its black shows. *Sanford and Son, Good Times,* and *The Jeffersons* are three of the most memorable. Interestingly, a number of these shows experienced clashes between white writers and African American actors.

✔ *Sanford and Son:* Despite conflict off-camera, Red Foxx scored as Fred Sanford, a cantankerous Los Angeles junkman who lived with his son. *Sanford and Son* was one of the most popular shows of its time. Its five-year run ended in 1977, but the series continues to air in syndication.

✔ *Good Times:* Built around a character played by Esther Rolle on the 1972 television series *Maude, Good Times* featured a family trying to make ends meet in a Chicago housing project. Originally, the show's producers wanted Rolle to play a single mother, but she refused. Unlike other shows, *Good Times* brought dignity and humanity to poorer African Americans. Sensitive to negative portrayals of African Americans, stage actors Rolle and John Amos, who played her husband, objected to the increasing prominence of Jimmie Walker's character J.J. To them, he appeared buffoonish with his signature exclamation "Dyn-o-mite!" and disdain for school. Amos eventually left the show, and Rolle soon followed. Problems and all, *Good Times* remains an important part of television history, as evidenced by its success in syndication.

✔ *The Jeffersons:* Another groundbreaking series for the time, *The Jeffersons* depicted wealthy African Americans. Like Archie Bunker from *All in the Family,* the show that first introduced the Jeffersons, George Jefferson was as bigoted against white people as Archie was against everybody else. In addition, *The Jeffersons* regularly depicted a committed interracial marriage through George and Louise's neighbors, Tom and Helen Willis.

Kiddie comedies

Sitcoms came and went throughout the 1970s and early 1980s. For a time, all-black shows like *What's Happening!!* (loosely based on the popular 1975 film

Cooley High) lingered, but they soon gave way to broader comedies featuring black characters, particularly children. Here are a few examples:

- ✔ Gary Coleman and Todd Bridges became fast celebrities from *Diff'rent Strokes,* a series about a rich white single father who adopts two orphaned black kids.

- ✔ Kim Fields played the lone black kid in *The Facts of Life,* a series about life at a boarding school.

- ✔ Emmanuel Lewis played a black orphan cared for by a former white football player and his wife in the hit series *Webster.*

Interestingly, the film shorts *Our Gang,* better known as *The Little Rascals,* which appeared before television, introduced black child actors to Hollywood. In the 1950s and into the 1970s, *Our Gang* showed up on television. Despite reinforcing stereotypes such as black children routinely eating watermelon and fried chicken, *Our Gang*'s Ernie Morrison who played Sunshine Sammy was the first black actor signed to a long-term Hollywood contract. Most people, however, are more familiar with Billie Thomas who played Buckwheat, known for his signature unruly hair, because of Eddie Murphy's parodies of him on *Saturday Night Live.*

Cue the Huxtables

It's really impossible to overstate the significance of *The Cosby Show* in television history. A sitcom about the lives of an upper-middle-class black family headed by a husband who's a doctor and a wife who's an attorney, *The Cosby Show* was the most-watched show by all Americans during its eight-year run in the 1980s and early 1990s. For years, Bill Cosby received "top television dad" honors. Beyond its entertainment value, *The Cosby Show* educated all Americans about African American history and culture in a noninvasive way: The family home showcased African American art; Cosby's character Cliff Huxtable was a huge jazz buff, and some episodes featured legends like Lena Horne; and generational story lines showed complete families on both sides. Overall, the show was simultaneously traditionally American and African American.

Attracting young black audiences

New networks Fox and the WB zeroed in on the young black audience in the early 1990s with several shows that included

- ✔ *In Living Color* (1990), an in-your-face sketch comedy show that incorporated popular culture, including a hip-hop DJ and dancers. The show made the Wayans family, most notably Damon in front of the camera and Keenen behind, and Jamie Foxx (not to mention white actor Jim Carrey) stars.

> ✔ *Martin* (1992), a comedy built around a Detroit radio personality (played by Martin Lawrence), his girlfriend, and their friends.

> ✔ *Living Single* (1993), a comedy starring Queen Latifah and Kim Fields revolving around six friends, four women and two men, that preceded the all-white NBC hit *Friends* by a year.

Interestingly, Fox, the WB, and even UPN, which created black shows like *Moesha, Girlfriends,* and *The Parkers,* began distancing themselves from the African American audience after they gained firm footing with TV audiences. NBC, ABC, and CBS have presented few African American-oriented shows since the 1970s and 1980s. Today, the merger of UPN and the WB to form the CW has left the fate of the black-oriented sitcom up in the air.

In contrast to network TV, cable has shown a dedication to black comedy through influential shows such as HBO's *Def Comedy Jam* and *The Chris Rock Show,* along with numerous stand-up comedy specials from Whoopi Goldberg, Chris Rock, Mike Epps, Cedric the Entertainer, and others. Comedian Dave Chappelle shook up basic cable with his sketch comedy program *Chappelle's Show* in 2003 on Comedy Central before discontinuing the show in 2005.

Where's the drama?

Very few networks have attempted all-black dramatic series. In television, ensemble casts, particularly for hospital dramas and cop shows, have been the winning strategy for including black actors. *Hill Street Blues, St. Elsewhere, Miami Vice, L.A. Law,* and others provided weekly exposure for actors such as Michael Warren, Denzel Washington, Philip Michael Thomas, and Blair Underwood. In the 1990s, the cop genre even became more hip-hop–oriented; *New York Undercover,* for example, which paired a black and Latino cop, relied heavily on hip-hop dress, slang, music, and attitude. By the early 2000s, shows such as *ER* had firmly established a standard for African American talent. Few shows, however, have embraced multiracial casting like *Grey's Anatomy* (created by Shonda Rhimes, an African American female) and *Lost.*

African American actors in dramatic serials have fared better with cable. FX's *The Shield,* featuring CCH Pounder and Forest Whitaker, isn't an anomaly. HBO's *Six Feet Under* broke all the rules with the character Keith Charles, an African American police officer turned private security expert in a homosexual, interracial relationship. HBO's innovative prison drama *Oz* featured many African Americans. *The Wire* continued that innovation by showing Baltimore's drug scene from the perspective of law enforcement and the drug dealers. Showtime had success with *Soul Food,* a family drama based on the hit 1997 film. In 2005, LOGO, a gay cable channel, launched Patrik-Ian Polk's all-black series *Noah's Arc,* based on the 2004 film.

African Americans on soap operas

Most people are surprised to learn that Cicely Tyson, James Earl Jones, Phylicia Rashad, and Laurence Fishburne are among the long list of black actors who appeared on soap operas at some point in their careers. Vivica A. Fox is fond of telling the story of how she got the role of Will Smith's girlfriend in the film *Independence Day* (1996) — the producer's wife saw her on *The Young & the Restless.*

In the 1980s, a storyline on *All My Children* involving the characters Angie and Jessie (played by Debi Morgan and Darnell Williams) broke the soap opera mold by prominently featuring an African American couple. On *Days of Our Lives,* actor-turned-screenwriter Tina Andrews's interracial relationship was so controversial with viewers that she was fired. Today, interracial relationships aren't automatic deal breakers on soap operas. Although there's still room to grow, today's black soap actors enjoy juicier storylines. Some of the more recent stars to appear on soaps include Nia Long, Lauryn Hill, and Taye Diggs. *The Young and the Restless,* however, made Victoria Rowell and Shemar Moore, who moved on to prime time television, recognizable actors.

Made-for-cable movies, particularly those by HBO, have been the real stand-outs, however, with many of them winning numerous awards. Highlights include:

- ✔ *Miss Evers' Boys* (1997), an intense film about the controversial 1930s Tuskegee Syphilis Experiment, which injected black men, without their knowledge, with syphilis and didn't treat them.

- ✔ *Don King: Only in America* (1997), a biopic of the infamous boxing promoter (flip to Chapter 18 for more details about Don King).

- ✔ *The Corner* (2000), a groundbreaking miniseries about a Baltimore family's struggles with crack and poverty.

- ✔ *Lackawanna Blues* (2005), a drama about a young boy's colorful childhood growing up in a roominghouse in civil rights–era Lackawanna, New York.

The Next Level: African American Television Empires

In just a few decades, two Mississippi-born media powerhouses, Robert Johnson and Oprah Winfrey, have broken through television's glass ceiling. Johnson built the formidable cable network Black Entertainment Television (BET), and talk show host Oprah Winfrey has become one of the most powerful individuals in television history.

America discovers its *Roots*

The success of the 1974 television movie *The Autobiography of Miss Jane Pittman,* based on the Ernest Gaines novel about a black woman whose life spans from Reconstruction to the civil rights movement, convinced ABC executives to greenlight the larger-than-life 1977 miniseries *Roots,* based on Alex Haley's best-selling novel. (Television's key black actress during the 1970s and 1980s, Cicely Tyson, who starred as Miss Jane Pittman, also had a role in *Roots.)* More than shattering television records during its unprecedented eight-night broadcast, *Roots* dramatically impacted the nation's racial consciousness, inspiring dialogue in schools and at work. On average, 80 million Americans watched each of the seven episodes, and 100 million (almost half the country) tuned in for the eighth and final episode.

With its multigenerational storyline and its intimate look at the institution of slavery, *Roots* underscored the idea that, despite enduring the brutality of beatings, rapes, and other atrocities during slavery, African Americans maintained a strong sense of family as humane and dignified as any other Americans. Although Haley later settled a plagiarism suit with Harold Courlander, who wrote a similar novel, *The African,* in 1968, the impact of his work never faded.

Roots didn't make the world perfect, but it proved that television could make a difference by entertaining, educating, and inspiring dialogue about taboo subjects. By today's standards, *Roots* is a tame and gross oversimplification of this critical period in our nation's history. At the time, however, it was a monumental step forward for race relations. Even today, it remains one of the few television programs watched by almost all Americans.

The billion-dollar BET

In 1980, former cable industry lobbyist Robert Johnson launched BET as a weekly, two-hour Friday-night block on USA Network (a 2002 divorce from his wife of 33 years, Sheila Crump Johnson, resulted in her recognition as a BET cofounder). Three years later, BET was a full-fledged, 24-hour network of its own. Even with its shaky history with African American viewers — the network is frequently criticized for its abundance of sexually charged rap videos — BET does have a few milestones. Three of its shows — *Bobby Jones Gospel,* launched in 1980; *Rap City,* launched in 1989; and *ComicView,* launched in 1992 — are among the longest running in television history. BET is also one of the first black-owned companies to go public. Over the years, BET has attempted public affairs shows such as the nightly talk program *BET Tonight* (which launched the career of PBS host Tavis Smiley), *BET Nightly News,* and *Teen Summit.* BET's success has inspired other channels, such as the Black Family Channel and TV One, a joint venture between African American radio giant Radio One and cable giant Comcast. In 2000, media giant Viacom purchased BET for $3 billion.

The big "O"

Born poor in Mississippi and raised in Milwaukee and Nashville, Oprah Winfrey landed her first media job in radio at age 17. Before leaving for Chicago in 1984 where she dethroned Phil Donahue, the then reigning king of talk, she cohosted a talk show in Baltimore. In 1985, *The Oprah Winfrey Show,* which tackles everything from sexual molestation to racism and sexism, went national. An avid reader, Winfrey gave the publishing industry a boost with her Oprah Winfrey Book Club; her recommendation literally sent books to the top of the best-seller lists.

One of the world's most generous philanthropists, Winfrey has raised millions of dollars for causes in Africa, where she opened the Oprah Winfrey Leadership Academy for Girls in January 2007, as well as Hurricane Katrina victims through her Oprah's Angel Network. Her magazine *O* remains one of the most successful launches in publishing history, and she's a partner in the Oxygen Network for women. As an actress, Winfrey was nominated for both the Oscar and Golden Globe for her role as Sophia in the film version of *The Color Purple* (1985), which she produced as a Tony Award–winning, Broadway musical in 2006. Winfrey also produces film and television projects, most notably *Beloved* (1998) and Zora Neale Hurston's *Their Eyes Were Watching God* (2005) starring Halle Berry for ABC.

Chapter 18

Winning Ain't Easy: Race and Sports

*L*ooking at the NBA, NFL, and other popular sports leagues today, it's hard to imagine a time when African Americans weren't welcomed in the general sports world. In a time when racism made no exceptions for talented athletes, barriers against African Americans were as prevalent in sports as they were in any other part of American society. Therefore, sports became an important civil rights battlefield with the success of early black athletes resonating far beyond the individual.

This chapter covers the many sports arenas, such as baseball, boxing, and track and field, in which African American athletes have not only participated but excelled. It also explores some of their milestones and highlights important figures, both historically and in the contemporary sports world, who contributed both to their respective sports and to overall social change.

Baseball

The first known African American baseball game occurred in 1860 when the Weeksville of New York and the Colored Union Club played in Hoboken, New Jersey. James H. Francis and Francis Wood formed the Pythians in the Philadelphia area in the 1860s, but when the Pythians applied to the National Association of Base Ball Players (NABBP) for official recognition in 1867, that organization resolved to ban any club that included African Americans. Other baseball organizations, particularly professional ones, didn't have an outright ban against African American players. As a result, Bud Fowler, William Edward White, Moses Fleetwood "Fleet" Walker, and his brother Welday Walker played baseball at a high level in the late 19th century.

Playing baseball in overwhelmingly white environments wasn't easy. At first, many white players tolerated the few black players. As the 20th century drew closer, however, antiblack attitudes intensified. In the International League, an early minor league in which Walker and Fowler played, some white players refused to play against the "colored" talent of opposing teams. Others wouldn't pose next to their own black teammates for team pictures. In 1887, International League owners voted against extending contracts to future black players but agreed to honor the contracts of existing players. When the Supreme Court officially sanctioned segregation in its 1896 *Plessy v. Ferguson* decision (refer to Chapter 7), African Americans didn't play alongside white players in Major League Baseball (MLB) until Jackie Robinson broke that color line in 1947.

Thanks to early player/manager/sportswriter King Solomon White, better known as Sol White, African American baseball history wasn't lost. White published his seminal work, *History of Colored Base Ball,* in 1907.

The Negro Leagues

Professional African American baseball players didn't solely turn to predominantly white baseball clubs to play. In 1885, the Babylon Black Panthers (of New York), later renamed the Cuban Giants, became the first black professional team. Shortly thereafter, the first Negro League took root. Others soon followed. These leagues, the key personalities that populated them, and other developments paved the way for Jackie Robinson's historic entry into Major League Baseball.

Players in the Negro Leagues came mostly from the East, Midwest, and South, but others came from Puerto Rico, Cuba, and other nearby countries. In later years, three women, Toni Stone, Connie Morgan, and Mamie Johnson also played in the Negro Leagues.

Famous leagues

The Negro Leagues, which included several leagues comprised of countless baseball clubs, some more successful than others, really shined in the early 20th century. But the idea of independent black baseball began before then with early organizations such as the Southern League of Colored Base Ballists, formed in 1886, and the National Colored Base Ball League, established in 1887.

Andrew "Rube" Foster

Considered the father of black baseball, Texas-born Andrew "Rube" Foster began as a pitcher with the Cuban X-Giants. When he led them to victory over the Philadelphia Giants in the 1903 Colored Championship, the Philadelphia Giants' white owner, H. Walter Schlichter, hired Foster, and the very next year they topped the X-Giants. In 1907, Foster left the Philadelphia Giants which early black baseball historian Sol Whilte led, to manage and play for the Chicago Leland Giants.

On the field, Foster created a more aggressive team known for seeking extra bases, He also fine-tuned the pitchers. Off the field, he took over bookings and increased the team's gate take from 10 percent to 40 percent. Confident of his skills, Foster threatened to leave the team if owner Frank Leland didn't step away from all baseball operations; Leland refused. Eventually, Foster gained legal control of the Leland Giants' name, thus forcing Leland to start the Chicago Giants. Foster's Leland Giants later became the Chicago American Giants.

In 1920, Foster created the National Negro League (NNL) but became mentally ill in the late 1920s and died in 1930. Without him, the league faltered and folded in 1931. Revived in 1933, the NNL thrived until 1948.

Equally important in developing early black baseball were the Colored All Americans, a traveling barnstorming unit pitting the legendary Cuban Giants against rivals the New York Gorhams, which both gained admission to the white Middle States League before later hitting the road. The following leagues, however, directly inform what most people think of as the Negro Leagues:

- ✔ **Negro National League:** The black workers substituting for the depleted white force during World War I gave black baseball enough of a financial boon to help create the Negro National League in 1920 with Andrew "Rube" Foster serving as league president. Founding teams included Foster's Chicago American Giants, the legendary Kansas City Monarchs, and the St. Louis Giants.

  In 1921, the semi-pro Negro Southern League, whose impressive roster included pitcher Satchel Paige, strengthened the NNL, but it still folded in 1931. The next year Homestead Grays' owner Cumberland Posey's East-West League tried to replace the NNL but also failed. In 1933, reputed gangster and Pittsburgh Crawfords' owner Gus Greenlee successfully revived the NNL until 1948.

- ✔ **Eastern Colored League:** Spearheaded in 1923 by Pennsylvania's Hilldale Daisies–owner Ed Bolden and Nat Strong, a white businessman, the Eastern Colored League (ECL) rivaled the NNL. The two leagues reconciled in 1924 and agreed to play each other in the Negro League World Series. The ECL folded in 1928.

✔ **Negro American League:** Considered the last great black baseball league, the Negro American League, formed in 1937, is the league for which Jackie Robinson played. Dr. J.B. Martin, a Memphis dentist who, along with his brother B.B. Martin, built a baseball powerhouse with the Memphis Red Sox, led black baseball during one of its most explosive periods. Even after Major League Baseball began raiding its rosters, Martin tried to keep the league going through the 1950s before folding in the early 1960s.

Key people

Cool Papa Bell, Oscar Charleston, Martín Dihigo, and Buck Leonard, all in the Baseball Hall of Fame, are just a handful of the great players that electrified the Negro Leagues. Two of the most famous players from that era, however, may just be Josh Gibson and Satchel Paige:

✔ **Josh Gibson:** Baseball historians regularly place catcher Josh Gibson, who played with the Homestead Grays and Pittsburgh Crawfords, among baseball's all-time greatest hitters. Often compared to Babe Ruth, the Georgia-born Gibson, who had a career batting average that exceeded .350, reportedly hit nearly 800 home runs throughout his 17-year career. Sadly, Gibson died at age 35, just months before Major League Baseball integrated.

✔ **Satchel Paige:** Born in Mobile, Alabama, Leroy "Satchel" Paige, the Negro Leagues' most well-known pitcher, had an illustrious career that included stints with the Pittsburgh Crawfords and the Kansas City Monarchs. His crowd-pleasing showmanship was such a draw that he was often loaned out to help struggling teams improve their attendance records and stay afloat. Paige reportedly pitched 300 shutouts. Major League Baseball's oldest rookie at age 42 in 1948, Paige became the first black pitcher to take the mound in the 1948 World Series, which his club, the Cleveland Indians, won.

Key events

In addition to regular play, the Negro Leagues hosted many special games. The early prototype for generating interest in black baseball was *barnstorming*, the practice of traveling around and presenting special events. Other crowd-pleasing contests also developed. As early as 1896, the first Colored Championships occurred, and there were similar contests throughout the Negro Leagues' long history:

✔ **All-Star games.** These games were the Negro Leagues' biggest draw. First held in 1933, the All-Star game allowed fans to select deserving players and often attracted more than 40,000 fans.

✔ **Contests between all-black and all-white teams:** Black players couldn't play alongside white players, but many did play against and beat white players.

Negro Leagues players in the Baseball Hall of Fame

It took years of intense debates, including a plea from baseball great Ted Williams and the 1970 publication of Robert Peterson's influential *Only the Ball Was White,* before the Baseball Hall of Fame began inducting Negro Leagues players. In 1971, Josh Gibson, Cool Papa Bell, Satchel Paige, and Oscar Charleston were among the first Negro Leaguers inducted. Hall of Fame recognition, along with the Negro Leagues Baseball Museum in Kansas City, Missouri, has ensured that this critical chapter in American sports history won't be forgotten.

Negro Leagues players and their many African American owners were well aware of America's racial climate, with many like the Newark Eagles, who hosted Anti-Lynching Day in 1939, often stepping up in civic matters.

The demise of the Negro Leagues

The integration of Major League Baseball (MLB) devastated the Negro Leagues as more and more players, following Jackie Robinson's lead, headed to the majors. Larry Doby, Don Newcombe, Willie Mays, Ernie Banks, and Henry "Hank" Aaron were just some of the distinguished MLB players with Negro League roots (see the section "The modern era" for details on some of these players). In 1958, the Negro American League played its last game. The Indianapolis Clowns, the team Hank Aaron initially played for, continued to play exhibition games into the 1980s, but black baseball never recovered.

Jackie Robinson: Integrating baseball

Brooklyn Dodgers President and General Manager Branch Rickey challenged Major League Baseball's unwritten policy against black players when he signed the Kansas City Monarchs' Jack Roosevelt "Jackie" Robinson. On April 15, 1947, the 28-year-old Robinson debuted as a Brooklyn Dodger and changed modern-day baseball forever. Over the course of his ten seasons with the Dodgers, the team won six pennants and a World Series; Robinson, who led the league in stolen bases his first year, achieved individual honors including Rookie of the Year and National League MVP.

While it has been generally acknowledged that Robinson wasn't the Negro Leagues' best player, Rickey believed that Robinson, who had attended UCLA and served in the military, could withstand the abuse that would accompany integrating MLB. Rickey made Robinson promise that he wouldn't retaliate against any racial provocations or publicly address them for an entire year. Well aware that Robinson once faced court-martial for protesting segregation in the army, Rickey sent Robinson to a minor league club in Canada to prep him for playing ball in the major leagues.

Before Robinson even suited up, white players from his own squad and others considered protesting his entry. On the field, white fans taunted him with racial slurs. He also received many death threats. Still, in the face of such pressures, Robinson persevered and excelled. By the end of his first season, Robinson, who enjoyed a faithful black fan base, could also count on his ever-growing white fan base.

The modern era

Major League Baseball wasted little time embracing black players. Following are a few prominent players from the 1950s to the end of the 1970s:

- **Willie Mays:** This legendary center fielder for the New York–turned–San Francisco Giants amassed an amazing 3,283 hits, 660 home runs, 12 Gold Gloves, 24 All-Star game appearances, and 4 World Series appearances (and 1 win) during a major league career that began in 1951 and ended in 1973.

- **Bob Gibson:** In the 1967 World Series, St. Louis Cardinals' pitcher and eventual two-time Cy Young winner Bob Gibson not only allowed just three earned runs in three complete game victories but also hit an important home run himself. In 1968, he set a World Series record by striking out 17 Detroit Tigers in the very first game.

- **Curt Flood:** Outstanding player Flood made his mark off the field when he refused a 1969 trade from the St. Louis Cardinals to the Philadelphia Phillies, taking his case all the way to the Supreme Court. Although he lost the legal battle, many agree that he opened the door to today's era of free agency. Because of his courage, the salaries of today's baseball players represent a much larger portion of their team's and the league's overall wealth.

- **Hank Aaron:** Before 53,775 fans, on April 8, 1974, Atlanta Braves right fielder Hank "the Hammer" Aaron broke Babe Ruth's long-standing home run record of 714 home runs; when he retired from baseball in 1976, he had 755 career home runs.

- **Reggie Jackson:** Known as Mr. October and considered baseball's first black megastar, Reggie Jackson played in five World Series and sealed his legend in the final game of the 1977 World Series. Playing for the New York Yankees, Jackson hit three home runs off three different pitchers. His two MVP World Series honors for two separate teams, the Oakland Athletics and the New York Yankees, also placed him in the elite company of Babe Ruth.

"Queen of the Negro Leagues": Effa Manley

Much more than an owner's wife, Effa Manley was a player advocate who took an active role in managing the Newark Eagles, often fighting for better schedules and salaries. Civic-minded, she served as treasurer of the NAACP's Newark chapter and involved the team in many civil rights causes. When MLB began raiding the Negro Leagues' rosters, Manley was outspoken about MLB compensating owners like her and her husband. Although Manley, who kept a scrapbook of black baseball's glory days, died in 1981, she became the first woman inducted into the Baseball Hall of Fame in 2006.

From the 1980s and 1990s into the 2000s, quite a few African American baseball players accepted the torch. In his first year of eligibility, longtime San Diego Padres right fielder Tony Gwynn got the go-ahead for the Baseball Hall of Fame. There's already a plaque awaiting longtime Oakland Athletics player Rickey Henderson, baseball's stolen base king. Former Seattle Mariner Ken Griffey, Jr., almost guaranteed his spot in Cooperstown when he surpassed Mickey Mantle on baseball's home run list. But becoming baseball's new home run king might not guarantee a place in Baseball's Hall of Fame for former Pittsburgh Pirates player and longtime San Francisco Giants franchise player Barry Bonds, who has been dogged by allegations of steroid use.

Basketball

It didn't take long for the U.S. to embrace basketball, invented by Canadian-born James A Naismith in 1891. By the 1900s, the U.S. had a few professional teams. In 1902, Massachusetts native Harry "Bucky" Lew became the first African American professional player. Harvard-educated physical education instructor Edwin Henderson, who many call the father of black basketball, introduced the game to black schools in Washington, D.C., in 1904.

Henderson recognized the sport's potential in the area of civil rights. Through the all-black Interscholastic Athletic Association of the Middle States (ISAA), established in 1905, Henderson encouraged competitive basketball among African Americans, as did New York's Smart Set Athletic Club of Brooklyn and the St. Christopher Club of New York City. The latter organizations, along with three others, formed the Olympian Athletic League in 1907. For years, these organizations fostered black basketball talent and took it to new heights, planting the seeds for both collegiate and professional play among African Americans. Even today, basketball's communal spirit thrives as basketball courts and programs are very prominent throughout the nation, particularly in urban areas.

Holcombe Rucker and Rucker Park

In 1946, longtime NYC Department of Parks worker Holcombe Rucker created a neighborhood basketball program to keep kids off Harlem's mean streets. Rucker, whose motto was "each one, teach one," emphasized education and checked report cards to decide who played in his program. He even tutored his charges in the fundamentals of English and life. With his help, over 700 program participants attended college on athletic scholarships.

Rucker's idea of pitting professional players like Wilt Chamberlain and Nate "Tiny" Archibald against celebrated local talent like Richard "Pee Wee" Kirkland and Earl "The Goat" Manigault (whom Don Cheadle played in the 1996 HBO film *Rebound),* however, made his tournaments legendary. Even after Rucker died in 1965, the tournaments survived, relocating to what became Rucker Park in 1974.

Concerned about injuries, NBA players stayed away from Rucker Park until the Entertainers Basketball Classic brought them back in the 1980s. Today, the park is the site of court battles between street ball talent and NBA royalty like Allen Iverson and Kobe Bryant. Music luminaries such as P. Diddy and Fat Joe sponsor teams. At the game, hip-hop DJs provide music and announcers provide colorful and frequently funny commentary. Through nationwide tours, And 1, an urban-oriented footwear company, and others have exposed larger audiences to streetball and its explosive players.

College ball

Basketball eventually evolved into a viable option for African American men in particular to attend college and then later as a means to a professional career. Below is just a quick glimpse into the college game and its overall impact.

Black colleges

Black colleges quickly embraced basketball and provided the first opportunity for African Americans, male and female, to play the sport. Although today black college basketball is an afterthought for most sports professionals, black coaches and schools were among basketball's early innovators, and the most enduring legacies have come from two head coaches:

✔ **Tennessee State's John B. McLendon:** A sports civil rights pioneer, McLendon, who cofounded the CIAA Tournament in 1946, black college basketball's premier contest, made a significant breakthrough when his team beat a white school for a national championship in 1957. Credited with creating fastbreak basketball and the half-court press, McLendon coached all-black teams that beat all-white teams during the height of racial segregation. In 1961, McLendon, who spearheaded other black college programs, became the first black coach of a professional mainstream team in 1961. In 1966, he became the first black coach hired by a white college, Cleveland State. He was also the first black Olympic coach in 1968, as well as the first black coach of the American Basketball Association's Denver Rockets in 1969.

> ✔ **Winston-Salem State's Clarence "Big House" Gaines:** Gaines's teams won 12 CIAA titles in his 47-year tenure as head coach, with him amassing 828 wins. Both black and white college teams absorbed his fast-breaking style of play with athletic and fast players. NBA great Earl "the Pearl" Monroe and sports commentator Stephen A. Smith are two players he coached.

Mainstream colleges

Prior to World War I, Fenwick Watkins, Cumberland Posey, and Paul Robeson played basketball on predominantly white teams at mainstream universities. Such strides continued into the 1930s when Columbia University's George Gregory, Jr., became the first African American All-American basketball player, and Long Island University's William "Dolly" King became the first black player to participate in the National Amateur Athletic Union. William Garrett continued that movement into the Midwest when he integrated the Big Ten at Indiana University in 1947.

Loyola University Chicago ended the customary practice of playing only three black players at any given time, regularly playing four players and sometimes five. In 1963, in the NCAA Championship game, Loyola started four black players and played five in its upset win over Cincinnati, which was looking for a three-peat. College basketball's racial walls were torn down completely when Texas Tech, as dramatized in the 2006 film *Glory Road,* went with an all-black starting lineup to defeat the all-white basketball powerhouse University of Kentucky in the 1966 NCAA championship. Until Texas Tech's monumental victory, there were still a number of Southern colleges that didn't play black players at all.

Since then, African Americans have dominated college basketball. Along the way, great coaches like Georgetown's John Thompson, former Temple University coach John Chaney, and former University of Arkansas coach Nolan Richardson have paved the way for other Division I African American college coaches.

Pro ball

Early black men's basketball flourished, especially in the cities, during what is often referred to as the Black Fives Era. Professional play emerged as early as 1909, with Pittsburgh's Monticello Rifles, owned by Cumberland Posey, being the most popular team. Countless college students emulated the players' fast-paced style.

In 1913, Posey created the Loendi Big Five in Pittsburgh. This team ruled black basketball until Robert Douglas formed the New York Renaissance, a Harlem-based basketball powerhouse. Known as the Rens, they proved their superiority by defeating the National Basketball League (NBL) champion all-white Oshkosh All-Stars in the World Professional Basketball Tournament in

1939. During the 1948–1949 season, the franchise moved to Ohio and joined the NBL, becoming the first all-black franchise in a white league. Although the NBL folded, the Dayton Rens/New York Rens are in the Naismith Memorial Basketball Hall of Fame in Springfield, Massachusetts.

Because the American Basketball Association excluded African Americans when it launched in 1925, players from Chicago's Wendell Phillips High School formed the Savoy Big Five in 1927. Renamed the Harlem Globetrotters when agent Abe Saperstein took over, the team suffered many racial indignities during its journey to become a credible basketball team. In 1940, the Harlem Globetrotters defeated the Chicago Bruins in the World Professional Basketball Tournament and then beat the World Champion Minneapolis Lakers, now in Los Angeles, two out of three times in 1948 and 1949. Despite those competitive beginnings, the Harlem Globetrotters became a novelty act in later years.

Integration on the court

Prompted by World War II's effect on the white player pool, the NBL chose to welcome black players instead of folding. In 1942, the Toledo Jim White Chevrolets in Ohio signed four black players, while the Chicago Studebakers signed five former Harlem Globetrotters. Curiously, though, the NBL had only one black player in 1943. Still the move was positive, as the West Coast professional leagues began integrating in 1944. The Basketball Association of America (BAA), which banned black players in 1946, merged with the NBL to create the National Basketball Association (NBA) during the 1949–1950 season, making integration the norm. Chuck Cooper, signed by the Boston Celtics, became the NBA's first black draft pick even though the Washington Capitols' Earl Lloyd became the first African American to play in the NBA.

Unlike other sports, the NBA has embraced black coaches and general managers quickly. Bill Russell opened the doors as the NBA's first black coach. Of the many who've followed in his footsteps, his former college teammate K.C. Jones, who also coached the Celtics, and Lenny Wilkins, who followed Russell as the Seattle Supersonics' coach, have both won NBA championships. African Americans in upper management aren't rare, either. Former players Elgin Baylor, Joe Dumars, and Isiah Thomas are just three attached to high-profile teams. In 2003, the NBA also made history when Black Entertainment Television founder Robert Johnson became the nation's first black majority owner of an NBA franchise.

Great players

Many great African American players helped build as well as sustain the NBA. Some notable Hall of Famers include

✔ **Bill Russell:** With legendary center Russell, who served as the team's coach as well as a player from 1966 to 1969, the Boston Celtics won an astonishing 11 NBA championships in 13 seasons. Russell set many playoff scoring and defensive records that remain untouched.

✔ **Wilt Chamberlain:** Although revered center Chamberlain is still the only NBA player to score 100 points in a single game, he also holds nearly 100 NBA records, making him arguably the greatest NBA player of all time.

✔ **Elgin Baylor:** Considered one of the NBA's purest scorers, many credit Baylor for saving the Lakers franchise, located in Minneapolis at the time of his draft. Baylor's double-digit scoring brought out the crowds and helped the Lakers make the playoffs. Baylor's many accomplishments include a 71-point game against the Knicks in 1960 and a 61-point playoff effort against the Celtics in 1962.

✔ **Oscar Robertson:** King of the triple doubles, Robertson, who earned Player of the Year honors for three consecutive seasons while a student at the University of Cincinnati (Cincinnati) in the late 1950s, became the NBA prototype for the all-around player.

✔ **Julius "Dr. J" Erving:** Dr. J's electrifying play changed the game of basketball forever. Thanks to him, the dunk went from a rare treat to a regular feature. He also combined energetic showmanship with dignity and grace. It's often been said that the NBA merged with the American Basketball Association (ABA) just to get Erving.

✔ **Earvin "Magic" Johnson:** Magic Johnson helped curtail declining interest in the NBA during the late 1970s when he and Larry Bird carried their college rivalry into the NBA in 1979. Playing in Los Angeles, point guard Johnson, aided by great center Kareem Abdul-Jabbar and a host of other all-stars, regenerated fan excitement and directly contributed to the NBA's survival.

✔ **Michael Jordan:** Few predicted that Michael Jordan would become the most famous basketball player on the planet when the Chicago Bulls drafted him in 1984. But his unbelievable rookie year scoring was only a glimpse into the player he would become. Jordan's spectacular offensive and defensive play on his way to six NBA championships put him in the running for the honor of greatest NBA player of all time.

Women's basketball

Black women in basketball have traveled a much harder road than men, but the black community embraced black women's basketball early. New York and Philadelphia had a few teams before World War I, and both the Chicago Romas and the Philadelphia Tribunes, the first professional sports teams for black women, were very popular. The Philadelphia Tribunes even traveled extensively throughout the South to introduce young girls to the sport.

As early as the 1920s — long before Title IX of the Educational Amendment of 1972 mandated federally funded colleges to provide women access to sports and scholarships — black colleges began investing in women's basketball programs. Games were well-attended, and black newspapers extensively covering collegiate women's basketball into the 1940s. At that time, white institutions and the white community in general didn't support female athletics in the same manner.

Title IX forced many mainstream universities to establish or invest more in women's sports programs. Coupled with ongoing desegregation efforts, the legislation benefited black female athletes, and college players like Lusia Harris, who attended Mississippi's Delta State University, received more opportunities to display their talents. In 1971, the women's game went from a half-court to a full-court game. Women's basketball grew in stature when it debuted at the 1976 Olympics, and the U.S. team, on which Harris played, won a silver medal.

Competition heightened further when the NCAA Women's Basketball Championship kicked off in 1982. Powerhouse women's programs at the University of Tennessee, University of Connecticut, and Louisiana Tech emerged. In addition to players, those institutions also snatched up black female coaching talent like C. Vivian Stringer, one of the all-time great women basketball coaches.

A surprising gold medal win at the 1984 Olympics gave women's basketball a huge boost in momentum. Key team members included Cheryl Miller, now a sports commentator, and Lynette Woodard, who was the first woman to play with the Harlem Globetrotters. At the 1996 Olympics, Team USA went undefeated. Teresa Edwards, Dawn Staley, and Nikki McCray are just a few of the outstanding players from those teams.

The NBA-supported WNBA started in 1997. In its early years, top talent such as the Houston Comets' Sheryl Swoopes, the first female basketball player to receive her own shoe from Nike, and Lisa Leslie, the Los Angeles Sparks' dominating center, attracted fans to the fledgling league. Leadership from modern-day women's basketball pioneers like Cheryl Miller made the league credible. Today, the WNBA is the nation's premier venue for women's basketball.

Throughout the years, new superstars have steadily emerged. Some of the most recent include Chamique Holdsclaw, Alana Beard, Tamika Catchings, and Seimone Augustus. And with top talent like Candace Parker, the first woman to win the McDonald's High School All-American dunk contest, expanding the appeal of women's basketball, the WNBA will continue its growth.

Boxing

Slave owners were notorious for staging fights between their slaves, and that's precisely how some early black boxers got the bulk of their boxing experience. As professional boxing developed in 19th-century America, promoters generally banned African Americans from challenging white fighters, especially in the heavyweight category. To gain credibility, fighters like Tom Molineaux, a slave whose boxing skill eventually freed him, went to England, boxing's mecca (the British championship was equivalent to the world championship). In 1810, Molineaux earned a shot at reigning heavyweight champion Tom Cribb. Although he lost that bout and a rematch with Cribb, to England's surprise, he proved a formidable foe.

During the late 19th century, a black boxing circuit developed, but competing for the titles that white fighters held was still difficult. That changed in the 20th century. Following are several of boxing's key African American figures:

- ✔ **Jack Johnson (1878–1946):** Although lightweight boxer Joe Gans's 1902 world title opened doors for other African American boxers, heavyweight John Arthur "Jack" Johnson's battles epitomized Jim Crow America. In 1903, he became the Colored Heavyweight Champion, but the reigning white world champion, Jim Jeffries, refused to fight him. When Johnson easily defeated Canadian Tommy Burns in 1908 to win the title and other white fighters failed to avenge Burns's defeat, Jeffries was lured out of retirement. Billed as "the Great White Hope" in the "Fight of the Century," Jeffries fell to Johnson on July 4, 1910. Johnson's victory sparked a wave of race riots and resulted in certain states refusing to film his victories over white fighters. The critically acclaimed 2004 PBS documentary *Unforgivable Blackness: The Rise and Fall of Jack Johnson,* directed by Ken Burns, explores Johnson's career in the context of American race relations.

- ✔ **Joe Louis (1914–1981):** From his boxing debut in 1934 and throughout most of his career, Joe Louis's signature was knocking his opponents out. In his prime, Louis, nicknamed the Brown Bomber, rarely lost a fight. An upset loss to German boxer Max Schmeling in 1936 rattled Louis to the point that he insisted on a rematch until he got one in 1938. With the U.S. on the brink of entering World War II, the fight reached an international audience via the radio. More than a personal achievement, Louis' win symbolized a win for democracy. From 1937 to 1949, Louis successfully defended his title 25 times.

- ✔ **Sugar Ray Robinson (1921–1989):** In his long career, welterweight-middleweight champion Sugar Ray Robinson won 202 fights (108 by knockouts) and only lost 19, most of them at the end of his prime. A hard hitter with quick feet and hands, Robinson, whom many still consider the best pound-for-pound boxer of all time, fought all over the world.

✔ **Muhammad Ali (1942–):** Through the 1960s and 1970s, no fighter captivated the public like Kentucky native Muhammad Ali (born Cassius
Clay); see Figure 18-1. The 1960 Olympic gold medalist's 1964 defeat of
Sonny Liston ushered in boxing's new era. Known for his fancy footwork,
his boastful, witty rhymes, and his stunning good looks, the Nation of
Islam convert paid for his outspokenness. When he refused his Vietnam
draft order on religious grounds, Ali was stripped of his title and
received a five-year prison sentence in 1967; the Supreme Court later
reversed the decision. Ali went on to defeat George Foreman in the 1974
Don King–produced Rumble in Jungle, where he won back his undisputed heavyweight title. In the following year's fight defending his title,
Thrilla in Manila, against Joe Frazier, the referee ended the fight out of
concern for the badly beaten Frazier. After a brief retirement, Ali returned
to the ring in 1980 and lost his heavyweight title for good to Larry Holmes.
Well past his prime, Ali finally retired in 1981.

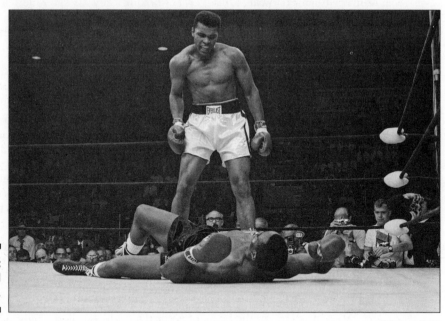

Figure 18-1:
Muhammad
Ali.

© Bettmann/Corbis

Don King

"Only in America," to use a phrase coined by Don King, could a former street hustler who served four years in prison for murder become one of sports' most famous figures. Known for his eccentric hair and creative use of the English language, the boxing promoter's career began in 1972 when he convinced Muhammad Ali to participate in a fundraiser to save a black hospital in Cleveland. In 1974, the Cleveland native staged one of the greatest fights in boxing history, the Rumble in the Jungle in Zaire, in which Ali fought George Foreman. Thrilla in Manila, in which Ali battled Joe Frazier in the Philippines, followed. Since the 1970s, Sugar Ray Leonard, Mike Tyson, Larry Holmes, Felix Trinidad, Evander Holyfield, and Oscar de la Hoya have been just a few of King's other headliners. King is credited with almost single-handedly turning boxing into a multibillion-dollar global industry that attracts record-breaking live and pay-per-view audiences. King has also survived numerous lawsuits, from Muhammad Ali to Mike Tyson, charging that he robbed his boxers of millions.

✔ **Sugar Ray Leonard (1956–):** At his prime in the late 1970s and 1980s, the North Carolina–born gold medal winner (1976) Leonard battled some of boxing's most formidable opponents, including Thomas "Hitman" Hearns, "Marvelous" Marvin Hagler, and Panama's Roberto Duran.

✔ **Mike Tyson (1966–):** In 1986, 20-year-old Brooklynite Tyson became boxing's youngest heavyweight champion. During 1987, "Iron" Mike defeated James "Bonecrusher" Smith and Tony Tucker to become the undisputed heavyweight champion of the world. Although Tyson beat the aging Larry Holmes in 1988, his unbelievable defeat of Michael Spinks in a fight that lasted only 1 minute and 31 seconds elevated his cult status. Troubles outside the ring, including a high-profile divorce from actress Robin Givens and a rape conviction, hindered Tyson's boxing career. After jail, Tyson appeared more troubled and, in a 1997 fight against Evander Holyfield, bit a part of his opponent's ear off, presumably frustrated by Holyfield's repeated head-butting. Although his career continued to decline, Tyson didn't call it quits until 2005.

Although boxing no longer captivates the masses the way it once did, Roy Jones, Jr., Sugar Shane Mosley, and Floyd Mayweather, among others, are recognized names. Muhammad Ali's daughter Laila Ali has also made a name for herself in the sport while blazing a trail for female boxers.

Football

As far as American traditions go, football is second only to baseball. Like baseball, pro football welcomed African American talent in the late 1940s. Curiously, college football, which had absorbed African Americans into its ranks early, lagged behind pro football from the 1950s into the 1970s, mainly because Southern colleges refused to embrace African American football players. At the same time, their football programs had increased in stature. Even in regards to African Americans holding leadership positions in coaching and upper management, the college level, in some respects, lags behind the pro game, which has been criticized often for its lack of diversity.

Pro football

The American Professional Football Association, renamed the National Football League (NFL) in 1922, didn't begin as an exclusionary organization in 1920. African Americans Robert "Rube" Marshall and Frederick Douglass "Fritz" Pollard played through intense racial harassment. As the NFL grew, it reversed its position and began excluding African Americans in 1933. That color line remained in place until the Los Angeles Rams signed Kenny Washington and Woody Strode in 1946. Penn State's Wally Triplett became the first African American draftee to play in the NFL in 1949. Arguably, in 1957, Jim Brown became the NFL's first African American legend.

Recognizing that segregation remained strong in the collegiate ranks, the NFL didn't bypass black college talent. Grambling's Paul "Tank" Younger, who played with the Los Angeles Rams, became the NFL's first black college star. Since Younger, black college all-stars who have excelled in the NFL include Jackson State's Walter Payton, Mississippi Valley State's Jerry Rice, and Grambling's Doug Williams, who was the first African American quarterback to win a Super Bowl.

Although the Chicago Bears' Willie Thrower became the NFL's first black quarterback in 1953 and Denver's Marlin Briscoe and Buffalo's James Harris were starting quarterbacks in the late 1960s, African Americans were largely restricted from holding the position. In the 1980s, stellar play from Warren Moon, who proved himself in the Canadian Football League first, and Randall Cunningham helped move other black quarterbacks to the forefront. But despite Doug Williams's Super Bowl win, the NFL's many outstanding black quarterbacks, particularly Michael Vick, have been repeatedly criticized for not emulating the white, "pocket" quarterback, despite their winning records.

Another point of contention for the NFL has been in coaching. Whereas basketball has integrated black talent in almost all areas of the game, such change in the NFL has come relatively late. In 1989, the Los Angeles Raiders made Art Shell the first black NFL head coach since Fritz Pollard.

The NFL really shook things up after attorneys Johnnie Cochran and Cyrus Mehri unveiled a report showing that, while the NFL's few black coaches typically had superior performance records, fewer head coaching opportunities existed for black coaches. In response, the NFL instituted the "Rooney Rule," named for Pittsburgh Steelers owner Dan Rooney, requiring teams to interview at least one minority candidate while filling a head coaching vacancy or pay a fine. The Detroit Lions paid a $200,000 fine for hiring Steve Mariucci in 2003 and not interviewing anyone, white or black.

At the top of 2007, however, black coaches got a huge boost when Lovie Smith (Chicago Bears) and Tony Dungy (Indianapolis Colts) became the first black coaches to lead their teams to the Super Bowl, with Dungy's team winning. Thirty-four-year-old Mike Tomlin's ascension as head coach of the Pittsburgh Steelers during that same time also signaled a major change. In 2006 and 2007, things also moved a little faster in the general manager ranks as Jim Reese (New York Giants) and Rick Smith (Houston Texans) joined Ozzie Newsome (Baltimore Ravens), who became the NFL's first African American general manager in 2002.

College football

African Americans have found a way to participate in college football almost from the beginning. William Henry Lewis, who played football at Amherst and Harvard, became an All-American in 1892 and 1893. In 1916, Fritz Pollard was the first African American college player to appear in the Rose Bowl. African American athletes in Northern colleges endured racial harassment in addition to segregation from other athletes; many predominantly white universities in the South refused to accept black students in any capacity, in defiance of the Supreme Court.

Black colleges developed strong football programs in response to this reality. None, however, would prove as great as that of Louisiana's Grambling State University, where Eddie Robinson, beginning in 1941, built a football powerhouse that sent 210 players, more than any other college coach, to the NFL. In 1985, Robinson broke Bear Bryant's record as college football's winningest coach, and by 1995, his 400 career wins put him in a class of his own. Upon retirement in 1997, Robinson had amassed an astonishing 408 wins, 165 losses, and 15 ties.

It took a luminary such as Bear Bryant, however, to open up predominantly white college football programs in the South to African Americans. In 1971, the University of Southern California opened its season against the University of Alabama. USC's integrated team trounced the all-white team from Alabama. Many have speculated that Bryant, who reportedly tried to integrate his football program at the University of Kentucky, intentionally scheduled the game to make a case for integration. Shortly thereafter, junior college transfer John Mitchell became the first black player to play for Alabama. When Mitchell joined Bryant's coaching staff in 1973, nearly a third of Alabama's starters were African American.

In recent years, there's been no lack of black talent on the field, but college football, like the NFL, has been accused of overlooking African Americans in other positions. Of the 117 Division I-A schools in 2002, only 4 had black head coaches. Those who applauded the iconic Notre Dame for signing Ty Willingham on as head coach were disappointed when the school dumped Willingham in 2004 after just three of his contracted six seasons. Although the University of Washington quickly snatched him up, the consensus was that, had he been able to succeed at Notre Dame, coaching walls could have tumbled for black coaches. With that grand experiment failed, the ball shifted to former Bear Bryant–player Sylvester Croom, who became the first African American head coach in the Southeastern Conference (SEC) when he accepted the top job for the Mississippi State Bulldogs in 2003.

Track and Field

African Americans have participated in track and field since the 1890s, with both black and predominantly white colleges in the North cultivating their talents early on (predominantly white Southern colleges refused African Americans admission well until the middle of the 20th century). Tuskegee Institute, which hired its first athletic director, James B. Washington, in 1890, was competitive in track and field by 1893. Notable 19th-century track stars include William Tecumseh Sherman, Amherst's 1890 champion half-sprinter; and Harvard's Napoleon Bonaparte Marshall, who ran the 440 dash in 51.2 seconds. Other notable track and field stars include:

- **George Poage (1880–1962):** The University of Wisconsin's Poage became the first African American to win an Olympic medal when he came away with two bronze medals in the 1904 Olympics.

- **John "Doc" Taylor (1882–1908):** The University of Pennsylvania's Taylor became the first black collegiate track and field champion in 1907 and the first black American to win an Olympic gold medal in the 1908 games in London.

✔ **Howard Drew (1890–1957):** Injury prevented Howard Porter Drew from competing in the 1912 Olympics, but he set the standard for running the 100-yard dash in under 10 seconds and was the first African American to be tagged the world's fastest human.

✔ **Jesse Owens (1913–1980):** Before dominating college track and field as a student at Ohio State University, the Alabama-born Owens broke world records in high school. His college success led him to the 1936 Olympics where, in the height of Hitler's assertion of Aryan supremacy, he won an unprecedented four gold medals, the first American to accomplish that feat.

✔ **Alice Coachman (1923–):** In the 1948 Olympics in London, master high jumper Coachman, whose talent was nurtured at Tuskegee Institute, became the first black woman to win a gold medal and the first American woman to win a gold medal in track and field.

✔ **Wilma Rudolph (1940–1994):** One of 22 children and stricken with polio early in her life, Rudolph overcame tremendous obstacles to set the bar for female track. Her standout play in basketball in junior high school attracted the track coach's attention, and at the age of 16, she won a bronze medal in the 1956 Olympics. In the 1960 Olympics, she became the first American woman to win three gold medals.

✔ **Edwin Moses (1955–):** In the late 1970s and early 1980s, Edwin Moses ruled the hurdles, winning gold medals in the 1976 and 1984 Olympics. Between 1977 and 1987, Moses won 122 consecutive races.

✔ **Carl Lewis (1961–):** One of the most accomplished athletes of all time, Lewis won 10 Olympic medals (9 gold and 1 silver) and set countless world records during his career. Voted the Olympic Athlete of the Century, Lewis competed and medaled in the 1984, 1988, 1992, and 1996 Olympics.

✔ **Jackie Joyner-Kersee (1962–):** A heptathlon pioneer raised in East St. Louis, Illinois, and aided by her accomplished track and field coach husband Bob Kersee, Joyner-Kersee scored gold while also setting an Olympic long jump record at the 1988 Olympics. That same year, she became the first woman to win the *Sporting News* Man of the Year honors.

✔ **Michael Johnson (1967–):** Competing in the 1992, 1996, and 2000 Olympics, the self-proclaimed fastest man in the world has amassed an impressive five gold medals.

✔ **Marion Jones (1975–):** Dubbed the fastest woman on earth, California native Jones made Olympic history in 2000 when she became the first female athlete to win five medals (three gold and two bronze) at a single Olympics. Although dogged in recent years by allegations of illegal drug use, Jones is still consider by many to be one of the world's greatest female athletes.

At the 2004 Olympics, Shawn Crawford, Justin Gatlin, Joanna Hayes, and long jumper Dwight Phillips all won gold medals, continuing the tradition of African American excellence in track and field events.

Making a statement at the 1968 Olympics

Emotions ran high at the 1968 Olympics in Mexico City when track and field gold medalist Tommie Smith and bronze medalist John Carlos raised black-gloved fists in the air to represent black power and black unity as the national anthem played. Inspired by sociologist Dr. Harry Edwards who had asked them and other black Olympians to boycott the games, Smith and Carlos paid for their silent protest with a suspension from the national team and a ban from the Olympic Village. Back home, they received death threats and struggled for employment for years. Since then, they've become heroes for using their grand moment to stand up for equality. HBO chronicled this pivotal event in the 1999 documentary *Fists of Freedom: The Story of the '68 Summer Games.*

© Bettmann/Corbis

Tennis

Black colleges formed tennis teams as early as the 1890s, but the American Tennis Association (ATA), formed in 1916 in response to the U.S. Lawn Tennis Association's (USLTA) policy banning black players, really nurtured African American tennis players. One of the oldest black sports organizations in the United States, the ATA sponsored its first tournament in 1917 in Baltimore, Maryland. Black tennis greats Althea Gibson, Arthur Ashe, Zina Garrison-Jackson, Lori McNeil, and Chanda Rubin all played on the ATA circuit. The ATA Junior Development Program, created by Dr. Robert Walter Johnson in the 1950s, continues to nurture new talent.

Tennis's color line was broken in 1950 when Althea Gibson, winner of ten ATA championships, competed in the now-defunct U.S. Nationals. In 1956, the New York–raised Gibson won the French Open. She also won consecutive Wimbledon titles in 1957 and 1958, as well as major doubles and mixed doubles titles. Other prominent African American tennis champs include:

- **Arthur Ashe:** Ashe pioneered men's tennis by becoming the first African American named to the Davis Cup team in 1963. He also led UCLA to the NCAA tennis championship in 1965. In 1968, Ashe became the first African American man to win the U.S. Open and followed that victory with wins at the Australian Open in 1970 and Wimbledon in 1975. Ashe was a very outspoken civil rights advocate and one of the first prominent HIV/AIDS activists (he contracted the disease himself through a blood transfusion), educating the public about the disease before losing his battle in 1993.

- **Venus and Serena Williams:** In the late 1980s and early 1990s, the Williams sisters raised African American awareness of tennis, especially among young people. The older of the two, Venus, won both Wimbledon and the U.S. Open in 2000 and 2001. In 2002 and 2003, Serena defeated her big sister to win the U.S. Open, French Open, Wimbledon, and the Australian Open. The sisters became the first two women in Grand Slam history to square off in four consecutive finals and often swapped the top ranking in women's tennis.

- **James Blake:** In 2006, male tennis player James Blake emerged from the shadows, becoming the first black male tennis player ranked number one in the United States since Arthur Ashe.

Clearview Golf Course

World War II veteran and golfer Bill Powell found his own solution to golf's discrimination: He created his own golf course. He began designing Clearview Golf Course in East Canton, Ohio, in 1946 and opened the first 9 holes to the public just two years later. The course became an 18-hole course in 1978. Named a National Historic Site in 2001, Clearview is the first golf course built, owned, and operated by an African American.

Golf

Established as a white-only organization in 1916, the Professional Golf Association (PGA) and its prestigious Masters Tournament (instituted in 1934) allowed African Americans in only as caddies and groundsmen. In response to their racist policy, the United Golfers Association (UGA) and its National Colored Golf Tournament took root in 1925. When black golfers Ted Rhodes, Bill Spiller, and Madison Gunther filed a civil suit against the PGA in 1948, the PGA adopted an invitation-only policy to continue its discriminatory practices. Finally, in 1961, the PGA bowed to public pressure and let African Americans play.

The following year, Charlie Sifford became the first black golfer on the PGA tour, and, in 1964, Pete Brown became the first African American to win a PGA title. Before the 1990s, Lee Elder, the first black golfer to play at the coveted Masters Tournament in 1975 and the first to play on the U.S.'s Ryder Cup team in 1979, had been the most successful African American player. In the 1990s, Tiger Woods emerged on the golfing scene, breaking record after record and becoming one of the greatest golfers of all-time.

Other Sports

African American sports milestones are plentiful and extend to sports not typically associated with African Americans. Below is a diverse sampling of those achievements:

✔ **Horse racing:** African Americans dominated horse racing in its early years, with 13 African American jockeys of 15 in the first Kentucky Derbys in 1875. (See Chapter 19 for more about this historic feat.) In fact, African American Oscar Lewis was the first winner of that race. Beginning in the late 1890s, the numbers of African Americans in the sport decreased due in part to racial discrimination, as well as African Americans moving from the country to the city during the Great Migration. When Marlon St. Julien competed in the 2000 Kentucky Derby, he was the first African American to do so since 1921.

- **Cycling:** In 1899, cyclist Marshall "Major" Taylor became the first African American to hold an international title when he won the world championship in Montreal. Al Whaley became the first African American cycling champion of the modern era when he won the Masters World Championship in 1997.

- **Winter sports:** Figure skater Debi Thomas's bronze medal at the 1988 Winter Olympics made her the first African American to win a medal at a Winter Olympics. Bobsledder Vonetta Flowers won a team gold medal in the 2002 Olympics. In 2006, speedskater Shani Davis became the first African American to win a gold medal in an individual sport (1,000 meters) in a Winter Olympics; he also won a silver medal.

- **Gymnastics:** Dominique Dawes's individual bronze medal in the 1996 Olympics made her the first African American to win an individual medal in gymnastics. At the 1992 Summer Olympics, she and Uganda-born teammate Elizabeth "Betty" Okino were on the U.S. bronze medal team.

- **Fencing:** Six-time Olympian Peter Westbrook won the bronze medal in fencing at the 1984 Olympics. In 2003, Westbrook protégé Keeth Smart became the first American male fencer to be top-ranked in the world. Elite African American female fencers include three-time Olympian Sharon Montplaisir as well as Smart's sister Erin, who made the Olympic team for the first time in 2004.

- **Volleyball:** Known as the Clutchman for her powerfully fast spikes, team captain Flora "Flo" Hyman led the U.S. Olympic women's volleyball team to a silver medal in the 1984 Olympics. In 1992, sisters Kim and Elaina Oden were key members of the team that won the bronze medal.

- **Rowing:** U.S. women's rowing team captain Anita DeFrantz led her team to a bronze medal at the 1976 Olympics. Denied a chance at gold, DeFrantz, an attorney, sued the U.S. Olympic Committee for boycotting the 1980 Olympics and lost; later, she received the International Olympic Committee's (IOC) Olympic Order medal, the IOC's highest honor for those who exemplify Olympic values. In 1986, DeFrantz became a lifetime member of the IOC, the first African American and the first American woman to serve on the committee.

Part VI
The Part of Tens

The 5th Wave   By Rich Tennant

"I marched in Selma, Montgomery, and D.C. But I'm not marching on a bleach company because their bottle contains the message 'whites only.'"

In this part . . .

This part offers up a quick glimpse into African American history. It starts with a list of ten African American firsts that may be news to you, followed by ten influential books typically studied in African American history and literature classes. Then it moves on to ten influential African American artists.

Chapter 19

Ten African American Firsts

*F*irsts are always milestones, but when a member of a traditionally under-represented group achieves them, the effects are even more profound. Jackie Robinson's breakthrough in baseball, for example, ushered in other African American players, changing the overall structure of Major League Baseball and, many would argue, American society overall.

Culled from various fields, the ten African American firsts presented here are far from exhaustive. Think of them as representations of the diverse impact that African Americans have had on both the African American community and America overall.

Medicine (1783)

Not unlike many physicians of his time, Dr. James Derham didn't attend medical school. Instead, Derham, born a slave in Philadelphia in 1757, received his training from his three slave masters who were all doctors. It was Dr. Robert Love, his third owner, who encouraged Derham to practice medicine. Working as both a medical assistant and apothecary, Derham purchased his freedom in 1783 and established his own medical practice in New Orleans, making him the first black physician in the United States. Impressed by Derham, Dr. Benjamin Rush, a signer of the *Declaration of Independence* and, perhaps, the most distinguished physician of his time, convinced Derham to relocate his practice to Philadelphia. There, he became a throat disorders specialist.

Law (1845)

Details of Macon B. Allen's life are sketchy, but he's generally acknowledged as the first African American to practice law legally in the United States. Some sources suggest that Allen passed the bar in Maine in 1844 but relocated to Massachusetts because there were few black people in Maine. Others maintain that he relocated to Massachusetts because he wasn't permitted to pass the bar in Maine. Regardless, Allen, who was admitted to the Massachusetts bar in 1845, is credited with forming the first African American–owned law practice with Robert Morris, Jr., as well as being the country's first black justice of the peace. After the Civil War, he moved to South Carolina where he became a judge in 1873.

Kentucky Derby (1875)

A little-known fact about the Kentucky Derby is that African Americans were an integral part of its early history. Oliver Lewis, who rode Aristides, a horse trained by Ansel Williamson, also an African American, wasn't just the first African American jockey to win the Kentucky Derby but the first jockey to win *period.* Interestingly, African American jockeys won 15 of the first 28 Kentucky Derbys. Isaac Murphy not only became the first jockey of any race to win three Kentucky Derbys, but he was also the very first jockey inducted into the Jockey Hall of Fame. (Read more about the African American contribution to sports in Chapter 18.)

Congressional Medal of Honor (1900)

Nearly four decades after his heroic actions, Civil War hero Sgt. William H. Carney received the Congressional Medal of Honor, the first given to an African American. Born a slave in Virginia, Carney's father reportedly escaped to Massachusetts via the Underground Railroad, and his family joined him later. An inspiration for the film *Glory,* Carney distinguished himself during the crucial 1863 battle at Fort Wagner in Charleston, South Carolina. He spotted a wounded soldier about to drop the flag, a signal of defeat, and although wounded, Carney picked up the flag and refused to let it drop, even after Confederate soldiers shot him several more times. Today, that same flag is enshrined in Boston's Memorial Hall. (Read more about the Civil War in Chapter 6.)

Rhodes Scholar (1907)

Philadelphia native and Phi Beta Kappa Harvard graduate Alain Locke was the first African American Rhodes Scholar. A Howard University professor for 40 years, Locke was a pivotal figure during the Harlem Renaissance (discussed in Chapter 14). Locke, who edited the Harlem Renaissance's key manifesto *The New Negro,* encouraged black artists, including artist Aaron Douglass and writers Langston Hughes and Zora Neale Hurston, to draw from their African heritage for creative inspiration.

Exploration (1909)

Born in Maryland in 1866 and orphaned at a young age, Matthew A. Henson became a cabin boy on a merchant ship, and by age 18, he was well skilled and well traveled. A chance meeting with Robert E. Peary changed Henson's life as the pair spent almost two decades trying to reach the North Pole. Without Henson, who quickly learned the Inuit language and culture as well as arctic survival skills, it's doubtful that Peary would have reached the North Pole. Peary, himself, acknowledged Henson's contributions, admitting he couldn't "get along without Henson" and even penned the foreword for Henson's 1912 book *A Black Explorer at the North Pole.*

Because of the pervasive racism of the time, mainstream organizations honoring the feat often excluded Henson. African American organizations, however, regularly recognized his significant achievement. Slightly before his death in 1955, Henson, who some claim reached the North Pole 45 minutes before Peary, did receive more mainstream praise, including a presidential commendation from Eisenhower in 1954. Posthumously, Henson's great honors include reinterment in Arlington National Cemetery near Peary as well as receiving the Hubbard Award, the National Geographic Society's highest honor.

Television (1939)

Noted film and television historian Donald Bogle credits Ethel Waters as the first African American to broadcast a show on network television. *The Ethel Waters Show*, which appeared NBC on June 14, 1939, featured several skits, including a dramatic sequence from Water's hit play, *Mamba's Daughters.* Years later, Waters, who often played an on-screen maid, became the first African American actress nominated for an Emmy. (To read more about African Americans in television, go to Chapter 17.)

Nobel Peace Prize (1950)

Ralph Bunche, a longtime Howard University professor and active participant in the civil rights movement, began working with the United Nations in 1946. From 1947 to 1949, he tackled the deadly conflict in Palestine, eventually persuading Israel and the Arab States to sign the 1949 Armistice Agreements, thus ending the Arab-Israeli War. In 1950, Bunche became the first African American to receive the Nobel Peace Prize.

Pulitzer Prize (1950)

Poet Gwendolyn Brooks was the first African American writer to win the Pulitzer Prize. Raised and nurtured on Chicago's South Side, a key feature in much of her work, Brooks published her first poem, *Eventide,* in 1930 in the legendary African American newspaper, the *Chicago Defender.* Her first book of poetry, *A Street in Bronzeville*, published in 1945 and set in the historic Chicago black community of Bronzeville, received critical acclaim. Brooks's second collection of poetry, *Annie Allen,* paints a vivid picture of life as a young black woman and won the coveted Pulitzer Prize. In addition to receiving a Guggenheim Fellowship, Brooks also became an American Academy of Arts and Letters fellow. (You can read more about African American literature in Chapter 14.)

Fashion (1988)

Vicksburg, Mississippi, native and fashion designer Patrick Kelly infused his work with the folk sensibilities of his Southern upbringing, including imagery some considered racist. In 1988, Kelly, born in 1954, became the first American designer inducted into the Chambre Syndicale, the elite French fashion industry organization to which Yves Saint Laurent and Christian Lacroix belong.

Kelly attended Mississippi's predominantly black Jackson State University before relocating to Atlanta, where he once hocked his refashioned thrift-store wares on the streets and worked as a window dresser for an upscale boutique. After a stint in New York where he attended the Parsons School of Design, Kelly went to Paris and found great success. Sadly, in 1990, Kelly, on the brink of fashion superstardom, died, reportedly of AIDS complications.

Chapter 20

Ten African American Literary Classics

*Y*ou're probably thinking there can't possibly be such a thing as a definitive work of African American culture. You're right! The ten classic books in this chapter, however, serve as diverse representations of the African American experience specifically and the human experience in general. Most of these works feature the timeless theme of freedom. Collectively, they also provide a broad overview of African American history into the 1960s as well as raise key questions such as the value of education, the role of communal responsibility, and the true meaning of personal happiness that are just as relevant today as they were at the time these books were written.

These ten books only scratch the surface. There just isn't enough space to include every phenomenal classic by an African American author. Therefore, absences such as James Baldwin's *The Fire Next Time* or *Notes from a Native Son* and Ernest Gaines's *The Autobiography of Miss Jane Pittman* are simply reminders that the African American canon is especially deep. To find out more about African American literature, visit Chapter 14.

Narrative of the Life of Frederick Douglass, An American Slave Written by Himself (1845)

Narrative of the Life of Frederick Douglass is written in the slave narrative tradition, a literary style important to the overall development of African American literature (refer to Chapter 14 for more on this style). A controversial best seller in service of the antislavery movement, Frederick Douglass wrote so eloquently that many white critics, as they had with Phillis Wheatley's work in the 18th century, questioned whether he was the true author.

In the book, which helped the one-time fugitive slave become the most important African American leader of the 19th century, Douglass detailed his experiences as a slave, including his escape at age 20. Fearing his recapture, friends encouraged Douglass to spend time in Europe. While there, he helped bring international attention to slavery in the United States. Although he published his own newspaper, wrote other books, and was a noted orator and statesman after he returned to the United States, his *Narrative* still reigns as one of his most notable achievements.

Up From Slavery: An Autobiography by Booker T. Washington (1901)

Without argument, Booker T. Washington was the most dominant African American leader of his time. When his autobiography *Up From Slavery* appeared in 1901, it became an instant classic. A slave until he was 9 years old, Washington was nearly a teenager before he learned to read, but graduated with honors from Virginia's Hampton Institute. While he was just a teacher at Hampton, Hampton's president recommended him to the founders of Tuskegee Institute. Washington's remarkable feat of building (literally and figuratively) Tuskegee out of nothing into the nation's premier African American institution often placed him in prominent political circles. His public statements that vocational education served the black masses better than intellectual education alone and that African Americans should be patient about full political equality created considerable controversy among African Americans for decades. Yet his own "up from slavery" odyssey, touching on many of those points, remains a treasured text.

The Souls of Black Folk by W.E.B. Du Bois (1903)

The cultural significance of W.E.B. Du Bois's *The Souls of Black Folk* was immediately apparent when *The New York Times* and other nationally respected publications reviewed the book. A poetic and eloquent tome of essays by the first African American to receive a PhD from Harvard, *The Souls of Black Folk* provides a personal, sociological, and philosophical examination of being black in white America. Its impact was so far-reaching that Du Bois's direct challenge of Booker T. Washington's accommodationist attitude toward segregation divided African American leadership into two camps for decades. In *The Souls of Black Folk*, Du Bois, one of the NAACP's 60 founders, rightly asserted that the "problem of the Twentieth century is the problem of the color-line." He also advanced the concept of the Talented Tenth, his belief that the top 10 percent of African Americans had a responsibility to lead the masses. To this day, Du Bois's many other publications have yet to surpass the popularity of this seminal work.

The Mis-Education of the Negro by Carter G. Woodson (1933)

Known as the "father of black history," Carter G. Woodson pioneered scholarly study of African American history and culture and is responsible for the establishment of Black History Month. In *The Mis-Education of the Negro*, Woodson questions the value of Eurocentric education for African Americans and advocates a more balanced educational system that doesn't ignore the tremendous contributions of African Americans to American history and the world. Sadly, the book's continuing popularity among both students and non-students stems from the harsh reality that Woodson's interrogation of the American educational system for African Americans specifically largely remains valid.

Woodson's work inspired the title of Lauryn Hill's 1998 Grammy-winning album *The Miseducation of Lauryn Hill.*

Their Eyes Were Watching God by Zora Neale Hurston (1937)

A major player during the Harlem Renaissance, Zora Neale Hurston studied with noted folklorist Franz Boas and even collected Southern folk music with famed folklorist Alan Lomax for the Library of Congress. This substantial study of "Negro folklore," coupled with her own personal experiences, permeate her timeless novel *Their Eyes Were Watching God.* Set mostly in Eatonville, Florida, the all-black town where she grew up, *Their Eyes Were Watching God* illustrates Hurston's poetic command of language. In recent decades, female scholars, in particular, have praised Hurston's ability to capture protagonist Janie Crawford's frustrations as she struggles to find herself in the 1930s during a time when a black woman, as Janie's grandmother Nanny tells her, is "de mule uh de world." Although once a heralded writer, Hurston died penniless in 1960. Largely ignored until celebrated writer Alice Walker resurrected her legacy in the 1970s, Hurston's classic novel reached an even larger audience when Oprah Winfrey produced the book's first film version starring Halle Berry in 2005.

Native Son by Richard Wright (1940)

Mississippi-born writer Richard Wright's "protest" novel *Native Son,* which deals head-on with racism and its sociological causes and effects, sold a whopping 250,000 copies during its first run. Set mainly on Chicago's poor and predominantly black South Side during the 1930s, *Native Son* tells the tragic story of 20-year-old Bigger Thomas as his life spirals into an uncontrollable and tangled web of fear and murder.

A one-time member of the Communist Party, Wright, who escaped the Jim Crow South only to endure intense racial segregation in Chicago, uses Thomas's despicable actions to dramatize racism's devastating effects. An influential titan of 20th-century African American literature, Wright's naturalistic literary style depicting African Americans as victims of larger social forces defined black writers for years.

Invisible Man by Ralph Ellison (1952)

Oklahoma native and one-time music student Ralph Ellison left Tuskegee Institute in 1936 for New York City. There he met Richard Wright and became affiliated with the influential Federal Writers' Project. In 1952, Ellison published *Invisible Man,* his first novel, to critical acclaim. In *Invisible Man,* the unnamed protagonist searches for his own identity, only to find it marred by American racism. Ellison mixes and matches American and African American cultural traditions as he reveals that African Americans, the unnamed protagonist included, are largely invisible in mainstream American society.

Through the fictional characters of Dr. Bledsoe and Ras the Exhorter (fictionalized versions of Booker T. Washington and Marcus Garvey and their respective positions), Ellison analyzes the various strategies African Americans use and have used to achieve racial equality. Ellison's decision to infuse jazz, a uniquely American art form created by African Americans, throughout the text, subtly establishes an aesthetic perspective that is simultaneously American and African American. Although Ellison published another novel, *Juneteenth*, posthumously, *Invisible Man* remains his American masterpiece.

The Autobiography of Malcolm X (As Told to Alex Haley) by Alex Haley (1965)

Published just months following Malcolm X's assassination in February 1965, *Time Magazine* deemed *The Autobiography of Malcolm X* one of the 20th century's ten most important nonfiction books. Dictated to Alex Haley, who later wrote *Roots, The Autobiography of Malcolm X* details Malcolm Little's life from once promising student to petty hustler as well as his rise from a prison convict to one of black America's most charismatic leaders. Unlike Martin Luther King, Jr., Malcolm X, who rose to prominence as a member of the Nation of Islam, didn't advocate nonviolence as a means of improving the overall condition of black people in America. He favored a more militant approach that proved especially popular in urban centers. Although incomplete, *The Autobiography of Malcolm X* provides an intimate window into one of the 20th century's most intriguing and controversial figures of any race.

The Color Purple by Alice Walker (1982)

In *The Color Purple,* longtime activist Alice Walker, who coined the term *womanism* to distinguish African American feminism, scored critically and commercially with the Pulitzer Prize–winning story of Celie, a young black woman who overcomes poverty and sexual abuse in the rural South to realize her own self-worth. In *The Color Purple,* Walker uses folkloric techniques reminiscent of her literary mother, Zora Neale Hurston. Infused with a womanist energy, *The Color Purple* questions taboo subjects such as misogyny, sexual abuse, and homosexuality, as well as the traditional religious beliefs within the African American community. Despite the critical acclaim Walker received for *The Color Purple,* many African American men, especially after the release of a film adaptation, accused Walker of portraying black men negatively. Controversy aside, *The Color Purple* remains a widely read staple of African American literature.

Beloved by Toni Morrison (1987)

Six years after she published *Beloved,* Toni Morrison became the first African American recipient of the Nobel Prize for Literature for her collected works. Partly inspired by the true story of Margaret Garner, a slave woman who chose to kill her children rather than return them to slavery, *Beloved* follows the life of Sethe, a woman haunted by both her slave past and the ghost of the infant daughter she kills to protect from slave hunters tracking her down. Shunned by the African American community and living quietly with her oldest daughter in a house presumably haunted by the ghost of the dead baby girl, Sethe gets another chance at life and love when Paul D, an associate from her former plantation, comes to town. That's all shattered when Beloved, whom Sethe believes is her dead child reborn, appears.

A beacon of achievement in both African American literature and literature overall, *Beloved* represents the maturation of a genre rooted in the critical slave narrative tradition by paying homage to and transcending those origins. Refreshing in its multifaceted approach to slavery and the Reconstruction period, *Beloved* examines the shackles, literally and figuratively, of Sethe's, as well as the United States', slave past.

Chapter 21

Ten Influential African American Artists

In This Chapter

▶ Creating African American art

▶ Destroying conventions

As a result of the special significance artisans held in African culture, woodcarving, pottery, basket weaving, ironworks, and other crafts largely characterized early African American art. While portrait artists did emerge prior to the Civil War, African American artists were relatively few until after the Civil War. It wasn't until the Harlem Renaissance, however, that African American artists embraced their African heritage. Today, many world-class museums include in their permanent collections work from African American artists.

The ten influential African American artists featured in this chapter are far from definitive. Instead, they serve as a representative taste of an African American art tradition that continues to grow and evolve.

Joshua Johnson (c. 1763–1832)

Believed to be the first successful African American artist, Joshua Johnson (sometimes Johnston), who was likely born a slave in the West Indies, worked in the Baltimore area between the 1790s and early 1800s where he painted prominent middle-class families, which included free African Americans. His talent and fame rivaled that of his white contemporary Charles Wilson Peale, whom some scholars believe Johnson knew personally. More than 80 of his portraits hang in some of the world's most prestigious museums, including the American Museum in Bath, England.

Edmonia Lewis (c. 1845–1911)

Born to an African American father and a mother with Native American ancestry and orphaned at a young age, sculptor Edmonia Lewis, supported largely by her wealthy older brother, was among the few successful female artists of her time. Unlike other black artists, Lewis didn't hide her heritage and liked being photographed with her work. A bust of Colonel Robert Gould Shaw, the white commander of the Union army's legendary all-black 54th Regiment, earned Lewis widespread acclaim. In Rome, then an intellectual center for writers, poets, and artists often visited by wealthy Americans, Lewis flourished but still exhibited her work in the United States. One of her most memorable works, *The Death of Cleopatra*, was lost for many years. After not selling the piece at both the 1876 Philadelphia Centennial Exposition and the 1878 Chicago Interstate Exposition, Lewis stored the piece instead of shipping it to Rome. Until its discovery in 1988, the famous piece spent time in a Chicago saloon and as a grave marker for a horse named Cleopatra. Today, the restored masterpiece resides in the Smithsonian National Museum of American Art. Sadly, historians are unsure exactly when and where Lewis died.

Henry Ossawa Tanner (1859–1937)

Because the bulk of Henry Ossawa Tanner's work features natural and religious themes, his early paintings depicting African Americans are especially rare and very valuable. The first black artist to achieve international fame, Tanner, the son of an African Methodist Episcopal minister father and a mother who escaped slavery through the Underground Railroad, studied art at the prestigious Pennsylvania Academy of the Fine Arts. After a failed photography studio in Atlanta, Tanner eventually made his way to Paris in 1893 where he studied at the Académie Julian. Inspired by the Paul Laurence Dunbar poem "A Banjo Song," Tanner created his most famous work, *The Banjo Lesson*, a moving portrait of an elderly man teaching the banjo to the young boy on his knee, in 1894. While Tanner held exhibitions in the United States, he lived the rest of his life in France with his wife and child.

Face vessels

Functional pottery such as jugs modeled in the shape of human faces, known as *face vessels,* emerged prior to the Civil War. Although first spotted in the North around 1810, during the 1840s slaves in Edgefield, South Carolina, for unknown reasons, excelled at creating them. Distinguished by their alkaline-glazed stoneware and simple, earthy tones, face vessels quickly spread to other parts of the South.

While people in various parts of the world, including Africa, use face vessel–like objects in specific rituals, scholars have been unable to determine whether the face vessels created during the antebellum period functioned beyond mundane tasks such as holding water. Given the number of face vessels recovered along key Underground Railroad routes, however, there is reason to believe that they served a greater purpose. For whatever reason, face vessel production waned after 1865.

Aaron Douglas (1899–1979)

Known as the "father of black American art," Aaron Douglas, born in Kansas, made a bold artistic and political statement by incorporating African and African American influences in his work. During the Harlem Renaissance, Douglas's work regularly appeared on the cover of the magazine *Opportunity* as well as in books by Harlem Renaissance writers such as James Weldon Johnson. Douglas served as the first president of the Harlem Artists Guild, which succeeded in getting black artists accepted for projects with the Works Progress Administration (WPA). Through the WPA, Douglas, in 1934, created one of his most famous murals, *Aspects of Negro Life*, which is still at the Countee Cullen Branch of the New York Public Library. First commissioned to create murals for Fisk University, Douglas later helped create the school's art department in the late 1930s but didn't become a full-time art professor there until 1944. Douglas, who also chaired the art department, remained at Fisk until his retirement in 1966. Today, his work, including his signature murals, remains a valued feature of the historic campus.

Another famous WPA alumnus Hale Woodruff created the extraordinary *Amistad* murals, depicting the famous slave ship rebellion, at Talladega College's Savery Library in Alabama.

Horace Pippin (1888–1946)

Pursuing art as a child was too expensive for Horace Pippin. At age 14, Pippin left school altogether to help support his family. Wounded by enemy fire in World War I, Pippin, a member of the famed all-black 369th Infantry Regiment, which fought honorably alongside the French, lost normal use of his right arm. Back home in West Chester, Pennsylvania, Pippin, his wife, and her son eked out a modest living on his disability, income from odd jobs, and her earnings as a laundress. Unable to erase the horrors of war from his mind, Pippin returned to art around age 40. Because of his injury, his first painting, *The End of the War: Starting Home*, took a reported three years to complete. Illustrator N.C. Wyeth, who lived in the area, spotted Pippin's work in a local shop and introduced him to a larger audience. The art world embraced Pippin's bold use of colors, his depictions of African American life, and his antiwar, religious, and landscape paintings. Four of Pippin's works were included in a 1938 traveling show for the Museum of Modern Art. Just as he was becoming more famous, Pippin died of a stroke in 1946.

Lois Mailou Jones (1905–1998)

Artist Lois Mailou Jones, a Howard University art professor from 1930 until 1977, developed her own gift while also nurturing younger artists such as sculptor Elizabeth Catlett and African American art advocate David Driskell. Jones began her impressive art career, which spanned over six decades, in her native Boston where she graduated from the School of the Museum of Fine Arts in 1927. Dissatisfied with the anonymity of life as a textile designer, Jones sought a teaching career to complement her art career but racism forced her south. She began developing the art department at North Carolina's Palmer Memorial Institute before Howard University wooed her away. Jones, who secretly entered her work in contests barring black artists and won, explored her craft freely during a sabbatical in Paris in the late 1930s where she studied, visited museums, and painted. There, she created *Les Fétiches*, her celebrated piece of African masks. In 1953, Jones married a Haitian graphic artist, and they traveled regularly between Haiti and Washington, D.C. Fascinated with Haiti's strong African retentions, Jones integrated that influence into her work and never stopped seeking inspiration from the African Diaspora.

Jacob Lawrence (1917–2000)

Jacob Lawrence directly benefited from the cultural richness of the Harlem Renaissance and, at an early age, took classes with respected artists Charles Alston and Augusta Savage. A child of the Great Migration, Lawrence used his personal experiences, along with historical research collected at the 135th Street Library (now the Schomburg Center for Research in Black Culture), to create his highly acclaimed series, *The Migration of the Negro*, also known as *The Migration Series*, in 1940 and 1941. Although Lawrence created several impressive series around historical figures such as Haiti's revolutionary leader Toussaint L'Ouverture, *The Migration Series* catapulted him into mainstream American art circles. Today, at least 200 museums house Lawrence's work. Elected into the prestigious American Academy of Arts and Letters in 1983, Lawrence, who painted until his death in 2000, created a large body of work documenting varying aspects of African American life in an astonishingly beautiful and provocative modernist style. One of the most well-known American artists of the 20th century, Lawrence, who also taught art, helped widen the parameters of American art and opened doors previously closed to African American artists.

Romare Bearden (1911–1988)

The Harlem Renaissance and the Great Migration greatly influenced the North Carolina–born and Harlem-raised artist Romare Bearden. Although early in his life, Bearden, whose mother was a noted journalist, created cartoons for mainstream and African American publications, the World War II veteran and longtime social worker didn't make his mark in the art world until later in his life. During the 1960s and 1970s, Bearden began cultivating his now famous collage technique, which resembles African American quilts on canvas. Greatly inspired by jazz, the one-time jazz artist incorporated that love into famous works such as *Jammin' at the Savoy*. Equally important, Bearden, with his insightful essays and books such as *A History of African American Artists: From 1792 to the Present* published posthumously by his coauthor Harry Henderson, helped elevate the African American artist as a thinking, creative person whose gifts extended beyond raw talent. Bearden also played key roles in establishing black institutions such as the Studio Museum in Harlem and the Black Academy of Arts and Letters. Recognizing Bearden's importance as an artist, in 2003 the National Gallery of Art hosted *The Art of Romare Bearden*, its first major retrospective of an African American artist.

John Biggers (1924–2001)

The youngest of seven children born to parents in Gastonia, North Carolina, John Biggers, under the guidance of legendary Austrian-born art educator Viktor Lowenfeld, began his artistic journey at Hampton Institute where another mentor Charles White served as an artist-in-residence. Following a two-year stint in the navy, Biggers, at the urging of Lowenfeld, came to Pennsylvania State University where he earned several degrees, including his PhD. In 1949, Biggers began developing Texas Southern University's art department. A 1957 UNESCO fellowship allowing Biggers to travel to Africa deeply affected him and his work. He shared that experience in his 1962 book *Ananse: The Web of Life in Africa* where he mixed his drawings with his personal observations of countries such as Ghana and Nigeria. Influenced by great Mexican muralists such as Diego Rivera, Biggers, who spent over 30 years at Texas Southern, left several treasured murals in Houston. Known for his rich and complex style, Biggers's works often highlighted black women. Distinctive for their mythic quality as well as their resounding beauty, some of Biggers's many well-known works include *Birth from the Sea* and *The Contribution of Negro Women to American Life and Education*.

Jean-Michel Basquiat (1960–1988)

Jean-Michel Basquiat's commercial success remains enigmatic, especially in the context of African American art. Born in Brooklyn, New York, of Haitian and Puerto Rican ancestry, Basquiat's rise to fame, aided by his stint as a graffiti artist and appearances on a public access show, coincides with that of hip-hop in some ways. His participation in the multi-artist exhibition, *The Times Square Show*, in 1980, followed by an article lauding his work by Rene Ricard in *Artforum*, served as critical launching pads for his meteoric international art career. A brief friendship with Andy Warhol only elevated his profile. Staple features of Basquiat's work, often characterized as "neo-expressionist," include primitive-looking figures and words. Descriptions of his work by some white critics as simply "primitive" conjured up racist images of African American artists as lacking true artistic merit for many. His unexpected death to a heroin overdose in 1988 only fueled his legend. Although Basquiat isn't specifically tied to African American cultural traditions in the same ways as pioneering artists such as Jacob Lawrence, his success raised critical questions about what constituted African American art while also expanding general notions regarding acceptable and unacceptable content for an African American artist.

Index

BUSINESS, CAREERS & PERSONAL FINANCE

0-7645-9847-3

0-7645-2431-3

Also available:
- Business Plans Kit For Dummies
  0-7645-9794-9
- Economics For Dummies
  0-7645-5726-2
- Grant Writing For Dummies
  0-7645-8416-2
- Home Buying For Dummies
  0-7645-5331-3
- Managing For Dummies
  0-7645-1771-6
- Marketing For Dummies
  0-7645-5600-2

- Personal Finance For Dummies
  0-7645-2590-5*
- Resumes For Dummies
  0-7645-5471-9
- Selling For Dummies
  0-7645-5363-1
- Six Sigma For Dummies
  0-7645-6798-5
- Small Business Kit For Dummies
  0-7645-5984-2
- Starting an eBay Business For Dummies
  0-7645-6924-4
- Your Dream Career For Dummies
  0-7645-9795-7

HOME & BUSINESS COMPUTER BASICS

0-470-05432-8

0-471-75421-8

Also available:
- Cleaning Windows Vista For Dummies
  0-471-78293-9
- Excel 2007 For Dummies
  0-470-03737-7
- Mac OS X Tiger For Dummies
  0-7645-7675-5
- MacBook For Dummies
  0-470-04859-X
- Macs For Dummies
  0-470-04849-2
- Office 2007 For Dummies
  0-470-00923-3

- Outlook 2007 For Dummies
  0-470-03830-6
- PCs For Dummies
  0-7645-8958-X
- Salesforce.com For Dummies
  0-470-04893-X
- Upgrading & Fixing Laptops For Dummies
  0-7645-8959-8
- Word 2007 For Dummies
  0-470-03658-3
- Quicken 2007 For Dummies
  0-470-04600-7

FOOD, HOME, GARDEN, HOBBIES, MUSIC & PETS

0-7645-8404-9

0-7645-9904-6

Also available:
- Candy Making For Dummies
  0-7645-9734-5
- Card Games For Dummies
  0-7645-9910-0
- Crocheting For Dummies
  0-7645-4151-X
- Dog Training For Dummies
  0-7645-8418-9
- Healthy Carb Cookbook For Dummies
  0-7645-8476-6
- Home Maintenance For Dummies
  0-7645-5215-5

- Horses For Dummies
  0-7645-9797-3
- Jewelry Making & Beading For Dummies
  0-7645-2571-9
- Orchids For Dummies
  0-7645-6759-4
- Puppies For Dummies
  0-7645-5255-4
- Rock Guitar For Dummies
  0-7645-5356-9
- Sewing For Dummies
  0-7645-6847-7
- Singing For Dummies
  0-7645-2475-5

INTERNET & DIGITAL MEDIA

0-470-04529-9

0-470-04894-8

Also available:
- Blogging For Dummies
  0-471-77084-1
- Digital Photography For Dummies
  0-7645-9802-3
- Digital Photography All-in-One Desk Reference For Dummies
  0-470-03743-1
- Digital SLR Cameras and Photography For Dummies
  0-7645-9803-1
- eBay Business All-in-One Desk Reference For Dummies
  0-7645-8438-3
- HDTV For Dummies
  0-470-09673-X

- Home Entertainment PCs For Dummies
  0-470-05523-5
- MySpace For Dummies
  0-470-09529-6
- Search Engine Optimization For Dummies
  0-471-97998-8
- Skype For Dummies
  0-470-04891-3
- The Internet For Dummies
  0-7645-8996-2
- Wiring Your Digital Home For Dummies
  0-471-91830-X

* Separate Canadian edition also available
† Separate U.K. edition also available

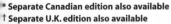

WILEY

SPORTS, FITNESS, PARENTING, RELIGION & SPIRITUALITY

0-471-76871-5

0-7645-7841-3

Also available:
- Catholicism For Dummies
  0-7645-5391-7
- Exercise Balls For Dummies
  0-7645-5623-1
- Fitness For Dummies
  0-7645-7851-0
- Football For Dummies
  0-7645-3936-1
- Judaism For Dummies
  0-7645-5299-6
- Potty Training For Dummies
  0-7645-5417-4
- Buddhism For Dummies
  0-7645-5359-3

- Pregnancy For Dummies
  0-7645-4483-7 †
- Ten Minute Tone-Ups For Dummies
  0-7645-7207-5
- NASCAR For Dummies
  0-7645-7681-X
- Religion For Dummies
  0-7645-5264-3
- Soccer For Dummies
  0-7645-5229-5
- Women in the Bible For Dummies
  0-7645-8475-8

TRAVEL

0-7645-7749-2

0-7645-6945-7

Also available:
- Alaska For Dummies
  0-7645-7746-8
- Cruise Vacations For Dummies
  0-7645-6941-4
- England For Dummies
  0-7645-4276-1
- Europe For Dummies
  0-7645-7529-5
- Germany For Dummies
  0-7645-7823-5
- Hawaii For Dummies
  0-7645-7402-7

- Italy For Dummies
  0-7645-7386-1
- Las Vegas For Dummies
  0-7645-7382-9
- London For Dummies
  0-7645-4277-X
- Paris For Dummies
  0-7645-7630-5
- RV Vacations For Dummies
  0-7645-4442-X
- Walt Disney World & Orlando
  For Dummies
  0-7645-9660-8

GRAPHICS, DESIGN & WEB DEVELOPMENT

0-7645-8815-X

0-7645-9571-7

Also available:
- 3D Game Animation For Dummies
  0-7645-8789-7
- AutoCAD 2006 For Dummies
  0-7645-8925-3
- Building a Web Site For Dummies
  0-7645-7144-3
- Creating Web Pages For Dummies
  0-470-08030-2
- Creating Web Pages All-in-One Desk
  Reference For Dummies
  0-7645-4345-8
- Dreamweaver 8 For Dummies
  0-7645-9649-7

- InDesign CS2 For Dummies
  0-7645-9572-5
- Macromedia Flash 8 For Dummies
  0-7645-9691-8
- Photoshop CS2 and Digital
  Photography For Dummies
  0-7645-9580-6
- Photoshop Elements 4 For Dummies
  0-471-77483-9
- Syndicating Web Sites with RSS Feeds
  For Dummies
  0-7645-8848-6
- Yahoo! SiteBuilder For Dummies
  0-7645-9800-7

NETWORKING, SECURITY, PROGRAMMING & DATABASES

0-7645-7728-X

0-471-74940-0

Also available:
- Access 2007 For Dummies
  0-470-04612-0
- ASP.NET 2 For Dummies
  0-7645-7907-X
- C# 2005 For Dummies
  0-7645-9704-3
- Hacking For Dummies
  0-470-05235-X
- Hacking Wireless Networks
  For Dummies
  0-7645-9730-2
- Java For Dummies
  0-470-08716-1

- Microsoft SQL Server 2005 For Dummies
  0-7645-7755-7
- Networking All-in-One Desk Reference
  For Dummies
  0-7645-9939-9
- Preventing Identity Theft For Dummies
  0-7645-7336-5
- Telecom For Dummies
  0-471-77085-X
- Visual Studio 2005 All-in-One Desk
  Reference For Dummies
  0-7645-9775-2
- XML For Dummies
  0-7645-8845-1